April Fool's Day

Bryce Courtenay was born in South Africa but has spent the greater part of his adult life in Australia. He lives in Sydney and is a creative director at George Patterson advertising agency. He also writes a weekly column in the *Australian*. *The Power of One* and *Tandia* are his first novels.

BRYCE COURTENAY

April Fool's Day

A Modern Love Story

Published 1994 by Mandarin
a part of Reed Books Australia
22 Salmon Street, Port Melbourne, Victoria 3207
a division of Reed International Books Australia Pty Limited

Reprinted 1994 (five times), 1995 (five times), 1996

First published in Australia 1993
by William Heinemann Australia
Reprinted 1993 (three times)

Typeset in Palatino by Bookset Pty Ltd
Printed and bound in Australia by Griffin Paperbacks

National Library of Australia
cataloguing-in-publication data:

Courtenay, Bryce, 1933– .
April Fool's Day: a modern tragedy.
ISBN 1 86330 335 9.

1. Courtenay, Damon, 1967–1991. 2. AIDS (Disease) –
Patients – Biography. 3. Hemophiliacs – Biography. I. Title.
616.1572092

This is Damon's book and it is
for Benita
and for
Celeste, whom he loved
with all his heart.

To his love and gratitude I add my own.

All at once the warmth fell away and the life passed
into the moving air.

Virgil *Aeneid IV*

Contents

Acknowledgments

As always with a book of this kind there are a great many people to thank who don't get a mention between the pages. Damon, my son, was fortunate in that he had so many people throughout his life who cared about and loved him and who often played a quiet but wonderfully supportive role in making his life easier. To all those who loved and cared for him but who are not mentioned by name — thank you.

Then there are those people who helped to shape Damon's life, some of whom are mentioned in this book but others, as important, who are not. Tony and John Wallace for their love and help all his life and especially at the end, Shirley Ham who made his limbs work again when they'd stopped, Michael and Roberta Wilson, the voluntary CSN workers, the Bobby Goldsmith Foundation, the nurses from the Waverley Community Health Centre, the doctors, nurses and staff of the Marks Pavilion, Prince Henry Hospital, Roger Tonkin, Bernie Carlisle and Wendy, Patricia Cook, Nola and the late Mark Bishop,

Sally and Peter Kalina, the late Pixie and Bruce Harris, Lana and Lucy. All contributed to the quality of Damon's short, sweet life.

Many other people gave generously of their time, knowledge or facilities to help me with the task of writing: Alan Barry, Lorraine Cibilic, Owen Denmeade, Steven Fearnley, Ethna Gallacher, Alex Hamill, Barbara Volk, Dr John Vivian Wells, Carol Shorter for her help to Celeste, George Patterson my agency, who were always generous in allowing me time and facilities when I needed them.

Four more names remain: Jill Hickson, my literary agent in Australia; Mic Cheetham, my agent in London; Laura Longrigg in London, who did the early editing; and Louise Adler, Publishing Director of William Heinemann Australia, who brought considerable skill, patience and tenacity to bear as the major editor responsible for thinning and shaping a book which sometimes threatened to overwhelm me and in which I was often too closely involved to see its substance with clarity and calm. I thank you all for your generosity of mind and spirit.

WRITERS' BLOC

THE READER IS ALWAYS RIGHT

Book One

Damon Courtenay is Not to be Touched,
Not Ever.

1

Death on a Saffron Morning.

Damon died in the third week after Pinatubo, a small, unknown volcano in the Philippines, started to belch smoke and spew ash, pushing smoke higher and higher into the stratosphere where the great up-draughts and crosswinds that swirl above the earth swept it to a height of twenty-two thousand feet and spread it like a blanket across the blue Pacific Ocean.

An hour before dawn each day the sunset on the light side of the earth reflected its glow against this great smokescreen and bounced it into the dark sleeping side to create a false dawn. The first of these false dawns occurred in Sydney on April the first 1991, the morning Damon died. An April Fool's dawn on April Fools' Day.

We all thought Damon would die sometime over the Easter long weekend, though God knows, he'd beaten the odds often enough before. The mighty Damon, just when you thought he was a goner, he would make it round the final corner on wobbly legs and totter down the home straight to be back with us again. But each time it was harder and each time he was weaker, a little bit of his old self left behind.

His brothers Brett and Adam were there with Celeste and Ann. Also Benita, his mother, with her anger at a son passing before his father, her love and the private, unreasonable guilt she'd carried for twenty-four years. We were Damon's family, Benita, Bryce, Brett, Adam, Celeste and Ann.

Celeste had been Damon's lover and had lived with him for the past six years. She had been his constant and devoted nurse. She dressed his bedsores, swabbed the thick yellow crusted thrush from his lips and the inside of his mouth and the pus from his conjunctive eyes. She washed him and cleaned up when he was incontinent and dressed his shingles. She had administered his morphine and the complex two-hourly cocktail of pills that kept his frail heart pumping and his mind more or less focused.

It was Celeste, more than any of us, who had watched his body slowly deteriorate, his ribs growing sharply more pronounced under his taut translucent skin and his limbs becoming so thin and dry that it seemed as though they might snap when he was lifted into bed.

Damon, whose body had never been his strong point, now looked like a walking corpse, a Jew in one of those flickering black and white newsreel pictures taken by the Allies when they liberated the concentration camps.

Funny how those pictures were somehow meant to be

in black and white, because the first thing you notice about approaching death is its lack of colour. Colour is an obscene pigment in the dying process.

Before death came to Damon, he appeared to fade, to be losing his colour. Damon's eyes were now smudged large, and set deep in his skull. There seemed to be no clear, clean hazel left to nourish them with life, they'd changed to a mottled brown, the colour of grape vinegar. Often, as he drank liquid morphine straight from the bottle, they would glaze over and lose focus, as though he'd pulled a shroud over them so he could hide his shame.

Then on April Fools' Day, a day which began with surprising, unexpected colour, Damon was ready. There was no colour left in him at all, he'd wrung the last drop out, used the last tiny bit to whisper that he loved us.

It was a great effort for him to talk and each of us took our turn in moving up close, "I love you very much, Dad." There was nothing more to say. It was everything contained in one thing, his whole life.

Brett, his oldest brother, silent and big as a barn door, was back from Kuala Lumpur with Ann. Adam, soft, big-hearted Adam who loved his little brother with a fierce, sad, bewildered face, had flown from London.

Both brothers waited for Damon to die, gentle and a bit clumsy in the small semi-detached cottage Damon shared with Celeste. Both were trying to be useful around the smoothly functioning Celeste who still spoke to Damon with a clear, laughing, indulgent voice as though amused that he'd turned a slight indisposition into an excuse for a day away from work.

Celeste was not prepared to let Death into Damon's

room and so she beat it back, threatened it with laughter and sheer, desperate bluff. At night she slept beside him, holding him tight, on guard against Death's surreptitious entry, ready to wake up and defend him the moment the curtains parted and the hot, dry breath of the Prince of Darkness billowed inwards.

Once, towards the end, Damon threw a sudden massive fit, not the first, but the first for a while and we rushed him by ambulance to the nearest hospital. In Casualty he experienced a second fit which caused him to evacuate. It was decided to keep him in hospital overnight.

Damon was removed to a tiny room, situated in a sort of twilight zone between the Casualty ward and a regular one. Though nothing was said, it was the room they kept for his kind. A room where they used yellow bags. Everything went into these bright yellow plastic bags to be incinerated. Swabs, tissues, syringes, uneaten food, the contaminated detritus of his broken life.

Taped to the door was the international infection warning; a yellow circle with a black cross in the centre. Beneath it, written with a red felt-tipped marking pen, a sign saying: Gown, mask and gloves must be worn.

The room was painted pale apple green and contained a single bed and the usual lights, plugs, switches and rubber tubing set into the wall, but nothing else. It was a holding place, a really sad space to have to come to die.

Two cheerful young nurses in rubber gloves, gowns and masks appeared at the door with a stainless steel trolley and we stood with our backs to the wall to make room for them to enter. They both had firm brows and nice brown eyes and looked as though they might be attractive under the cotton squares which hid the remainder of their faces. When they smiled their stretched lips sucked up the thin mask, creasing it with a horizontal line. Pulled tight like that against their faces, they looked like pretty bank robbers in a kids' funny movie.

They kept up their chatter as they removed Damon's soiled pyjama bottom and placed it into a yellow bag, then they swabbed him clean. They showed no surprise when they turned him on his stomach to do the same on his flip side and saw the open bedsore the size of a large man's fist spreading up his back from his coccyx.

The bedsore was an obscenity on his pale skin, not just for what it was, but also for its colour: the raw, angry flesh tainted with his excrement seemed somehow to be the physical place, the hole torn into his lower back where the colour was leaking out.

The two young nurses cleaned him carefully and dressed the bed wound, placing the cotton wool swabs into a yellow bag clipped to the end of the trolley. Then they worked him into a fresh pair of pyjamas, his arms floppy and awkward, his head lolling, a gangly rag doll being treated to a fresh pair of striped pyjamas in an apple green playroom for the condemned.

One of the nurses examined Damon's drip, squinting expertly at the tiny clear saline drop poised at the top of the pipette then adjusted the pressure, forcing the reluctant droplet to let go so that another might immediately follow it to oblivion. The second nurse stood at the doorway waiting with the trolley and they left together, still chatting, their trim belted waists, starched hips and strong young legs revealed where the over-gown was split and carelessly tied down the back, were full of fierce, fecund life.

Damon, who was heavily sedated and barely aware of his surroundings, immediately fell into an exhausted sleep. It was over for another time, we could go home and pretend, for a few hours, to pick up the tattered remnants of our normal lives. We'd learned not to lie awake in the dark and stare at the ceiling, not to think, to postpone the sadness, shunting the future without Damon into a disused siding.

We were all just hanging on, telling ourselves that Damon had beaten the grim reaper once again, our private thoughts perhaps different. Mine I knew were filled with guilty questions. How much more? How much more did he have to take? Couldn't it have ended tonight? Was it wrong, wicked, to think like this? Such a little-boy word, wicked. Was I thinking of me and not of him? Was life precious, even now when there was nothing left except pain and memories? With the old good memories corrupted and the images defiled? This time it was a couple of severe fits which threatened to stop his dicky heart. If his heart had gone tonight, would I have allowed them to use the cardio- resuscitation equipment or would I have screamed at them to leave him alone to die, to let him become a sudden blinding nothing?

The fits were just the latest in a litany of remorseless assaults to his battered body and he'd made it through to the other end still with us, still able to come out of his corner for another round.

The mighty Damon, it hurt such a lot just to think about him. I wanted to be proud of his courage and at the same time to cry out at the shame that someone so beautiful could fight so hard, to die so badly.

A nursing sister entered the room carrying a clipboard. She moved directly to me, the only male in the room. "Overnight admission." She handed me the clipboard. "You need to sign it before you leave." She glanced at the fob watch pinned to her uniform.

I took the clipboard and handed it to Celeste who was half- seated with one hip resting on Damon's bed. The nursing sister's eyes followed, she was short and wide, powdered too white and with her cheekbones over-blushed. She had large breasts and wore heavy duty support stockings and flat, white, crepe-soled shoes.

Her instinctive demeanor and appearance brought back memories of a past hospital system. It was as though she was serving out her time and had reluctantly given up her starched nursing sister's veil and the unspoken authority it had carried.

She indicated Damon by slightly lifting her chin, "Is he a relation?" Her question was directed at Celeste.

"I'm his defacto," Celeste replied. The word suddenly sounded coarse and illegitimate as though it was a part of what was wrong with Damon.

The woman was momentarily caught by surprise, Damon's kind were not supposed to have female part-ners. "That won't do," she said and looked at me. "You're his father?" I nodded and she turned back to Celeste and gave her a quick, paper-thin smile, as though an electric impulse had caused her lips to twitch involuntarily. Then she reached for the clipboard and handed it back to me, tapping the spot with a biro where she wanted me to place my signature.

I took the pen and scribbled my name. Benita and

Celeste looked at me and I indicated with my eyes that we should leave; there was nothing further we could do now that Damon was asleep. We turned to go, but Celeste shook her head, "I have to sleep here." Her pretty face was pale and drained and her blue eyes were bloodshot from crying alone in the toilet.

"You can't, dear. Not in this room. It's too small and against regulations, this is an infection risk area." The sister paused then added, though not unkindly, "You can wait in Casualty, there's a TV and a coffee machine. We'll call you if you're needed."

Celeste's eyes welled, but her voice was steady, though slightly high pitched when she spoke, so that the words came out like a child's, all at once, "Is he more of an infection risk here than he is at home?"

Her logic was irrefutable, but the sister wasn't having any, "We, we can't take all the necessary precautions."

"I don't care about precautions! He needs me to fight for him, he won't make it alone!" Celeste frowned, seeking further reasons, "You see, he can't fight the dark on his own, he'll just die and I won't be with him."

The older woman was an experienced hand in Casualty and familiar with the behaviour of traumatised families. She had the good grace not to sigh, but her downcast eyes indicated her impatience. "He won't die, dear. He is over the worst, his heart fibrillation has stopped and his pulse rate is steady. The doctor says he'll be all right, he can't be moved, movement can sometimes bring on another fit." Her response was practised and fast and was followed by her thin, electric smile, "All he needs now is a little rest."

She made this last statement as though Damon was

completely cured, that is, but for a few hours needed to gather his strength. "You really must go now, you can't stay, you can't do anything more for him here." She cocked her head and looked directly into Celeste's eyes, folding her arms and hugging the clipboard to her bosom.

Celeste looked down and took Damon's limp hand in her own as if she was about to tell his fortune. She was quite still and a tear rolled down her cheek and then her chin and dropped into Damon's hand.

The sister stood her ground, not moving, allowing the silence to gather momentum. Her confrontation was experienced and dismissive, the stance she'd learned to use to shut things down quickly when trouble threatened. She was accustomed to having her own way and more than a match for this pretty little blonde with the cropped hair, high cheekbones and soft, generous mouth.

I was the first to capitulate. Embarrassed, anxious not to make a scene, I said, "C'mon, darling, I think perhaps we should go." I moved over to the bed and took Celeste by the elbow. "You're tired," I appealed to her softly, "we're all a bit tired, we haven't eaten, c'mon, let's go home, I'll cook."

The mention of food was crass. I told myself this wasn't the right time to make a fuss. But I knew it was. I was aware I was being as weak as piss. I didn't care, I wanted to leave, to run rather than walk away. My sensibilities were repulsed at the baby sweet odour of lanolin and talcum powder, at the inappropriate nursery innocence of the smell in this tiny room where they used only yellow bags. I had to get away from the bright light bouncing against the enamelled semi-gloss apple green walls and beating up from the polished vinyl floor.

The confrontation going on was gnawing at my gut and I could feel the day's grime and the slightly damp sweat deposited around the rim of my collar. It was one o'clock in the morning and I hadn't eaten since breakfast. I wanted to gulp outside air, to be swallowed by the street dark. I wanted time off from my son's slow dying. Almost at once I was overwhelmed by guilt of this thought as well, the wanting to eat, feeling sorry for myself when my son was dying and I was so very much alive.

Celeste jerked her elbow free and releasing Damon's hand she shot from the bed. "Get the doctor. Get the fucking doctor, now!" Her eyes were crazy, inches from the older woman's. Taken completely by surprise, the nursing sister stepped backwards, her plump shoulders bumping against the wall and bouncing back.

Celeste too was a pro, six years with Damon and there wasn't a hospital system in the Sydney metropolitan area she didn't know. She'd been screwed by experts a hundred, maybe a thousand times before, this nursing sister was just another of the countless obstacles she'd come against.

In retrospect, the hospital sister wasn't being particularly bitchy. She was simply exercising her judgment, getting through a tough shift the best she could. She was the product of an age when hospital visitors responded unquestioningly to her authority, but this time she was up against a new force, a young urban guerrilla armed with six years of anger, frustration and fierce, remorseless love.

Benita pushed forward, her face darkly angry. She too was a veteran. With a sweep of her arm she brushed Celeste out of the way and pinned the woman back against the wall. She is a big, classy-looking woman with a voice when she's angry which cuts like razor ribbon.

"Excuse me, but she stays. The law says relatives can stay. So Celeste stays! Okay?" But she wasn't really asking permission or even a question.

Benita pulled back and the sister lowered the clipboard and snorted, one eyebrow slightly raised, "And you excuse me, madam! She is not a relative."

"Get-the-bloody-doctor!" Benita spat the words out, advancing again. Whereupon the sister pulled the clipboard hard against her breast, protecting herself unconsciously. "Ha!" she huffed, her large breasts jumping in surprise. Then she stormed out of the doorway. We could hear the angry squeak of her crepe-soled shoes on the vinyl as she moved down the corridor towards Casualty.

"Jesus, now what?"

Both women looked at me but said nothing. I knew they were thinking that I should have said something. That I'd gone to water. Fuck them, I'd had enough.

Quite soon afterwards the two young nurses returned wheeling a gurney. This time wearing only masks. They were silent, their eyes serious, aware no doubt of the conniption. On the gurney they carried a doubled over mattress and I helped them lift it and place it on the floor beside Damon's bed. The mattress almost completely filled the tiny room so that Benita and I had to stand outside the door to say goodbye to Celeste.

When we'd gone and she was left alone with Damon, Celeste relocated his drip to the side nearest the door and lifted him from his bed, placing him on the mattress. There she slept with him safely in her arms. Celeste was not prepared to give Damon up, not to Death, not to anyone. So she held him tight all night, protecting him just the way she did every night at home.

2

Birth, Weddings and Bloodlines.

Brett and Adam were both born reddish pink and creased-up looking, the way a normal baby should look, tiny hands turned into protesting fists, eyes closed tight to the sudden, shitty, air-filled space around them.

Both, by some miracle, missed out on the blood lottery which found Damon and stamped him at birth with its deadly imprint. He was born with a large bruise under his armpit which ran down his left side, across his ribs to his hip forming a deep, mulberry-coloured birthmark.

"Congratulations, you have another boy, Mrs Courtenay. A bit bruised, but that will soon pass. He's pale, so we've given him a blood transfusion. You can bring him back in ten days and we'll do the circumcision then."

"A blood transfusion? Is that usual doctor?"

"Not normal, but not unusual . . . probably caused by

the forceps . . . nothing to be concerned about."

In those days, the mid sixties, there was still a definite role you were expected to play around doctors. You were the awed and grateful parents of the newborn. You waited to be spoken to, not wishing to appear stupid by asking questions. People dying of cancer of the colon were afraid to ask how long? How bad is the pain going to be? What does the blood in the stool mean? What further symptoms can we expect?

Doctors, with their scrubbed pink nails, perfectly trimmed cuticles and soft-looking hands that smelled of Phisohex were the high priests of the social temple. In our hospitals they were surrounded by the homage and adulation of the nursing staff and the pliant, schoolboy obedience of the interns. They responded, for the most part, by being bad tempered, intimidating, ill mannered and pompous.

Damon was a lovely baby with a fright of soft blond hair that stood up like a long brush cut from the very beginning. After a week at home the bruise down his side had blotched green and purple and we looked forward to the time when he'd be perfect again. After the evening feed he slept through the night, missing the three o'clock feed altogether and he almost never cried. Damon, even then, was no cry baby.

Benita, we used to say at the time, was stacked up front and there was milk for two babies and then some to spare. Around feeding time the aureole of her nipples showed dark against her wet shirt. After two kids in twenty-one months, we were pretty expert. Though I'd almost forgotten about the pooey "curry bum" nappies (How can one small baby hold so much shit?) and the clotted, milky chunder down the back of my shirt as I worked for a burp.

By the time we'd had Damon home ten days and he was due to be taken back to hospital for his circumcision, we were into a routine. Benita was Jewish and by Jewish law, therefore, my sons were born Jews. However, the circumcision of our boys was not an observance of the ancient ritual of Brith Milah, when Abraham is commanded by God to circumcise his son by his wife Sarah as the sign of His covenant with the Jews. I think it was simply a common social custom which we took more or less for granted, happy to let the hospital undertake the inconsequential operation. After Brett and Adam, we knew circumcision wasn't a big deal and we brought Damon straight back home from the hospital.

"Don't worry if your baby bleeds a little, a few drops won't hurt, it happens with circumcision." The doctor's voice was casual and reassuring.

Damon, we felt sure, was going to be an easy baby and his brothers, Brett, who was five, and Adam, who was three, seemed to like him a lot. They could often be seen standing at his bassinet with Damon's tiny hand clutched around a dirty, extended finger while they talked serious brother talk to him.

We were going out on the evening of the day Damon was circumcised, to what promised to be a lavish affair, the twilight wedding reception of one of Benita's girl-friends, Gemma Rubens. The invitation had arrived, not by post, but personally delivered, slipped under the front door. It came in a double-sized, expensive-looking, ivory-coloured envelope with our names scripted in silver by a calligrapher. The card, too, was edged in silver and embossed with two doves holding up a heart-shaped garland of roses. Inside the heart, printed in matte embossed silver, were the names, Dudley and Gemma.

The Goldberg family were third generation, highly successful and sophisticated Australian Jews at the respectable end of the rag trade, with a chain of successful shops. The bride's family were Polish born, in the chicken meat business and also very rich. Benita assured me that old and new money were on a collision course — expensive understatement versus sheer ostentation.

We'd taken the elaborate invitation over to show Benita's ageing grandmother, a tiny, birdlike Jewish lady with beautiful manners, who'd once been rich and in the same social milieu as the Goldbergs but now was poor again. She was no longer a member of the Jewish glitterati. She looked at the wedding invitation and observed wryly, "When you got it, why not show off a little? Tomorrow you may not got it again."

I was fascinated with the prospect of the wedding. The idea of meeting these people, who had arrived in Australia with nothing more than the dirt under their fingernails and had made it really big, gave me hope for my own future. My mother, a small-town dressmaker, raised me and my sister without a father and we were just about as poor as a white skin allows you to get in South Africa. Like most people who've escaped this condition I was both fascinated as well as daunted by the idea of wealth. Money really scared me. People like the Goldbergs, who'd had it a long time, made me feel inferior.

Not so the Rubens, they were different, they'd been through the horror of the Holocaust and now were having to start all over again. They seemed to me to be the world's best role model for someone like me; they had brains and an old culture, but they were not above buying respectability in a new country with a little marrying up and a little quality mixing. Everyone has to start somewhere and what I liked most about Australia was that it was odds-on that the most refined had once been among the vulgar. I saw the Rubens as my role models and the Goldbergs as my social destination.

We'd picked a hand-thrown fruit bowl glazed in a dark green with a Margaret Preston style of Australian wild flower motif. It cost more than we could easily afford and we'd comforted ourselves that, while ours would be the cheapest wedding gift there, it would make up for this by being overwhelmingly in good taste. Good taste was something I was also learning about. I guess I was already headed in the wrong direction. Pretension and smugness in the young is generally a great disadvantage to the quick accumulation of cash.

The Chevron Hilton, where the twilight reception was to be held, was showbiz and frequented by the glitterati. It was Sydney razzamatazz in the very best of bad taste. Sammy Davis Junior and Lennie Bruce had both performed there; the place was hot to trot.

As the day of the wedding was the same day as Damon's circumcision, Benita was worried about leaving him in the care of Sarah, our regular baby-sitter. Worried was probably an understatement; Benita was fiercely protective of her children and it was only after my carping insistence on our going and a gentle extolling of Sarah's virtue as a baby-sitter that she finally agreed to go. She left a bottle for Damon's evening feed, though she expected to be back before this time.

Sarah was what was known in those days as "an unspoilt convent girl" and was in her final year of high school. She was going through a personal crisis, having lost her first real boyfriend and broken out in acne all in the same tragic month. She was the ideal baby-sitter, with three-year-old twins in her own family by dint of her mother's second marriage. She knew her way around small children and we trusted her completely.

Benita was right about the ostentation, you could pick the Goldberg faction from the Rubens in a flash. Despite the early summer temperature, stoles of mink and silver fox were worn by the Rubens ladies over gowns, for the most part, of baby blue and pink satin, richly embroidered with seed pearls and diamantés. The matriarchs on the Goldberg side were outfitted several rungs up on the haute couture ladder in a preponderance of black, brown and burgundy. They wore no furs whatsoever.

Necks on both sides were neutral, equally expensively braced with pearl chokers. Ears, too, showed no discrimination and were splashed with diamonds that matched sister stones on carefully manicured fingers.

The men, on the other hand, looked much of a muchness and for the most part wore double-breasted, grey pin-striped or navy business suits. Theirs was a division created by accent, the nasal twang of the Australian vowel fighting with the guttural inflections of middle and eastern Europe. Male and female, everyone appeared to be talking at the same time so the band at the far end of the ballroom could only be heard in occasional snatches.

I don't remember a great deal about the first half of the reception. I recall a young doctor sat next to Benita and totally monopolised her. I was more or less forced to speak exclusively to a middle-aged guy on my right who, it turned out, had made his money in chicken guts. When I showed a polite interest in the subject he seemed immediately keen to recruit me into the offal business.

Israel also proved to be very big on the agenda. This was a year before the Six Day War and the world was yet to discover that, lying dormant under two thousand years of Jewish passivity, was a formidable aggression. The Jews would take no more backward steps. This, however, was a metamorphosis yet to come, the great exodus from Europe and the return to the Palestine homeland was still a romantic idea, but every Jew in the Western world felt responsible for the rehabilitation of this narrow strip of sand and rock sandwiched between ancient enemies.

Jewish doctors and lawyers, professors and fish-mongers, rag traders and, as it turned out, even Jews in the chicken guts business, all sent their daughters and their sons to help out. Gemma herself, fresh from a master's degree in English Literature at Sydney University, spent eighteen months in a kibbutz growing and pickling cucumbers. Privately, she admitted that life as a kibbutznik was hell and her love for the promised land was quickly cured in the brine vats, where tiny green gherkins floated like baby turds and left her hands swollen and stinging for the entire time she was a daughter of the soil.

The greening of Israel was psychologically very important. The New World Jews, those who discovered freedom and prosperity in the lands of America, Canada, South Africa and Australia were, for the most part, within one or two generations from central and eastern Europe.

For generations, Jews had been driven from the land they were to own. Yet the Torah taught them that they were a people of the land and that ownership of the soil was part of this deep, spiritual yearning at the core of the Jewish ethos. This, more than anything, was the reason for their return to the land of Israel.

If the Jews who prospered in new lands were not prepared to return themselves to Palestine then they were emotionally bound to its rebirth by occasionally lending their sons and daughters and by paying for the flowering of the desert. And so the book of trees was devised, The Golden Book. At weddings it became traditional to donate to The Golden Book. It was this aspect of the wedding of Dudley and Gemma that I most clearly remember because it was connected directly with what happened to Damon.

The bloke who dealt in chicken offal, the innards, giblets and guts, which he supplied by the truckload to pet food factories seemed very grateful to have someone seated beside him who was prepared to listen. He was a natural enthusiast, proud of his success, and he wore a huge canary diamond signet ring which he told me was set in New Guinea gold and worth twenty-five thousand pounds. Although Australia had fairly recently converted to decimal currency and the dollar unit, he still spoke in pounds. He also mentioned that his daughter was an archaeologist but was working in a kibbutz in the Negev. It seemed that archaeologists, like violinists, were fairly thick on the ground in Israel and money for digs wasn't high on the priority list in a nation frantic to establish a viable agricultural base. It turned out she was his only offspring and not interested in the offal business. He seemed happy to chat on and have me do the listening so that one thing led to another and, to my surprise, he ended up offering me a job. "Not everybody likes to work with a Jew. But we could make a good business. A nice boy like you could go far."

There's not a hell of a lot you can say to an offer like that. Nobody actually thinks specifically about joining the chicken offal business. I certainly recognised that here was a living example of how I could make a reasonably quick, if unprepossessing, fortune. Which, of course, was the main reason why I was anxious to attend the wedding reception in the first place. I had the theory that if you stick around money and success it rubs off a little. I'd always been poor and was still reasonably so. My career in advertising hadn't advanced to the point where it couldn't be curtailed if the right offer came from elsewhere. I had brains but lacked know-how.

The chicken guts man assured me that chicken offal was money for old rope. He had every chicken farm tied up within a day's refrigerated trucking distance from Sydney and Melbourne. He talked with great enthusiasm and I must say I was becoming more and more impressed, until he mentioned in passing that you couldn't get rid of the smell of chicken shit, that it stayed with you all the time, when you went to bed at night and when you awoke in the morning, even when you went on holidays.

The moment he said this I could smell it on him. Funny how the mind works. I was done for. Poor boys with ambition do not want to grow rich to the smell of chicken shit. As you can plainly see, already there was too much of the good-taste wedding present in me and not enough chicken guts. Too much Goldberg and not enough Rubens.

My mind, always apt to embroider, immediately took me into the future as an offal man, to a time when my three boys would go to Cranbrook, an expensive private school for the so-called better born. In my mind's ear I could hear them asking to be let off a block from the school gates, embarrassed about a father who, at a distance of ten feet, smelled of chicken guts. Such was my need for security and respectability, that it never occurred to me that no boy at Cranbrook would have the faintest idea of how the insides of a chicken smelled — that the closest any of them had ever come to a dead chicken would be the strips of odourless white meat cushioned on shredded iceberg lettuce on their sandwiches. I am ashamed that, at the time, I lacked the imagination and the courage to accept what amounted to a very generous offer from an extremely nice man.

In fact, though much too polite to show it, I was somewhat upset at the offer. It wasn't the way I pictured myself. Nor was this the way I'd imagined the wedding reception would be. I'd quite clearly seen myself seated among several high-flying operators who were impressed by my beautiful Jewish wife and my own obvious intelligence and who were offering me inside tips on the money market which would enable me to convert a meagre bank balance into a sizeable fortune almost overnight.

I knew this could be done. A bloke in the agency had told me that the casting director had told him about this well-known model whose name, naturally, he couldn't divulge, but who'd slept with this Jewish multi-millionaire who hadn't paid her because that would have made her a whore. Instead, he'd told her to sell everything she owned, even her house, put it all into a particular company's shares, and then keep the shares for six weeks — no more — before she sold them again. She'd followed his advice and was now worth a squillion; she would never have to work again, either on the catwalk or on her back.

It was all a matter of who you knew and a lot of the who-to-knows were right here at this wedding. But I, for one, wasn't getting to meet any of them. Instead, I was saddled with a guy who was doomed for the remainder of his life to smell of chicken shit. Years later, when I was in hospital undergoing a spinal fusion, I met a pathologist who confirmed this phenomenon. He explained that a bug that lives in human excreta attaches itself to the olfactory membranes in the nose so that you can never personally get rid of the smell of excrement, even though others around you are unaware of it. Whether this is true of chicken shit I've never found out, but it seems to explain what had happened to my would-be benefactor. I recall feeling strongly that it was time to cut my losses and remind Benita that we had intended being home before nine.

What I had no way of knowing was that the battle of the bulging cheque books was about to begin. Crossed, double, triple and quadruple digits would be dashed from flashing pens in the war of The Golden Book. I was just going to nudge Benita and suggest that we kick the dust, when a stout, jowly, little guy with receding hair swept straight back and plastered with Brylcreem jumped up waving a cheque book. He walked importantly up to a microphone which was placed in front of the bandstand.

Instead of adjusting the microphone he stretched up high, almost on tip-toe, then turned his head towards the top table. "A big surprise!" he said, grinning and waving the cheque book above his head. "A big surprise, ladies and gentlemen, compliments Myers Chickens." He paused and, grinning again, looked around scanning the tables in front of him, "Roasters, boilers and friers! Treat yourself tenderly, take home a Myers!"

There was laughter and some applause at his recital of the Myers Chicken slogan, though mostly, I must say, from the chicken meat side.

The little guy brought his gaze back to the distant top table, "The beautiful bride and the groom, may your names be inscribed in the book of life. My compliments also to the bridesmaids." He was still holding the cheque book aloft. "You wondering maybe about the cheque book? No, I don't think you wondering, I think maybe you got your pen already ready already." He cleared his throat and brought the cheque book down. "Maybe somebody here doesn't know me, so now I introduce myself. I am Morris Myers." He paused as though waiting for a response and when this didn't come added, "Myers Continental Chickens? You tried maybe a little Myers chicken? A little soup with loxchen? Or a nice breast?" Now there were smiles all round and Morris Myers happy, pushed home the advantage, "We got kosher also, our Bondi shop, Campbell Parade." He gave us all a big smile, his head slightly tilted, "Be nice, *treat yourself tenderly*, maybe you heard already on the television our advertising?"

Morris Myers was being unnecessarily modest. Myers

was to chicken what Donald is to duck and every child over the age of three could sing the Myers Chicken jingle. Now, with both hands aloft, he held the cheque book again and tore a single cheque from it. "From Mrs Myers, my wonderful wife, also my boys, Joseph and Lennie, I pledge two thousand dollars for The Golden Book!"

Next to me the chicken guts man sighed, "Morris has got two boys and already both work in the business. Oh, my . . ." I could sense the longing for an offal heir in his voice.

Two thousand dollars was a great deal of money in those days and there was a gasp of appreciation from the audience and then tremendous applause. Morris waited for the clapping to die down, holding up his hand to quell the last of it. "My friends, let me tell you something maybe you haven't thought a lot this subject. For two thousand years when the *shophar* is blown and we drink the wine of redemption at Rosh Hashanah we are saying: 'Next year in Jerusalem!'" He looked about him. "Next year in Jerusalem," he repeated quietly, though the microphone carried his words clearly to the hushed audience.

He paused again. "Now the time has come. God has kept His promise to His people, Israel belongs now to the Jews again, to you, also me. If we cannot go to break the rock, to dig the irrigation canals to bring water to the kibbutzniks who make ready the soil for trees that will make Israel a green, beautiful land again, then we must use this." He held the cheque in his hand aloft, "Here is our spade and our dollar-muscles!" Morris Myers paused again, looking about him, "Who will be the next to honour the beautiful bride and the groom?" He wasn't quite ready for a response and continued, "A tree. A tree that grows strong and tall and reaches to touch the blue sky. A tree that is one day so big it will make a great shade and has also a trunk so a man's arms cannot come around it. A tree that can stand strong when the wind comes from the desert and has roots like iron that can bind and hold. Who will put his name on such a tree? A glorious name and also, you are getting a nice little brass plate by this tree, so the people who are coming by that tree, they will see your name, they will know who is giving this tree for Israel!" He pronounced it, Is-ray-el, as in the Hebrew language and his middle European accent seemed no longer slightly comic, but sounded mellifluous and ancient, almost biblical. I wondered how it must feel to be a Jew and return home to your promised land, after two thousand years. How it must be to begin the task of making the desert bloom again, carving the new Garden of Eden from the rock and the heat and the loose grains of dead sand.

There was the scrape of a chair on the parquet floor beside me and the chicken guts man leapt to his feet waving his cheque book. "I have here a spade! I have here muscle cash!" he cried, moving over to the microphone.

Poor old Dudley and Gemma, their wedding, hijacked by Morris Myers for The Golden Book, never recovered. That night a dozen square miles of eucalypt forest were pledged to Israel as the Jewish cheque-book horticulturists from Down Under worked themselves into a planting frenzy faster than the speed of write.

Benita claims that it was a combination of my

desperation, boredom, poor manners, indifferent upbringing and, probably, inebriation that caused what happened next. In a way I suppose she is right, although I wasn't conscious of my physical actions at the time and I'm certain I wasn't drunk.

The pen ploughing and cheque-book planting had been going on for at least an hour, with each cheque attached to a long, boring speech. It showned no sign of abating and like most of us at times of extreme boredom I found myself daydreaming. Only, I have never completely lost the ability of childhood to become totally lost, going so deeply down into my subconscious that I forget where I am and the dreaming becomes more real than the reality around me.

I suddenly became aware of Damon as he lay in his bassinet at home. His lips were blue and puckered, his skin so white it was almost translucent and his eyes tightly closed. It was much more than a premonition or a vague discomfort, it was a clear, clean image in the mind's eye as though I were standing over him. There was something terribly wrong. I leapt from my chair and grabbed Benita, gripping her by the arm with both hands, attempting to pull her to her feet. "Come, we've got to go!" I hissed.

Taken by surprise she rose to her feet to the amazement of the doctor seated beside her. I released her arm and grabbed his. "You have to come, our baby is at home dying!"

The doctor stood, he wasn't much bigger than I was, though broader about the shoulders. "You came here, to this wedding and your baby is dying?" He looked at Benita.

"Of course not!" Benita protested. She put her hand on his arm and smiled, trying to cover her embarrassment, "Mark, I'm sorry." She threw a dirty look at me, "He's not used to wine."

"Please, Mark, please come, it's true." I tried to pull him by the arm but he pulled away. I was unaware that the entire table was looking at me.

Benita had had enough. "No, *you* come!" she spat, then she grabbed me, her sharp nails digging into my upper arm.

I grabbed her by the wrist, pulled her grip from my arm and made for the doorway. I was close to tears but no less convinced that something was terribly wrong with Damon. Benita must have stopped to get her handbag, then I heard her heels following me to the lift.

"Jesus! Are you crazy? What's wrong with you?" she shouted, catching up.

"It's Damon, there's something wrong." I offered no further explanation.

The lift pinged and the doors opened. It contained an elderly couple, so nothing further was said on the way down. As the lift opened into the hotel foyer I moved out first. "Wait outside on the pavement, I'll get the car." I started to run.

"Wait!" I heard Benita shout, but I kept on running, ignoring her call. I pulled up outside the front of the hotel where Benita waited and leant over to open the passenger side door. She jumped in, slamming the door violently behind her. "What's the matter with you? How dare you humiliate me in front of everyone!" I pulled away fast. "Go on, kill us! Don't go so bloody fast! What am I going to say to Gemma? You spoilt her whole wedding!" It came out in sharp, vituperative bursts. Then she started to sob, though I think, more from anger and humiliation than distress. "You're drunk! Jesus! Don't drive so bloody fast!"

I was not drunk; driving fast, yes, but not stupidly: concentrating on the road which was sheeny wet from a thunderstorm following the afternoon heat, though the rain had stopped before we'd come out of the hotel. "I'm sorry. I had this sudden premonition about Damon." Even as I spoke it reappeared sharp and quite clear, though I knew it sounded really crazy.

"Oh, you! I suppose you think it's funny! You're a . . . " She seemed lost for words. "You're a bloody anti-semite!" Benita's anger was now mixed with the frustration of knowing that I wasn't going to explain any further. She folded her arms and sucked her bottom lip under the top one, then she hunched her shoulders and jammed into the corner, distancing herself as far from me as the car would allow.

The image of my dying baby son was still sharp in my mind. How could I explain to her that what had happened was a childhood response. A thing I'd learned sucking at a black breast. I was simply being African which had nothing to do with reason and there was nothing I could do to stop it. I was reacting to an instinct so deep it didn't occur to me to question it. In some unexplained things I was still a child of a different, darker place and I was responding to voices of a different kind.

Fifteen minutes later, I turned sharply into the little dead-end street where we lived and pulled up in front of our two-bedroom cottage. I cut the ignition, grabbed the keys and leapt from the car.

The front door opened into a small passageway, with the doorway to the lounge on the immediate right so that you could look directly into it. The television was on low with light pumping from the screen, giving the room a bluish, semi-translucent darkness. Sarah must have heard my key rattle in the lock and she walked out of the lounge room into the lighted hallway. "Hi, Sarah. The baby? Everything okay?"

My words were an attempt to sound casual but I was breathing hard. Sarah looked confused, accurately sensing my anxiety and immediately thinking she must be guilty of something. "Yes, Mr Courtenay. What's wrong? Have I ... done something?" I made no reply; instead I brushed rudely past her and went into the lounge.

Twenty-four years later, I can still recall the picture on the black and white television screen, though I wasn't conscious of looking at it as I crossed the room. The ABC nine o'clock news was on and showed uni students and the usual left-wing rat-bags and trade unionists carrying banners and placards passing the town hall in George Street in an anti-Vietnam demonstration. (Or that is how I thought of them at the time.) The long shot of the marchers cut suddenly to a close-up of Dr Jim Cairns, a popular Labor politician who parted his hair down the centre and seemed always to wear a slightly hurt expression, like someone who believes himself constantly misunderstood.

I crossed the room opening a pair of slim louvre doors on to the small closed-in verandah we'd converted into a nursery for Damon. I turned on the light and moved over to the bassinet. Damon lay neatly tucked in under a blue blanket. He was a bit pale and I thought his lips lacked colour, but they were nothing like I'd seen them in my mind; his eyes were closed tightly, like a newborn kitten's, but he seemed contented enough and quite naturally asleep. My first sensation was one of enormous relief. I placed my hands on the edge of the bassinet, tossed my head back and let out a huge sigh. I'd been wrong, my mind had been playing tricks. My relief was followed immediately by a feeling of incredible stupidity. My face started to burn, the heat rising to my forehead and breaking into sharp prickles. How was I ever going to explain myself to Benita?

I decided to pick Damon up and bring him to her for his evening feed. With her baby asleep in my arms, my wife couldn't very well shout at me. And after I'd returned from taking Sarah home and she'd fed him and handed him to me for de-burping she would have calmed down somewhat. Feeding her baby would make her eyes go soft and, by the time Damon was put down again, I'd have thought of a way to explain my bizarre behaviour.

I could hear Benita saying something to Sarah as she entered the house. I pulled the blanket away from my sleeping son and reached down for him. Then I saw that his nappy was soaked with blood.

3

*Butterfly Needles, Hospitals and Sir
Splutter Grunt.*

It was a month after Damon's circumcision, in fact, well
after Christmas, when our appointment came around to
see Sir Seymour Plutta, knight of the realm, paediatrician
and specialist at the Children's Hospital, Camperdown.
We were later to learn that his nickname among the staff
was, predictably, Splutter Grunt or, further abbreviated,
S.G. The grunt was added to the splutter for reasons I
was to discover some time later.

He was a greying, bristle-haired, stiffly put together
little man in his mid fifties in a blue serge suit with fully
buttoned waistcoat, starched cutaway white collar and
navy blue club tie. If he'd been an animal he'd have been
a rather irascible fox terrier. He also had a most peculiar
walk. As he moved forward he would tug at the ends of
his suit sleeve to cover an inch of protruding white cuff.

First he'd pull one sleeve forward to bury a flash of miscreant white and then the other. The moment he released one sleeve to attend to the second cuff, the first reappeared, forcing him to repeat the motion.

It was this peculiar sleeve-tugging action that gave his walk its jerky appearance. As he tugged at his sleeve the movement seemed somehow synchronised with his neck and back, which would immediately straighten with a small, almost imperceptible jolt. All of this gave him the rigid appearance of an old-fashioned, wind-up tin soldier.

If I seem to be belabouring this description of Sir Seymour, it is because in all the years we were to know him this entire outfit, including his silk hose and immaculately shone, expensive, handmade black shoes, never altered. His clothes were himself and he gave the impression that they dressed a body as spindly and insubstantial as a Giacometti sketch. But for his blue serge suit and his pettish manner he might hardly have been there at all.

Despite his size, fear followed Sir Seymour like an invisible vapour. You could sense nurses and young doctors scurrying like small forest animals down corridors into dark corners and disappearing through escape hatches at the sound of his entourage approaching.

For he never walked alone. He was constantly accompanied by a dozen fawning, white-jacketed interns and the charge sister for the ward, at whom he would bark instructions or point out faults in cleaning or general administration. A dripping tap or an empty saline drip above a child's cot or bed would send him into a fearful state.

Nevertheless, his reputation as a doctor was formidable and, in particular, he was famous for his diagnostic skills. While on his rounds he would often approach the cot of a small child, glance at the infant with a cold blue, clinical eye and, without the slightest acknowledgment of the child, finger its limbs, place a cold stethoscope on its tiny chest or examine its ears or eyes. When the bewildered infant commenced to cry he would look carefully at its tongue. Then, still oblivious of the distraught child, he would whisper his findings into the ear of the ward sister as if she were unaware of the child's illness. Turning to some luckless intern, he would demand that the student examine the bawling infant, diagnose its illness, explain the typical symptoms and articulate the usual treatment.

It was as if Sir Seymour had seen every slapstick British hospital comedy ever made, had missed the melodrama and taken seriously the role of the legendary and fearsome head of hospital. If the intern failed to satisfy with the diagnosis, in a pettifogging voice, tinged with scorn, Sir Seymour would ridicule the student in front of his peers, whereupon he would instruct the sister to reveal the correct diagnosis. On the other hand, if the intern got it more or less right, Sir Seymour would grunt in a highly pronounced way and move on. This grunt, which provided the second part of his nickname, was known among the interns as Splutter's grunt and was considered the ultimate sign of approval, the imprimatur to go forth and practise medicine with divine confidence.

Benita and I were ushered into a small waiting room by a nurse and left to wait for Sir Seymour. The small room contained no windows and a single ceiling light lit the interior. It was furnished with four, rather scuffed, bentwood chairs, a child's wicker chair and a low table on which lay a pile of tattered children's books with most of the covers separated from their innards.

The door leading into Sir Seymour's surgery was closed. Screwed on to it was a varnished teak plaque with his name, "Sir Seymour Plutta", lettered in gold in Times Roman, complete with black drop shadow. It was very quiet in the waiting room and, though I strained to hear any signs of life, no noise at all came from the other side of the heavy teak door.

We'd been exactly on time, Benita in a salmon pink Chanel suit and me dressed for work in navy blazer and tie and Damon ready to chuckle, as usual. In fact we'd arrived at Camperdown early, not knowing how long it would take to get across town. We'd even waited for several minutes outside the hospital gates in order to arrive precisely on time. Now we sat for forty minutes, whispering to each other for fear of disturbing the medical silence.

We were both a little overwrought, our minds filled with speculation about our baby boy. Benita had become convinced that Damon was a bleeder. I tried to comfort her, pointing out that since the time of the wedding when I'd grabbed him and rushed him to Crown Street maternity hospital for a transfusion, saving his life by less than a hour, he'd been perfect. His birth bruise was gone and he was the pinkest, fattest, loveliest baby with sticky-up hair you've ever seen.

"What if he is a bleeder, what will we do?" It was a question Benita asked constantly and to which I had no answer. Instead, I would hide my frustration by feigning irritability.

"Well he isn't, that's all! Don't you think they'd have told us by now?"

"Well then, why are we seeing the specialist at the Children's Hospital?"

"It's just routine. Obviously it isn't serious. They transferred him there from Crown Street. The appointment isn't until after Christmas . . . It's just routine."

"Well, what if he is, that's all!"

I knew what she meant but it had become a thing between us. "Is what?"

"A bleeder!"

"Jesus! I wish you'd stop carrying on like a bloody old woman! Damon is a perfectly normal baby!"

I could hear myself inventing the protesting words in an attempt to smother the speculation coming from my wife and, secretly, from my own eroding confidence. Finally the door to Sir Seymour's surgery opened and a nursing sister emerged carrying a very small baby wrapped in a white hospital blanket. "You can go in now," she said, not looking at us as she crossed the waiting room. I hurried to open the outer door for her and she passed through it without acknowledging me, her attention on the baby in her arms.

Sir Seymour was seated in an old-fashioned swivel chair behind a large desk in the centre of the room. "Sit, please," he said without glancing up. In that universal way of all doctors he appeared to be writing on a small filing card. We sat, lowering our bottoms quietly on to the two bentwood chairs facing his desk, companions to those in the waiting room. He continued to write for what seemed like several minutes, sufficient time anyway to examine our surroundings.

The surgery was unremarkable and gave an overall impression of brownness. Brown teak panelling, a single, large, ugly, brown, framed picture showing a bleak, autumnal, Scottish landscape on the far wall. Against the wall to the left of the desk stood a brown, rather lumpy looking, vinyl examination couch with brass studs around its perimeter. Directly above this were several cheaply framed, though important looking, certificates and diplomas. The floor was uncovered and made of dark, frequently polished parquet, the tiny oblong blocks barely visible where years of waxing had filled the spaces between them and smoothed their individual grain to a surface anonymity. Even the olfactory aspect of the surgery gave a hint of gloom, the vague paraffin smell of built-up floor polish seemed entirely appropriate to the sombre nature of the space surrounding us.

Adding to the general sense of depression was a large creamy-yellow porcelain basin against the right-hand wall, with centred stainless steel spout and elbow nudgetaps jutting out of the wall on either side. The lead S-bend under the sink was dented and somewhat lopsided and a paper towel dispenser was fitted high up onto the wall to the side of the sink. Directly below it on the floor stood an old-fashioned scale with T-bar and sliding cast-iron weight counter.

It was just the sort of room in which you expected to hear bad news. I could sense Benita's growing depression. Sir Seymour looked up at last. "Ah, yes, Mr and Mrs ..." he glanced down at his appointment diary, "Courtenay?"

"How do you do, doctor?" we both mumbled, Benita smiling nervously.

Sir Seymour continued without acknowledging our greeting. "Yes, let me see. Your son, Damien, isn't it?"

"Damon, doctor."

He ignored my correction and opening a drawer withdrew a small wooden index-card box. Walking his fingertips over the tops of the cards, he removed one and placed it on the desk. "Yes, well. How was your Christmas?" He looked up and flashed us a thin smile adding, "I wanted you to have Christmas first."

"Fine, thank you, doctor." I was immediately anxious at his clumsy phrasing.

Sir Seymour continued to look directly at us. "Yes, well. He's a haemophiliac, I'm afraid." His expression was almost matter of fact. "I wanted you to get Christmas over first. Any others in your family?" His eyes moved to Benita.

Benita was clearly stunned, not prepared for his question. "A haemophiliac?"

I sensed that she knew what a haemophiliac was, though I had no idea. We'd used the term bleeder without ever putting a medical name to it. At the sound of that word, I grew cold. I knew just enough Latin to know it had something to do with blood. Our worst private fear was about to be plucked from dormancy in our subconscious and planted into our real lives.

"It's not a disease, so you must put the idea of a cure away from your minds immediately. Haemophilia is caused by a factor missing in your child's blood, the ingredient which causes it to clot." He turned his palms upwards and gave a small shrug, "It's not something we can ever fix."

Benita is a feisty woman and though clearly distressed she looked directly at the doctor. "I know what a haemophiliac is, doctor. It's been over a month since his circumcision. Why didn't you tell us before this?"

Sir Seymour looked at her, surprised at the pique in her voice, or perhaps the idea that he was being asked to explain. "My dear young lady, I thought it best to let Christmas pass."

I could feel a sharp stab of anger rise up in me. Unknowingly, I was standing at the source of the Nile, the thin first trickle from under rock and fern, the beginning of twenty-four years of a great river of anger and frustration at the arrogance, the careless disregard for feelings and the patronising manner of the Australian medical profession. Nevertheless, I remained silent, too timid to rebuke the great doctor.

Benita's eyes welled up and her voice was tearful as she spoke. "We had a right to know earlier. He's my baby!" I put my arm around her, more to stop any further outburst than to comfort her. I was hurt and angry too, but I didn't want a scene. In fact, I couldn't imagine one with this vainglorious aristocrat.

"Can anything be done, doctor?" I asked, anxious to sound co-operative.

Sir Seymour seemed oblivious of Benita's distress. "No, Mr ... er ... Courtenay. I repeat, there is something missing! In fact it's the *Factor VIII* in his blood. He hasn't any, or damn little. You'll have to bring him in for a blood transfusion every time he bleeds."

"Bleeds? You mean if he's cut?" My mind raced ahead.

It didn't seem too bad. Babies, even small children, don't get cut too often and we could be super careful bringing him up. In my mind I was already groping for the comforting phrases I would later use to Benita. She was blowing her nose on a tissue, Sir Seymour waiting for her to complete the task so that the nasal noise wouldn't compete with his voice.

"Bruise, not cut. When he bumps himself he'll get a haematoma, a bruise, internal bleeding. In his case this generally won't stop spontaneously and he'll need a blood transfusion. Superficial cuts and scrapes are of no major concern, it's the knocks and bumps that do the damage."

"If it isn't stopped, this internal bleeding ... will he die, doctor?"

"No, not unless the bruising is extensive. A bad automobile accident, for instance, and you find you can't get him to a hospital for a transfusion fairly quickly." He picked up his fountain pen and leaned back in the swivel chair tapping the capped pen onto his kneecap. "I think the sooner you face up to the fact that your son won't have a normal life and that life expectancy in his case is limited, the better." He clearly approved of his direct no-nonsense manner. "He'll start to develop arthritis in his teens. Haemophiliacs seldom live beyond their mid forties, though treatment is improving slowly."

I wasn't really hearing any of this, my mind still focused on whether Damon could bleed to death. Internal bleeding seemed so much worse than the outside kind. "A blood transfusion, what does it involve?"

"We use a frozen solution called cryoprecipitate, which is basically *Factor VIII*. We administer it intravenously using a butterfly needle to get into the vein. It usually stops the bleeding in three or four hours."

Benita had recovered sufficiently to look up at the doctor who had adopted a slightly arch expression, as though he was growing impatient at my questions but felt it was perhaps too early to terminate the interview.

"Is he in pain when it happens, when he bruises?" Benita asked.

"Yes, well, it's rather a nasty business. The pressure builds up under the skin and the skin can only expand so much. I imagine it would be very painful, although a child's pain centre isn't as highly developed as our own." He glanced at his watch. "Look, I've made an appointment for you to see Dr Robertson. He has an interest in haematology. Your son Damien will be under his immediate care."

He paused, leaned forward and gave us another tiny, sharp smile. "You are in good company. Tsar Nicholas, the last of the Russian tsars, his son was a haemophiliac." He smiled thinly again. "You may be assured I'll keep my eye on the boy. Haemophiliacs are not that common and a classic haemophiliac with virtually no clotting factor whatsoever, well, it's a bit of a find really. The pathology is damned interesting."

He leaned forward and, as though he were reinforcing the glance at his watch moments before, he now tapped his fountain pen on the edge of the desk, bringing the interview to a conclusion. "I anticipate we'll be seeing quite a lot of your young lad here at Camperdown." He picked up the phone and dialled a single digit. "Sister is Dr Robertson available to see Mr and Mrs Courtenay now?"

Fuck you, doctor! But the expletive in my mind remained mute: I needed to know one more thing before he dismissed us. "How will we know when he's bruised himself? I mean, he's a tiny baby."

Sir Seymour raised an eyebrow fractionally. It was obvious he thought me rather dim. "Why, he'll cry, of course." He rose from his chair. "See Sister at reception. Dr Robertson will answer any further questions you may have."

I went to shake his hand, but both hands were now clasped behind his back, as though he'd anticipated being touched and had wished to avoid any further personal contact. "Thank you, doctor," I said lamely. "Thank you for seeing us." I hated my obsequious manner, yet so intimidated was I in the presence of the "great" Sir Splutter Grunt that I seemed not to be able to help myself. Doctors were, after all, second only to God in those days.

"Yes, thank you," Benita whispered as we turned to leave. I put my arm around her and we crossed the room. I could hear the protesting squeak of the swivel chair as his bum returned to it. Then the rattle of the telephone receiver being picked up, followed by the "zirrrrit" of the dial face as it triggered a single digit. All this before we'd reached the door. It was just another routine day for Sir Seymour Plutta.

At the door I turned and said again, "Thank you, doctor."

The handpiece held to his ear, Sir Seymour grunted, a single sharp sound, like a resonant burp. Unknowingly, I'd become a recipient of Splutter's grunt, though I felt none of the divine confidence it was meant to inspire.

It was almost eighteen months before Damon's life as a haemophiliac got truly underway. Not yet crawling, but able to stand in his heavily upholstered cot and despite the fact that it stood well away from the wall, he'd managed somehow to bang his head.

We were to learn that bruising is a mysterious thing and often seems to happen without a remembered incident. Human beings are a clumsy lot; we whack and knock and thump and bump ourselves unknowingly a hundred times every day. Only, with a haemophiliac, the clotting factor in the blood doesn't rush to the rescue in seconds, blotting up the blood to prevent internalised bleeding.

Benita woke to Damon's crying and nudged me with her elbow. Because I'm an habitual early riser we'd agreed that I'd do the early morning nappy change and allow her to sleep in a bit. It was early, just before five a.m., still dark on a crisp autumn morning. I made my way blearily to Damon's cot and picked him up, which seemed to comfort him for a moment but, when I laid him down to change his nappy, he started to cry again. I dried him, powdered his pink little bottom and changed him. Then I brought him, still crying, into bed with Benita and went into the kitchen to prepare his bottle. He really was the easiest of children and seldom cried for no reason. I prepared his bottle then ran the cold tap over it, testing it on the inside of my wrist before bringing it in to him.

"He doesn't seem well, his head feels hot," Benita said as I entered the bedroom. Benita is notoriously cranky in the mornings, when nothing ever seems to be right. I drew the bedroom curtains to let in the light, but it was still rather dark and so I switched on the light. "What do you mean?" I asked.

"It feels wrong." She had one hand resting on top of Damon's head as she reached for the bottle. "There's something wrong with his head, it's bigger or something." She fed the bottle to Damon who resisted taking it and continued to cry.

"Don't be silly. It's just the angle. Babies' heads always look big. Babies' heads are big, their bodies have to grow into them." I took the bottle and tried it on him again and, somewhat to my surprise, he took it, which stopped him crying. "There you are," I said smugly, confident that I'd solved the problem.

He cried intermittently for the next couple of hours but seemed all right again as I left for work at seven-thirty. "It's colic or something," I said expertly. Though his head did seem to have expanded a little, I was reluctant to admit this even to myself. "Call me if anything happens," I said to Benita as I kissed her, anxious to escape from her growing concern into the crisp autumn outside.

At noon Benita called me at work, but I was out at the time producing a television commercial at a North Sydney studio. The script called for two voices, with all dialogue on camera, requiring a locked sound stage. The director had called for absolutely no interruption. By the time we'd finished it was after five and the studio receptionist had left for home, having failed to give me Benita's lunchtime message, relayed through to the film studio by Suzanne my secretary.

I was the creative director at McCann Erickson, a job which I'd inherited almost by default and for which many thought I was both too young and too inexperienced. It meant long hours and a great deal of hard work; I seldom got home before nine at night and often much later.

I justified this to Benita as the break we'd been looking for, the "make or break", I called it. Privately, I told myself that I'd make it up to my kids by rising early each morning to get them off to school and by devoting my entire weekend to my family. To some degree, at least, I was to be successful in this. A big career, success with all the trappings, was important to someone with my background. It was up to me to keep the ball in the air. Poor boys don't get too many second chances. After all, I told myself, "I'm doing all this for them."

The professional demands on me, as I saw them, were not only for hard work. I had progressed very quickly in my advertising career and had been appointed creative director of a large agency just five years after starting in the advertising business. I was a young executive launched on a spectacular career path and I was prepared to pay my dues. If this meant late nights and less time for the kids, it was a price I was prepared to pay. The Western world was booming, the consumer society was upon us, the steaks were thick and tender and pink in the middle, the geese were laying golden eggs and opportunities in the Lucky Country for a young bloke with no formal training and some talent for words were spectacular. All it was going to take was drive and ambition, two words which should have been appropriated and sandwiched between my Christian and my surname — Bryce "Drive & Ambition" Courtenay. It fitted perfectly. I was learning to tap dance and I was to become very good at it, the Fred Astaire of the local propaganda industry.

The decade and a half from the early sixties to the mid seventies in Sydney advertising were hard-drinking years. As Australia's youngest creative director, running a big reputation creative department, I suppose I was under a fair amount of pressure to perform. A few drinks after finishing work at seven or eight was easy to justify as part of the job, part of my career, part of being a good bloke and, though I would have had trouble admitting it, also a part of my ability to cope.

I should add that nobody is easier to convince himself than I am. I tell myself lies and soon I believe them. I had a hot team of creative people and I convinced myself that the task of sharing their after-hours life was included among my professional responsibilities.

It wasn't too hard for my inflated ego to reach this conclusion and I don't remember needing any outside persuasion. The pub was fun, a nice warm cocoon, a great place to hide. How easily it all rolls off the tongue and how bloody arrogant and pompous it now seems. Increasingly, I found myself driving home late at night, half — no three-quarters — smashed, to wake up the following morning with a sore head and a yellow, furry, nicotine-coated tongue.

But somehow I always got the boys up early. Brett and Adam and, later, Damon also, that is, if he hadn't been up most of the night with a bleed and wouldn't be going to school as usual. I'd make their breakfast and we'd have a bit of a play or we'd talk or discuss their homework. In the summer we'd even occasionally go fishing in the bay or kick a ball around. This was almost entirely out of guilt. While I think I did have the makings of a very good father, I didn't give the task the priority it demands in life. As a father I was all smoke and mirrors, a nice guy who was never around at night but who always came to breakfast.

The shoot I was on the day Damon's head exploded finished late. After the director called a wrap we all retired to a pub up the road. It was the place where all the northside ad men, film people, musos, jingle merchants, production people, freelance artists, illustrators and the like, did their drinking. The beer was always fresh and suitably cold and the girls from the local agencies who dropped in after five usually started pretty and drank prettier and prettier as the evening wore on.

Australia had very few dedicated young artists at that time and the older, well-known ones had all escaped overseas. We were the commercials — the young talent who had opted for money rather than a damp basement lodging and eventual recognition.

This pub was across the Bridge from McCann Erickson, my own agency. Sometime during the evening a bloke named Singo from a local agency, who'd had too much to drink and took exception either to me, or my intrusion into his territory, invited me into the lane at the back of the pub.

The pub emptied to accompany us and, soon after squaring up, Singo tore my collar and I biffed him a couple of times and spilled a bit of blood. I could box a little and blood on a white shirt is always a quick way to stop a meaningless fight. This was a trick I'd learned in the copper mines in Central Africa at a much earlier stage in my life and it has subsequently saved me from any real damage to my physical person on a dozen different occasions.

At the sight of a generous splash of nose blood down Singo's shirt-front we were immediately parted by several of the more sober of the spectators. Ten minutes later Singo and I, arms around each other's shoulders, were singing a rugby song together and feeling absolutely no pain.

I drove home that night thinking the yellow line down the centre of the road was specially placed there to guide me. That is, as long as I was careful to straddle it with the front wheels of General Motors finest, my light brown (Northern Territory Gold) Holden Special. I followed it conscientiously and home is precisely where it led.

It was after midnight when I pulled up outside our cottage, where I was confronted at the door by a raging, screaming, tearful, berserk, biting, scratching, delicious-looking wife with heaving breasts, whom I could only think of as stunning. Someone whom I would have dearly loved to sleep with but who, alas, wasn't going to let me.

I awoke the next morning feeling very second-hand and scratched about the face and arms from Benita's welcome the previous night. I woke Brett and Adam for breakfast, fresh orange juice for vitamin C, cornflakes and toast soldiers for dipping into the small, oval, calcium-encased Vesuvius in their egg cups, which erupted every time they pushed toast fingers into its disgusting yellow goo.

At breakfast six-year-old Brett told me how Damon's head had grown bigger and bigger until they all thought it was going to pop. "We waited for you, Daddy, but then Mummy had to take him to the hospital. It's probably popped by now! Will he still be alive?"

Benita, who wasn't talking to me, did at least say Damon was okay. I called the hospital when I got to work and asked how he was. "He's had two transfusions and seems quite cheerful," the ward sister told me.

"May I visit him at about eleven?" I asked.

There was a pause. "Sorry Mr Courtenay, but you'll have to wait until Dr Robertson comes in. He's instructed no visitors, but he may be prepared to make an exception for the child's parents. Can you call back in an hour?"

An hour later I called to be told that I was allowed to see Damon, but that Benita was not permitted to do so. "Why Sister?" I asked fearfully.

There was a pause on the phone. "I think I'd better put you through to Dr Robertson," she said.

After she connected me I could hear the extension ringing for quite some time; finally the receiver lifted, "Robertson!"

"Doctor, it's Bryce Courtenay, Damon's father."

"Oh, yes, Mr Courtenay?"

"Sister tells me my wife may not visit him."

"Ah yes, a matter of judgment. You see your son has a very bad haematoma. To be perfectly frank, we've never seen anything quite like it. The cranium is grossly swollen and is very unsightly. I'm afraid your wife may react badly if we allowed her to see him in his present condition. Why did you wait so long to bring him in?"

I couldn't tell him about my being drunk or that Benita was a new driver and afraid to drive through the city traffic. "You instructed us always to wait a few hours, to make sure it was a bleed," I said, knowing that this was true but taking his instructions to the extreme. Knowing how long to wait was always a problem, Benita is apt to panic too quickly and I remain calm too long.

"I think you took my instructions to the extreme, don't you?"

I remained silent, not knowing what to say and angry that he wanted me to admit my mistake like a schoolboy confronted by his housemaster.

"Well, be that as it may, I don't want your wife visiting the child," he said.

What a fucking nerve! Who the fuck does he think he is? Whose fucking baby is it, anyway? I was filled with righteous indignation, but when the time came to speak all I could manage was, "That's considerate of you, doctor, but she *is* his mother, I think she'll be more upset if she's not permitted to see him."

I was taking Robertson on for the first time. My head started to pound and, with the sudden rush of blood, my hangover hurt like hell. I wanted to throw up, the mixture of anxiety and the previous night's drinking not a good one. I could taste the sour, raspy burn of sudden sick in the back of my throat.

There was a lengthy silence on the other end of the phone, at last Robertson answered, his voice controlled, "Nevertheless, that is my decision, Mr Courtenay."

My head roared and I couldn't hear myself think: I'll insist! No I won't, I'll back off. Christ, no, not this time! This time I'll make a stand!

"I see, er, yes, very well doctor, I'll tell her."

"Thank you, Mr Courtenay, I'm sure it's for the best." The phone went dead.

I arrived at the Children's Hospital half an hour later

not knowing what to expect, fearful of what I might see. What I saw as I entered Damon's room was so vastly in excess of my imagination that I immediately went into shock.

That day in early Autumn, in the tiny private room in the Children's Hospital with the walls painted with a mural of pixies, fairies and mushrooms, was to be the worst day of my life, that is, until April Fools' Day twenty-three years later.

I want you to imagine an alien creature with a small baby's torso, fat and chubby and pink, but on its shoulders a huge, deep purple, oval head about three times the size of a normal head, soft and mushy-looking like an overripe plum, with the skin stretched so tightly that it created a totally smooth surface with no features. Where you looked for eyes, there were only tiny slits and where there ought to have been a mouth, there was a small aperture that looked like a deformed belly button. And where there might be ears, there was nothing, except two dents in the side of the great, oval sack of purple blood.

My beautiful baby son with his large, bright, happy eyes and soft sticky-up hair had been turned into a monster. He stood holding on to the side of the cot rocking back and forth, tiny bubbles coming from the twisted, navel-like aperture that should have been his soft little rosebud mouth.

I stood, unable to comprehend. Nothing had prepared me for this. In Africa, in the mines, I had once seen a black man's skull split like a ripe tsamma melon by a fall of rock, brains and blood leaking from its shell. All I could do was light a cigarette and put it in his mouth;

and when he'd smoked it he said quietly, "Thank you, Bwana." Then he died. Once, I had been present when a shooter I was with shot a male baboon in the stomach and I'd observed it tear its own guts out, pulling out its entrails as it screamed in agony on a dark mottled rock against a blue African sky. I took the rifle from the man who'd made the shot and who now stood watching, his eyes agate-sharp with cruel glee. I worked the bolt, bringing a fresh bullet into the chamber and shot the almost human ape at point-blank range through the head. The bastard had shaved the nose of the .303 cartridges he was using, turning them into dumdums. The head of the baboon exploded as the bullet struck, leaving the great ape without a head on its torso; but with its hands still buried in its bloody guts.

And now my son's head. My son's head filled with blood and pain by the failure of a tiny chromosome trigger, a certain *Factor VIII* gone missing in his otherwise perfectly ordinary blood. The ingredient that turned off the tap for other babies wasn't there and my son's head filled and filled with blood until it looked as though it might explode. Explode like the head of the baboon, leaving a perfectly normal baby torso standing headless against a mural of red, floppy-capped pixies, gossamer fairies and pink-gilled toadstools.

I knew the nightmare of heads. I'd seen how vulnerable heads could be. The quiet death of the black man deep inside the dark, flinted earth of a copper mine and the raging death in the afternoon of a baboon with no head, its blackness and agony silhouetted against a flawless African sky. Now this new nightmare — the head of *my son* filled with the blood of his unstoppable bleeding.

There is some pain which is too great for a spontaneous outcry, too awful for the sobs that so nicely soak our agony in tears. It is a pain that comes from deep inside and so completely fills you that you become motionless, noiseless, without tears, just one or two that squeeze out and run across your chin like thin, carelessly spooned soup.

I didn't hear Sir Seymour Plutta and his entourage as they entered. Perhaps I heard him talking, but it was as though in a *dwaal*, a dream, in which a black and white fox terrier, balancing an open umbrella on its nose, dances on its hind legs in a circle made by strange, elongated, grinning men in white coats.

"Extraordinary! Gentlemen, you will spend your entire medical careers and never see anything like this again. Mr . . . er, the photographer here, will record it for a case study I intend to write. What's the umbrella for? I see . . . lighting, bounces light back into the subject. Ah-ha, I see, a reflector, a photographer's reflector. Will you use flash? We want all the details. You must shoot every angle, we may never get another chance. See how perfect, gentlemen. See here, you can poke your finger into the cranium. It's all blood, a massive, quite outstanding haematoma. Here, come on gentlemen, touch it. What do you think is the cause? Anyone like to hazard a guess?"

The flash bulb on the photographer's camera brought me back. White-jacketed interns were lined up in front of my son, each prodding a finger into the huge, purple, blood-filled balloon. An animal wail came from the back of my throat, perhaps like the baboon on the mottled rock, I don't know. Then I hit the blurred face nearest me. It went down. It was a lousy, mistimed punch; the bastard should have stayed down but, instead, Sir Seymour Plutta hit the floor and then sat up astonished, his hand clamped over his bloody nose, unable to comprehend what had happened.

"Get up, you shit, I'm going to fucking kill you!" That's what a medico I met years later told me I'd growled, though I don't recall saying anything at all and no official report of the incident was ever made. I was grabbed and held by a number of the interns as I bent to pull Sir Seymour to his feet by the lapels of his jacket. He continued to sit bewildered on the floor with his back against the photographer's lightbox, his head directly under the lighting umbrella. I saw a terrified little man in a white shirt and blue serge suit who reminded me of a fox terrier with blood coming from its nose. But at least the fox terrier was no longer yapping.

The long nightmare of the bleeding had begun.

4

The Art of Dreaming.

I'm not at all sure I was a good father. I often think that I messed up the task of being a parent. Though I try to tell myself parenthood is still too close to me and, certainly, I feel unable to write a chronological account of our family life. The time we are given for parenting is so short, passes so quickly and is jumbled up with so many other priorities and disruptions that, in the end, we come to doubt that we used it in the best interests of our children.

There is so much which, in retrospect, I feel might have been added. I feel most guilty about letting my children's childhood pass without sufficient play. I was too preoccupied with myself, my career and, I told myself, Damon's haemophilia. Before I was fully aware of it, their childhood was over and I was talking to young adults

56

whose voices had suddenly become a couple of octaves lower.

At thirty-one, Brett still recalls with some chagrin that every year I promised we'd go camping and that we never did. I promised to go fishing with him at The Gap and I never did. Partly because I'd once watched in terror as he scampered, like a mountain goat, across the cliff face, but mostly because I was otherwise occupied. Damon wanted to learn to skin dive, but we never got around to it; again, I told myself, because I was afraid he might be hurt, but mostly it was because I couldn't find the time. Adam wanted badly to teach me how to ride a surfboard, but this too never came about.

Now, as I try to write about Damon's childhood, to re-create a time where his small life was crowded with events, these are hopelessly confused in my own memory.

For instance, Brett and Adam achieved quite a lot in their not unusual childhood. At school and in sport, both achieved most of the academic and sundry accolades, the badges and the prizes and the leadership roles which institutions invent as the character-building trivia of which school life is composed. As a consequence they often made us feel proud of them. But now, barely a decade later, few of these formal pictures remain in my mind.

Instead, I carry around a bagful of emotional clutter among which is a picture of Brett at ten handing me his end-of-term school report. While he'd done well enough overall, his English mark was a C. Language in our family has always been important; I sternly demanded an explanation. He looked up at me and bringing his hand up to his head he scratched it, bemused, "I dunno how it happened, Dad, I thought I done good!"

Another is of an eight-year-old Adam, whose room had acquired a peculiar smell, which he seemed not to notice. One evening, quite late, I walked into it to tell him it was bedtime. Sitting happily on his bed chewing an apple was a wide-eyed and totally relaxed possum. "Dad, this is Willy," Adam said casually, not looking up from his homework. It turned out he'd spent months enticing the small arboreal creature into making visits into his room from the bush reserve abutting our garden.

Of Damon there is yet another, a sliver of emotional memory which, like those of Brett and Adam, carries no significance and no importance and exists, some might say, at the saccharine end of memory. Damon, perhaps five years old, woke me early one summer morning shaking my shoulder with both hands. "Wake up, wake up, Daddy, it's the world's best day and guess what?" He leapt on to me. "Hooray! We're in it!"

I find that the person I am or even have become is, in a large part, formed from this same sort of trivia.

It was perhaps my African background that allowed me to see Damon as a temporary gift. The fact that he had been born with a chronic condition and that his life couldn't be taken for granted, that a really bad fall or a relatively minor motor accident or some other cause of severe internal bleeding could take him away from us meant that he was special. While we were not really well off at this time, we were on our way and, certainly, we could afford to give our children many privileges. It could be possible to conclude that Damon was advantaged by his family's wealth. But it is important, I think, to understand neither wealth nor privilege eases the pain, nor can they finally prevent death. Both pain and death are as difficult to bear in a privileged child as in one less so. In the end, money cannot and does not help.

Haemophilia is an extraordinarily painful and protracted disease. A bleed is usually treated eight or ten hours after it has started, for it takes this long for a knock to become more painful than the initial bump. People bump themselves around sixty times a day and so it is impossible to notice a bump and transfuse it immediately. You have to wait and see if an ordinary, casual bump has caused internal bleeding. But once a bleed starts the pain continues long after the blood transfusion has been given. The clotting *Factor VIII* takes at least seven hours to stop continuous bleeding and often as long as a couple of days. This means that internal blood, seeping out of thousands of capillaries, builds up pressure under the skin. Unable to break the skin, the blood soon has nowhere to go and pushes inwards. The result is not dissimilar to being squeezed tighter and tighter by a vice. Imagine your hand, arm or knee in a vice which is squeezed relentlessly for eight or ten hours. The pain would become unbearable.

Haemophilia *was* a handicap for Damon. How could he lead the life of a small boy? He would never jump from a wall or cross a ditch or kick a ball properly or romp about and fall into a delighted heap of squealing young bodies on the front lawn.

Damon was a capricious gift to us, one we knew we must delight in while we may. We cherished him so much. We knew that if he joined in physical play with other kids he would certainly end up in great pain with an internal bleed which would need a trip to the hospital and a blood transfusion. So we lived those early years with our hearts constantly in our mouths.

But, despite this, Benita and I decided that he should make his own "physical" decisions as soon as he was old enough to understand the full consequences of his actions. If the simple act of kicking a ball was a calculated cost, if the price of being a normal kid, if for only a few minutes at a time, came very high then the decision to do so must be his. We had no right to impose our anxiety on him or claim to know what was best for him.

At least in this regard we were intelligent parents, for I truly believe this difficult decision on our part allowed him to grow up a wonderfully well-adjusted person. His frustration at not being able to do the physical things other kids took for granted was enormous, but it was never to turn into resentment or self-pity, or worse still, a derring-do attitude that would put him in deliberate jeopardy. I can never once remember Damon ever feeling sorry for himself.

Because he spent so much time away from school, physically disabled in some way, his mother and I became closely involved with his intellect and imagination — she by introducing him at a very early age to books and me by teaching him how to use his mind in an idiosyncratic fashion. We started early with our toddler, when he had his purple head and I'd go in to see him every evening.

He'd sit on my lap and I'd talk to him about Africa and about the life that goes on in our heads. It wasn't simply idle dreaming, but another sort of reality such that, when things got bad, there would be a place to go to inside your own head. It wasn't stuff he'd understand for a great many years to come, but I told it to him anyway so that, when comprehension eventually came, it would seem as though he'd always known it was there waiting for him, his own private country.

Then I'd sing to him, silly little songs in Zulu and Afrikaans and even one in English. The English song was always George Gershwin's "Summertime" from the folk opera *Porgy and Bess*. It was my favourite and I knew all the lyrics, but alas, with my decidedly unremarkable voice, I was banned from singing it at home. As far as I know this is a lifetime ban that's never been lifted. But Damon allowed me to sing it and he didn't seem to mind in the least when I sang off-key or when, trying to sustain a particularly mellifluous note, my voice broke. Sometimes I would sing it to him twice, careful to get the croaky bits correct the second time around. His purple head would blow spit bubbles and he wouldn't mind at all. Damon was a pretty tolerant sort of guy even then.

I am convinced that the need to dream is critical, to visit the private country in your head is an essential part of thinking, a natural problem-solving gift we are all given if we choose to use it. What I was really creating in Damon was simple self-hypnosis. Used intelligently to take us into ourselves, into parts of the brain we don't sufficiently use, it allows us to see problems from a different perspective and often to solve them in an original and more imaginative way. In reality, there really wasn't any need to teach it at all. I simply allowed Damon's dreaming to continue on, to stretch beyond his early childhood, careful only from time to time to add a little direction and to guide its haphazard and uncharted early childhood ways.

As it turned out, he was to lose two days in every week of his school life and to keep up with his classmates he was going to need something extra going for him. No matter how clever he might be, a little more than half of his school life absent from his school desk did not augur well for the examination-based curriculum of modern education. He would need another way to learn and so teaching him how to use his mind more completely seemed to me to be a suitable way to go about the task.

Because Benita and I spent so much more time with him than is usual, we had more responsibility for the things which influenced Damon than the conventional mélange of teachers, peers and siblings. Benita taught him the joy of books and of music and art. She taught Damon how to see and hear with intellectual clarity. I am not suggesting that Damon was exceptional in these things. While he developed a more sophisticated sense of art and music and, perhaps, even books he didn't ever show any artistic bent. Adam, his brother, was intensely musical with a good ear for languages and Brett showed an early ability to paint which seems to have since diminished. Damon was none of these things. He grew up to be someone who got a great deal of pleasure being a user. He seemed to delight in things. He, more than anyone I've met, seemed to use both the left and the right brain without conscious effort. He was always curious and wholly interested in just about everything around him.

At twelve, Damon was reading Franz Kafka and asking his mother questions she was barely able to answer. He seldom asked me questions of the intellectual kind, mostly for fear that I'd dad fact his query — I'd use my intuition where the answer was unknown. My ability to answer any question ever asked of me, Brett had labelled as a dad fact. These spurious, though often well-surmised and often coincidentally accurate answers, played an important part in the lives of my children. They would take some of my more outrageous creative answers or assertions to school to the delight and astonishment of their schoolmates who collected dad facts as eagerly as my own children did.

Even some of the masters wished to be informed of any new dad facts which might emerge. I became the prince of pure speculation and the master of the plausible impossibility. Even today among their friends, Adam or Brett, not sure of all of the facts of a matter, might paraphrase a statement by saying, "This may well be a bit of a dad fact, but I recently heard that . . ." One of the more important outcomes of dad facting was that all my kids grew up to make certain of facts while also accepting that pure speculation has a part to play in thinking.

Damon wasn't especially gifted. As he grew older he wanted all the yuppie things. He spoke of an expensive apartment, beautiful things around him and always of the Ferrari he would drive. He was convinced that he would be a millionaire by the time he was twenty-five. Quite how he would make this happen he was less clear about. Perhaps I had taught him to dream too well. His head was filled with business schemes all involving overnight success, not a great deal of effort on his part and the making of unlimited money. In the meantime, magically, he seemed to enjoy his life even though he was in constant pain.

From the very beginning Damon had a great many problems: his body didn't work; he was constantly disappointed by missing out on parties or excursions he'd looked forward to for weeks because he'd have a bleed and couldn't go; and his body was always covered in unsightly bruises. But one of his problems wasn't loneliness. He attracted people around him effortlessly, those of his own age and others closer to their dotage; all saw themselves as his friend and never tried to patronise him. Somehow, he had mastered the gift of friendship without making gestures, but by the giving of his spirit. People just liked being with Damon; he made them feel strong and hopeful and alive.

He wasn't an expert at anything. He was a conspicuous consumer and there is a big difference. He wasn't a snob, though he wanted the best because it seemed to him to work better than the less good. So he would spend his time with people who had something to say and with things that required more than superficial thinking. Nobody enjoyed people quite as much as Damon. Even at a young age he liked to listen. Perhaps he knew instinctively he was only going to be with us for a short while. But he sure had a great appetite for life, he rattled it as a baby might a favourite toy. Damon was completely alive every day of his life.

5

Knee Bone Connected to the Thigh Bone.

With two healthy little boys, I guess the attempt at a third child was really a try for a girl. Had Damon been a girl there would have been no haemophilia and this story would never have been told. The gene with its missing *Factor VIII* (the stuff in our blood which causes it to clot), while carried by the female, cannot transmit to female children. Only males are born haemophiliacs.

Blood tests have shown that Benita carried the affected gene from birth and by some enormous, unexplained miracle it missed both Brett and Adam. In terms of a lottery, the chances of this happening are around ten million to one, to have missed twice makes the odds almost impossible to contemplate. Had Brett or even Adam been born haemophiliacs, naturally that would have been the end of children for us. I don't suppose one can speculate in such matters, but, in retrospect, the idea of not having Damon, who made such a rich contribution to our lives, is unthinkable.

Apart from the incident concerning the circumcision, Damon's purple head episode was the first real warning that family life was going to change for us. When he began to crawl, the wheels immediately fell off our nice, calm, family life. We kissed Dr Spock and all his good middle-American advice goodbye forever and started to learn the new reality of living with a child who bleeds internally at the slightest knock.

All the hard corners on the furniture had to be rounded or padded and our tables and chairs carried so many bandaged corners most rooms looked like a casualty ward for accident-prone furniture. In fact, this precaution turned out to to be more for our own peace of mind than as a protection for an active crawler and, later, toddler.

Unless your child has marks to show where they've been, you simply have no idea how often they bump into the world around them. Learning to walk is, to say the least, a hit-and-miss business for us all — more hit than miss.

Soon Damon's chubby little body was covered with patches of purple, green, mottled brown and a peculiar muddy sort of red. In the twenty-four years of loving him we were never again to see him as a clean skin. He wore his "coat of many colours", the dozen or so large bruises in the process of ripening or fading, like a tramp wears a cast-off jacket. They never left him and almost every one of them commemorated a trip to hospital to receive a blood transfusion.

Throughout his life Damon was to have at least three

blood transfusions a week and sometimes more. We would put him to bed at night not knowing how long it would be before we were wakened to his cry. Later, when he could walk, he would come to my bedside and tug on my arm, "Wake up, Daddy, I've got a bleed."

I'd wake up to find him with his blue baby blanket, known as "Blanky" held against his cheek with his thumb in his mouth. "Hospital?" Damon would nod his head solemnly and I'd switch on the bedside light, scribble a note to Benita in case she woke up, then scratch around in a drawer for a T-shirt and jeans and rumble about in the bottom of the wardrobe for a pair of sandshoes. In nearly nine years of going to the hospital, mostly very late at night, I never put out any clothes in anticipation. Quite why not, I can't say. Perhaps it was an African thing from my past. An old Zulu proverb says, "Never put the herdboy's porridge out at night, for the demons also get hungry." Perhaps, deep inside, I thought by leaving my clothes ready I was inviting a bleed, inviting the demons to visit. It's stupid, I know, but very few things in this world are wrought by logic alone.

It was always my job to wake up at night and attend to Damon. I don't know quite how this happened; I know that there were times that I resented it enormously. I'd be dog-tired after a hard day or I'd have arrived home a little worse for wear and having to wake up in response to Damon's crying wasn't easy. But the implication of Damon crying was that he had a bleed and this would inevitably end in his having to go to hospital. Benita was genuinely scared of driving in the night and has never done so. Somehow along the way we'd negotiated that she did the days and I did the nights. If I said that I didn't often think that I'd gotten a raw deal, I'd be lying. I'd flop into bed exhausted only to be wakened two hours later by a Damon tug on the arm. Sometimes my head would be splitting and my mouth tasting like the inside of a parrot's cage. But I had no choice; I often found this hard and felt sorry for myself.

Even so, there is something that happens to you when you have a critically ill child. You learn, or at least I did, to keep things in separate compartments. Every task is clearly defined and kept in its own box. Damon's haemophilia called for an emotional neutrality. We decided it must never interfere with the opportunities available for Brett and Adam. They must not feel its impact on their lives. And so you couldn't in the end allow yourself to react emotionally to the circumstances around you; his bleeds and the procedure they involved took precedence over everything else — but they must not be seen to be doing so. After a while you simply gave up trying to work out who did what at home, what was fair and what wasn't. All the quarrelling and bickering and feeling sorry for yourself served no useful purpose. When you were in the Damon box, the haemophilia compartment, you simply got on with things and tried to create as little fuss as possible. There was an emotional price to pay for this, sometimes I appear very cold, precise and unfeeling. However, the discipline involved in conducting one's life in this way is not good for the human soul.

Looking back, those long nights were my real time with Damon, the time a father should spend with his sons, but never really allows time for in everyday life. Damon and I grew up together in the dark hours when most of the world, and almost all of the kids in it, were asleep.

To distract him from his pain we would talk. From the beginning he was curious about almost everything and a good listener, whereas, at the drop of a hat, I tend to go on a bit. We were a good combination. I think, of all his pleasant ways, the things people seemed to like most about Damon was his genuine curiosity and concern and the fact that he was a world champion listener.

Even from an early age Damon listened with his eyes and his whole face and his entire body in such a single-minded way that it was as though the two of you were wrapped together in a silken cocoon. It was this rare ability to concentrate that made it so much easier for him to discover his inner mind and to use it to control his often very severe pain.

Bleeding for a haemophiliac is not a question of receiving a severe knock; though a severe knock can create a bad bleed, this is not always the case. A light tap on the elbow, such as a toddler might experience a hundred times a day, can set up a bad bleed, while a much harder fall, observed with dismay, might create little or no damage. Bleeds seemed to come from nowhere and were always internal. Small superficial bleeds, from a light cut or a scratch say, were seldom dangerous and quite easy to handle with an ice pack and a little pressure applied.

It sometimes seemed to us that bleeds were most magical things, appearing often for no reason, for Damon could have a bleed while confined to bed with a cold. Even when he was old enough to monitor his own physical actions, many of his bleeds seemed spontaneous and without explanation. This was very hard to live with, the cause and effect we all rely on instinctively wasn't present. It was such an unreasonable disease, such an unfair one on everyone, but most particularly on Damon who could plan nothing in his life with any certainty.

Before he could walk I would wake to him crying in his cot, mostly well after midnight, and I would go to him and feel around until I located the hot spot, the spot on his body which was warmer to the touch and therefore indicated that he had started to bleed internally.

I'd go to the phone and call Dr Gett, the young Chinese doctor who was Damon's needle man. Gett, small and lightly built, was one of those doctors who make you want to forgive the medical profession for all its transgressions.

In a ghastly irony, the very thing he did for us so many times was to strike at his own family a few years later. His brother, also a doctor, was on a visit to New York to attend a medical convention. A mugger accosted him late at night at his hotel door and, it is thought, demanded his wallet. The young doctor must have resisted and was stabbed. He was found just inside the door of his hotel room the following morning, his cries for help having been ignored and, unable to reach the telephone, he bled to death.

When Dr Gett first cared for Damon he was still very young, about the same age as myself and had just been elevated to assistant haematologist under Dr Robertson. It was Dr Gett's job to undertake the medical procedure which, in those days, constituted a transfusion of *Factor VIII*.

Why Dr Gett was the only person allowed to transfuse Damon we were never quite able to understand. While he was a whizz with a butterfly needle, the process of putting a hypodermic needle into a vein is hardly a major medical procedure. Watching it three or four times a week it didn't seem all that complicated and, apart from actually putting in the dreaded needle, to save time and the services of a nursing sister in the small hours of the morning, I did most of the procedure anyway.

Several opaque plastic bags about seven inches long and five across of yellowish-coloured cryoprecipitate, the name given in this form to *Factor VIII,* would be taken out of the hospital freezer and lowered into lukewarm water for fifteen or so minutes to thaw. Then it would be removed and gently hand-massaged until the *Factor VIII* was completely dissolved to make a viscous, mucus-coloured substance. This would then be drawn out of each of the bags with a syringe and added to a single bag attached to a dripline which was suspended on a hook above Damon's head. When the bag of "cryo" and the dripline were in place it was time to use the butterfly needle. It had two small plastic wings fitted to the end of the needle which could be brought together by the fore-finger and thumb so that the needle would be secure and at more or less the correct angle to enter a vein. From the end of the hollow butterfly needle ran a tiny, eight-inch plastic tube with its end designed to clip into the dripline. A tourniquet was wrapped around Damon's upper arm and pumped until the veins in his arm "came up". The butterfly needle was then inserted, usually into a larger vein on the back of Damon's hand almost at the junction of the wrist.

If the butterfly needle was correctly inserted, the blood would quickly shoot up the tiny tube which would then be attached to the dripline and the drip flow tap turned on. Drop by tiny drop, the *Factor VIII* would enter his veins until an hour or so later the plastic bag above his head containing the precious clotting factor was empty and it was time to go home. It would be some time after we arrived back home before the clotting factor would take full effect and begin to terminate the bleed and alleviate the pain sufficiently for Damon to fall into a fitful sleep. The whole round trip to hospital and back might take three hours and, often, another two or three more would pass before the pain subsided enough for Damon to sleep.

We soon grew accustomed to seeing the light grow steadily and Damon could recognise the various bird calls in the garden as each came to feed. We must have held the father and son world record for seeing the sun come up over Parsley Bay.

On bleed nights, I seldom got back to bed and would count myself fortunate if I managed to get two or three hours' sleep prior to a bleed coming on. Most bleed nights merged into morning; often I'd just have Damon down and finally asleep when it would be time to wake Brett and Adam for breakfast. After we'd talked a while I'd shower and shave, make their school lunches and drop them at school on my way to work.

My advertising career was continuing to blossom, the trade press even referred to it sometimes as mercurial — and my social drinking with it. I was earning quite a reputation in the business, not all of it good. Where commonsense should have dictated that I come home early and hit the sack for a few hours sleep before the inevitable bleed occurred, instead I stayed out, telling myself I was only doing my job, not letting one thing disrupt the other. This was, of course, untrue. What I was doing was being unfair to my wife, decidedly sorry for myself and something of a coward, unable to face what waited for me back home.

Benita, who is a pretty feisty woman, didn't take too kindly to my nocturnal working habits, when my elbow seemed to be doing most of the work. We began to quarrel. I knew it was my fault mostly, but in the nature of these things I was essentially male and stubborn and not a little stupid. The worse things grew at home the more I stayed away, so that I would often get home late to find Damon sitting in front of the television in his dressing gown, holding Blanky to his face, thumb in mouth and waiting for me to take him to hospital. His large hazel eyes would look at me, "Hello, Daddy. I'm sorry, I've got a bad bleed." Of course, this made me feel even more guilty, with (Why are grown men so bloody stupid?) a resultant increase in my absolutely reprehensible behaviour.

But more of that later. The process of doing a transfusion wasn't all that complicated. While it was a fairly tricky business getting a butterfly needle into a tiny vein, all this really seemed to need was a steady hand and I felt sure that doctors don't have a monopoly on those. Besides, Dr Gett, mostly dog-tired and as short on sleep as I was, would often take two or three attempts to get the needle correctly placed. I was convinced that I could learn the whole procedure without much difficulty.

I had worked out that to do transfusions at home would make an enormous difference to Damon's life and began to work for this to happen when Damon was only two years old. The longer a bleed continued the worse and more sustained the pain and the permanent damage to his joints. Most haemophiliacs are semi- or permanently crippled by their early thirties due to constant bleeding into the joints and the subsequent severe onset of arthritis this brings about. Home treatment would not only save Damon a great deal of immediate pain but it promised to delay the fusing (locking) of elbows, knees, wrists and ankles by several years. As far as I was concerned, the stakes were pretty high and I had to try to persuade the hospital to let me put in a deep freeze for the bags of cryoprecipitate and to allow me to do transfusions.

Benita and I went to see Sir Seymour Plutta (Sir Splutter Grunt) and attempted to explain our point of view. It was the first time I'd confronted him since the time I'd knocked him down, but when we entered his consulting room he looked up at me as though we'd never met before. "What is it you want," he looked down at his pad, ". . . er, Mr Courtenay?"

I pointed out that I'd been through the entire transfusion procedure hundreds of times and, apart from putting the needle into the vein, it was simple enough. I felt sure I could be trained to use a needle in a matter of a few days.

"That's an arrogant and preposterous suggestion! Your physician, Dr Gett, has been trained for nearly seven years. It's a highly skilled task." He looked up at us. "I'm not sure I'd attempt it myself."

"I'm younger, my hands are much steadier than yours, doctor."

"No, no, I'm sorry, we simply cannot entertain the idea."

"Why not, doctor?" Benita asked, speaking up for the first time.

"Precedent, we'd be setting a precedent, a most unfortunate one, too, I might add. Start that sort of nonsense and people will soon believe they don't need the services of a qualified physician for all sorts of things!"

We looked at him, astonished, and I think Sir Splutter Grunt himself realised how reactionary this must have sounded, but he seemed unable to think of any other objection. Suddenly, his eyes lit up. "Teenagers! If they saw their parents using hypodermic needles in the kitchen they'd be encouraged to try heroin!"

Heroin was not exactly at epidemic levels on the streets of Sydney in the late sixties, even *pot* was a drug just beginning to be used by the so-called hippies. There could scarcely have been a teenager in Australia, except perhaps for the younger street prostitutes, who could have afforded hard drugs and the one most talked about at that time was LSD. This second reason was, if anything, more bizarre even than his first.

"Damon is just two years old, doctor. But we're not the only haemophiliac family. How many haemophiliac parents do you think there are?" Benita asked, then replied herself, "We've contacted them all, there are fifty-six families, they all want to do their own home transfusion."

"They all believe themselves capable of learning how to use a butterfly needle," I added.

But Sir Splutter Grunt had closed down, he'd listened to us long enough. We already knew of his personal anger at the idea that we'd lobbied the families of other haemophiliacs, but now he was smart enough not to be drawn into a fight on two fronts.

"My dear Mr and Mrs Courtenay, your proposal is out of the question! It's . . . it's . . . quite unthinkable! I would have thought people of your intelligence would know better." This last statement he said quietly, as though speaking to himself. Then he rose decisively from his chair and came around to where we were sitting. Gripping my arm just above the elbow with both his hands he practically tugged me upright and then proceeded to escort me to the door.

"You must please not ask me again, Mr Courtenay. I assure you, your son is getting the best possible treatment at this hospital. I don't think you fully appreciate what we are doing for him. I simply cannot understand your attitude!" He was plainly upset and, I sensed, even a little hurt at our obvious lack of gratitude. Sir Splutter Grunt reached for the brass door knob and opened the door, allowing Benita to follow me out. "Good day to you!" he said, his voice as neatly clipped as his moustache.

"Goodbye, Sir Seymour," we both said as he pushed the door shut with a great deal more haste than good manners dictated.

Benita is a woman who is not easily daunted and in the matter of her youngest son she was not about to give up. We tried to go over his head to the hospital board. However, the hospital system proved completely intransigent; no one but a fully qualified physician was entitled to place a needle into a patient's vein, this despite the fact that most of the nurses and certainly all of the nursing sisters could have learned to do it with consummate ease, thus saving the institution a great deal of time and money.

What this arcane dictate meant was that Dr Gett, who lived even further from the hospital than we did, was the prisoner of Damon's bleeds. In addition to insisting that the placing of a needle into a human vein was the sole prerogative of a doctor, Sir Splutter Grunt would not allow any other doctor but Gett to transfuse Damon.

When Gett was out of town, perhaps on vacation, a special doctor was appointed, but once Gett returned the old routine continued. Quite why this was so, was never explained. Dr Gett would often work a sixteen-hour day at the hospital and then receive a call from me at one or two a.m. to meet us at the Children's Hospital in an hour. We kept this routine going for more than seven years but never once did he complain or even suggest that Damon was causing the slightest disruption to his life. Though I do recall that sometimes I'd look into his smooth, unlined, Oriental face and wonder which of us was the more weary. The difference was that he was always sober and I, quite often, was not. Damon was having a marked effect on both of our lives.

Then in 1971, I had a short trip to the United States to attend an advertising workshop in Chicago and an interview with McCann Erickson for a big creative job in New York. While in New York, I visited the two hospitals which treated the greatest numbers of haemophiliac patients. To my horror I discovered that American haemophiliacs had either to pay for the blood they used in transfusions or supply it themselves from donations by family members and their friends.

I also discovered that, while the blood collected was

processed in the hospital blood bank, it was returned
to the home of the patient where it was kept in a normal
deep freeze. Home transfusion was a reality in the
United States and had been for some years. When a
bleed occurred, the parents or, if he was a teenager or
adult, the haemophiliac himself would administer the
transfusion.

When I commented on this to a New York doctor at
one of the hospitals he looked at me amazed, "For Chris-
sakes, the kids doing morph out on the streets don't have
any trouble working a blunt syringe. A butterfly needle
is infinitely easier to use than a dirty hypodermic in a
badly lit alley!"

I was so excited I phoned home to Australia that night.
I remember it cost me seventy dollars, two days' living
expenses, so that I was forced for the next two days to
stoke up at breakfast, which was part of the tariff at the
cheap hotel I was staying at.

We had the answer we needed. I also had the job in
New York. I was nearly on the way to being a really big-
time ad man. But the one answer cancelled out the other.
I worked out that if we moved to New York we weren't
entitled to join Blue Cross and I couldn't possibly rely on
new friends to become blood donors and it would cost
in the region of thirty thousand dollars a year to buy
sufficient blood to keep Damon alive. As a classic haemophiliac (a very rare grouping), he used almost fifteen
times the blood product of a normal haemophiliac. Thirty
thousand dollars in those days was a fortune; even the
brightest young career on Madison Avenue couldn't
finance his sort of blood demand.

I shall be grateful to Damon for this outcome to my

dying day. Being a big-time American ad executive is a doubtful ambition to say the least and, with my kind of tunnel vision, would have completely screwed up my life and the lives of my family with it. As it turned out, it was touch and go anyway. Raw ambition and a chronically ill child are not a good mix in either family life or in the corporate world. Long hours, hard drinking and the constant pressure of work in an ideas factory, coupled with a chronic lack of sleep and the stress of a haemophiliac child, make for an explosive mix.

I returned to Sydney from New York more determined than ever to do whatever it took to get permission to give my son blood transfusions in his own home. Needless to say, every fibre in the tiny body of Sir Splutter Grunt was opposed to this happening and so also was the hospital board. The fact that I carried testimonials from several New York physicians and affidavits attesting to the efficacy of the routine obtained from the parents and several American haemophiliacs themselves was irrelevant.

Sir Splutter Grunt, we were to learn, *was* the hospital board. The pompous old men of the old school tie brigade who nominated each other to this prestigious board would never dream of contradicting their very own medical knight of the realm.

One old guy, a member of the board, phoned us one night to ask me to stop bothering them. He made no attempt to understand our point of view and, as I recall it, his monologue went somewhat like this:

"Good God, old chap. How could they possibly go against the sensible wishes of a man who, upon the announcement in the New Year's Honours List, next day booked passage by P&O steamer and travelled to England and thence to Buckingham Palace. A loyal subject who wanted to kneel before Her Majesty. Such are the old-fashioned values of Seymour Plutta that he wanted his knighthood from the lips of the Queen herself, with his commoner knees dutifully bent."

Perhaps, in retrospect and because I've told the story so often, I have come to wildly exaggerate his amazingly pompous pronouncement, but I don't know by how much.

Nevertheless, our egos were dented and our courage mostly spent. The medical profession, as usual, was having it completely its own way. By the meek and mild patient standards of the time, we were making an impossible bloody nuisance of ourselves; doctors and hospital boards didn't expect to be badgered, nor did they take kindly to constant interruptions to their rubber stamp meetings.

But it didn't help. We even recruited parents with similar problems to make the same request.

Eventually, by a statutory device some clerical ingrate in the system managed to dig up, the hospital board managed to invoke a state law which went back to the late nineteenth century making the placing of hypodermic needles directly in the veins of a human subject the sole prerogative of a qualified physician.

The bastards had us on toast! Now the very law of the land would need to be changed if ever we were to succeed in doing blood transfusions in our own homes. Hospital — 10. Patients — 0.

Dr Gett and I never spoke of my ambition to transfuse Damon's bleeds at home. I accepted that he had no meaningful influence over the system, as much captive of its absurdity as we were, and I wanted to save him the embarrassment of a confrontation he could do nothing about and which could possibly compromise him. Doctors still were not expected to share confidences with their clients and Gett could not be seen to be too friendly, as this might have been regarded as a conspiracy by Sir Splutter Grunt's people.

So we suffered mutually, while being forced to stand on opposite sides of the fence. The dark circles around Dr Gett's dark almond eyes grew more pronounced. After seven years, Damon was coming close to wearing us both out.

It was at about this time, when Damon was in junior school, that Sir Splutter Grunt and those who advised him decided to put a calliper on his left leg. This was done without consulting an orthopaedic specialist; we were just sent off to the hospital workshop to have him fitted.

What came back was a clumsy sort of black orthopaedic boot with metal rods inserted into the thick sole on either side and running halfway up both sides of the leg. Halfway up the thigh, a wide, stitched leather belt looped around the leg to hold the steel rods firmly. The knee was encased in a stitched leather cup, which was attached to the rods and buckled in the back. Thus, the leg could not, under any circumstances, be bent.

The reason for the calliper was Damon's left knee. And it was the circumstances surrounding this knee which had perhaps allowed us to let Sir Splutter Grunt get away with the calliper without asking for a second opinion from an orthopaedic specialist.

Secretly, we felt terribly guilty about Damon's left knee, damaged in an accident which should never have occurred and for which I blamed myself. We were building a swimming pool, mostly for Damon, as swimming was essential therapy to build up his body and keep his joints flexible. We'd gone pretty deeply into hock to afford it, as we'd not long previously purchased a rather rundown, though bigger, old home with an overgrown garden, the cottage having become too small for a growing family. The superstructure had been removed from the concrete pour on the Friday and I had persuaded the builder not to cover the pool so that we could all admire it. Our kids were old enough, anyway, not to be in any danger of falling into an empty swimming pool.

We decided to have lunch the next day beside the pool, to sort of get used to the grand life this suggested in our minds, when it would be finally tiled and filled with water so clear you would be able to see the Queen's head on a five-cent coin resting on the bottom. The pool, I have to admit, was a big deal and we were all walking pretty tall around the place. Certainly, nobody in my family had ever owned a swimming pool, or even thought of owning a swimming pool. While Benita had rich relatives with private pools somewhere down in Melbourne, the only thing in the backyard of her parents' semi-detached cottage was a bit of a lawn, a patch of big-leafed red-stemmed rhubarb, a compost heap of lawn clippings and kitchen peelings and a magnificent trellis of sweet peas, for which, every year, her old man grumblingly dug the three-foot ditch required — but only after an entire winter of persistent nagging from her diminutive nana.

Though we told ourselves the pool was for Damon, we even referred to it as Damon's pool, we nevertheless felt pretty damned smug about it. The house was falling down around us, the garden was a wilderness but we had the best pool-to-be in the neighbourhood, no doubt-ski aboutski!

To cut a long story short, I was doing the sausages and chops on the barbecue when Damon had a go at Brett, who, unthinkingly, gave him a playful shove. Damon lost his balance and, moving rapidly backwards, fell into the deep end of the empty pool. I hit the bottom of the pool so soon after him that, for years, we used to say that I caught him as he bounced. But Damon was badly hurt and we soon discovered that his left knee and arm had taken the brunt of the fall.

We rushed him to hospital where he was given a massive transfusion, but his knee and elbow bled for nearly three weeks and both limbs would never be the same again. The elbow eventually stiffened so that Damon forever afterwards was unable to straighten his arm fully, but it was the knee which became a constant source of bleeding and brought him a great deal of pain. In one fall, he had done ten years' damage to it. The pool, which was meant to keep his growing limbs straight and true, had brought him undone even before he was able to swim in it.

When the hospital suggested that a calliper was necessary to give the knee a chance, to stop the incessant bleeding and, with it, the pain, we agreed without thinking. With our past experience of Sir Splutter Grunt we really should have known better.

Damon wore that horrible calliper, dragging it around

without complaining much, for two years until it grew too small for him and we decided to visit an orthopaedic specialist to have him examined privately. We wanted to find out if something less rigid and physically limiting might be made to replace the heavy iron rods. It was apparent that Damon's leg had atrophied and was markedly thinner than his right leg. We'd worried about this and had been told that this was perfectly natural. As the price of saving the knee, some atrophy was to be expected and, though the leg might never fully return to normal size, it would eventually be strong again.

Through means I don't recall, the specialist we saw was a noted professor of orthopaedics at a well-known teaching hospital. To my shame I don't remember his name, though I recall that interview as traumatic in every little detail. The doctor was a big, raw-boned man with a shock of sandy hair and fierce, bushy eyebrows. He asked us why Damon was wearing a calliper. "Why is this leg atrophied?" He removed the calliper and dropped it on the floor next to the examination couch on which Damon was lying. Then he held Damon's thin little leg below the knee and, using both his hands, he worked his big thumbs into the slack, useless calf muscle.

I was confused by the question. "Well, because of that," I pointed to the floor, ". . . the calliper, doctor."

"No, no," he said impatiently, "*Why* did the leg atrophy?"

Confused, I pointed to the calliper again. "It was a perfectly good leg until his knee went and he was made to wear that." I then told him about the empty pool accident two years previously and the subsequent constant bleeding in the knee. He looked down at the ugly worn boot with its inserted callipers. Without Damon's little stick leg to give it life, it seemed like something created to do deliberate physical harm.

"Did it work?" he asked.

I was forced to admit we didn't know, but Benita added that Damon still got plenty of bleeds in this particular knee, many more than occurred in the right leg.

The professor grunted and turned his back to us and started to examine Damon. During the course of the examination, I sensed that his demeanour was changing. The short grunts he had begun with had become sighs, then huffs, then little expostulations of air and gruff growls.

He turned and faced us, and I saw that his face had grown quite red. If what followed wasn't a medical breakthrough, it was certainly a breakthrough in doctor-patient communication.

"Those bastards have destroyed your son's leg!"

His anger was such that he was now shaking; he stood at attention in his long, white jacket, with fists clenched tightly at his side, as though he were trying to avoid bursting into little bits. Then it came again, his voice loud and angry and he pointed directly at me.

"For Christ's sake! You should have known better! This lad will never again walk without a pronounced limp, the knee is totally fused and without any movement. His left leg is shorter than the other and will continue to atrophy and its usefulness has been greatly reduced!"

He was shouting at us. "In my opinion, the calliper would not have stopped a single bloody bleed!" He gulped, pausing for a single moment, "In all probability, it would have caused a great many to occur!"

He stopped, shook his head and sighed, though it was more a wince than a sigh and seemed designed to bring his temper back under control. "I'm sorry, Mr and Mrs ..." he dropped his chin and brought his forefinger and thumb up to pinch at his frown, trying to recall our surname.

"Courtenay," I said softly, not quite knowing what next to expect from this big, angry man standing over us.

He brought his hand down from his head, his open palm facing us in a gesture of reconciliation. "I apologise Mr and Mrs Courtenay. How could you have possibly known? I'm quite wrong, I apologise." Then he added, "It's this damned place; after a while you think everyone you see is an incompetent bloody doctor or intern." He brought his hand up again and wiped the back of it across his mouth. "I know you can't tell me who the stupid, callous men are who did this to your beautiful boy. Even if you did I wouldn't be able to do anything but, on behalf of the medical profession, I apologise and I am deeply ashamed."

Damon, who had not yet spoken, looked up at the professor and then pointed to the calliper on the floor. "At least wearing it I could sometimes kick a ball, sir," he said.

6

*Politics, Sim the Man and Beating the
Needle Ban.*

The chairman of McCann Erickson, the American advertising company for which I worked, was a naturalised
Australian named Sim Rubensohn. He was small, irascible and walked with a pronounced limp which was
caused by a car accident when he attempted to drive
home too drunk and senseless to leave his big American
car, the "Yank Tank", and call a cab.

Rubensohn had sold his own advertising company to
the giant McCann Erickson when, in the sixties, international expansion of Madison Avenue advertising agencies
became the popular thing to do and global marketing
was the catch-phrase of international business.

An alcoholic in remission, Rubensohn was simply the
most difficult and unreasonable man I have ever met.
His more or less sole job in the agency, apart from being

the chairman, was to run one or two very large accounts at chairman to chairman level and the advertising and election affairs of the Australian Labor Party, the political party in office in the mid sixties in the state of New South Wales and, also, in long-term opposition in federal politics.

Sim ran his ill-tempered life at top speed and expected everyone working with him to fit into his time schedule, which was to start at seven a.m. each morning. This wasn't too bad, except that he left work promptly at four p.m. to tend his magnificent camellia and Japanese garden at his property in Dural, an outlying district some thirty kilometres from the city.

With a roar of the big, green V12 Jaguar, over whose steering wheel the diminutive Sim could barely see, he would head for the hills, leaving behind sufficient work to keep his minions working back, often until late at night. Overnight was the longest time frame in which Sim could think; he expected every task to be completed by seven the following morning when his new working day began.

Despite his small, lopsided size, Rubensohn was tough, an ex-alcoholic and ex-gambler who, when forced to give up both vices, fell into a foul mood from which he never recovered. Despatch boys, since grown into senior account executives in the agency, spoke in awe of Sim's previous gambling exploits. They bragged of having been part of the regular Monday morning delivery of a brown paper parcel the size of a shoe box to an SP bookmaker to settle Sim's losses at the weekend races. The SP bookmaker would make them stand as witness as he carefully counted the ten-pound notes, handing back Sim's marker to the boy at the correct conclusion. Occasionally, the traffic would be the other way, the despatch boy would arrive empty-handed and leave with a couple of shoe boxes crammed with cash in the form of big denomination notes.

But mostly it was a one-way traffic, to pay the bookmaker. Sim was a great tactician with a brilliant, political brain, but he was a lousy drunk and an even worse gambler. When he mixed both he was a disaster. He had eventually to choose between drink and power. Power was the more intoxicating, he loved it even more than the bottle. Not the kind that goes on parade, rather the stuff that remains unseen and lasts; faceless power, that makes and breaks and casts no shadow where it walks. Power usually needs money to back it and Sim was giving too much of his to the SP bookies, so he was forced to give up gambling as well as drink.

Gambling and its contingent sin, prostitution, had become so institutionalised in New South Wales that they were hardly regarded as crime at all, but rather more as the tidy and profitable containment of bad, though inevitable, social conduct. It was a grand life and somewhere in all of this was Sim Rubensohn, the king-maker.

Sim the Man, as he was known in some circles, pulled a great many of the strings and he also ran the political advertising for the party. I was the unfortunate person picked by him to work on the Labor Party account. That is, I was expected to run the creative department of the agency as well as work on Labor advertising. My days already long, grew progressively longer and I, increasingly, neglected my wife and growing family.

Running a political advertising account is not unusual in an advertising agency. For a few weeks prior to elections the agency works hard, but the money is good and comes in a lump sum, so it is very profitable. Under Sim Rubensohn, however, it was nothing of the sort. It was a year in and year out business with elections only being the most impossibly frenetic part. Sim didn't take a brief and then go away and make a few advertisements. Sim told the party what to say, how to say it and when to say it; he also personally raised the money in order to say it in the newspapers, on radio and television.

Sim knew everyone in politics and the unions, he knew all their scams and who was getting what and how and, finally, how much. He never abused this position or betrayed a confidence. Most importantly, he also never asked for advertising funds but made himself personally responsible for raising the money to run the Labor advertising campaign at election time. This gave him enormous power and influence in the party. Sim was the money box.

In this money-raising quest he was a remorseless, greatly feared operator with a long and dangerous memory. Moreover, he wasn't on the take himself and, while he was ruthless as a money collector, he was known to be utterly discreet; a favour promised to an anonymous, though generous, industrial or business donor was always delivered on time and in good measure.

Whereas no Labor politician would have trusted the man who sat beside him in parliament, even though they had probably raced billy carts together in the same working-class street, they all trusted Sim. They discussed things with him and they told him everything. Sim could move upwards or downwards or sideways in the party room, in broad terms, he was a Labor Godfather.

This was Tammany Hall politics in the best, second and third generation local Irish tradition. It was curious, therefore, that the man most trusted by the socialist party to deliver them to power and glory was a tiny Jewish alcoholic with a gammy leg, who was born in Cape Town, South Africa.

Alas, I was the man under Sim most trusted to deliver the advertising designed to do all this. During the months leading up to a state or federal election, Sim regarded me as his personal twenty-four hour property. This continued for five years and I was to get to know every aspect of local state politics in that time, including the sergeant who operated as the bag man, for Sim reckoned, quite logically, that a part of the "extra salary" the politicians paid themselves, should go towards their re-election.

These were perhaps the most difficult years of my working life and also the most exhilarating. I quite often hated Sim with a passion, but I loved the way he got things done and the power he exercised. I admired his pure selfishness, how he let nothing and nobody stand in his way. With Sim, everything was possible, you just had to know which button to press, who to call and what to say. It was a marvellous exercise in the power of quiet and persistent malevolence. The results were achieved through discreet suggestion; a gentle reminder of an indiscreet incident in the past, always carefully couched with a promise for the future. Sim would threaten a man with a promise. The technique was simple: *I know something about you. I need something from you. I have something for you.* He called this the Holy Trinity of Political Persuasion and he was its ultimate master.

With Sim an election campaign was a war declared, where the rules went out the window and the winner took all. Coming into politics at this level I found I had to grow up awfully fast but that elections were a source of pure adrenalin. I was completely caught up and, as usual, I soon had my priorities totally screwed up.

All this happened before Damon was born and I was neglecting my young family shamelessly in the name of building a career. By the time Damon came along in 1966 we'd lost the NSW Labor account after holding it for twenty-four years and we were still in the political wilderness with the federal Labor Party.

Sim may have seen me as a new force in political copywriting, but my record was pretty dismal — I'd lost two out of three elections we'd fought. In 1968, with Damon not yet two years old, three state elections took place — New South Wales, South Australia and Queensland — the first in February, the next in March and the Queensland election in August. Sim was relentless. More often than not, I would get home after midnight from mixing a radio or television track or getting a newspaper advertisement to the paper just before the midnight deadline. I'd arrive home bleary-eyed, my stomach soured from too much beer and cheap fried food taken on the run, knowing I faced the likely event of a rip-roaring row with Benita.

I'd crash into bed to be wakened an hour or so later by Damon crying. Twenty minutes later we'd be on our way to the hospital, where we'd spend much of the remainder of the night in watching the good Doctor Gett put the dreaded needle in.

I'd practise at home. I'd pump up Damon's little arm with a tourniquet until the veins at the back of his hand and in the crease of his arm started to surface, the tiny little serpents of his distress, blue against his smooth, white skin. Then, with the tip of my forefinger and with my eyes closed, I'd trace the direction of each vein until I knew the length and direction of every transfusable vein in both his hands and along the inside of his arms. We simply never gave up hoping that one day, when he was old enough, Damon would do his own transfusions in his own home.

To claim that I became involved with Sim Rubensohn and politics as a part of an astute career plan would be lying. I wasn't politically minded; in fact politics had made me flee my own country. I found myself simply seconded to the job. To have refused to work with the cantankerous Rubensohn of the eternally bad spleen would have put my precious little career in jeopardy. The poor boy in me was still too frightened to chance it on his own. I needed the security a big multinational advertising agency afforded me and, perhaps more honestly, I loved the recognition it gave me. I was the youngest and the brightest working for one of the biggest and now, with Sim Rubensohn, the fiercest.

Sim had me by the short and curlies from the first moment he summoned me to his over-large office with its genuine Louis Quinze furniture and antique kilims, and he never gave up tugging. His greatest strength was that he was an utter and complete bastard without a breath of compassion in his entire person. Sim proceeded to work me like a dog and I responded like a dog, mostly wagging my tail trying to please my master; doing as I was told when I was told to do it, without much regard for my family or my wife, who was trying to cope with three children conceived within five years.

In fact, at first, I liked meeting the rich, the powerful and the corrupt and it seemed that I had a real talent for writing political advertising, since only the legendary Percy "Pip" Cogger had ever lasted more than one election with Rubensohn.

But after five years, with a federal and several state elections behind me, coupled with my normal work as the creative director of the agency, I was just about worn out. By now I was totally disenchanted with politicians and politics, my family life was in tatters, my drinking getting steadily worse and, moreover, I was beginning to realise that I was losing my sense of self. I, too, was beginning to turn into a political animal of the kind I saw around me, the mediocre men who ran on a high octane mixture of power and fear and who constantly compromised their integrity to gain more than they were legitimately entitled to receive.

The phone at home would begin ringing at five a.m. when Rubensohn made his first calls of the day, so that my first impression of most days was an irascible, high-pitched voice barking instructions at me. Quite often I'd still be trying to get Damon back to bed from hospital when the first call came. Sim never said "please" or "thank you" and he never introduced himself, he simply barked out his demands and accepted a polite, acquiescent reply prior to slamming the phone down in your ear. I had no idea whether he knew of Damon's condition. Rubensohn was interested only in the things he could use; being aware that I had a chronically ill child was probably not to his advantage to know.

Although Rubensohn, in the five years I worked for him, never once paid me the slightest compliment, my career continued to blossom, my salary was increased and I was made a director of the agency which, at that time, was considered a pretty big deal.

But I'd had enough and one morning during the five a.m. phone call I told Rubensohn to get stuffed and I resigned. This time I slammed the phone down. The phone rang every five minutes for the next two hours and finally, in exasperation Benita, who'd been awakened by the continual calls and had been told of my decision, picked it up and, before Sim could say anything, shouted down the phone, "He's not coming back! You hear. He's not bloody coming back. Ever!"

She hung on just a fraction too long and Rubensohn shot back at her, "If Bryce will stay for the next federal election, I'll see that the law is changed and you can do your son's blood transfusions at home!" Game, set and match! The perfidious political master had once again demonstrated the Holy Trinity of Politics. *I know something about you. I need something from you. I have something for you.*

But it wasn't quite as easy as that. The nation's health came under the Federal Government, where the Labor Party was in opposition and where the Liberal minister for health at the time was one of Sim's more particular enemies.

When I arrived at work on the morning of my resignation there was a message from Sim's ageing and long-suffering secretary, Miss Gorman, to come up and see him immediately. I walked up the two flights of stairs from the creative department to Sim's outrageously large office. "You'd better go in," Miss Gorman said, not glancing up, her voice as usual flat, without emotion. Working with Sim Rubensohn had set her face in a permanent deadpan, her expression neither hopeless nor hopeful, the best that could be said for it being that it was permanently neutral. Miss Gorman was the only person in the world who had Sim completely foxed.

I entered, taking large steps over the very expensive kilims, thinking obsequiously to save them needless wear and tear, and came to a stop opposite Sim's huge, ornate, Louis Quinze desk behind which he sat in a huge, slightly raised chair of the same period. He didn't look up from the folder he was reading, though when he spoke his voice was surprisingly friendly. "Sit, Bryce." I moved to sit in one of the chairs which appeared to have shorter than usual legs, so that Sim, seated behind the desk, actually towered above me.

I had learned with Rubensohn, that short of becoming totally impervious, like Miss Gorman, attack was the best way to approach him. "You can't do anything for my son, Mr Rubensohn, the law allowing only doctors to do transfusions is a federal one." But my heart was beating rapidly, Sim Rubensohn always kept his promises, maybe he'd worked something out? Perhaps he knew someone in the Libs? He'd once worked for the Liberal Party until he'd had a fallout with Bob Menzies. You never knew with Sim.

Rubensohn looked up, "That's just the point isn't it? We've got a federal election coming up next year. Labor could win this one, the country's sick of the Libs."

"Not sick enough to vote Labor in."

"You're wrong!" Rubensohn shouted, becoming his natural self again. He shouted loudest when he was least certain of himself. "Dead wrong! That's your problem, Bryce, you have absolutely no political judgment. Government's are voted *out*! The people want the Libs *out*! After nineteen years people have had enough of them!"

"See me through this one last election, Bryce." Sim's voice lowered a tone and he once again sounded quite human, almost pleading. "This is the one I've worked for all these years. This one's ours!" He brought his fist down on the desktop. "Labor *will* make it this time and the first thing, the very first piece of legislation they pass, will be to allow blood transfusions to be done in the home." He looked up and must have seen the uncertainty in my face. "I'll give it to you in writing. We'll win the next federal election and you'll get your blood transfusions." He leaned forward and took a piece of his personal note paper from a small wooden box on his desk and removed the cap from his gold pen.

"Labor can't win, Mr Rubensohn," I said softly, half-ashamed of myself for the disloyalty I was showing.

"Eh? Bullshit, Bryce! You're not listening! Don't you ever listen? A bloody chimpanzee could win the next election from the Libs. People are fed up, they're going to vote them *out*!" He paused momentarily, "Not Labor *in*! The Libs *out*! Don't you understand anything?"

He was silent as he wrote, then he handed me the paper. "Here, it's a personal promise. When Labor win the next election you get what you want if you help me to fight it."

The promise wasn't worth the paper it was written on, but I took it anyway, too weak to tell him where to shove it. I resigned shortly afterwards to take up a position with J. Walter Thompson, another international advertising agency, who had offered to treble my salary.

Labor lost the next election. I'd been right; Sim's note wasn't worth a busted fart.

In 1972, Labor finally swept into power in the federal election. But, of course, it was much too late for me. I comforted myself with the thought that, if I'd remained for the next four years with Sim Rubensohn, my life and my family would have been totally wrecked. I sent a note of congratulation to the old bastard but received no reply. I expected none, Sim wasn't a forgiving man.

My final parting from Sim Rubensohn had been pretty acrimonious. He admitted, though very reluctantly, that I was to be his protégé. Of course, with Sim you never knew, this admission might simply have been a last desperate ploy to keep me. He told me I was ruining my life, that if I stayed with him I would one day take his place as chairman of McCann and have the same sort of influence at the state and federal level of politics. "You will be very rich, Bryce."

All this took place in a private room at the Royal Prince Alfred Hospital where he was to undergo an emergency kidney operation. Sim Rubensohn knew a good bedside scene when he saw one. He was, or he pretended to be, in considerable pain as we spoke, so that he could hardly shout at all, which meant he could barely communicate. But he still had enough venom left in him to tell me to go to hell when he saw I wasn't going to change my mind.

"Life gives us all only one chance, my boy, *one* chance, *which taken at the flood leads on to fortune.* You've had yours and *you'll* never get another. You, my boy, have settled for too little! You could have been anything!" He said all this in a hoarse, raspy voice, every once in a while wincing at the pain I was causing him. Finally he dismissed me with a backward flip of his hand, "Go to hell! I'm finished with you!" Sim Rubensohn was an extremely poor loser.

Two years after I'd sent him the congratulatory note on Labor's historic win, I received a return note from Sim Rubensohn. It was his first contact with me since I had been summarily dismissed from his hospital bed. The note was short and written in his usual large, impetuous scrawl in the centre of the page.

> Bryce,
> I have spoken to
> Gough Whitlam
> about your son.
> *Sim Rubensohn.*

Six months later, just before Damon's ninth birthday, a law was passed allowing parents and hospital-registered patients in need of routine blood transfusions to perform these in their own homes.

This single act transformed Damon's life. It was just how I imagined it would be, the needle was easy to master and in no time I was an expert. At nine Damon was transfusing himself, becoming a great deal more expert than I was and using me only when his hand was bruised and he couldn't grip the wings of the butterfly needle.

However, all this came in a sense too late for Damon; by the age of seven his little body was pretty badly beaten up. His left leg was shorter than the right, badly atrophied and permanently damaged with the knee almost completely fused so that it gave him only very limited movement. His left arm was the same, permanently locked at the elbow into a slightly bent position and so thin that you could join your thumb and forefinger around the top of his biceps. From constant bleeding, all his joints were damaged and arthritis was beginning to set in, bringing him a great deal of additional pain.

Some of this, of course, was a direct consequence of being a haemophiliac. We had seen haemophiliacs in other countries as badly afflicted as Damon, but who'd received home transfusions from the very beginning. The physical difference was quite profound and for us, desperately sad. We felt as though, as Australians, we had somehow contrived to mutilate our beloved little boy.

While medical practice is markedly better today, stupidity of the Sir Splutter Grunt kind continues and, in the treatment of AIDS, we were to experience a new level of incompetence and plain, old-fashioned ignorance.

The making of a Sir Splutter Grunt begins very early in the medical system and, even today, when doctors thankfully have much less clout and status in the community, they are generally socially inept, inclined to be superior, careless in their human relations and, finally, are tied down by a bureaucratic and reactionary hospital system which gives them very little room to exercise initiative.

Damon, and others like him, are the victims of stubborn old men who wield enormous and unreasonable power in a system which largely still continues today.

Doing the transfusions at home was enormously beneficial to Damon's emotional well being and general health. The time from the onset of a bleed to the actual transfusion was now less than three-quarters of an hour. We soon discovered that the earlier you treat a bleed the quicker it stops and, often, he would have some relief within a couple of hours of receiving *Factor VIII*. This meant his ongoing pain, as the bruise began to heal, and total discomfort were greatly reduced and, more importantly, less permanent damage was done to his joints from sustained bleeding.

Compare this to going to the hospital for his transfusions. The entire process, including travel for both the doctor and ourselves and the transfusion, would often take three hours just to turn around and it might be another three or four hours before the clotting factor became effective and the bleeding began to diminish. With Damon's average of three bleeds a week, the hospital treatment effectively produced about three times as much bleeding time as a home transfusion. Or put in a different way, it had the equivalent effect on Damon's body of having a four-hour bleed every day of his life!

It was becoming harder and harder not to see ourselves as victims of an uncaring system.

7

Damon

*This letter was written on Good Friday, 1979, when Damon was
twelve and just before his grandmother was due to visit us from
South Africa.*

Dear Nana,

I hope you are very well. Mum, Dad, Brett and Adam
are all very well, although Adam has had a very bad
cold. I have just come out of hospital, and have had a
small operation on my right knee. But don't worry, it
was was such a small operation that it took only ten
minutes. All they did was stick a needle into my knee
and draw back some fluid out of my knee joint, so as I
won't have any trouble with that knee again. I was only
in hospital for two days, so I didn't miss much school.

We are on holidays for one week because of our
Easter break, and it is Good Friday today. Dad is at
home till Tuesday, but then he has to go back to work.

He has just come back from New Zealand, he was there for four days on business. We are all getting a real New Zealand wool jumper from Dad, but we won't get them till May because they haven't been knitted yet!

Speaking of May, I don't think I can wait to see you! Only another three weeks till you are here!!! I've been looking forward to seeing you for years and years and years!!!! It was a shame that you couldn't have come this month because down here we have an Easter Show, which is on from the sixth of April to the seventeenth of April, and we could have taken you there because it has a lot of fun things, such as big fruit and vegetable displays, electronic displays, all sorts of horse riding and displays of animals. There is also an arts and crafts centre. You can always buy show bags, or sample bags, which contain all sorts of sweets and toys and books and lots of other things.

Yesterday I went to see a movie about a plot to assassinate a Greek president! It was called *The Thirty-Nine Steps*, and was great. The plan was that when the Greek President was addressing the British Houses of Parliament, a bomb would explode and kill him. Two Prussian agents had planted a bomb in the Houses of Parliament, and it was attached to Big Ben, and when Big Ben struck 11.45, the bomb would explode. The hero climbed out onto Big Ben and held onto the minute hand to stop it reaching 11.45, I went with a friend and had a really good time.

I have some very big tests coming up at school. They are maths and science.

Maths will be easy, but science will be hard because it was based on a week away from school when most of the class went to the bush for a week and camped to study the wild life around Canberra. I couldn't go because of my Haemophilia, but I shall still have to do the test by studying all the worksheets that were given out.

Anyway, I must go now, and I'll wait till after I see you to write again. Just think, I'll really see you! So till May, send my love to Aunty Rosemary and everyone else.

Yours with love
Damon

X X X X X X X X

P.S. Everyone over here sends their love!

8

Damon

This is a compilation of various conversations Damon had with his friends and myself. I have tried to capture his essential "voice" although, of course, the continuity is my own.

I can't really remember when my dad wasn't telling me stories because he was just always telling them.

With my mum it was books. Books seemed to be everywhere in my life. They lay in stacks beside my bed, I'm sure she must have tucked them up with me in my cot. I don't even remember learning to read. I could certainly read before I went to kindergarten and I can remember being astonished to discover that reading wasn't something everyone could do, like breathing. I just thought human beings could always read.

Books are very important to me because they often took away my pain. Not the very severe pain, but the early pain and the last of the pain when a bleed is coming on or beginning to lessen. My mum would sit me on her lap when I had a bleed and read to me. "One day you just started to read the words aloud," she claimed, as though one minute I wasn't reading and the next there I was pronouncing the words out loud.

Loving books isn't just about reading, when I was small and until I was about five when the last little bit wore out, I used to have a small blue blanket which I used to hold against my cheek while I sucked my thumb. You see lots of small kids doing it, but "Blanky" was very important to me and I don't think I could have been able to cope as well without it. Books are a bit the same. They bring back the times when I felt safe and secure. My mum used to read with me nestled on her lap. The warmth and intimacy of her lap and her special smell and reassuring voice as she read to me and the story itself, they all became, in a sense, what books meant, really a tremendous comfort. I can still just pick one up and run my hands over it and immediately I start to feel better.

I remember once at Sydney University when I got a bad bleed but I had to stay all day; I don't remember why. When the pain was getting really bad I went into the library and took out three books and just sat for a while with them in my lap, touching them. I know it seems dumb, but it helped a lot.

I also loved the stories my dad told me. They were mostly about Africa and things that happened to him, fantastic things that you believed when you were little and then had some doubts about when you got a little older and when we called them "dad facts". He always told them as though they were true, even if we begged him to say they weren't. But it didn't really matter, because you wanted to hear the story anyway.

Like once we were in the Botanic Gardens and Mum pointed to a funny looking plant with it's name on a little plaque. "Oh look, a lobelia, I've always wondered what a lobelia looked like," she said.

"In the Mountains of the Moon in the Congo, high above the rainforest where the gorillas live and just above the snowline, where it's always misty and wet, the lobelias grow to be twelve feet tall," Dad said.

We were looking at this funny little plant about thirty centimetres high and I saw Adam looking upwards along a tree trunk to gauge how high twelve foot was. Shortly afterwards I could see his lips silently saying, "Ah bull!"

When we got home Adam went straight to the *Encyclopaedia Botanica* and came and sat down in my room and we looked up lobelia. *Lobelia alata* was only half a metre high, *Lobelia cardinalis* was a metre high, *Lobelia erinus,* a native of South Africa was a mere 0.15 metre. A native of South Africa? Kapow! Gotcha! Rat-tat-tat-tat! We had Dad squasherated, exactly were we wanted him!

All the taller lobelia grew in Australia and they weren't anything like three and a half metres high which was what Dad said in his dad fact! The one in South Africa was a dwarf, the smallest of them all, not even twenty-five centimetres!

Adam was very happy at this win for truth and justice. He was about to march off to challenge Dad with this undeniable lobelia truth, when we both saw it right at the bottom of the page:

Lobelia deckenii, a native of Mount Kilimanjaro, Kenya, a frost-resistant evergreen shrub which grows to a height of 4 metres. Also found on the slopes of the Mountains of the Moon in Zaire.

Four metres was even taller than the twelve feet Dad said. That was the trouble with dad facts, sometimes they turned out not to be dad facts at all. And then there were the dad facts you knew in your heart were dad facts but you couldn't prove it. They were the kind that drove Adam crazy. Like the story of The Great Cockroach Regatta when, using bits of bacon, miners trained blind albino cockroaches underground in the copper mines in Africa to race in paper boats along the water canals and gambled thousands on the results.

Now that was one of my dad's greatest unprovable dad facts which, no matter how much Adam cross-examined him, he couldn't fault. But the worst part for Adam was when my dad would sum up a dad fact with a sort of moral. It was as though my dad was using an untruth to announce a truth.

Brett, on the other hand, would love these moral summaries, always insisting on one after a dad fact. He needed them because when he got to school he would begin with this end bit, with the moral summary of the dad fact. For instance, he'd begin by saying casually:

"In this cruel world it's the blind leading the blind in a case of sink or swim, where it's roach eat roach, and where big gobbles up small; in life there is no such thing as plain sailing and if you want to bring home the bacon you must be prepared to do things differently and never ever give up."

Everyone would immediately know that a gi-normous dad fact was coming on and they'd gather around to be suitably confounded. They used to like to have Adam present so that afterwards he could try to prove to them how the latest dad fact couldn't possibly be true.

Unfortunately their wasn't such a thing as an *Encyclopaedia Cockroachi* at home or in the school library so Adam couldn't check the great blind albino cockroach probability and so this particular dad fact remains, even today, the greatest of them all.

But I bet one day when Adam is a famous journalist or foreign correspondent he'll go to Africa, to those very same copper mines in Zambia, and he'll go underground and see if the cockroaches are white and blind and can swim *and* then he'll check in the British Museum or some place like that to see if cockroaches can become cannibals.

That's how Adam is, where facts are concerned *he's* the one who never gives up.

9

The Lover with a Limp and a Red Ferrari.

With children who cannot physically do the things other children take for granted, secrecy becomes a matter of self-protection. In a sense, they *are* abused children, though not in the generally accepted meaning. The world of little boys is largely physical and being unable to be a part of it is a mental trauma which must have significant effects on a small child. Damon would have gone to great lengths to protect a frail ego.

Though I told myself that I understood how Damon must feel about his inability to play with other kids, to wield a cricket bat, kick a soccer or rugby ball, run a race or simply join in the rough and tumble of growing up, I clearly didn't. While I was able to intellectualise his anxiety and even sometimes keenly feel his disappointment, I never fully understood his emotional pain.

The truth was that he became so skilled at covering up, at concealing his setbacks, that we all simply forgot how he must feel when he saw Adam and Brett with surfboards under their arms happily heading for the beach. Or watched at the edge of the playground as the other kids had a rollicking good time, chasing around, crashing into each other, grabbing and falling about in the way of small boys.

The big trouble with Damon was that he never complained. Not even as a small child. He simply watched and then got on with something else. He would sit and listen and laugh as Adam talked of cracking a big wave, hugging himself as Adam told us how frightened he was but how, when he finally stood up on his board, he felt like every good thing that could possibly happen had just happened to him.

Damon would make Adam tell the story in every detail, his eyes shining at his brother's triumph and he'd ask questions so that he soon knew all the surfing jargon and the meanings of the various board manoeuvres and the ways of the cantankerous waves. He knew the reef break on South Bondi almost as well as Adam and they soon spoke a surfing jargon I was unable to comprehend. Adam often quite forgot that Damon didn't ride a board and they would discuss technique and mistakes and chances taken and missed, the state of the waves and the effect on the surfing when the king tides ran.

Nielsen Park is a small harbour beach where for the most part the waves are too flat to earn the respect of even beginner board riders; but a couple of times a year, for reasons no one seemed to be able to explain, the waves would run at Nielsen. This would usually happen around midnight or even later, but when they ran, the northern end of this tiny beach featured a board ride which was legendary. It was fast, tricky and required great skill; in return it gave up one of the best right-hand breaks in the surfing business.

The phone would ring, often at two in the morning and Damon would answer. "Nielsen's running!" a voice would shout down the phone and hang up. Nobody ever knew who was the first to know this. A tiny beach which started to pump in the small hours of the morning, how would a kid know that? But someone always did.

Damon would get Adam and Brett up and send them running, surfboards under their arms, for Nielsen which wasn't much more than a kilometre from home. When, some hours later, I rose, Damon would usually be up and dressed and we'd jump into the car and race for Nielsen to watch the boys do the last of their surfing in the dawn light. We'd watch from the sandstone cliff top looking down, anxiously trying to find Brett and Adam among the heads dotting the water and pushing surfboards into the swell.

Damon would get terribly excited when Brett or Adam caught a wave and groan with disappointment when they missed. The waves at Nielsen broke to the right or, in surfing parlance, it was a right-hand break, and, when the harbour swell was huge, would cover a series of tall pylons which stood fixed into the sand as supports for the shark net which turned a part of the far right side of the beach into a safe swimming area in the summer. Riding the pylons meant taking the wave over them and not dropping short; this took a great deal of courage. Adam was a goofy footer, which meant he surfed with his right foot forward which, again, meant he had his back to the breaking wave and therefore couldn't see the pylons so easily as the waves ahead dropped to reveal them. Damon would have his heart in his mouth as Adam moved backwards towards the giant kauri posts, knowing that his brother's skill depended on his choosing a wave that wouldn't die moments before arriving at the pylons and send him crashing disastrously into one of them. He'd yell with delight, victory shining in his eyes, when Adam *gassed* his board over the dangerous stumps, riding it imperiously into the beach, his back to the wave. I'm sure, from seeing the look on his face, that Damon felt nearly the same rush of triumph and sudden charge of adrenalin as his older brother.

Years later Adam was to admit to me that he only attempted the pylons when Damon was on the cliff. "I came to believe that I needed the extra courage he gave me. He'd stand up there on the cliff top with his leg-iron and his arms raised and I'd feel that, if Damon wanted it, I could do it."

We'd return home about seven, the two brothers red-eyed and happy from the salt and exhaustion and from having being dumped ten times for every wave they caught. These were bacon and egg mornings, with thick slices of tomato fried in with the bacon and sometimes, if we were lucky, we'd even have sausages in the fridge. Nielsen-running was a sort of annual celebration, like the coming of the sardines in Portugal.

Quite how the two boys got through school that day I was never game to ask, although half the class would probably have been asleep with them. It was a sort of tacit understanding, negotiated in the first instance by

Damon, that when Nielsen was running the boys could go, even though it was mostly well past midnight.

Damon was never to feel the surge of a wave as it lifted the board nor the sweet, hard, exquisite pain of his arms working like pistons tearing at the swell to get set on to the lip of the thundering water, then to rise and ride the tiny, waxed plank cutting a streak of side-foam along the green, glassed edge of a wave riding it all the way into the fizzing white water on the shoreline.

Yet Damon was, or at least pretended to be, as enthusiastic and expert on the subject of surfing as his brothers and he would listen for hours as they discussed the vagaries of Nielsen, Bondi (North and South), Tamarama and Coogee, the more or less accepted surfing boundaries for the Eastern Suburbs kids. He also knew his cricket and his rugby and discussed them at great length with Adam in particular, for Brett wasn't interested in these two team sports. Brett liked his combat man-on-man or alone, so he chose tennis and surfing as his sports or fishing off Watson's Bay Gap with his mate, Gary. The two of them were like goats on the high, vertical sandstone cliffs and I constantly expected a knock on the door to tell me something bad had happened. But you've got to let kids be intrepid. With Damon denied the freedom and exhilaration of a strong, resourceful body, I could hardly be over-protective of his brothers. Brett often came home bleeding, but he never broke anything. As an adult he still fishes off The Gap and can be counted on to bring back a brace of fat bream or leatherjacket.

When eight-year-old Adam started playing rugby at the Cranbrook Prep. School oval on Saturday mornings, Damon would drag his leg-iron up and down the touch-line cheering Adam on and shouting instructions every time he touched the ball.

"G'arn Adam! Tackle! Tackle him! Go low! Low!!" or "Pass! Pass the ball! Ah gee, Adam! (Sigh) Dad, you've got to tell him to wait for the gap to open, he thinks it's always there!"

Afterwards, they would discuss the game and Damon would offer his serious advice as to how Adam had gone wrong, the nature of the opposition, Adam's tactics and form on the day and how he might improve as a five-eight.

"Your hands are good, Adam, the best, but you see a gap where there isn't one and get sucked in every time."

Adam, who was pretty serious about everything he did, would spend the next game passing the ball to his centres, sometimes ignoring a gap in the opposition line he could have strolled through with his eyes closed. The two of them were very close as brothers, but you got the impression that Damon was the one in charge.

In the summer we would sit under the jacaranda trees and watch Adam playing cricket. Damon, as usual, was both his harshest critic and his biggest fan. Only once did I hear him say, "You know, Dad, I think I could've been a *really* good batsman." The wistfulness in his voice brought a sudden and unexpected stinging to my eyes and Damon, glancing up, saw my distress and he never again volunteered another "I could've been".

In fact he *just might* have been good at the kind of sport which requires good hand-eye co-ordination, he was an absolute whizz at ping-pong, a game which requires very little movement if your eye is sufficiently fast. But arthritis in his wrists soon took care of even this small sporting triumph.

Because he was so vital and involved and enthusiastic his brothers forgot that he was a haemophiliac. He stopped wearing short pants at the age of eight and so his bruises were usually covered. Besides, Damon never alluded to his bleeds, so that it was easy to think of him as a kid who chose not to play sport, rather than one who was unable to do so.

When, at around ten, he was doing his own blood transfusions, he would get a bleed and quietly prepare the *Factor VIII* and then close the door to his room and transfuse himself so that his brothers were unaware of the pain. He would simply announce that he was going into his room to read and would prefer not to be interrupted. He'd retire, often for three or four hours, until the worst of the pain was over, then he'd come out as though nothing had happened, same old cheerful Damon.

To help him in all this, most of the bleeds continued to come at night, so that he could keep a great deal of his pain and discomfort to himself and appear to be in pretty good shape by the morning. We dreaded each full moon, Damon always got the worst bleeds when the moon was full. His diary showed this quite clearly, yet when I mentioned it in the notes we prepared with each batch of cryoprecipitate the hospital haematologist laughed derisively. "Does he feel the urge to howl, as well?" he once quipped to the nursing sister.

If Damon was quiet about his physical problems he made up for it with his extroverted nature. Damon had an opinion on everything and demanded that it be heard. He loved to argue and to use his mind and his fast tongue. Because he was so often away from school with a bleed, he learned to read widely under his mother's direction and he was soon pretty hard to beat in an argument or discussion. For a start he knew more though, surprisingly, he never became a know-all. Adam tended to be a bit of a know-all, or at least a Mr know-all-the-facts, but not Damon. He must have instinctively known, or discovered somewhere along the way, that the secret to covering up his physical problems was to divert people's attention to his mind. He was sufficiently acute to realise that this wasn't simply a matter of being a big mouth who had all the answers, though the temptation to be one must have been enormous. After all, he had nothing else to show off. But he seemed to know when to draw back, satisfied that he'd beaten his opponent without shaming him, prepared to listen as well as talk. In fact, Damon developed into an expert listener.

I think Damon genuinely liked to listen, to truly listen. He would listen with everything he had, his eyes, his shoulders, his hands and his entire demeanour and then remain silent and consider what he'd heard, ask one or two cogent questions and then finally offer an opinion. This mannerism was charming and so he made his friends seem important and their opinions valuable. Such perspicacity was astonishing in a child so young. Damon, even at an early age, seemed to know the difference between advice and the polite offer of an opinion. Pretty soon other kids, including his brothers, started to seek his advice on the things that troubled them.

The point was that Damon was, or appeared to be, an entirely positive person who could tackle a wide range of the subjects which were of concern to small boys. He was an expert on parents, school teachers, the rules of everything, what was fair and unfair, how to solve problems with older brothers, spiteful sisters and difficult parents. It was plain that many of his schoolmates left for home armed with Damon's logic to confound their enemies. Even his older brothers, who quarrelled with each other as all kids do, would sometimes be prepared to accept Damon as arbiter.

Damon, unable to go out and mix it with the other kids, had found a way to attract people to him. Adam tells how, in junior and senior school, you could always see a bunch of kids gathered around Damon under a tree. His disposition was such that he was almost never left entirely alone except when the other kids went on excursions and he was left behind. Although we accepted his gregarious nature as a blessing, thinking him always to have friends around him, we were too busy to realise ourselves that the nature of his illness meant that he spent a great deal of time on his own. In a letter sent to his grandmother when Damon was ten years old and which she returned to me knowing I was writing this book, he says, explaining his life to her, ".... I don't really need friends".

Somewhere along the line, and when he was still very young, Damon must have decided to be what Brett later referred to as "supernormal" and to carry his physical disadvantages with so little mention that he feigned surprise when anyone brought the matter up. Being normal, I now realise, was a full-time job for him. To seem like everyone else Damon had to work like hell to cover his considerable pain, his anxiety and above all, never, ever show the slightest sign of self-pity.

Damon soon began to realise that his mind could compensate for his body in other ways as well. The early training in imagination and visualisation was beginning to be helpful as he matured. By his early teens he had developed enormous mental discipline and the kind of concentration that can only come from the practice of self-hypnosis or, to give it a more friendly name, meditation.

Damon could diminish his pain level by becoming so deeply immersed in a book or a discussion that it seemed to mask his trauma. When it got really bad he would sit quietly, his arms folded in his lap, his eyes closed, his mind deeply in his subconscious controlling the pain. Damon was becoming an expert at self-hypnosis.

The medical staff at Prince Alfred, the hospital to which he transferred when a haematology unit was created, would claim that Damon seemed able to tolerate a great deal more pain than their other haemophilia patients. If this was so, then it was essentially mind power, the value of knowing how to enter his mind at a different level. We never spoke much of this aspect of pain control, though sometimes I'd ask him how a bleed was and he'd grimace. "It needed a trip to Africa," he'd say. So it seemed Damon must have had his own version of the night country, though he never explained and I didn't ask.

Damon had a very good mind and his mother was doing all she could to see that it got even better. Intelligence is a great healer and Benita added to his natural precocity by constantly keeping his mind sharp, never allowing it to grow lazy. The dictionary and encyclopaedia were well-thumbed books in our home, both were used almost exclusively by Adam and Damon. Adam, everlastingly a seeker after truth, used the books to confirm facts; Damon was as constantly in the business of expanding upon them.

Damon used me rather differently. He liked the way I could expand on a subject and think out of the square. "What we need here is some of *Dad's thinking*," he'd sometimes say. This, I was to learn, was not because he regarded my intellect as superior, a final opinion placed on a somewhat higher plane after an argument may have become deadlocked. In fact, I don't think he had a great deal of respect for the extent of my knowledge at all. *Dad's thinking* interested him because I could often reach conclusions that were plausible without necessarily being the most logical or truthful explanation of a situation or event — hence the inglorious *Dad Fact*.

While Damon obviously liked discussing things with me, he was also aware of my limitations, often declaring my version of how something might have come about as less likely but more interesting than the cold hard truth. This limitation he perceived in my intelligence was demonstrated to me early one morning when I think he was about seven.

He'd invited his friend, Jamie, from his prep school to spend the night. We were still in our cottage, where the inside walls were made of fibre board and therefore not very soundproof.

I woke at about five the following morning to hear the two small boys talking animatedly. It soon became apparent that they were discussing their fathers. Damon seemed to me to be more articulate about his father, or at least appeared to know me rather better than Jamie did his own male parent. As though aware of this and to equal up the points taken or go one better, Jamie suddenly announced, "My dad owns a television station!"

This was perfectly true, he was the son of a powerful media family who owned both Australia's leading women's magazine and the country's most successful commercial television network. I waited, anxious to hear Damon's comeback. This was, after all, pretty heavy stuff. How does a seven-year-old, even one with Damon's inventive mind, come back after a piece of one-upmanship of this quality?

There was a pause, which seemed to continue for quite a while, then Damon replied, perhaps even a trifle tartly, "My dad knows *everything*!"

This was said with absolute conviction, as though the ownership of a television station was a poor substitute for the ownership of positively limitless knowledge of the kind that caused the stars and the planets in the universe to spin and shine.

I silently applauded. Maybe, in a court of his peers, this reply would have lost out against the sheer impressiveness of owning your own television station, but as a comeback it was both sagacious and had a lot of class. Damon had neatly changed direction, brought the argument around from the ownership of things to the personal qualities of the two people. Not bad, not bad at all!

I beamed silently from the other side of the wall, proud of the classy kid we'd reared; then Damon added as though an afterthought, "But he doesn't know *very much* about everything!"

Although both Damon's brothers seemed to like him, Adam seemed the closer of the two to his little brother.

Brett was a pretty independent type and somewhat happy-go-lucky, content to cruise through life doing just enough to be left alone and to be seldom singled out for either responsibility or reprimand.

Adam was different, he was a trier and a perfectionist, constantly anxious about his progress, a born nail-biter. Adam soon learned to respect Damon's mind and he'd bring his anxieties to him as often, if not more often, than he would either to his mother or myself. He seemed constantly confounded by life's complexity and was increasingly subject to self-doubt and depression. This was particularly true during his puberty and it was at this time, in particular, that he took his anxieties to his little brother.

I discovered with all my sons that one morning they wake up and their world has changed. Instead of being happy kids, they become morose and silent. Instead of quite liking their parents they now see them as practically mentally retarded. Everything "sucks" and nothing can be done to please them. Their angst, confusion, malice, ill-temper, thoughtlessness, despair, superiority and disinterest comes out in the form of arms locked across their chests and brows so deeply furrowed as to be practically prehensile. Their voices drop an octave and they temporarily lose the ability to speak, this faculty being replaced with a Neanderthal grunt which covers every possible situation they may confront.

Angry-looking pimples, which they squeeze into even more angry-looking, raised red circles, appear on hitherto smoothly tanned faces. Though they don't openly blame their parents for this unseemly pustulence or for everything else that's suddenly gone rotten in their lives, it's obvious that in the allocation of mothers and fathers they got a pretty raw deal, a couple of near idiots with absolutely no redeeming features whatsoever.

Morose anger is suddenly a constant in the home, not just their own, but the backlash of hurt and spite they instil in the other members of the family. No reconciliation is possible and, certainly, at times I seriously wondered where I'd gone wrong, and how, in each case, we could have been responsible for raising such an unmitigated little bastard.

Then, one morning three or so years later, the monster who has created such bitter enmity within a perfectly nice family comes up to you at breakfast. The troglodyte grunt followed by the rude stretch across the table for the milk and then the silent, aggressive spooning of Mr Kellogg's crispy corn flakes into an open, munching, masticating mouth, suddenly kisses you for the first time in three years. Then he starts to chat and laugh as though nothing untoward has taken place in the preceding thirty-six months. The very idea of you as his mortal enemy, so permanent a part of his demeanour the previous day, week, month, year, forever, is now a preposterous thought, an invention of your own over-imaginative mind. He even manages to tell you, in a perfectly sincere voice, "I love you, Dad". And, of course, the little shit is instantly forgiven and his mother, who has been communicating with him via his brothers for the last umpteen months, hugs him, bursts into tears of gratitude and asks him joyously what he'd like for dinner.

Adam followed Brett into this state of pubescent insanity and, in due course, Damon followed Adam. While Brett was perfectly awful and Damon argumentative and irritable and over-precocious, Adam, as usual, managed to find a complication in his state of recalcitrant depression which made the adolescence of the other two seem like a couple of smallish wobbles in a more or less straight line of paternal harmony.

Shortly after going to see the film, *The Exorcist*, Adam developed an almost manic depression. He became convinced that he was in conflict with the devil and that if he didn't hang on to his thoughts very carefully the devil himself would take him over and rule his mind.

Quite where this came from I'm not sure, certainly not from any formal religious training. The devil played no part in his childhood, good and evil in the accepted catechism was not high on the list of his childhood instruction. I tried to cope with this devil fixation, pointing out that puberty was a pretty tough time, that it was quite okay to masturbate and have sexual fantasies for which he had no need to feel guilty. But I'd guessed wrong as usual. Nothing I said helped. This thing seemed to be over and above the expectations of puberty, an extra bombshell thrown in to confound his already perplexed and somewhat bewildered parents.

To suddenly find that the devil, in a very real sense of evil, was preoccupying Adam's mind, almost to the exclusion of everything else, was reminiscent of my own upbringing. But this wasn't darkest Africa, there was no witchcraft in Adam's pubescent life and I had certainly not introduced the subject to them as children. Only Damon had been shown how to take himself down into his own private country and, anyway, this technique had never been presented as though it contained any supernatural or mysterious qualities, let alone any quasi-demonic witchcraft.

At first Benita and I told ourselves it would go away, that this particular obsession was simply a different aspect of puberty, unlike that of his older brother, simply another manifestation, one which Brett, with his more happy-go-lucky pre-pubescent personality, had fortunately escaped. But there was little doubt that Adam's fears were palpable. Damon, however, was not prepared to indulge Adam. He would argue with him, confound his doubts, build up his ego and get him back on track. Damon, more than any of us, seemed to be able to cope with Adam's obsession; almost single-handedly he got Adam out of his depression with his logic, his caring, his compassion and even, once in a while, with his capacity for profound sympathy. He was able to calm Adam's fear and help to alleviate his depression and even, on occasion, to sit at his bedside until he fell asleep. Adam continued to need both the company and counsel of Damon long after he'd come out of his fear-of-the-devil stage and the two remained very close to the end.

It was curious that Adam, who was a good athlete, a good scholar, tremendously popular with his peers and his teachers and seemed to have everything a child could possibly want, needed the constant counsel of his younger brother who, though himself severely handicapped, never asked for a reciprocal shoulder to lean on. Much as they both loved Damon, I doubt very much if it ever occurred to Adam or Brett to show anything but the most casual, brotherly compassion for Damon's condition. This was not simply because they were preoccupied with their own lives. Both boys, if you exclude that horrid period during puberty, are and were considerate people and by no means egocentric. It was just that Damon was such a positive personality that he was simply not someone for whom you could possibly feel sorry.

Damon had another characteristic which made it difficult to see him in anything but a positive light. He overflowed with confidence. In his own mind, nothing in the non-physical sense seemed beyond him and he became convinced at a quite early age that he was destined to be both great and rich. Though, of these two things, wealth was the more important. We are not a materialistic family, doing things has always been more important than having things and so it was difficult to understand this desire on Damon's part for material wealth. He never really lacked for anything in the material sense and his preoccupation with money seemed strangely incongruous in someone who had such intelligence and, I think, real depth of personality.

It only became understandable if you thought about what Damon didn't have and how he might compensate for this. His body was frail, already he walked with a pronounced limp, movement in his elbows, knees and ankles was restricted, his joints partly fused by arthritis by the time he was in his mid-teens. Only wealth of a fairly excessive kind could turn him into the kind of hero he secretly longed to be. We always cherish the gifts we don't have and make light of those we've been given. Damon wanted to be somehow physically important and he must have decided that wealth could achieve this; that an aura of culture and wealth would compensate for his inadequate physicality in the same way that truly rich people seem larger in stature and physically more impressive than those of us who merely make ends meet.

While Damon went through the usual childhood stage of deciding to be a great doctor and scientist and to find a cure for haemophilia, as he grew into his teens the famous Nobel laureate scientist he intended to be was also seen to be filthy rich, wore Ray-Bans and drove a Ferrari Dino, having achieved all this before he reached the age of twenty-five and while only just out of Med. School. It is a curious thing that Damon always projected the coming together of àll his ambitions at the age of twenty-five, that he never talked of himself beyond this age. In part, his mother is to be blamed for Damon's rather overblown state of mind. Not only did she fill his head with books but also with images. She acquainted him with paintings and buildings, places and people. She told him what it was to be a Renaissance Man. She imbued in him what was good taste and what was thought not to be. Being a strong woman, she is fairly arbitrary in her likes and loyalties and, besides, she is outrageously Eurocentric in terms of fashion, architecture, painting, design, intellect, lifestyle and just plain chic, panache, élan, sophistication and tradition. She used a big spoon to ladle all this on to Damon's dreaming plate and he, one of the great listeners, imbibed all this romantic and esoteric nonsense and came to the correct, though disastrous, conclusion that it added up to a lifestyle which required a great deal of money, brains, talent and style — but not a lot of physical ability.

He assured himself that he possessed all the required characteristics save the money and, with the addition of a red Ferrari Dino (which, I suppose, compensated in his mind for his inadequate body), he would cope effortlessly with the business of being rich, brilliant and a dilettante. He would think faster, be more charming and, his natural self-confidence assured him, as soon as he was old enough to qualify for his learner-driver plates, he would drive faster and better than anyone who ever sat behind the steering wheel of a high performance Italian sportscar.

All this would make him extremely sexy, the young, good-looking Australian (with a slight but very sensual limp) who had come from the Antipodes to conquer the Old World.

The Ferrari was important; not a brand new one, which I suspect, using his mother's social barometer, he sensed would be not altogether in good taste, but a Dino, a machine which epitomised Enzo Ferrari's genius before he compromised his engineering soul and started building cars for rich, coke-sniffing hairdressers, advertising men and the new breed of Wall St. bratocracy.

As Damon grew into his later teens he lost the ambition to become a doctor. While, if he applied himself, he certainly had the brains for medical school, he may have known that his body would almost certainly let him down. The constant time missed from school because of his bleeds would be no different at university and medicine would certainly not easily allow for this.

If Damon was going to be rich, it was clear he wasn't going to be a rich doctor and someone else was going to find the cure for haemophilia, which Damon now knew was not to be his claim to fame.

In fact, when he was about fifteen, we read an article which claimed that research at Oxford University had made it possible to diagnose haemophilia in the womb.

What this seemed to mean was that there would be no more haemophiliacs, that a foetus found to be missing *Factor VIII* in the blood would be quietly aborted. Goodbye all future Damons, it was a sad but real thought. Beethoven's father had venereal disease and his mother was placed in an insane asylum; by today's standards the family gynaecologist would almost certainly have recommended that Mrs Beethoven's pregnancy be terminated.

It's an old argument and a tired one and, in a world where there are too many children, where forty-four thousand die every day of starvation, the anti-abortion stance is difficult to justify. How would we have reacted had we known of Damon's condition while there was still time to abort? I feel almost certain that I would have agreed to this happening. After all, we had the gift of two healthy sons, two children is blessing enough for anyone.

Yet, as it turned out, the idea of not having Damon in our lives is almost unthinkable. He heightened our sense of life and taught us all the meaning of love. He showed us how important it was to live each day, to squeeze the essence from the hours we are given. He was no saint, yet he gave us all a sense of living beyond ourselves. He had no strong beliefs, but he made us more compassionate and understanding in those human virtues we have the arrogance to refer to as Judaeo-Christian.

It is too easy to eulogise someone you have loved and lost and Damon's life of twenty-four years was insufficient to make him a remarkable human being. He was just a great kid, then a young man who had dreams that were bigger than his suffering and hopes bigger than his fears. He might also have had plans bigger than his frail body could accommodate, though I think not. Damon, the schemer, the dreamer, the optimist, was too used to overcoming obstacles, too big on fortitude not to have been a formidable competitor.

But when he was seventeen we learned that he was HIV positive. In the latter part of 1983 we didn't know quite what that meant. The only thing we knew was that it wasn't AIDS, the new disease which was beginning to kill homosexuals, quite a few in San Francisco and New York, though only the hint of a handful in Sydney. Not even Uncle Robert, a homosexual friend of the family, knew of anyone who had AIDS.

But looking back, I think we all knew that time was now a finite factor in Damon's life. Less time was now on his side. Damon had to make his mark rather sooner than later. Perhaps that's why he wanted to be rich while he was still young? Perhaps all this is nonsense? Certainly, I never discussed it with him, but at about this time, when it was announced he was HIV positive, Damon lost interest in long-term plans such as would be necessary if he were to follow a career in medicine.

I must also be truthful, Damon from the age of ten, when he began to deliver parcels for Bernie Carlisle, our local chemist, was always involved in a get-rich scheme. Because of his bleeds he couldn't always ride his bicycle or get to the chemist shop after school, so he developed a network of local kids who could stand in for him. At first, this was simply a matter of expediency and of not letting Mr Carlisle down, but it soon became the basis of Damon's working philosophy, as he was seen to take a small commission from each of the kids for supplying them with job security.

I recall late one night, in fact it was early one morning, perhaps two or three a.m., when Damon was about ten years old and we'd not long started doing home transfusions, he had a bleed in his right arm so he couldn't manage the needle himself. He'd woken me and I'd put the needle in and sat with him while the drip went through, when suddenly he asked, "Dad, what's a commission agent?"

It was always as well to ask Damon where his questions were leading, his mind was so quick that he'd take leaps and you'd find yourself explaining at length something which was meant only to be a bridge to another subject queuing for attention in his mind.

"Why do you want to know?"

"Well, when Brett was writing that essay you were helping him with on modern communications, you said advertising was a commission agent for the media. What did you mean?"

I explained how advertising agents accepted work from manufacturers and, instead of charging them a fee for making the advertisement and placing it, they charged them a percentage of the money it cost to buy the air time or the space in the magazine or newspaper. Then I added that the media, that is, the television station or radio station, magazine or newspaper also sold the air time or space on the page to advertising agencies for ten per cent less than if the client wanted to buy it directly from them.

This meant that advertising agents got commissions both from the manufacturer and from the media and were therefore agents who received commissions. Putting the two things together, they were commission agents.

"You mean they get this money for doing nothing?" Damon was clearly interested.

"No, I wouldn't say that, they have great skills, they have to think of ideas and make them into ads for the paper or radio and TV commercials. Then they have to find the right place to put these ideas, the right magazines or TV programs to make people buy products." I had to admit to myself, it didn't sound too intellectually challenging put in this way and Damon was quick to respond.

"They sell ideas? Is that what you do being the creative director, Dad?"

I agreed that this was pretty well it. "I think of ideas and my company gets paid a commission for putting these ideas into the media in the form of television or radio commercials or print ads," I repeated.

I could see a light go on in Damon's eyes. "You don't really *work* do you? You just sit there and have ideas and people pay you commissions?" He glanced up, "How much? How much do they pay you, Dad?"

"Well, it's not quite as easy as that!" I said a little defensively. "Having ideas isn't all that easy you know! I mean, if a client is going to spend a million dollars he wants a pretty good idea!"

"A million dollars! How much of that do you get being a commission agent?"

I could sense that I was in trouble, that my days as the hero who went forth each day to slay the commercial dragon and bring home the family bread were about to end. "Well, the client pays you seven and a half per cent and the media gives you ten per cent, that's . . ."

"Seventeen and a half per cent! A commission agent gets seventeen and a half per cent of a million dollars?" He was clearly blown away.

"Shhh! You'll wake everyone up. It's three o'clock in the morning," I hissed, hoping to bring the subject of commission agents to an abrupt end.

But Damon had already reached for the calculator which he kept beside his bed. Holding it between his knees, he tapped out the calculation.

"It's near enough to one hundred and seventy thousand in a million dollars, you don't need a calculator to work that out," I said scornfully. But Damon was the first generation to be raised on the calculator and he used it as a matter of course, just as my generation had turned on the radio to hear news we'd already read in the morning paper.

He whistled in amazement, "One hundred and seventy-five thousand!" The jerk of his body as he reacted to this surprising figure stopped the flow of the drip.

"Now look what you've done," I said annoyed. "Hold still." I gently wiggled the needle hoping to get the drip flowing into the vein again. "Yeah, one hundred and seventy thousand odd, that's what I already said. But it's not as easy as that, you know!" Fortunately the drip started again; had it not I would have had to find a new vein and put the remainder of the cryoprecipitate through it.

"Just for having ideas." Damon said this as though to himself and I knew I'd lost him and, in his head, he'd found the way to his first fortune.

Damon's various business enterprises never lasted too long, they were all based on himself as the negotiator and middleman with a dozen or so of his friends actually doing the work. In the environment I had grown up in he would have made a fortune, but the kids around where we lived had trouble enough attending to their own swimming pools, let alone the three each they were allocated to clean over the weekend. Damon brought in lots of business but his employees always let him down. He was always out making good some enterprise or other by doing the job himself. He'd clean four pools and come home with a massive bleed, or deliver messages till mid evening and come home with a bleed, or have to work all day cleaning and detailing a couple of Mercedes because his team was out surfing or at camp or away with their parents for the weekend or just plain lazy and, of course, he returned home with a bleed. His most successful business was a Sunday morning croissant door-to-door delivery service. This was basic bicycle work and physically not too demanding, so that when his workers didn't get up at five a.m. to collect their croissants from the baker at Rose Bay, Damon could usually get Adam and sometimes even Brett to help him deliver. But this too failed after a year or so, when people increasingly forgot to put out their croissant money and Damon found himself out of pocket.

Damon's modus operandi was twenty-five per cent of the take in return for which he negotiated the business, collected the money and maintained the quality control. Though the "human factor", which was what he called the basic indolence of his friends, destroyed each of his business enterprises, he still managed to create enough income to buy a hi-fidelity record and tape unit with two speakers, which would have sufficed for a major concert at the Sydney Opera House and which he valued at five thousand dollars, and a record and tape collection which he assured me was worth at least two thousand.

Under his mother's guidance he'd learned all about classical music and his collection was impressive, but the ebullient Damon discovered hard and then acid rock and the music coming from his room would change from the Brahms violin concerto to a couple of hard rock numbers and back again to Vivaldi's *Four Seasons* in the time it took to play these in sequence.

Damon, as usual, knew all about the music he played and every detail of the equipment on which he played it. Fed up with hired labour, he put a proposition to the hi-fi shop whose equipment and *integrity* he respected the most that they should pay him commission only, in fact seventeen and a half per cent, on sales of equipment he sold to customers he himself brought in.

The shop owner could hardly believe his ears, the bargain was struck and Damon, with work at last that didn't tax his body or depend on his mates, started to clean up. Working his Cranbrook contacts, mostly the kids whom he'd so disastrously employed in the past, he soon had their parents' homes installed with the latest and the best hi-fidelity gear. Damon, of course, spent everything he earned, most of it in fact going directly back to the owner of the hi-fi shop, as Damon's audio equipment started to compare with that of a small, high-tech FM radio station. We were discovering that there was no such thing as perfection in sound, but that the urge to try to create it was obsessive and was akin to throwing money into a bottomless pit. Damon's head-phones alone cost more than the Toshiba equipment the rest of the family used to play its tapes and records.

Damon's matriculation year, 1983, came and went more or less the same as all the others, he was still only managing three days at school a week and he seemed never to study. He had a spurt of growing between fifteen and seventeen when his bleeds were worse than ever, but nothing else seemed untoward, until he sat his final school examination. Midway through his Higher School Certificate examination we received a call from the Haemophilia Centre asking us to make an appointment to see the head haematologist. Benita nominated a day two days hence when Damon wasn't sitting for an exam and when I could take a couple of hours off work.

We arrived at the Haemophilia Centre not particularly anxious; from time to time we'd been in to hear a progress report on Damon's general health and Denise, the sister-in-charge, hadn't indicated that this visit was anything very special.

For a while the doctor talked about Damon's bad knee. We'd heard of an operation which was being performed overseas to cut away the calcium deposits inside the kneecap that were fusing the knee and causing arthritis. His opinion was that the operation was difficult and problematic and we shouldn't attempt to do anything and now he was once again stating his objection.

Finally he came to the point, "Damon has developed a blood condition, a viral condition known as HIV positive."

Benita looked anxious, "What does that mean, doctor?"

"Well we're not *absolutely* certain, he probably got it from a blood transfusion."

"Well, what happens? What can we expect?"

The haematologist shrugged, "We don't precisely know, we think it has a very long incubation period and, in fact, it might never develop into anything at all."

I looked at Benita and we both relaxed. Damon had been through so much, a seemingly benign virus in his blood wasn't the end of the world.

The doctor tapped his biro on the blotter in front of him. "I wouldn't worry too much, haemophilia is always going to be his major worry in life." He looked up and smiled. "Almost half our haemophiliacs have contracted this virus which seems to have shown no overall effect."

"I've read about HIV. Isn't it something happening to homosexuals in America?"

The doctor looked up quickly. "Yes, well, that's where they isolated it in the blood. Too little is known to be exact. As I said, there isn't any cause for alarm."

Of course, with our past experience of the medical profession, we should have become panic stricken immediately, but once again we listened and accepted an opinion which, as it transpired, was based on less research and reading than we'd done ourselves. We promptly forgot about Damon's new HIV-positive state.

Of course we took him in to have a T-cell count every month, but he always returned a count well within the safety margin. We were much more concerned about his arthritis and the ever-recurring left knee bleed. The old leg-iron knee caused him as much pain as the rest of his body put together and now the right knee was giving him trouble, bleeding more frequently than it had done previously. Damon looked like becoming a cripple and all our energies were spent on trying to prevent this from happening.

We'd found a good surgeon who would aspirate his knees, that is, open them up to remove the old, coagulated blood and permanent pus and gore around each knee. While this wouldn't do a great deal for the damaged knees, it was thought that it might stop some of the bleeding and, in this way, prevent further damage. The operation, though simple, required a great deal of blood product. We would often have to wait several weeks for blood to become available. Operating on a haemophiliac was a tricky business and very few surgeons would even attempt it. Because of the potential use of so much blood, the hospital did not encourage surgery on haemophiliacs and Dr MacDonald, the surgeon prepared to operate, was at constant loggerheads with the department head and the hospital board.

MacDonald wasn't an easy man to like. He was very outspoken, aware that his fellow surgeons were simply too afraid to operate on a haemophiliac. But he was a good man and cared a great deal about Damon and, indeed, all the other haemophiliacs who had to rely solely on his surgical skills. He spent half his professional life trying to get permission to perform even the most simple operations on haemophiliacs who badly needed his attention. Even a tooth extraction is a major event with a haemophiliac, where the bleeding from having a wisdom tooth extracted is a highly dangerous procedure which, if it goes wrong, can cause the patient to die. The hospital simply couldn't be bothered with the complex procedures involved. As usual, the haemophiliac supporters were only a handful of families with no political clout or influence and they were, it seemed, more trouble than they were worth. Moreover, they were represented by a surgeon who observed almost no medical decorum and constantly overstepped his authority. It was ironical that, for once, we had a doctor on our side and he was being rendered almost ineffectual by his peers and the hospital system.

MacDonald was a highly skilled surgeon who kept abreast of the latest surgical techniques in haemophiliac procedure. Although the aspiration was a small help, Damon's knees were not responding well and needed to be opened up and scraped. The constant bleeding had formed calcium deposits in the joints which acted like rust. The elbow and knee joints were fused and the idea was to try to cut away the sharp calcium deposits which caused much of the bleeding and to attempt to restore some movement to his knees. Similar operations had been successful overseas and MacDonald was hopeful that the same results could be achieved here.

He was an impetuous man by nature, but a careful surgeon, and had studied the procedure carefully. Despite the objection of the head haematologist, he became convinced that it was a feasible operation for Damon with a good chance for a positive result.

Only two problems existed, permission to save sufficient blood product for the operation and a particular piece of equipment needed to perform the operation. The German equipment was long overdue and useful in a great many other surgical applications, but the head of department and then the hospital board vetoed the request to purchase it. They had greater needs than this particular equipment and it was made perfectly clear to

MacDonald that these "greater needs" would continue to exist for a long time to come. MacDonald was becoming more and more frustrated, but he was only an "honorary" and, as such, making much too much of a nuisance of himself.

I managed to raise the thirty-three thousand dollars for the equipment through a generous donation from the trust fund of a leading financial organisation, who happened to be one of my clients; as well, we managed to scrape together a bit ourselves. MacDonald went back and requested permission to operate, acquainting the hospital board with the good news of the donation of the very latest equipment to the hospital surgical department.

He was promptly told that blood product wasn't available through the Red Cross for such an operation and that he couldn't, in the foreseeable future, expect that supplies would be forthcoming. MacDonald, after three years of this kind of frustration, had had enough and he resigned his position as an honorary. His resignation was accepted, we have been told, with alacrity by his department head. This man later coldly explained to one of the sisters at the Haemophilia Centre that *his* area had rather greater priorities than the surgical task of restoring the knees of a haemophiliac from a privileged background just so that he could gallivant around a tennis court. Game, set and match to the doctors in the surgical department of The Royal Prince Alfred Hospital.

Almost ten years later, no haemophiliac has undergone such an operation to his knee, though it is commonplace overseas. Several of those haemophiliacs who might have benefited from such an operation are still alive but are permanently confined to wheelchairs. Also, it is now known that the amount of blood for this particular operation is reasonably easy to obtain, given a few weeks' notice. The system had caught up with us again and Damon, it seemed, was well on his way to becoming a permanent cripple. The sexy little limp was becoming a bit of a hobble and, as far as we knew, Mr Enzo Ferrari hadn't yet designed the world's fastest fire-engine red wheelchair.

But, of course, Damon didn't become a cripple. Two new events came into his life, one of them was bad and came in the form of a peculiar nocturnal condition known as "night sweats" and the other was simply divine and came in the shape of a leggy, seventeen-year-old, blue-eyed blonde, named Celeste.

10

Of Books and Dings and Other Things.

When someone we love dies there appears to be some sort of healing mechanism triggered in our minds which effectively binds up our hurt. After the initial overwhelming onslaught, the hurt visits us in small, just bearable portions, slowly leaching out our grief so that we may eventually resume our former lives. These sudden inoculating jabs of grief intended to build up our resistance, are thankfully soon over and we can cope until the next one strikes and we feel again the paralysis of loss.

Alas, this natural process is not designed to cope with writing a book where the pain is deliberately made to linger so that it can, in some part, be trapped for the page. I started to write just two weeks after Damon's death, knowing that if I delayed I might not be able to keep my promise to him. Damon's last but a few words to me were to ask me to write this book. His voice was tediously slow and his eyes glazed from the effects of the massive doses of morphine he took to shield what had become almost incomprehensible pain, yet his mind seemed surprisingly clear.

Our conversation, which here appears so precise and organised, took almost forty minutes with long pauses, some extended to five minutes, as he fought for clarity, choosing carefully these almost last of his words to me through the miasma of drugs, the combination of pills and brightly coloured capsules Celeste called his drug cocktail.

The simple text I've put down here involved a gigantic effort at concentration on Damon's part and was a supreme example of sheer willpower. Towards the end, the task of concentrating for more than twenty or so seconds at a time became almost impossible for him. I would sit beside him on his bed as he spoke to me in a low rasp; I had to strain to hear him, my ear as close to his mouth as I could get. "Dad, I was too young and, in the end, too weak to write about all this." He waved his hand feebly in front of his face, the gesture intended to take in what his life had become. "But people *must* be told about AIDS. Ordinary people must understand it's just something that happens. That it's not wicked or a punishment and that it needs a lot of love."

Here came one of his long pauses and I could see he was upset, but his concentration was so fierce that I dared not attempt to comfort him for fear that his fragile mind might collapse. At last he continued, "Some of the people in hospital, the gay guys, their parents come to visit them at the last moment — for the first time —

when they are going to die." Damon started to weep and all I could do was to hold his hand. "Rick calls them," he said through his tears, "You know Rick? Rick Osborne your friend. He calls them ... and gets heavy." Damon sniffed and I wiped the mucus from his nose and upper lip. "Rick gets really shitty on the phone and demands they come. And they come ... and they're scared and you can see they're ashamed ... and afraid." Damon's eyes filled again with tears. "They don't understand, Dad, they think *they're* being punished. That God is punishing them! They don't know what to say, how to behave, it's all new stuff. Some stay only a few minutes, ordinary working people who look down at their hands and around the room, but they don't, can't look at their own son! And then they leave, confused and frightened." Damon lay panting, his hand still in mine, the effort to get all this out was enormous, he looked up at me, his eyes red with conjunctivitis. Somewhere along the way his long, beautiful eyelashes had fallen out; one morning he just didn't have them. It was such a little thing in all the other things that we hardly noticed.

"Dad, you've got to write a book to tell people not to be frightened, not to run away, not to be ashamed. It's just a thing you get. You have to tell them that."

It was the longest conversation Damon had sustained for at least a month. Apart from the great difficulty he had concentrating, with a body no longer able to resist any sort of infection, thrush, the yellow fungus, had attacked the tissue of his mouth and spread down his throat and into the lining of his stomach and large intestine, so that it made each word actually painful to pronounce. It must have been like having a huge, spongy, suppurating sore spread on the inner lining of his food tract. After we'd talked he was completely exhausted and I thought he might actually die. Almost immediately he fell into a deep sleep, his breathing alternately soft and then suddenly furious and struggling, then so soft again it couldn't be heard and I'd put my ear to his heart, not able to hear his for the beating of my own.

Damon slept frighteningly, his eyes, pussed and swollen were half-open, staring up at the ceiling in the manner of the dead. My beautiful son was alive and dead at the same time.

This had been the last conversation. We'd started talking together so long ago at the time of his purple head. We'd talked and talked, through nights when the moon was full or the rain beat darkly against the window panes and the wind howled outside. We talked through the traffic swish of rainy streets with red and green light caught in the slicked road. Through hot nights or with blankets wrapped around us as we waited in emergency for Dr Gett, the needle man, to arrive. We talked the seasons away, winter and summer, old Damon and I; we'd seen a thousand mornings arrive, seen them sneak up on our conversation unannounced, the window grown suddenly and surprisingly light. We'd talked through the hours and days, the months and years. We'd chased pain away with chat a hundred times at least. We'd built word castles in the air so powerful with rhetoric and laughter that they'd been known to banish the pain of bad bleeds in their tracks.

Now the mighty Damon could talk no more. This was the last time for the duo who'd slain the great dragon Splutter Grunt and so liberated the butterfly needle.

These were the final hours coming up.

Damon knew that he'd come home to die. He'd asked that Adam return from London and Brett from Kuala Lumpur and that all his friends come to say goodbye. His request for this book was the last piece of tidying up he had to do with his short, sweet life.

I'm certain he didn't think of this book as his epitaph. Damon never borrowed gratuitously from anything in his life. I'm not saying he wasn't an opportunist, he knew how to get what he wanted and he wasn't above the odd scam. But any glory going had to be of his own making. The idea of a book which would act as a memorial to his own pain and struggle would have been abhorrent to him.

The book he wanted written was about being in love with life, about love and understanding and about not being afraid when you were dealt the joker in the pack, or at the least, facing your fears despite your fear. His final, but four, words to me were about Celeste. "Promise me, Dad, that you'll always look after Celeste, whom I love much, much more than my own dumb life."

Afterwards I found several attempts he'd made to write his own story on his Apple Macintosh. I'd like to say they were especially good words, a literary talent lost to the world, but Damon, though always articulate, was an ordinary maker of prose. He dealt too often in the reality of pain to be much good with hyperbole. From the very first sentence he feels the need to explain, to minimise, to make a small deal of what was truly a very big one.

As a writer he can be said to have lacked, completely, the sense of his own drama. His words are written as if he has gathered a few people around him for an informal lecture on the causes and effects of being a haemophiliac or on what it means to have AIDS. They contain no hint of self-pity and his pain remains private, not open to discussion, even by himself. To the vary last Damon was supernormal.

Well, I suppose his writing wasn't really best-seller material, but it's the stuff from which Damon was well and truly made. Damon was an explainer, a natural seeker after the truth, he wanted to leave behind something which someone else could use without seeking to earn any sympathy or glory for himself. Though, of course, he would have wanted his book to be a best-seller; in Damon's mind there wouldn't be any point in writing a book if the whole world wasn't going to read it.

It may seem natural enough that Damon would urge his readers to cherish their health. But there was more to it than a simple injunction not to take a wonderful gift for granted. Damon was always fascinated by energy. He loved to see people use it. The fact that he himself was always physically incapacitated to some degree, and often completely, made him crave action. It is hardly surprising therefore that the automobile provided the perfect answer. Had his knees been any better it might well have been a motor cycle. So we were lucky, I suppose. The idea of the mighty Damon on a Honda 1000 is the ultimate nightmare.

Damon could barely wait to turn seventeen so that he could obtain his provisional driving licence. I think it was the only thing he really studied for in his life and he was uncharacteristically in tears when, having achieved one hundred per cent in theory, he made some error or other in judgment during his road test and he was failed.

It didn't console him to be told that both Brett and Adam had failed the first time, in fact, that everyone failed the first time, that it was virtually *compulsory* to fail the first time, that the system quite definitely required it. Damon simply couldn't conceive that the automobile wasn't specifically designed for him and the failure was like being rejected by a lover for whom you are prepared to lay down your life.

We shared long faces and did all the appropriate tutt-tutting but, I must say, we were rather pleased at the time. Damon talked and dreamed speed and the idea of arthritic-stiffened arms and legs, none able to react as fast as normal limbs, behind the wheels and pedals of his mother's Alfa Sud, had all the ingredients of the usual nightmare. It wasn't difficult to predict that Damon was going to use a motor car to make up for a whole heap of physical and psychological hangups and perceived lost opportunities. The automobile was going to make Damon as normal as anyone else; it would be at once the leveller and the opportunity to demonstrate his daring and his skill.

Unfortunately he passed his test the second time around with a perfect performance; as far as I'm concerned it was the last time he ever drove a car with any sort of commonsense. No fighter pilot ever received his wings with more excitement. Damon was free to fly at last.

While waiting for fortune to present him with a red Ferrari he had to make do with his mother's Alfa Sud. At least it was Italian and had some pedigree, which was important. After all the successor to Fangio shouldn't be seen driving a Datsun Bluebird station wagon, my car at the time.

Sealed into what was little more than a neat, little, Italian bubble of metal and glass, Damon could dream of winning at Le Mans with laurel wreath from neck to knees, squirting a jeroboam of Bollinger over his pit crew and on to the adoring, mostly (beautiful) female, crowd.

His mother's constant nagging and my pedantic lectures didn't help, he drove the little Sud hard and fast and with no knowledge of what made the underside of the bonnet work. He was keen enough to be shown how to brake a car first by using its engine as well as some of the other niceties of driving an automobile intelligently. But I'm sure he saw me as someone who simply didn't understand that he was naturally gifted, the embodiment of a Fangio, Berger or Prost, or nearer to home, the retired, three-times-world-champion, Jack Brabham. The gift of a pair of English pigskin driving gloves and a new pair of Ray-Ban aviator, mirror lens sunglasses for his eighteenth birthday earned us the accolade of: "Probably the best parents in the history of the civilised world."

There wasn't much we could do. Damon behind the wheel of his mother's little Italian car was happier than we'd ever seen him. The knowledge that one half-serious accident which, in someone else, might only mean lacerations and bruising, would almost certainly kill him was difficult to overcome. The night Damon got his driving licence I woke suddenly, the old instinct in me still intact, someone was crying! It was Benita in bed beside me. "What's the matter, darling? Why are you crying?" She turned her back on me and buried her head in her pillow, trying to stifle her sobs.

I pulled her towards me and held her in my arms. "Shhh, stop now, whatever it is, I'm sure it's something we can fix."

This brought a fresh wail. "No, it isn't!"

I pulled her into my chest and held her tightly. "C'mon now, tell me. I'm sure there's *something* I can do."

Benita stopped crying and pulled away from my embrace. "Do you know someone at the police who can make him lose his licence?" She was right, there was nothing we could do and I felt like bawling myself. I called the Government Insurance Office and asked what the accident statistics were for young male drivers? They told me that males average five accidents before they reach the age of twenty-five, one of which would be serious. I didn't share this knowledge with Benita but signed Damon up for an advanced driver's course with the police driving school.

This proved to be the worst thing I could have done. All the talk about safe handling and caution on the road went completely over Damon's head; the ability to make a car do extraordinary things at high speed was all Damon cared about.

I had hoped, even expected, that the police instructors would discover the damage to his joints which made his reactions too slow for this type of driving, that they would emphasise that he wasn't Fangio material and, with his physical handicaps, should be extra careful, even under normal circumstances, when handling a car. Coming from them he might respond. I explained all this to a very doubtful Benita, who thought I'd taken leave of my senses. I remember concluding my argument with: "I'm telling you, it's dead cunning. It may not be good for his ego but it will make him understand he's not God's gift to the automobile."

But Adam was right when he'd claimed that Damon, but for his haemophilia, was a natural athlete and the speed of his reactions, first observed when he played ping-pong, now showed as he drove a car. They were fast enough to fool the police instructors into passing him the first time. The Advanced Driver certificate he received was framed and placed on the wall next to the huge, framed picture of a red Ferrari Dino. Damon was now superqualified to do stupid things with a motor car. With the national accident statistics stacked against him I was pretty certain it was only a matter of time before he rewrote the book of needless risks taken in the quest to make a small Italian sports sedan go faster than its factory specifications.

About nine p.m. one Saturday evening several months after he'd obtained his licence, the phone rang in the hall and I answered it. It was Damon. "Dad, I've had an accident."

I had been prepared for this moment for some time and all the scenarios I'd mentally conjured up now came rushing to the fore. The fact that it was Damon himself speaking on the other end entirely escaped my panicked mind. "Are you hurt? Have they called the ambulance? What hospital? I'm coming over directly? Are you in Emergency? Do they know you're a haemophiliac? Has someone contacted the Blood Bank?" It all tumbled out, the perfectly rehearsed sequence I'd mentally been through perhaps a hundred times without consciously being aware of what I was doing.

"Dad, it's me. It's Damon you're talking to! I'm all right, nothing wrong."

"Bruises! Shit! They're going to need ice, lots of ice. Have they been told? You must be packed in ice immediately. What hospital? I forget what hospital you said!" I cried.

"Dad! I haven't got a scratch."

Benita must have heard me on the phone and came running. "What? What is it? Damon? Is he all right?"

"He's had an accident." I was not conscious of how I said this and my own anxiety carried enough meaning for her to panic as well.

She went pale and began to shake and then sob. Clutching me on the shoulder she screamed down the phone, "Where is he! Where have you taken him!"

Benita's reaction brought me out of my own panic and, as though it was a delayed soundtrack, I now heard Damon's voice replay the past minute or so, assuring me that he was unhurt.

"It's all right. He's okay, apparently unhurt." I clasped Benita's shoulders with my free arm and pulled her to me, the phone still cupped to my ear.

"Dad? You there, Dad?" Damon yelled down the phone.

This incident, Damon's first accident, served to make me aware of how tension is built up over the years. I had always been able to meet each crisis with Damon as it came, my mind so finely tuned to his condition that nothing, I told myself, could phase me. *Never show any emotion. Never complain when you have to take him to hospital.*

Smile. Make light of things. Give comfort. Never admit you're tired. Never show how distraught you are. Never think of the consequences. Just act. You must be like a rock. In fact, I used the analogy of a rock to myself. I imagined myself as a nice, warm, sunny rock, sheltered from the bitterly cold wind, a sort of private place to which Damon could always come. I admit, this sounds pretty melodramatic, but the rock symbol was obviously a metaphor which gave me strength.

I also know precisely where it came from. On the wall beside my mother's sewing machine was a small, framed print given to her by an American missionary friend. It showed a young maiden clutching a wave-lashed pinnacle of rock which appeared to be positioned way out to sea, for there was no land anywhere visible. The wind tore at her skirts and hair as she gazed heavenward, one arm stretched towards the sombre skies in desperate supplication. Around her, the furious waves swirled at her skirt and it seemed to me it was only a matter of time before they completely engulfed her. But beaming down on her was a single ray of light which pierced the dark, ominous skies, lighting her frightened face. The caption at the bottom read: *I am the rock.*

Even as a small child it didn't make sense to me. I wasn't sure whether it was meant to be an assurance or a threat? Or was the girl about to be saved or doomed by this rock which had some sort of metamorphic property allowing it to trap young maidens who were silly enough to venture fully clothed far out to sea — when it was as plain as the nose on your face that a mighty hurricane was brewing. Later, when I first heard the hymn, "Rock of Ages", I wondered if it was the same rock at work again? What the hell did "I am the rock" mean?

But I must have worked it out somewhere along the way and decided that the rock was on her side. Though, of course, my rock for Damon was well away from the swirling waves and the howling wind and always dappled with sunlight. Corny as it must seem, this notion of being a rock held me together over the years. I was prepared to take anything Damon's illness could dish out and to cope with it, solid as a rock.

Or so I thought.

Now I discovered that tension is something you can handle for years, learn to live with so completely, so entirely sublimate, that it never shows on the surface. But it's there all the same and sooner or later it will overpower you as it now did me on the phone to Damon. My first reaction after my initial panic was to shout. To call Damon every kind of a bloody fool I could think of, as well as a few other words parents seldom use in front of their children. Now these issued from my lips faster than I could think, or care, to halt them.

I told him that he would never be allowed to drive a car again. "You hear? That's it! Never again! You can't be trusted, you're a bloody irresponsible maniac! You're practically a bloody cripple, you hear!" It was a threat, which, had I carried it out, would have been tantamount to a death sentence, worse even than the result of an accident. Finally I calmed down and sat down in a corner of the lounge room and started to weep, ashamed at what I'd said. It was also the first time since his purple head in hospital that I'd cried over Damon.

Two days later I was to inspect Benita's little Alfa Sud

at the garage where it had been towed. I arrived and the panel beater, without first warning me, led me to the car. It was a complete wreck. Damon had had a head-on collision pushing the engine past the dashboard and far into the front passenger seat. The roof post and roof itself on the passenger side had collapsed and what was left of the windshield was a large hole surrounded by crazed and buckled glass. Even the steering wheel was snapped into three pieces. But except for this, where the driver would sit was completely undamaged.

The panel beater looked at me morosely. "You're lucky, mate, you're still alive and the insurance company is going to give you a nice new one." He paused and spat on the ground at his feet. "Some bastards get all the fucking breaks."

Damon had survived his first accident; if he was going to measure up to the national average for under twenty-fives, he had four more to go. This time all he had to show for the experience was a week of severe pain and multiple blood transfusions to stop the bleeding in his shoulder sockets where the safety belt had jerked him back into his seat as it harnessed him against the impact of the collision.

Damon was to transcend, in fact wholly eclipse, the national under twenty-five accident average, believing himself always to be entirely in the right, though almost entirely in the right at considerable speed. He was never indicted for a driving offence but, nevertheless, I am not proud of his record, even though I was told often enough, once by a policeman, that it was his skilful driving which, in some instances, turned what could have been a disaster into a mere accident. I also suspect that Damon's smooth tongue and ingenuous manner helped enormously at the scene of an accident.

Damon was not entirely on his own, and he easily out-bingled his brothers. The three boys managed, several times over, to eliminate my twenty years of accident-free, no-fault insurance bonus and place a hefty premium on my annual car insurance which I think I'm still paying.

Whenever he passed me in his mum's car (a new Alfa), always with a sharp, cheeky toot and a wave of a leather-gloved hand, I would intone softly, my eyes directed upwards through the tinted windshield, "Please God, don't ever make him successful enough to own a Ferrari."

Book Two

Learning to Love the Needle.

11

Celeste

Loving a Boy with a Burt Reynolds Complex.
Celeste Swaps the Ray-Ban Kids.

I met Damon through Toby a few months after I'd left school. Toby was my first real experience of a proper boy, someone who lived in a real home with a mum who did mum things and a dad who went to work. Toby, like Damon, was a Cranbrook boy, which was pretty suspect for someone like me, but he was nice and played the electric guitar.

I mean he was a *really* gifted rock 'n' roll player. I liked the idea of going out with a musician, even though he was at university and didn't play professionally or even pretend to. At the Cross, where I lived, lots of guys tried to play guitar and act like they were pros in a group, but you knew they were would be's if they could be's. Toby,

who was really good, didn't want to play as a professional and I found this pretty amazing.

In my mind I equated rock 'n' roll music with a time
well past midnight. Davo, my inherited, sometime actor
and only other boyfriend experience, who was always a
bit drunk, would wake me by tapping on my window
and I'd get out of bed and we'd go to the Piccolo Bar. So
rock 'n' roll for me was speckled brown froth at the
bottom of a chocolate-coloured cappuccino cup, the acrid
smell of dope in a smoke-filled room and bourbon fumes
on Davo's breath. It certainly wasn't a polite, private
school boy with calm hazel eyes.

I should really tell you about Davo, who was what
passed for a boyfriend before I met Toby and, shortly
after that, Damon. Davo was the sort of boyfriend you
have when you're not really having a boyfriend, because
I kind of inherited him from my sister by mistake when
I was fifteen. She went away and Davo kept coming
around and tapping on the window and I was the only
female person whose window you could tap on at our
boarding house.

Davo was in his mid-twenties, an addict and, I suppose, an alcoholic. He was supposed to be an actor and
could have been before his brain sort of gave up on him
and he couldn't learn his lines any more. He'd be good
one moment and the next they'd scramble, the words
would come out but they'd be out of sequence. It was
amazing. I'll tell you more about him later.

Now here was Toby, a young guy with pink one-
shave-a-week cheeks, curly blond hair and serious hazel
eyes, who, I was pretty sure, was still a virgin, and played
electric guitar like he was permanently spaced out,

although I felt sure he didn't even take aspirin.

Anyway, Toby's music acted as the bridge I needed to cross into his nice, neat world. His guitar made him acceptable as a boyfriend. Although that's a bit funny coming from me; I was terribly shy and I wasn't exactly doing the choosing around the place. But if I was going to have a proper boyfriend, one more or less my own age but from the cleaner side of life, then Toby was acceptable because he was a rock 'n' roll musician.

I forgot to say that, after leaving school and before I met Toby, Muzzie, my grandmother who was terribly important in my life, suggested I take a modelling course with June Dally-Watkins. This was only a three-week course and I guess the closest a kid from Kings Cross gets to a finishing school. We learned how to sit and walk and do a bit about modelling clothes as well as how to look after your nails, hair and make-up. It was really sort of intended to turn you, after the ubiquitous typing course, into (wait for it), *a secretary with a future*!

On the strength of my June Dally-Watkins training I was accepted by a model agency. They must have seen something in me which I was quite unaware of, for I thought of myself as quite ugly. But only about one in a thousand girls made it into a model agency, so I was supposed to be very lucky to make it and this too gave me a bit of confidence. My main job at the time was as check-out chick at Harris Farm Markets and I also worked at Miss Chapman's bookshop and I now found myself doing a bit of modelling as well.

But I've got to say, the modelling was nothing big deal, the usual in-store catwalk stuff, mostly out in the western suburbs. You'd travel two hours in the train and then some totally apathetic shopping mall manager would show you the clothes you were going to wear, which were usually to be found hanging in a tiny box room which had to act as dressing room. Usually the toilets and washroom were at the other end of the complex and so you did your make-up in your compact mirror.

At first you think you'll be smart and do your make-up before you leave home, but you soon learn to stop that. The yobbos on the trains pick-up on you and hassle you and they can get really nasty. So you *dress ugly* and wear no make-up to a job, which can be difficult when you get there and find no change room facilities.

When you arrived you'd pick through the gear, hoping to find something that suited you. I was always running late and the other girls would have grabbed all the reasonable looking stuff, which didn't enhance my modelling career a whole lot as I was the one who was always being pinned at the back. Models are all supposed to be a size ten, but the variations in the rag trade on a size ten are astonishing and naturally the girls left the stuff that was too big. I became an expert with a safety pin, or walking on to the catwalk with my hand clutching a bunch of material pulled in at the waist and at the same time trying to look natural.

You'd do the best you could then they called your name and you walked towards the catwalk, going through the June Dally-Watkins litany in your head: "Watch the step, pause at the top, step forward, swing your bottom, pause at the centre of the catwalk, look left, smile, look right, smile, continue (Bottom! Swing your bottom!), walk to the end, pivot, hold, smile, turn, throw head back slightly, walk to the centre, pivot, smile left, smile right, walk to the end, mind step, disappear!"

You'd do all this trying not to throw up on to the heads of gross looking housewives in pink tracksuits and sheepskin ugg boots eating chips and yelling at toddlers in strollers who were painting their noses and foreheads with ice-cream cones. I don't know why, but they always seemed to give their kids green ice cream! It was quite awful and I hated it from the very first day and it never got any better. I can still sometimes hear it in my dreams.

"Now we have Celeste in a charming black and tan, naturally the colours for this autumn, romper suit, in beautiful wash 'n' wear lycra. Show the ladies the baggy cut around the hips, Celeste. The cut is generous for those of us with . . . er, just a little more breadth around the thighs. (Wait for the laugh, grin yourself.) Under her lovely autumn romper suit by Delvita of Melbourne, Celeste is wearing a pumpkin Merribelle American cotton T-shirt! Pumpkin is also this season's big colour. This divine T-shirt is not quite winter weight, but lovely for this time of the year, don't you think, ladies?"

I much preferred to work as a check-out chick at Harris Farm Markets, there at least the Italian growers would come in and they'd sing and muck around, fall on their knees in supplication, exaggerating their dismay when you refused them a kiss in return for them promising to be your devoted slave for life. One old man, who was known as Papa and always had three or four days' grey stubble on his chin, would touch a large peach or some other exotic fruit to his lips. "Tomorrow this'a peach is'a gonna be ripe and my kiss gonna taste-a beautifool in your mouth, signorina Celeste!"

It was comic book Italian-English, but that's how he *really* spoke. I always took the peach home, washed it and gave it to David, my brother, who was unaware that he was being kissed by a fat, ageing Italian in a sweaty navy singlet.

I wasn't much good at faking things and maybe I wasn't grateful enough to the model agency so, by the time I met Toby, my in-store parades were getting few and far between and I was virtually a model in name only. The occasional photography job came along when an art director in an advertising agency picked my mug shot from the model directory. It was just enough to enable me to claim a career in modelling without telling a bare-faced lie.

I think Toby quite liked taking out someone who was a model, just as I liked being with someone who played good electric guitar. He was so talented and if he'd known how rotten I was at modelling he'd probably have found someone else.

I hadn't entirely outgrown my childhood neurosis with boys but it was nice having someone really intelligent to like. Even though I'd grown up in somewhat different circumstances to most of the girls at my school, my family are all rather a brainy lot; my sister got brilliant marks in medicine, my mum had taken a law degree just for the sake of it, Daddy (my grandfather) was pretty strange but brilliant, Muzzie, too, and I'd done pretty okay myself in school. I wanted to be intellectually stimulated and to share my mind with someone else, but the kind of boys around the Cross were either street kids or as good as, they played rough and thought of girls as good for only one thing. Growing up without a father and with only the men in our boarding house, had made me pretty wary of men. The young ones were all stupid or drugged out and, since I'd been a small child, I knew to watch the roving hands of the old men around me.

So when I met Toby and started to see him I was still incredibly shy and a bit suspicious, much more so than I had been with Davo because it was a totally different fear. With Davo I wasn't surprised at where or how he lived or that he didn't have a job, or that he was a friend of the Bourke Street pros and that he had a drug habit. I wasn't surprised by any of that stuff and it didn't shock me; whereas going into a normal boy's life, that was exhilarating but also far more confusing for me.

Meeting Toby's family and being in a normal house and eating their food at a table, it was all very lovely, but also frightening. The first thing you do in those circumstances is not say anything. So I didn't. I was shy and out of place and awkward, I watched and observed until I felt happy enough with what was happening around me to be able to fit in. But secretly, I didn't really feel as though I fitted in at all and routines such as meals confused me a lot. All my life I seemed to be an onlooker and not a participant.

I was quite proud of my background. What I mean is I didn't feel the need to apologise for what I knew. Most people my age didn't have any idea of Davo's sort of life. My sort, too, I suppose. Though even in this I was an onlooker, a kid who understood the culture but was not essentially a creature of the Cross.

My grandmother, Muzzie, ran a boarding house for single men. "Male Guests Only" was what the sign on our dilapidated front fence was supposed to say. But the white painted background on the tin sign had long since cracked and scabbed in the sun and bits of it were peeling off, taking some of the black letters with it, so that the notice actually read:

M le Gues s ly

Daddy, who wasn't my dad at all but my grandfather, was Belgian. He spoke French to Muzzie, my grandmother, and English to me and he told me, when I was about five or six, that the sign stood for "Maison le Guessly" which was the name of the house they had in Paris before the war.

It was the only joke Daddy ever made and I didn't even know it was a joke and after a while it wasn't anyway and, to this day, the name of the house in Victoria St, Kings Cross is known as Maison le Guessly. If you asked her, I know my mum would swear on a stack of bibles that the house is named after the one Muzzie and Daddy had in Paris, even though she lived with them in Paris until she was eleven.

We weren't very good at the boarding-house business, so there were no rules. I don't mean no strict rules, just no rules. There were never any rules for us and no rules for the boarders, except that they had to pay their rent. They came and went, drunk, sober, sick, dying, crying, crazy or drugged, it simply didn't matter. One old man died and it was a week before anyone discovered him. Surprisingly, there were seldom any fights, I think mostly because the men who stayed with us knew that the police would never be called, no matter what, and so they were safe.

Maison le Guessly sort of ran by osmosis. It was dirty,

it stank, sunlight never entered the broken shades, taps leaked, bathrooms had the damp and peculiar smell of old men; but it wasn't a flop house and the people in it were mostly beaten up by life, not dead beats. Some even had jobs, but no families, and they came and went; some stayed for years and lived and died and hardly ever spoke.

Nobody told me to be suspicious of men, I just knew. I always just knew that I mustn't get too close to them. I learned very early, before I was five, that they liked to put their hands in all sorts of places and that I mustn't accept presents from them. By the time I was eight I was a real hard case and, if they came too close or smiled with their yellow teeth, I'd give them a burst of bad language and they'd always back off. By now you must be thinking that I was a disadvantaged child, which wasn't true at all. Nobody ever beat me, I can't ever remember being hungry and I always had clothes.

My mother was somewhat eccentric so Muzzie was just about everything for us, she looked after us in an unconventional way, but made up for this by being a fabulous person. She trusted me, even at the age of four she'd never tell me what to do, she just sort of guided me. Muzzie always treated me as an equal, even when I was a small child and she made me feel as though she and I were running Maison le Guessly and doing a pretty good job. I loved her fiercely and she became the force in my life, who made all the big decisions concerning me and who, right from the beginning, was interested in my mind.

Before the war, Muzzie had been a nearly famous concert pianist in Paris and so naturally knew nothing about a boarding house or children or cooking. She seldom cooked and we just ate things out of the fridge when we were hungry. As I said before, there wasn't any routine. Not even washing the dishes, we just didn't wash dishes or clean up or clean *anything*. Muzzie was interested in our minds not our manners.

I learned pretty early to fend for myself and, at seven, I was taking my clothes to the laundrette at the top of the street and doing my own laundry.

Sometimes the woman there would iron my school clothes. "You're a real little ragamuffin and so pretty, I wish you were mine," she'd always say. But I didn't wish I was hers, it was always hot and puffy in the laundrette and her hands were red and swollen and so was her face. A wisp of damp hair always stuck to her forehead and it didn't look like much of a life to me.

So we just lived in Maison le Guessly like everyone else, nobody ever shouted at us or screamed the way mothers do at their kids. In fact nobody said very much at all. I even had to learn basic hygiene from watching the other kids at the pre-school to which I took myself at Woolloomooloo at the age of three. Later, I learned more at kindergarten and, when I was older, of course, I taught what I'd learned to David, my baby brother, who was four years younger than me. I suppose my sister, who was four years older than me, must have learned from someone but she didn't bother to show me; we were not very close at the time.

Growing up at the Cross I was aware of what it meant to be a disadvantaged child and I knew that I wasn't one, because I knew Mummy and Muzzie loved me which wasn't the case with the other kids. I can't recall when I didn't know what a drunk or a prostitute was, but it was just a part of life. I was a street kid, in the sense that I played on the street in an environment where the street was a pretty tough place and you just knew these things.

All around me were the really disadvantaged children, the kids of prostitutes and addicts and alcoholics, children with black eyes and teeth missing and bruises all over them and cigarette burns on the inside of their arms and on their legs. There were kids my age, six and seven, who were abused hideously and who smoked habitually, holding a cigarette clamped between forefinger and thumb and doing the drag-back absently, without posing, like an adult. They almost never went to school and were drop-outs before they'd even dropped in.

Maison le Guessly was ruled by a matriarchal society, that is, Muzzie and sometimes my mum. They were the only grown-up women there except for Mrs Brown, who was an alcoholic who wouldn't leave and refused to be thrown out. The rest were "male guests". Even Daddy, Muzzie's husband and my grandfather, had no discernible influence around the place.

My grandfather was like a pale shadow and a most amazing contrast to the rest of the place. He was always immaculately dressed in a neatly pressed, three-piece, blue serge suit with knife creases in the trousers and with a watch chain across the front of his waistcoat. He looked like something out of another time altogether. Daddy was small and dapper with a clipped moustache, he had eyes so pale that the blue in them looked as though it had drained away over the years, maybe from seeing too much. He was an engineer once and he made the money to buy Maison le Guessly by working on the Snowy

Mountains Hydro-electric Scheme in the fifties where, according to Muzzie "he suffered incredible hardship for a man of his sensitive nature".

Daddy spent all day, like a mad scientist, in a room at the very top of Maison le Guessly where things bubbled and where he pored over plans and washed strips of film in a darkroom with a red bulb in the ceiling. He fancied himself as a photographer and took life behind the camera very seriously, only his photographs never came out properly, heads and pieces of people were always missing. I think there must have been something wrong with his drained-out eyes, though he refused to wear his rather thick glasses when he was taking photographs.

But he was a real dab hand at rosary beads. Daddy was a devout Catholic, though the only one in the family, Muzzie being sort of Church of England and we, of course, being nothing. When I was small I was made to live in Daddy's room, for some sort of protection, I suppose. I'd lie in bed at night trying to outlast the clicking beads as he said his catechism to the Blessed Virgin, Mother of God. In the process I'd picked up a fair amount about her and Jesus, her son, how she was his mother and obviously quite a person, being the mother of someone like that as well as God's mum.

One night, I managed the almost impossible and stopped Daddy in mid-bead to ask him, "If the Blessed Virgin Mary is the mother of Jesus, then who is his father?" Daddy explained curtly that Jesus didn't have a real father, that God was his father and that Jesus' was an immaculate conception; whereupon he continued with his beads.

Naturally I found this a bit confusing. The Virgin Mary

was God's mother and God was Jesus' father through an immaculate conception, whatever that was. The following morning I cornered my sister. "If Jesus didn't have a real father and was born anyway and we don't have a father and were born, what does that make us?" I asked.

She didn't know and we agreed to ask my mum, even though she wasn't to be relied on for most things. But as she was about to have David and was hugely pregnant without there being any sign of a father around, we agreed that on this one subject she must definitely know something, having done it two times before and about to again.

My mother, confronted with the question of who our father was, seemed quite calm. "You were both immaculate conceptions," she said, looking us straight in the eye. Then she poked at her distended tummy and sighed, "He is also an immaculate conception." She was always certain that my brother David would turn out to be a boy. "He is the most immaculate conception of all!" she added, pleased with herself.

We waited for more but that was it. My sister and I and brother-to-be were immaculate conceptions.

I asked my sister, who was eight, what an immaculate conception was. "It's like the Holy Virgin. Like baby Jesus. You don't have a father, you're just born with a mother."

This more or less confirmed what Daddy had said and so this seemed to be okay. I knew all about the Virgin from the clicking of the rosary beads, so I was forced to change my opinion of my mother whom I now thought must be smarter than I'd previously supposed.

As I grew older it fitted in nicely with everything. I

already knew I didn't like men, they had yellow teeth and groping fingers and usually smelt of cheap sherry. Most of the other kids around the Cross who had a father were shit-scared of them. So I was dead lucky, being an immaculate conception. I felt that you couldn't get much luckier than that!

But I soon learned you couldn't go around claiming you were an immaculate conception. When I went to kindergarten in Double Bay with mostly rich kids from proper families and later to Woollahra Demonstration, which was a partly selective state school for very bright children, I realised that the other kids demanded that you have a father or at least a plausible explanation if you didn't. A virgin birth, I was smart enough to realise, wasn't something you talked about too openly.

I accepted the immaculate conception theory completely. There was absolutely no doubt in my mind, even though I suppose I should have known better. I didn't equate birth with sex. I was a kid who grew up on the streets of Kings Cross and sex was something women with lots of make-up on and high-heeled shoes and short skirts did for money on the street corners to American soldiers and sailors and lonely migrant men and hoons from the western suburbs in tricked-up Holdens. So I lied when people asked me about my father, I simply told them he was dead. I used to quite like the look of sympathy on their faces while at the same time being glad I didn't have one, not even a dead one.

So you can see I had a rather different background from most kids with my education. I started to tell Toby about it one day and saw a look of doubt cross his face. I don't think he believed me. It was so completely outside his personal experience that he seemed quite shocked that I would even pretend to know about some of the things I seemed to know about. When I saw Davo once or twice and told him about Toby, he seemed shocked too. "Why are you playing with little boys?" he asked seriously. He said it in the same way that one might chastise a child abuser.

I was not yet eighteen but, around the Cross, seventeen can be a lifetime and you don't measure lives by years.

That was the last time I ever talked to Davo. I know he's still alive. Until recently I was quite prepared to think he must be dead, he was always sharing needles and he must be HIV positive by now. But I saw him again not so long ago. I was driving through the Cross and he crossed the road in front of me; he looked completely spaced out and didn't even look up when I blew the horn. I couldn't stop or I would have. Or maybe I wouldn't have? I don't know. Anyway, I couldn't stop so that's that with Davo, I suppose.

Before Toby realised I was intelligent, I don't think he really understood where I was coming from. I was quiet and shy, he was a new, unknown experience to come to terms with. Still I think he was a bit arrogant to think that because I was a model I was dumb. Admittedly, most of the girls doing modelling are pretty dumb. I'm almost convinced that you need to be pretty unimaginative to get through the jobs and the routines on the catwalk. Either that or you have to be incredibly ambitious. Although I doubt if even that is entirely right. You also have to be the right age. The girls who were getting the top fashion magazine work were mostly around fifteen. If you hadn't cracked television by the time you got to eighteen you were on the scrap heap in terms of modelling. Eighteen is pretty old for a photographic model these days, so I suppose Toby was quite lucky having a seventeen-year-old, semi-working model to go with his electric guitar.

Not that I looked seventeen, my breasts were still as flat as a pancake and I was still pretty gangly, though my bottom had filled out a bit. With make-up I could fake it and look my real age if ever I went into The Sheaf, the trendy Eastern Suburbs pub all the yuppie kids went to. It was in a pub that I met Toby. On the morning the Higher School Certificate results came out in the paper all the Eastern Suburbs kids would congregate at the Watson's Bay Hotel, a huge old pub with a beer garden that spilled down on to a small Harbour beach. It was a tradition so even I felt compelled to do so, knowing all the girls from final year at school would be there. Even though I was somewhat of a loner, some things you have to do and going to Watto Bay pub when the HSC results came out was one of them. It was the place you went to celebrate if you did well and get drunk if you'd done badly.

I'd started high school at Sydney Girls High and, even though I'd done well, I'd hated it. I was out of step with the other kids. I asked Muzzie if I could go to Kambala where my sister had gone after being expelled from Sydney Girls High. Muzzie agreed. The point was that we were not poor. I think Muzzie had quite a lot of money, but she wouldn't have thought about sending me to an exclusive private girls' school unless I asked. At Kambala I was known as "The Strange One" and there, too, I was essentially an onlooker. Although I was one of the clever kids and did very well in most things, especially in art, I was never really accepted. I felt like an intruder and I suppose in a way I was. I had absolutely nothing in common with anyone at that school. I never spoke about boys or going to parties and in the last few months of my final year a rumour spread that I was a lesbian. Never speaking about boys, having a punk haircut and a reputation for pretty weird drawings in art class probably all contributed to the rumour. I was into semi-anatomical drawings and painting and I'd paint a woman's torso and one breast would show the skin removed and all the veins and arteries showing. All my women looked vaguely like Morticia in *The Addams Family* and I suppose it led to me being thought a lesbian in some minds. I did nothing to deny this. I mean, how do you even go about denying you're a lesbian?

To be perfectly honest, it hurt a bit, a lot really, but it was also very convenient. I lived in constant dread that some of the girls would call on me at Maison le Guessly and discover the dump. Some of them lived in mansions and certainly all of them in well-ordered, upper-bracket homes. I know they thought that my living in the Cross with all that evil going on was very exotic, but I also knew that the discovery of *how* I lived in the Cross would lead to my ultimate destruction. Strangeness and being exotic was one thing, but lack of hygiene and plain dirt was quite another. At the time, Mummy and I were fighting a lot about cleaning up the boarding house. Though I *did* want it cleaned up, I now realise I really desperately wanted it clean not because of any sensibility, but rather out of a terror of discovery. The so-called "exotic" me would soon disappear under an onslaught of rancid cooking fat, dirt, rotting vegetables, cockroaches and smelly bed linen.

I now had my own room which you could enter without going through the house. It was painted, pretty, spotless and bright, the only clean room in the house. But just getting to it was a trip in itself: a wading through weeds, old junk, broken drainpipes, dirty windows, damp and rotten wood. Even the most casual glance at the house told all.

So, being thought of as a lesbian, though hurtful, was also quite useful. It meant no kid from school, seeking gratuitous thrills and high adventure by coming to the Cross, was about to come visiting.

But, being accused of being a lesbian did have one sad consequence. Eva, who'd been my friend since day one at Kambala, cracked under the pressure. She came from a straight family and the idea of being called a lesbian was too much for her. She began avoiding me, making it obvious in front of others that she didn't want me around. I lost my only real friend. I was incredibly hurt that she would listen to that sort of gossip and respond by destroying our friendship. We'd never even held hands! Davo said she must have been a shit of a friend to split for something as dumb as being a lesbian. It was okay in the end, we all grew up and we became friends again after school, which was very good, because I like her a lot.

The big event of our final year at school, as with most private schools, was the senior formal. For weeks it took up all the gossip and occupied every available thinking moment. Girls talked of dresses that cost thousands and the top beauty parlours and hairdressers in Double Bay were booked out. Nails were grown forbiddingly long, for once, ignored by teachers until after the big night. Male partners were the Who's Who of Sydney's private schools, with Cranbrook, Scots and Grammar the biggest suppliers of male hunk.

Taking Davo my surrogate boyfriend was of course out of the question. Even at two o'clock in the morning in the pink neon flush of Deans Coffee House he looked a highly unsavoury character; besides male earrings and needle marks were definitely not in vogue at Kambala Private Girls School.

I elected to go alone, something which had evidently never in living memory occurred before. But, as usual, I was oblivious of this. I wanted to go to the formal, it was the way you said goodbye to the school and I didn't want to miss it for anything.

I designed a stunning Elizabethan dress with a collar that went up my neck and ended in a ruffle under my chin. Muzzie gave me the money for it and I went into town and bought six metres of grey taffeta which I took to Maria, the Portuguese dressmaker, who worked in a tiny shop next to the dry cleaners. While she mostly did alterations and repairs, she was an exquisite dressmaker and she was thrilled with the idea of making my prom dress, finishing it entirely by hand.

I had never thought of myself as good looking, just the opposite, although Davo often said I was beautiful, but coming from Davo this wasn't exactly a confirmation from the editor of *Vogue International*. I must say, though, standing in front of Maria's mirror while she knelt beside me with her mouth filled with pins, I felt that at least I wasn't ugly. I have a long white neck and with the high collar and ruffle it looked amazing! I bought the highest heels I could find; they let me down a bit because they were cheap, but the hem of the dress mostly covered them.

I arrived at the formal by taxi, my wide taffeta skirt swishing and rustling as I entered the ballroom. I felt as though every eye in the place was on me and I suddenly felt incredibly nervous. Amazingly, I hadn't thought about the lesbian thing in connection with going alone to the formal but now, suddenly, it occurred to me. My being alone was positive confirmation of the fact and I could feel myself beginning to shake all over. At that moment I heard a voice behind me and turned to see Mrs Crompton who taught English. "Why, Celeste, what a fabulous gown!" she exclaimed. Then, taking a moment to look me over, she said, "You're quite the prettiest girl here tonight."

I knew quite suddenly that I looked really great! If I was forced into being thought a lesbian, I was going to be the most glamorous lesbian at the Kambala formal. An Elizabethan lesbian in a grey taffeta gown with a high ruffled neck, imperious and super-aloof and oh-so-very-sophisticated.

For a lesbian, I sure got a lot of dancing done and none of it with girls. For the first time in my life I sensed that I wasn't ugly or awkward.

But I was a little like Cinderella after her ball; the Kambala formal had exhausted my capacity to be a *femme fatale*. After that night I hung up my grey taffeta dress for good and retired back into being a loner.

So when Toby happened it was rather nice. He didn't

make any huge demands on me and I didn't encourage much groping — a bit of hand-holding and light kissing with my head on his shoulder in his father's car after we'd been somewhere. I liked all this enormously. It was suddenly like growing up properly without any fears. It was just having a good time and talking about things that were pretty serious, a big change from the usual drug culture with people staring at you with red, unfocused, dilated pupils and saying nothing that made sense. Toby talked about lots of things and it was nice just going on about normal things, like how we could change the world and stop people cutting down trees. We definitely wouldn't eat hamburgers because, just to grow beef, McDonald's were destroying the Amazon Basin at a rate of two miles an hour, twenty-four hours a day, every day, seven days a week!

McDonald's and the Amazon was one subject Toby shared with Davo. Davo too was very concerned about what he called, "The McDonald's Conspiracy". It was about the only thing Toby and Davo had in common that I could share with both of them. Davo would say, "We have to blow up McDonald's. Every fuckin' McDonald's in Australia . . . in the whole fuckin' world! Those hamburger hoods must be brought to justice! We must eliminate them before they eliminate us from the face of the earth. No more Green Peace, Green *fucking* War!" The Hamburger Conspiracy was Davo's most profound thought. When he started to declaim, I learned that this was the signal that he was about to switch to straight bourbon or go out on to the street and find some yobbo from the western suburbs who was hassling one of the girls, and beat him up or get beaten up.

More than stirring my teenage conscience, going out with Toby made me feel suddenly and entirely normal, a condition which I had begun to think of as unachievable. This was a wonderful new feeling. Boys were turning out to be pretty nice after all and I was learning my way around them in the shape of a blond, soft-eyed rock 'n' roll guitarist with a willingness to discuss just about anything that really mattered. Toby was, and still is, a very nice guy whom I love very much. Then Toby introduced me to his best friend, an overwhelming walking ego, named Damon Courtenay.

"This is my friend, Damon," Toby said. We'd gone to The Sheaf one Saturday afternoon, a rare visit, for Toby was aware I wasn't too fond of pubs. Damon ran his eyes slowly over me and they didn't seem overly impressed. "Who do you think *I* look like?" he asked suddenly, looking directly into my eyes.

He was sort of darkish with a short beard, which I thought of immediately as an affectation. First-year uni students with a beard really were a joke! He had large hazel eyes and a roundish face. You wouldn't call him handsome, but again he wasn't ugly either. It was an uncommon sort of face but nothing to write home about and much too immature to wear a beard. I hadn't a clue who he was supposed to look like and was not a little surprised at such a direct and egocentric question.

"I don't know. Who do you look like?" I raised one eyebrow a fraction and smiled, trying to look terribly cool and sophisticated, hoping the nervous me wasn't showing through Mr Revlon's carefully applied make-up mask. Damon looked at Toby and Toby smiled sheepishly, not liking the way things were going. He'd talked an awful lot about Damon and I know he wanted me to like him and now I could see he was concerned about this unpropitious start to our friendship.

"A movie star, think. A movie star," Toby said hopefully.

Damon waited, a small, superior smile playing at the corners of his mouth. The upsetting part was that he was not even a tiny bit embarrassed. How could anyone be such a prick?

I shrugged, "I don't know too many movie stars."

Damon gave a short laugh. Now he took a pair of Ray-Ban aviators from his leather jacket and put them on. He grinned, "One last try?"

He had an attractive grin, warm and open and one which didn't seem to go with the arsehole who was confronting me. "Marlon Brando?" I said, though without too much conviction, then added, "In *The Wild Ones*?" At least I had the black leather jacket and sunglasses right. Marlon Brando in *The Wild Ones* was a cult movie every kid around the Cross had seen four or five times and it was Davo's all-time favourite movie, speeches from which he could recite without the words ever scrambling.

Toby sighed and nervously lit a cigarette. "Jesus, Damon, forget it, will you?" He turned to me, squinting through his cigarette smoke. "It's Burt Reynolds. He thinks he looks like Burt Reynolds."

I wasn't sure who Burt Reynolds was and I tried to conjure up a picture in my mind, but nothing concrete came. I smiled. "You do, you know. You look just like Burt Reynolds," I said flatly, my eyebrow more than slightly arched, hoping my sarcasm would register.

"Whoever *he* is!" My heart was pounding, this wasn't a bit like me. Toby was so nice! I'd been lulled into a trap. This guy, Damon Courtenay, Toby's best friend, was everything bad I felt about private school boys. What a shit!

It was a very unimpressive beginning for both of us. What I didn't know at the time was that Damon was totally in love with Gina Bloom, a girl who was one of the coolest of the cool, with a blue aura around her you could practically see. At school she was known as brilliant; she didn't have a special name, she was simply Gina, the brilliant, Jewish and beautiful one. Later I was to learn that Damon was going to marry Gina Bloom; she was in his scheme of things.

Unimpressed was a mild word for what I felt about Toby's best friend and I remember hoping that our future relationship didn't include too much best friend. Some part of me must have reacted, because a few days later I looked in the *Herald* entertainment page and found a movie which starred Burt Reynolds and took myself off to see him.

In fact Damon *did* look a little bit like him, though not a lot, a bit, if you squinched your eyes. He also seemed to have adopted the same smart-arse mannerisms and both of them wore Ray-Ban aviators, another affectation I guessed Damon had taken from the movie star. Toby also wore them, assuring me in his defence, that they were the world's best sunglasses and cut out one hundred per cent of the infra-red and ultra-violet rays.

To my regret Toby, it seemed, came with friend and Damon seemed to be with us quite often as a threesome. Toby and Damon matched intellects all the time and carried on like a couple of schoolboys, though I must admit, fairly intelligent schoolboys. They were both at university and a bit up themselves. In fact, it was all a big wank.

But they were so far removed from Davo and his milieu that I couldn't help but enjoy myself. They seemed happy enough for me to join into their arguments, although this wasn't always easy. They understood each other very well and talked a sort of shorthand, something I'd noticed and admired in people who've been friends for a long time. I'd always hoped that one day I would have such a friend, so totally on the same wave-length that you almost don't have to talk at all and when you do, it's practically epigrammatic.

I was always a very quiet person, so whenever I went out with them they'd dominate the conversation and I'd mostly listen. I was really interested in their talk, it was not the sort of conversation I'd ever listened to before. It was schoolboys discussing deep, dark and mysterious philosophy. I knew I was their equal in intellect, I'd had an education every bit as good and I think I'd read as many books as Damon. I'd started reading very young to try to drown out Maison le Guessly and what was happening around me. Later Damon and I would discover that we'd read much too grown-up books at around the same age.

I soon realised that Damon wasn't really so full of himself but simply someone who was positive about everything he set out to do. I had no idea he was hiding something, as Toby had never mentioned this. The first time I noticed his difference, I mean his physical difference, we'd been out and it was fairly late and I said,

"Let's go and have a coffee at the Cross?"

So we went to have coffee at one of the places we used to have coffee. Not Deans, I only introduced them to Deans later, maybe it was Teazers. We were out in Damon's father's car and Damon had gone to park it while we waited for him on the pavement outside. I remember seeing him walking towards us with a limp. I thought nothing of it. Perhaps he'd knocked and hurt his leg or something. What I did notice was that he walked with his arms wide and slightly bent. I turned to Toby and laughed, "Damon really thinks he's incredibly macho, doesn't he?"

Toby looked at me quizzically. "Damon's a haemophiliac. One arm's permanently bent, one leg too, from bleeding into the joints. He does that with his arms so people won't notice the bent one." He smiled, "Better to be thought macho than deformed, heh?"

I had very little idea what a haemophiliac was. I could sort of work it out from biology but, like everyone else, I thought if you cut yourself you bled to death. I had never associated it with joints or physical handicap. Of course, I'd never even thought about it at all. I began to realise that there was more to Damon than met the eye.

We'd been out several times and I was an artist who prided myself on my observation yet, only now, did I discover that Damon had huge physical problems. He had such a strong personal presence, such enormous confidence, that I realised that I hadn't really looked at him at all, I simply felt him being there. It was always like that. Later, when we were together, Damon might have a very bad bleed and his pain would be almost unbearable for a couple of days. But he never talked about being sick, he never associated himself with sickness, so he wasn't. You just thought of Damon needing someone to do his fetching and carrying and to look after him for a little while. You never thought you were caring for a sick person, just that Damon needed you. That was all it was. Damon needing a little help for a little while.

Damon had a thing about cars which I'm sure deep down had something to do with his inability to do physical things. The car gave him a sense of physical control. Damon needed to feel in control of the world about him and a car was something he felt he could control. The rest of the world outside cars and his other love, stereos and music, was too uncontrollable. It's not an original thought, I know, but he really saw cars differently from most people. They were alive to him, really beautiful, and speed was something they had to express their beauty. We'd come across a Ferrari in the street and he'd walk around it almost in tears and I'd notice that his hands trembled. Cars were a physical extension of Damon, making up for the parts of him that didn't work very well.

This was the first time in my life that I started to be driven around in cars. Daddy's 1956 Peugeot 203 had exploded when I was still quite young and had joined the junk in the front yard and, besides, excursions in it were sufficiently rare not to qualify as regular driving around. So the whole idea of a motor car as casual transport was really new. Damon driving his father's beautiful Alfa GTV Sports wasn't a status symbol to be enjoyed, it was just like a surprise, "Wow! These people can drive and look at their cars! Oh my God!"

I mean it didn't affect the way I thought or anything.

But going out with Daddy in the Peugeot 203, though a seldom enough childhood experience, had always meant the family together, a rare and important occurrence. So a car had some sort of "togetherness" significance for me. Driving around with Toby and Damon was a nice experience. Nice and warm and together.

The sleek black Alfa with its grained leather seats was a beautiful car and I started to look at the design of cars from a purely aesthetic point of view. So Damon's love of cars was to be my bridge to him, just as Toby's electric guitar had been my crossing-over point with him.

Increasingly I was drawn to Damon, he was such an assured person and compared to him I felt very weak and uncertain of myself. Toby and I had been going out for some months but we hadn't done anything. I've never been the sort of person who jumps into bed with somebody the first time I meet them, I've never been like that and I never will be. I tend to regard it as, well you know, almost sacred. Not holy, but not something you throw away either. It's something you enjoy far more if you really know the person you're sleeping with. I'd been around sex indirectly all my life, it wasn't something I was ambivalent about.

Toby and I stopped seeing each other. I was pretty upset, tears and drama and that sort of thing. He'd admitted to me that he really loved a girl called Rebecca. Although we'd only been seeing each other for a very short time, Toby felt that it wasn't working the way it should be. I couldn't deny this, I had no real idea of the way it should be. For me it was wonderful and I was terribly hurt and upset and my old insecurity with men came rushing back. I was later to meet Rebecca, she was so lovely that when I saw her I didn't blame Toby for having her as his ideal.

I'd never been a jealous person, I don't think I had the self-esteem to be properly jealous, so I accepted Toby's right to love someone else, though of course I was upset.

Damon and I started seeing each other without Toby. Gina Bloom seemed to have disappeared or at least he didn't ever mention her. I must explain going out with Damon without Toby wasn't a guilty thing, Toby and Damon used to work nights for a locksmith in Vaucluse who had an all-night service for people who lost their keys. Toby had started the job and been trained while he was still at school and he, in turn, had trained Damon. They'd been doing it for about two years at school during the weekends and now they were doing it at uni too, but more often. It was good money for them both.

It was all pretty simple. The locksmith had taught them how to change locks in an emergency. Mostly they just manned the telephone in the small flat above the locksmith's and waited for calls from people who'd locked themselves out. Friday and Saturday night were the big nights when people got drunk and lost their keys. Toby or Damon, whoever was on night shift, radioed the addresses through to a mobile van, logged the call and that was about it. Often with Toby I'd spend the night at the locksmiths and Damon would come by and we'd play music or just talk all night. It was wonderful.

In fact the six months or so with Toby was to become my whole adolescence, the most marvellous time between being a child and an adult. I was still just seventeen and, although I knew all about drugs and prostitutes and how to chill-out in a sleazy cafe all night, I knew none of the things normal seventeen-year-olds took for granted.

Damon started taking me out after Toby and I had split up and I found myself holding hands with him. Not really even thinking about it. We'd go out when Toby was working and we'd find ourselves holding hands. One night, after Toby and I had parted, Damon was working at the locksmiths and I was with him, Toby dropped in to see Damon and found us together and he was incredibly upset seeing us together like that.

But it wasn't really like that! We weren't doing anything. We all loved each other and were very good friends. But it was Toby's *shitty* at seeing us together that made me realise that I felt differently about Damon than I ever had about Toby. I suddenly badly wanted Toby to understand that I was now Damon's girlfriend and loved him in a different sort of way. Differently than I had ever felt about anyone before.

For a while Toby was hurt, hurt quite a lot. But I doubt if he was really humiliated. After all, he'd wanted the separation, Damon and he loved each other much too much for me to get in the way and he knew that we weren't going to split the threesome.

So Damon and I started our relationship. It was built firmly on a friendship, so it was easy. Damon was the sort of person who made everything easy.

Two months later we were living together.

Damon was also working part time at Woollahra Electronics selling the best hi-fi gear and he met a photographer named Colin Beard who owned ten thousand classical LP recordings and was a nut about having perfect sound. Damon was equally fanatical in the search for the perfect tonal quality and they soon became hi-fidelity friends. One day Colin told him he had to go overseas on a six-month assignment and wanted to rent his tiny house in Woollahra but that he was terrified for his record collection which couldn't be moved, as it covered every available bit of wall space in the only room downstairs. At a rent of fifty dollars a week he'd found his man and woman.

Damon didn't exactly ask me to live with him. I stayed one night and then again a few days later, then I just stayed. The most magical time of my life was about to begin.

The house consisted of a front room, then a sort of fibro lean-to kitchen, that led into a make-shift toilet and bathroom which took up the remainder of the ground floor. An almost perpendicular staircase led up to an attic bedroom with a dormer window in the roof. The backyard was overgrown and roughly the size of a pocket handkerchief with an inwardly leaning, rusted corrugated-iron fence over which a morning glory creeper draped itself. The purple trumpets were spilling over the side of the fence to cover an ancient motor cycle before starting their invasion of the backyard, finally climbing the opposite iron fence and becoming someone else's morning glory. It was as though we had a whole backyard filled with purple flowers. A sort of hallelujah chorus of blooms trumpeting away as hard as they could to welcome us to our first home.

The bedroom in the attic had been painted white a long time ago and now the peeling paint was the colour of skimmed milk and lifted from the walls in hundreds of curiously shaped scallops. In the morning the sun would come streaming through the dormer window and bounce off the walls, the flaking paint making patterns that were lovely to look at. It was the most enchanting room you could possibly imagine and I'd wake up and just lie on my back and smile and wish I could die without anything else better happening to me.

Quite suddenly and out of the blue I had everything I ever wanted. A home of my own which I could keep clean, space I could regard as my own which was invasion and dirt-free and so quiet it was like the inside of a chapel.

Leaving home had been difficult. Mum had thrown a monstrous, snot-nosed tantrum claiming I was deserting an ailing Muzzie and leaving her to cope. In a sense this was true, Muzzie wasn't well. It was strange, but she'd always been young and bouncy and you never thought of her as an old woman. Then she turned seventy-seven and on the very morning of her birthday she turned old and frail and lost her will to fight my mum. She never again mentioned her plans to clean up and get Maison le Guessly going again.

So things were pretty ghastly. My mum now had the upper hand and the place was now at the point where it was a major health hazard even for us, who were immune to everything. I just had to get out and Muzzie understood when I asked her permission.

"Is it a man, darling?" she asked. I didn't quite know how to reply, I mean it was and it wasn't. I was now in love with Damon, but we still hadn't consummated our love and what we were giving each other made a statement like that seem inappropriate. I wasn't leaving because I had found a man. I was leaving because suddenly my life was happy and living with Damon was a part of that happiness. I'd found Damon and he'd found me, Celeste Laetitia Gabrielle of the immaculate conception.

Muzzie's question really hurt me. Now that I think about it I don't know why, after all, it was a sensible enough question to ask. But my grandmother was very important to me and the way she thought of me was important. We'd sort of been in partnership at Maison le Guessly and I expected her to trust me.

"I have to go, Muzzie, that's all. Do I have your permission?"

She nodded, "I know, darling, it happens to all of us."

"Muzzie, it's not how you think it is!" I insisted.

Muzzie suddenly looked sad and wistful. "I should never have married Daddy," she whispered. Then she looked at me and smiled and I knew she loved me very much. "Be nice to him, darling." She hesitated a fraction. "But be careful. Use those things you can get from the chemist."

I went into my room to take a few things I loved with me, mostly books and pictures. My mum was waiting for me. "You take nothing! Nothing! You hear? It all belongs to me. It's only yours if you live here!"

"Why?" I asked. I was suddenly terribly upset.

"I gave you these things when you were my daughter. Now you are no longer my daughter, so they don't belong to you any more!"

I arrived at our new house in Woollahra with two white plastic shopping bags which contained my street clothes. Even the grey taffeta Elizabethan dress was forbidden because Muzzie had paid for it. My mother claimed it belonged to the house, to the family, to the daughter I no longer was. Books I'd loved all my life, my very best friends, had to stay behind in shitty old Maison le Guessly with no one to love them.

But none of this mattered as I opened the rickety gate in the one-metre-wide front yard of the tiny cottage. The front wall had developed a large crack which zigzagged from the dormer window to the ground just missing the front door. The crack traced its way through a passion-fruit vine which seemed to be collaborating with a pink climbing rose to prevent it from separating any further and so causing the wall to collapse altogether.

It was the nicest house in the entire world and inside it was Damon, determined to work his way systematically through ten thousand classical records and wondering how he was going to fit them all into six months.

"Hi," I said coming in and putting my two plastic shopping bags down on the worn carpet. Damon looked at the bags and then up at me. "One day I'll buy you a house and everything in the whole world you could possibly want, even your own Dino Ferrari!"

"I don't want a Ferrari, I just want you!" I hugged him and started to sob, the effects of leaving Maison le Guessly suddenly overpowering me. Damon held me tightly and shushed my tears until I was okay again and I drew away from him. "I'm sorry," I said, "I'm not really the crying type." He'd shaved his beard and he was the handsomest thing you could possibly want. I put my arms around him again and kissed him, drinking him in and loving him terribly and wanting to cry and laugh and never die.

"Listen to this," he said, pushing me gently from him.

"It's Brahms Violin Concerto, my dad's favourite, mine too, I think."

One record down, nine thousand, nine hundred and ninety-nine to go. The opening strains of the violin concerto mixed with the sunshine, the bright clean air, the solitude and private niceness of being in love. Wow! Talk about immaculate conceptions, this was one all right!

12

Celeste

Madam Butterfly Needle starring in
The Love Transfusion.

I know this is going to sound silly but the very first
magical thing that happened between Damon and me
happened with our hands. The hand holding in the car
started to get more and more sensual. We both had this
great feeling within our hands. We'd hold hands and it
was a very serious thing. I know it sounds dumb and
naive and even silly after what I've told you I knew
about life and things, but Damon and I were aware of
making love while we were holding hands; it was safe
but it was also *not* safe and it all happened with our
hands. I mean, believe it or not, it was several weeks
before we actually kissed and there wasn't any other
touching or anything.

I suppose people will think that we were just a couple

of innocent kids, but that wasn't true. Damon wasn't shy and he certainly didn't have any terror of girls and there were hardly any surprises for me; I'd seen it all second-hand, almost since I'd been a child. Sex held no unknowns for me and I didn't get the feeling Damon was, you know, panting to conquer me.

But I was wrong. He told me later he was totally preoccupied with sex. Sex, he admitted later, was this *huge* thing with him. When you're a virgin you don't know how to admit you don't really know how things work. He'd study full frontals in *Playboy*, but they didn't seem to make him any wiser; so he pretended indifference when, really, he was going wild.

Once, when we were talking about sex, he said that the trouble with men's magazines that show all and talk about seduction is that they never talk about the preliminaries. Exactly how you actually go about undressing someone, or whether they undressed themselves and you did the same, or whether the girl was supposed to unbutton your shirt or pull down the zip of your fly as a sign of her agreement. To be totally sophisticated was terribly important to their image and they couldn't imagine sort of fumbling about and learning on the job like other guys. So they acted dead casual, when inside they were going crazy with lust and stuff.

Damon also had something else to contend with. In the middle of his final-year school exams, the most difficult period in a teenager's life, he had been called to the Haemophilia Centre and told he was HIV positive. Imagine finding out in the middle of HSC exams that you have AIDS!

When we started to go out in April 1985, he told me.

He explained carefully that he wasn't sick and that there was nothing wrong with him, but he was HIV positive and that sometimes developed into full-blown AIDS but that it wouldn't with him, he'd definitely beat it come what may.

I remember thinking nothing of it. If Damon said he'd beat it, he would. Damon was very proud of his mind, he believed it could beat anything. He talked about it a lot, how if you can control your mind you can beat pain and discomfort. It was something he'd gotten from his father from a very young age. So the news of his HIV positive diagnosis wasn't like a clap of thunder in my consciousness.

No one outside the medical profession knew very much about AIDS in 1985 and I didn't ask him a lot of questions. I don't think he knew too much himself, so I just accepted the news and our lives went on. I felt very privileged that he'd told me, because obviously it was an incredibly private thing to be told by someone. Of course it was very important that I know. Later I realised that Damon would never *not* have told me, he just wasn't like that. But there must have been something in the back of his mind, a real fear of harming me which made Damon very careful about sex, because we didn't have sex for a long time after we started going out. Damon was worried for me and scared inside, though he couldn't show any of this. His hands loved me and said things I could feel very strongly.

I now realise Damon had a real fear about his HIV as far as it involved me, but at the time I didn't understand this. I sort of vaguely understood that it was something which could be sexually transmitted but I didn't really know, I mean, no one at the time seemed to know. Damon's doctors hadn't told him he couldn't have sex. One of them had simply said he should always use condoms, but there was nothing new in that. And then he had to overcome the trauma around condoms and all that sort of stuff and that took a while.

I had no problems about sex at all, I really didn't. I just thought we'd leave it up to time and so on; when it happened I'd be happy but not overwhelmed, it just wasn't this big thing with me. I was so happy moving in and knowing I was being loved, so it didn't really matter; I honestly didn't think about it that much. I was a bit shy about my body, but not for the usual reasons. I was ugly and gawky and skinny with small breasts, these were things that troubled me greatly.

Damon was also a bit shy, maybe for the same reasons and, although I loved his body, he was no Arnold Schwarzenegger or even Burt Reynolds. He'd brought a set of weights from home and he used to work hard, puffing and huffing without any discernible result, though he never told me how long he'd been at it. One morning unbeknownst to me he'd been doing his exercises and had just finished and he'd left the weights on the floor. I entered the room humming happily and I saw they were in the way, so I reached down with one hand and picked them up and started swinging them around like a circus strongman, shouting "Wahee! Look at me!" swinging the weights around in a big arc and puffing my cheeks out. Then, without thinking, I put them somewhere out of the way and caught Damon looking at me as though he was about to cry. Instead, he burst into laughter; and that was the last time he ever used weights. I was glad about this, because I was pretty sure they were giving him bleeds and I loved him just the way he was, a bit crooked in places. He certainly was no Greek statue but I loved his body.

And so for some weeks after we'd moved into the little cottage in Woollahra we'd get into our pyjamas and go to bed and just lie there and hold hands. Sometimes, I'd wake up in the middle of the night and the moonlight would be shining through the dormer window and it would fill the room with silver light and we'd still be holding hands; I'd bring Damon's hand up to my lips and kiss it and begin to cry, it was just so lovely being with him.

That was the wonderful thing, there'd been no discussion, I'd just sort of moved in. It seemed, at the time, to be the most natural thing in the world to do. Damon sort of felt worried for me that I'd missed out on things; we'd exchanged confidences with one another and I know he felt upset that I'd never had a proper family like his own. In fact I was jealous of his childhood, his parents and brothers and his happy home. Of course I had no idea at that time how tough it had been for him growing up as a haemophiliac.

He told me what it was really like to be a haemophiliac, the pain and the hours alone and wishing you could just do things other kids did. He told me how he imagined himself doing things, being terrific at something physical, but then not allowing the fantasy to build up too much because he had to keep a grip on the reality of who and what he was. "The only thing I could play was ping-pong and I was terrific!" he'd sometimes boast, but always with a sad little smile on his face.

He didn't tell me any of this out of self-pity, but I knew he'd never told anyone before. Despite his haemophilia Damon was very sure about himself; compared to him I felt very weak. I too had never shared confidences and, when I told him about my life, I felt sure he'd never tell anyone else and that he'd look after me.

It was truly amazing, things about myself that had worried me all my life didn't seem to concern him in the least and things about him that worried him, like his atrophied leg and bent arm and stiffened elbows and wrists, I didn't even notice. I certainly wasn't shocked by his HIV status.

It was simply a case between us of, "Is that all?" We both realised that our worries and fears were just so petty. Damon gave me a lot of strength and made me glad to be who I was and even proud of growing up as I had. But I think he wanted us to be a family, so that I could know what that was like, too.

At last I had my own house to play in. All the dreams of cleaning up Maison le Guessly were taken into that tiny little cottage. It sure got a going-over. I scrubbed and polished and cleaned the windows and borrowed his parents' vacuum cleaner and hoovered the fading, ratty old carpet with its barely recognisable pink rose pattern about eighty times, until the threads of its threadbareness practically pleaded for mercy.

I remember waking up and hugging myself because today was the day I was going to scrub the bathroom walls and floor and inside the cupboards. I'd bought some Brasso to shine the ancient copper shower rose, green with verdigris and the copper pipe that led to the small gas heater on the wall. In my mind's eye I could see the shower rose and the pipe shining with a bright coppery glow against the flaking calcimine wall. It seemed like the biggest adventure possible and I hoped that I'd find the bathroom *really* filthy when I examined it on my knees. Eighteen years of frustration were building up into a cleaning frenzy and itching to be let loose and no bathroom on earth was going to be able to withstand my scrubbing brush and heavy bombardment bleach.

Housekeeping was no hardship, I can tell you. I'm sure I've got a very strong mother-program in me. I'd treated my mother like a child, and Daddy, in some ways even my grandmother Muzzie as I grew a little older and, of course, my brother was always like my own child. Now I had Damon, I'm pretty sure there was a pattern happening there somewhere inside.

We didn't know at the time how upset we were making a lot of people because we were together. Damon's closest friends were Toby, Paul, Bardy and Christopher. They were all characters in their own way, but Damon loved Christopher for being an eccentric right from the moment he'd met him in primary school. While his other friends were never very close to floppy, gangly, totally absent-minded Christopher whom Damon thought of as a genius, they would spend hours together and really loved each other.

All the friends were told about his HIV status and, like me, they'd accepted it without any trauma. But, for some reason or other, they'd told this to their parents. Parents who knew the Courtenay family were deeply shocked. How could Damon and his parents allow me to put myself at risk? They felt that he was committing a terrible sin.

Only quite recently Damon's dad told me how he had begged Damon not to take the house and, under no circumstances, allow me to move in. Despite the fact that he trusted Damon and he knew he'd use condoms, he also knew that young people have a sense of their own immortality, even Damon. We might grow careless, if only once, which could be enough to infect me.

Like me Damon hadn't even thought about my moving in and assured his dad that he wanted the house for only one reason, to listen to the best collection of classical and jazz LP records in Australia and, by looking after the house, he could do this for a token rent.

The idea that I might become infected never worried me in the slightest. I didn't even think about it, so I can't even say that I was knowingly and lovingly taking a risk. It never occurred to me to worry. I suppose Damon's dad was right, it must have been a kind of immortality you have when you're young. I now know that Damon's parents were pretty worried and must also have been aware of the disapproval of the other parents. But when I did move in, apart from talking needlessly to Damon about condoms and instructing him to be very careful, they never again interfered. They both trusted Damon and loved him and they just had to rely on this trust and love.

Of course, I never told my mum that Damon was HIV positive. If she'd known, she'd have made my life *unbearable*. I suppose you can't really blame her, any mother would be pretty upset, but when my mum gets something into her head she's unstoppable, she is capable of anything. If she'd known about Damon's HIV she might have phoned all the television stations.

As it was, I'd told her Damon was a haemophiliac and this alone led to a pretty traumatic incident. Somehow, my mum got it into her head that the reason why Damon wanted me and the real reason we were living together was that Damon needed my blood, I was to be his permanent blood supply. She would threaten to take the story on to television, that's why I was so scared to tell her about Damon's HIV status.

I didn't know that Bryce already knew about her, that she'd invaded his office and created a huge fuss on two occasions. Bryce didn't tell Benita or any of us until after Damon's death when it couldn't upset anyone any more.

Living with Damon at close quarters in the cottage I began to realise just how fragile he was. He was missing a lot of university because he'd wake up with a bleed in a knee or ankle and couldn't walk for a day or two. Or his hand would blow up and he couldn't pick anything up for days, not even a pencil. When he got a bleed in his hand or arm he sometimes couldn't do the transfusion himself and he'd have to go home so his dad could transfuse him or, sometimes, we'd be forced to go to the hospital.

Ever since the time I saw the drunken father of one of my Cross kids beat his small son to bloody pulp on the pavement I have been repelled both by blood and fathers. But now I wanted to help, to take Damon's father's place. Damon hated going into hospital where there were no good memories for him. I asked Damon to show me how to perform a blood transfusion.

I'd seen some of prostitutes using a syringe in the public toilets around the Cross and several times I'd observed someone at a party or in a back lane giving themselves a hit. I was familiar with the tourniquet, usually a tie or a strip of cloth, pulled tight with one end held firmly in the mouth and the little syringe pushed into a vein on the inside of the arm. It always seemed such a simple and, at the same time, a defiant, incredibly daring and wrong thing to do. In a perverse way, I found it both glamorous and repulsive. Syringe drugs are the end of the line and are sort of heroic as well as being awful, so you can't help being awed.

But now it was different. Damon was someone I loved terribly, who was in pain and who couldn't always help himself and he needed me to get the butterfly needle into his veins. The inside of his thin arms and the top of his hands, just in front of his wrists, were lined with scar-tissue from years and years of two or three transfusions a week since he'd been a tiny baby. I knew I must learn to get into those veins first time, every time. That was the most important thing I could do for him.

I'd force myself to watch, repulsed and wanting to throw up, as the needle probed into Damon's soft white arm. I'd grow increasingly dismayed as he'd sometimes try five or six places. The very best place for him was the crook of the elbow, the same vein addicts like to use. He'd refer to it as "Old Faithful" but it had been used so often from childhood and was so heavily scarred that he liked to keep it for a super emergency when all other veins failed.

But even Old Faithful didn't always work and I'd watch his despair, often wanting to cry out as each carefully aimed jab missed its mark and nothing happened. Then, when he'd finally get the short, stumpy, wicked-looking butterfly needle to centre in a vein and the blood, almost black, would suddenly shoot up the tiny plastic tube which led from the rear of the needle, that was happiness and I'd want to jump for joy.

I realised that forcing myself to watch him over the weeks I'd lost my revulsion for blood, lost it at the joy of seeing him get the needle into a vein. This sharing in the resolution of yet another crisis, knowing that one more needle was home and relief from pain begun, was much more powerful than the impulse to throw up at the sight of his blood. When this finally happened, that's when I knew I was ready to take on the task myself.

I'd watch as Damon quickly connected the end of the tiny plastic tube to a large syringe which contained the stuff that began to stop the bleeding, the clotting factor. I felt certain that I could learn, even though Damon claimed his mother had never been able to put a needle in because she had an almost pathological fear of blood. I said nothing to him, though I was positive it would be different with me. It really did seem relatively easy and I told myself that his misses were because it wasn't easy to transfuse yourself, that someone else doing it would probably be less clumsy.

After all, he was often putting a needle into an arm, hand or joint that was already bleeding and swollen and very painful. It seemed logical that my undamaged hand would be more steady and more skilful if I could control my initial fear. To this I added the thought that people with a heroin habit manage it and most of them are not exactly Albert Einstein. Sometimes, when Damon had a bad bleed in his right hand, he had to attempt to get the butterfly needle in using his left hand. Only after he'd tried this several times would he give up and call his dad or go to the hospital. Often he'd used up all the good veins attempting to get the needle in and it was a real battle when his dad or the hospital finally had a go.

I felt sure that if I could overcome my fear of blood and the desire to throw up, that I'd find transfusing him a relatively easy thing to do. I'd be on the spot and have first go and that could save Damon a little pain. I begged him to let me attempt the task.

But when Damon actually took me through the steps that first time I realised it wasn't at all as easy as it appeared. He was very casual about it, his voice light and relaxed as though he were teaching me a trick with a length of string, how to make a cat's cradle or something equally amusing and inconsequential. The first transfusion he asked me to attempt was in the back of his hand. This is about the second place to use because the fist can be clenched and placed at almost any angle and because it is rested on something it can be kept very still. He placed a tourniquet around his upper arm and pumped his fist furiously until the veins stood up blue and bold on the back his hand.

I'd already practised under his instruction, sliding the butterfly needle into a smooth-skinned lemon, which is roughly the thickness and resistance of human skin, or so Damon claimed. Now he made me run my fingers down the two or three biggish parallel veins which ran across the back of his hand pointing towards his wrist.

I'd made love to his hands, held them a thousand times, I felt I knew every vibration, every dent and curve and pulse in them, but suddenly this hand, placed so quietly down, ready to accept the needle, was a strange new surface where I'd never been before.

"Feel each with your forefinger, feel each vein, see if it's got *bounce*, is smooth and has, you know, *tension*." He took my forefinger and made me stroke along two or three veins, "Can you feel them, they're not all the same, are they?"

I nodded, I was breathing hard, trying to hold back a small panic rising in my chest; the veins all felt the same and all seemed very small. "Choose the one you think is biggest and is nice and firm and smooth." He pressed my finger down again moving it along a vein. "What about that one, it feels pretty good?"

"Okay," I gulped and brought the needle towards it, my fingers gripping and bringing together the plastic butterfly wings attached to the top of the needle.

"No, no!" Damon cried suddenly. I pulled back in shock. "Sorry, babe. The swab. Swab the area first. It must be sterile."

I gulped, breathing heavily. I knew that, I'd seen him do it dozens of times and I'd even swabbed the back of his hand for him in the past. Already things were going wrong. I broke open a swab and rubbed the area around the vein we'd selected. Then I picked up the needle and, inhaling silently, hoping Damon didn't sense how anxious and terrified I was, I moved the butterfly needle forward.

"Jesus! We've forgotten the gloves!" It was Damon again, this time his voice raised. I burst into tears, the tension too much. Damon released the tourniquet and took me in his arms. "I'm so sorry, darling, I didn't mean to, I guess I'm as nervous as you are."

But I had started to shake. Simple things were going wrong; in my anxiety my mind was blanking out and I was neglecting the most basic procedures. Sniffing I drew away from him and crossed the room to his medical cupboard, the top drawer of an old dresser where he kept all his transfusion stuff. "I'm sorry, I'm so stupid, I *know* what to do," I sniffed. I found the box of ultra-thin, clear plastic gloves which surgeons wear, but which now everyone who works with anyone who is HIV positive automatically puts on when they approach. "They could make the needle slip, make it hard to hold?" I said lamely.

"They won't," he assured me. "Surgeons have to do delicate things with them on, delicate operations." He paused. "They'll definitely help you. You'll see."

The gloves were very necessary for another reason: the HIV virus is carried in blood and if some of Damon's blood should enter, say, a cut on my hand, I could become infected. It wasn't much of a risk, perhaps a chance in a million, but he didn't want to take *any* chances. I realised that he was trying not to remind me of this possibility, simply suggesting the gloves would help me to get the needle in.

With the pale, protective latex gloves pulled tightly over my hands so that my hands looked as though they belonged to a ghost, Damon placed the tourniquet back again, pushing it high up his arm before pulling it tight around the biceps. Then he pumped his fist again to make the veins on the back of his hand stand out. I took a deep breath and, taking the butterfly needle and squeezing its wings together, I felt for the most propitious vein with my free hand.

To my consternation, this time the best prospect seemed to be a different vein from the last, a slightly smaller one which now seemed the more "bouncy". I angled the needle and felt the momentary resistance as its tiny, hollow, elliptical point broke through the surface of the skin and moved along the vein. I prayed for the sudden, glorious moment when the blood would shoot up the tiny plastic tube leading from the end of the butterfly needle. But nothing happened, the needle was stuck an inch into the back of Damon's hand without any result.

"Jiggle it," Damon grunted. "Jiggle it a bit. Just gently ... try to reposition it, you could be almost in without knowing."

I tried to move the needle around, almost withdrawing it and taking a different direction, but nothing happened. Damon, I could sense, was trying not to show any reaction, to keep from wincing.

"Pull it out. Try again. Use the same vein before it dies." He said this quietly, though I could sense the urgency behind his casual tone. Drops of perspiration covered his brow, I knew he so badly wanted me to succeed.

Perspiration formed on my own forehead making it itchy and I wanted to blow my nose which seemed suddenly to have filled with mucus. I felt sure the sweat on my brow would run into my eyes and make it impossible to see. I withdrew the needle and tried inserting it again, keeping it flat and in line with the blue-green vein, but again nothing happened and I was now very close to panic.

Damon sighed, "Pull it out, babe, that one's shot. Never mind, you nearly got it that time. We'll try another vein, perhaps the big one you were going to use before?"

I used an alco-wipe to wipe away the speck of blood

where the needle had been withdrawn, surface blood that didn't come from a major vein. Damon removed the tourniquet while I broke out a fresh butterfly needle from its protective plastic wrap. My hands were visibly shaking as I forced myself to stay calm.

"Just sit down for a moment and wipe your face." Damon looked at me kindly, "It's just a knack, you'll soon get the hang of it. If it was hard I wouldn't be able to do it, would I?"

I nodded, feeling sick in the stomach. I wanted so badly to do it right but I was scared, not only of missing, but also of the blood when it came. I tried to smile. "I'll get it this time, you'll see." *Please God, I'll do anything you ask! Anything! Just let me get it in this time.*

Damon applied the tourniquet and began to pump his fist. I felt along the veins, trying to decide which one felt right, none of them as big or bold as the one that I'd just missed, not even the original big one.

I selected one again, running the pad of my index finger along it, making sure I wanted this one. The plastic glove made it feel smooth and it seemed pretty bouncy, though I had no idea whether it was. I resterilised the top of Damon's hand and took up the butterfly needle, pinching its two tiny plastic wings together between my forefinger and thumb and hoping I could hold it steady enough.

"Relax, it's really quite easy," Damon said quietly. "Come at it at a slightly flatter angle; feel the vein and then try to push the needle into the centre of it, like inserting a smaller pipe into a larger one — nice and steady."

I flattened out the needle and pushed it in. Almost as

I broke through the surface of the skin, the needle pushed in up to its hilt and a sudden rush of blood moved up the tiny tube. "Beauty! Quick, connect it to the syringe," Damon shouted excitedly, he was grinning like an ape, hugely pleased for me.

I frantically reached for one of the syringes already filled with AHF and clipped the end of the tiny plastic pipe leading from the butterfly needle to the point of the syringe. My heart was beating furiously and I thought it was going to break right through my chest. I was too preoccupied to care about the blood. Now it was done and I was holding the syringe in my hand I wasn't squeamish at all. Seeing his beautiful dark blood shooting up the tiny capillary tube was one of the most beautiful moments in my entire life.

Damon released the pressure of the tourniquet around the top of his arm.

"Well done, babe! Madam Butterfly Needle, star of The Love Transfusion!"

I grinned, I was pretty proud of myself. "Wow! How about that?" I cried excitedly.

"Careful, don't move the syringe, the needle might slip out."

The idea of this happening calmed me instantly, I imagined having to do it all again and the thought was too awful for words. "Very slowly, push the plunger down very slowly," Damon instructed quietly.

I began to push the precious clotting liquid into his vein. I suddenly felt incredibly close to him, as though we were one person and I was giving him my own blood so that he could live. If only my mother had known how willingly I would have let him have my blood. I felt as though I was going to cry. I was now able to look after Damon when he couldn't transfuse himself. I can't tell you how good this felt, like being Queen of the Universe.

When I'd emptied the first syringe and connected the second and emptied it as well, the moment arrived to remove the needle. I took up an alco-wipe. "What now?"

"Just pull it out smoothly and quickly and put the alco-wipe down on the spot and hold it down, it won't bleed for long."

I held the alco-wipe in my left hand right next to where the needle entered the vein, ready in an instant to blot any drop of blood that might follow the needle as I withdrew it.

Damon looked up at me and smiled, "Keep your free hand away from the point of the needle, babe." It was another quiet warning that his blood was potentially deadly. The needle came away, slipping out of his vein smoothly. I blotted the entry point with an alco-wipe and put pressure on the spot to stop it bleeding. Suddenly a large tear splashed on to the back of Damon's hand and to my surprise I found I was crying, but I was also grinning like mad. Oh God, it felt so lovely!

13

Celeste

Tortilla Brings the Love out in a Man.

The reality of Damon's existence and the way he chose to live were very different. He was just so outgoing and expressive and talkative but now that we were living together I started to see him differently. A new Damon I didn't entirely know began to emerge. Before we'd lived together, sometimes he'd call and cancel a date or make some excuse which meant he wouldn't see me for a couple of days. This didn't concern me, I was a pretty private person myself who needed a bit of breathing space and so I thought it was natural enough. I now realised that on these occasions he'd been confined to bed or, at least, at home unable to walk. I now started to see what the bleeding was doing to him; a knee or an ankle would go wrong and I began to realise how much pain he was required to, almost constantly, endure.

One morning, soon after we'd moved in, I woke up in our lovely, sexy, wonderful bedroom and just lay there for a while watching the light play patterns on the crazy, white-washed, flaking wall. Suddenly I was filled with the *too muchness* of it all, the joy of everything, and I leapt up and bounced on the bed and grabbed my pillow and bashed Damon on the head. "Wake up, Grumpy. It's a beautiful day and I love you!"

He smiled and just lay very still and then I collapsed on him and hugged him and started to smother him with kisses. Suddenly I heard a terrible, involuntary groan. I pulled away from him in alarm, my arms propped on the bed on either side of his shoulders so that his torso was directly under me. He was fighting to hold back the tears, blood running down his chin where he'd bitten his lip, trying not to cry out from my embrace. "Babe, there's blood on your chin. Don't lick at it and go and wash now!" was all he said. Through his own pain came this one urgent instruction to me.

Damon had developed a shoulder bleed during the night and was in the most awful pain. I returned from the bathroom where I'd gone to wipe his blood from my chin to find that a drop of his blood must have run down his chin and spotted the white bedspread. It never quite came out, even though I washed it and bleached it a dozen times. Now, I love that old bed cover and the faded brown spot can just be seen where the spread covers my pillow. I must have kissed that spot and cried on it a hundred times.

We still hadn't made love. Damon and I were developing our loving relationship before we attempted a sexual relationship. I know Damon was scared, but that he felt the same way; we both wanted something special.

As part of this development, I started to see Damon as an old man sometimes. In the mornings his arthritis was usually bad, he was stiff and sore and barely able to move even though he didn't have a bleed. Getting down the stairs from our attic bedroom was hell for him and often just getting to the bathroom to have a pee was a major problem.

He'd sometimes be pretty grumpy and even short-tempered when the pain was very bad. Sometimes he'd even shout at me, though this was very seldom. Compared with what I was used to this wasn't exactly earth shattering and he'd always apologise later. I found this strange because, as I had grown older and into my teens at Maison le Guessly, we did a lot of shouting at each other. There was often terrible frustration, particularly between my mother and me, but also with Muzzie too; and sometimes we all genuinely hated each other, but we seldom apologised. Damon would get frustrated with his pain or his inability to do something and I guess I was sometimes a bit over-cheerful. He'd shout at me or tell me to grow up, but he was sorry almost immediately afterwards and always said so.

He was missing a lot of uni with his bleeds, mostly from an ankle or one of his knees, that had been playing up since childhood. I sensed that when they happened he couldn't get down from the bedroom and he was too proud to tell me, so he missed a lecture instead. He hated having to pee in a plastic bucket and then have me take it downstairs. Once, when I'd been forced for some reason to go over to Maison le Guessly, I brought one of

Daddy's bed pans, but Damon wouldn't use it. At least the bucket was a bit macho I suppose, the bedpan was hospital, a place he'd been a thousand times too often as it was. He didn't want me as a nurse even though in fact I thought nothing of it. Daddy had gone senile in the months before he'd died and had caused me a great deal more indignity than a silly old plastic bucket. Anyway, there really wasn't anything Damon couldn't have asked me to do.

The upstairs room was both wonderful and awful for him and I suggested we make the front room (the room with all the records) into the bedroom. Damon was genuinely upset. "I've had this arthritis all my life, we've only got the best bedroom in the world for six months!"

I learned that everything in Damon's life was a trade-off, he could never guarantee anything happening and so he'd learned to use things while and when he could. He knew how I loved that bedroom and the whole house and he wasn't going to compromise me just because *he* had a bleed or was in a bit of pain. Damon lived with pain like someone learns to live with an awkwardly placed birthmark, he seemed to just make it a part of his life and get on with things.

Most young people want to leave home, it's the ultimate fantasy of anyone going through school: to be free to be themselves, be untidy, never cook, stay out as long as they like, have noisy parties and not have to answer to their parents any more. I had always been able to do all of these things so I wanted to leave home to make a home. A place where people could come over for tea and scones and I'd bake an apple pie and we'd listen to records, a house which I'd be proud to share with friends.

I just couldn't cope any longer with Maison le Guessly, it was just too much. I'd finished school, I had no reason to stay at home. I was working part time and had a little bit of money, I was probably making about $120 a week and, for me, that was a *lot* of money. Damon, too, had a bit of income from Woollahra Electronics and also the Vaucluse locksmith. So we had enough.

We hadn't expected to find the cottage or even live together; I mean we were so young and Damon had a nice home. So the cottage came along just when I couldn't stand being at home any longer and would have had to find a place and run away from Maison le Guessly anyway. But, now, it had happened and we had enough to live on and have friends over for home-cooked meals.

Ha, ha! Home-cooked meals! Damon couldn't "boil water" except for two things he could make and I, too, hadn't any idea about cooking much beyond a fried egg sandwich. I mean, not the foggiest! It was really lucky that Damon liked just about anything I made and, before I learned to cook, our friends put up with some very funny things to eat and joked about being poisoned.

After a few goes Damon would beg for spaghetti bolognese which I'd made well by mistake one night. He also made his only two dishes, a sort of a curry which he said his dad used to make and of which he was pretty proud and Maggi 3 Minute Noodles. He called these "Notorious Noodles" because, when all my skills failed and I was in tears, he'd get up and go into the kitchen and we'd have this for dinner.

But slowly I got better and I even started to keep a recipe book, writing down those things that hadn't been a disaster and which we liked. One day, several months after Damon's death, I found the book and flicked through it, the memories flooding back to me as I remembered each recipe, even the first time I'd made it. Suddenly and quite unexpectedly I came across Damon's neat hand-writing; this is what he'd written:

Notorious Noodles

Boil half-full kettle, empty packet of Maggi 3 Minute Noodles into two equal portions in two soup plates and pour half the boiling water into each plate. Stir.
Delicious and good in an emergency!

Damon once, after a particularly awful meal, told me that, when he was very young, they had a maid called Dina who was Spanish and who used to make tortillas for them. He raved about this tortilla. It became sort of our joke: "Good, but not as good as Dina's tortilla," he'd say after another go of practically poisoning him.

Reyes was a Spanish boarder at Maison le Guessly all my life. He was the only male we were able to be near as kids and he would sometimes cook a meal on the hotplate in his room and invite us to share it. So I made a reluctant trip back to Maison le Guessly to ask him if he could show me how to cook a tortilla.

We went shopping together and bought special pota-toes and extra virgin olive oil and eggs and bits and pieces of this and that and two, beautiful, shiny, deep red Spanish onions and a proper tortilla pan. Then Reyes made me make a tortilla to his instructions right there in his tiny kitchenette on the little green and cream Early Kooka stove. I must say it smelled wonderful and when it was finished it looked like a beautiful yellow moon in a pan.

That night I took it home to the cottage in Woollahra and at dinner . . . da-da-dah . . . I presented it to Damon. We really pigged out and I was so proud when he said it was even better than he ever remembered Dina's being.

That was about two months after we'd come to the cottage and that night, after the tortilla, we made love for the first time in the beautiful, big bed with the white quilt. I don't really remember whether it was marvellous or anything. I think Damon was so preoccupied with the condom staying on that the earth didn't have time to move much. But, afterwards, we lay in each other's arms in our own home with the moon coming through the window and it was the happiest single hour I think I'd ever had.

Book Three

Friends Gather Round.

14

The Return of the Prodigal Son.

The owner of the cottage returned, delighted to find his small home spotless and in better condition than when he'd left it, his precious record collection dust-free and intact, the shower rose over the ancient bath shining with coppery brilliance. But for Damon and Celeste it meant a parting, they had nowhere else to go where the rent was sufficiently low for them to be together without the need to share premises with others.

I was unwilling to help them. I had reluctantly given Damon fifty dollars a week to cover the token rent they paid for the cottage, now I withdrew even this. Benita and I had been living in a sort of suspension of judgment, we wanted Damon back with us and we worried for his girlfriend whom we still didn't know very well. Occasionally, they'd come home for dinner and on these occasions Celeste would seem ill at ease, sitting very straight in her chair and speaking only when spoken to, the portions she took on her fork were very small and she proceeded to chew them too thoroughly to avoid contributing to the conversation around her.

We saw her as very young and pretty, though milky pale, as though she might suffer from anaemia. I brought the subject up on the second occasion she came to dinner. With a sharp, nervous little laugh and a toss of her head, she countered my suggestion that she see our family doctor. "I'm just pale and I don't expose myself to the sun and never have. You think I'm pale because I've never had a tan." It was the longest sentence she'd ever completed in our presence and it wasn't of course why I thought she was pale. I have to confess that if she'd agreed to a test for anaemia I was planning to ask Irwin Light, our family doctor, to persuade her to have an HIV test at the same time.

We were terribly worried, though Damon continued to assure us that they always took the right precautions. The very fact that they were sleeping together was of sufficient concern and I'd read somewhere that condoms have about a fifteen per cent failure factor. While legally of age to make their own decisions about sex, in our eyes they were still babies and I felt sure had both been virgins before coming together. Although we didn't admit it, even to each other, Benita and I hoped that this forced separation would mean the end of Damon's affair with Celeste. While he openly professed to love Celeste very dearly, it is in the nature of parents not to take the first great loves of their children too seriously. We were confident that a break away from each other would force them apart and keep Damon where he belonged, which was, of course, with us.

Later, when I realised how deeply in love they were, I would be ashamed of my lack of sensitivity. In time we would come to see Celeste as a most wonderful gift to our son, almost as if she were a divine inspiration, a final and benign gift from a merciful God. They would be together until the very end and no other love I have witnessed could have endured what transpired between them and still remain intact.

But at the time, I·was not taken in by my youngest son's protestation of an enduring love; their *affair* was simply an attempt by Damon to assert his independence with a very pretty young girl in tow. Damon loved to do things with style and here was a perfect example of his need to show off and to compensate for lots of other things.

His need to leave us, I told myself, was perfectly natural. Damon had been beholden to his parents in a way that must have been very difficult as he grew older. Parents are not consciously aware of how much time their teenage children spend away from their home environment, at school, excursions, camps, holidays and during their own leisure time. This was not true for Damon; he could almost never truly escape from his home, even for twenty-four hours, so it was understandable that he should now want to assert himself and claim his independence. His emotional need was one thing but the practical reality was another. His dependence on his home environment was implicit; we could best look after him and we knew what was best for him. Benita and I comforted ourselves with the assurance that we'd been more than generous and understanding for the six months we'd allowed him to be away from us and, in return, he'd abused his freedom by cutting university lectures.

We were not pleased and, although we were terribly worried about Celeste, we also secretly thought that she was probably responsible for Damon's neglect of his studies. The longer the two of them were together the more likely that something would happen and the less happy the final result for everybody.

We felt personally guilty that she had been placed in an environment where an opportunistic infection could come about from a simple accident. Over the years we'd all accidentally pricked ourselves with one of Damon's needles on several occasions. We'd indulged Damon enough, the adventure was over; in our eyes the experiment was not a success, it was time for him to come home and for his girlfriend to go away. In retrospect we were short-sighted and over-protective and even patronising. We had no real idea of what lay ahead for Damon. He seemed well enough, that is if you discounted the effects of his haemophilia and the growing agony of arthritis that years of bleeding was causing in his prematurely ageing joints and, unconsciously (though now I think perhaps it was consciously), we made no attempt to learn more about AIDS.

When Benita would bring up the subject of Damon's HIV status, I'd immediately muffle her concern with a counter that nothing had happened as yet. It was pointless worrying because too little was clinically known about the disease. There was no proof that everyone who became HIV positive matured into a full-blown AIDS patient. Other viruses, smallpox for instance, could lie dormant in the bloodstream of some people all their lives, why not this one? We were reverting to our accustomed roles: Benita over-concerned and I under-concerned. And so, mostly at my insistence, we did nothing to learn more about AIDS in the hope that some day we'd wake up to find it had all been a bad dream.

We would talk about Damon's problem as "The Virus" as though its kinship with other viruses, such as the ones that caused influenza, somehow made it more benign, not as dangerous. Benita and I were used to coping with chronic illness. We were veterans of the daily disaster, the sword of Damocles had been poised over Damon's head all his life, we were experts at taking things one day at a time. Haemophilia was something against which no precautions could be taken and, it seemed, this new thing we called The Virus was the same. In a sense we were true professionals. We were firemen sitting around in our singlets smoking and playing cards, completely relaxed when the symptoms were at rest, but ready to pull on our brass-buttoned jackets and spring into organised alert at the first sound of an alarm.

It always did with haemophilia. Both of us secretly knew that the crisis would come, that was our experience, confirmed a thousand times with Damon's bleeds. The idea that this pallid, frail-looking, little girl would be able to cope when it did come was, of course, nonsense. Damon needed our kind of nerve, our kind of calm, our expertise. So we wanted him back where he belonged, where he could get the proper care he needed for his arthritis, his bleeds and anything else he was going to have to face with this new thing we so casually called The Virus.

Damon was talking about quitting university and getting a job where he would start to make his first million before he was twenty-five. I wasn't at all happy with this idea. He was starting to compromise with his life and that wasn't the way I'd taught him. We were not quitters: we never gave up, life was about hanging in, the last man clinging to a single thread of rope was the one who won.

How pompous it now sounds! How often had I told him that life was to be likened to climbing a sheer cliff-face; as you climb you can hear the swish of the bodies falling, the people who have given up, who have lost their grip on the tenuous cracks of their ambition. "Nobody climbs this cliff without preparation as well as determination," I would say to him. "It's a combination of know-how and guts. Sometimes you can win by hanging on a split second longer than your opponent and you do this by being better prepared and more courageous."

I now see it for the bleak and futile analogy it was, filled with winning and scheming but containing no joy except the satisfaction of triumphing in a pointless conquest. But at the time it seemed like a good way to sober up a young man who thought he'd make his first million by the time he was twenty-five and, moreover, expected to have a great deal of fun in the process.

Damon believed, with a divine optimism, that owning all the grown-up toys was his absolute prerogative and that, with his good brain, it would be comparatively easy to do so. A penthouse in an exotic watering hole, the dreaded red Ferrari *varooming* out of an underground garage in the James Bond tradition, beautiful women desiring him, late nights, endless bottles of French cham-

pagne, utter sophistication, real power — all this would
be brought about, of course, by the personal charm, wit
and brilliance of a young man who ignored his considerable physical handicaps (in fact never mentioned them)
— when he was only halfway through his twenties.

I came from the school of hard knocks and I knew
with an equally stupid certainty that life wasn't meant to
be easy. I was also slowly beginning to realise that doing
things, not having things, is the whole point of life. That
by the time you finally get all the grown-up toys you've
largely forgotten how to play with them — the joy must
come from what you do, not from what you do with the
money you make from what you do.

This desire for the things that money can buy was a
fairly recent part of Damon's character. As a child he had
wanted to be a doctor, then later, in his teens, he decided
on a career in science, in medical research where, naturally enough, he would find a cure for everything on the
planet, his own condition probably first on the list for
purely practical reasons — to be fit enough to push the
frontiers of medical science further than they'd ever been
taken before. I suppose this kind of glory-dreaming is
common to all children, but we believed along with him.
Damon was a very clever and imaginative child and his
ambition to go into medical research was certainly not
beyond his intellect.

But now he had faltered, he was sounding more like a
con man than someone who was about to make a serious
attempt to enter adult life. Damon, who had only managed three days at school a week, wasn't going to find
the going easy when he stepped out on to the street to
compete. I told myself that it was my job to make him

get real, to make sure that he was intellectually equipped for a vocation he was both physically able to do and one which he would enjoy for its own sake before he was permanently crippled with arthritis.

And so, in my mind, there was simply no room for discussion. I decided he must complete university to put some order and discipline, if not commonsense, into this hopelessly romantic and naive child whom we had brought so tenuously to the brink of manhood. Celeste wasn't at university. Having been accepted to study architecture, she had postponed her entry for a year so she could play housewife (or that's how I saw it) and I was quite sure, in the way parents are always quite sure, that her being with Damon was one of the major causes of his not attending lectures.

It's always easy to blame other people's children for the faults of one's own and I was quick to blame the blue-eyed blonde who had taken over Damon's life. And so I insisted, with very little tact and in a decidedly peremptory manner, that if he failed he would be forced to return to university to repeat. I delivered this ultimatum shortly after his return home from living in the cottage. I was in Damon's room helping him with a difficult bleed. It wasn't a big room and it still carried the scars of his childhood: the navy blue ceiling with stars painted on it, his teddy bear propped up on the top of the small, somewhat rickety wardrobe, the doors of which were decorated by the cut-outs and stickers that marked his progress in childhood. These scissored and pasted memorabilia started with the bunny rabbits, gnomes and cartoon animals we'd used to celebrate his infancy and moved through each stage of his life: motor bikes and surfboard logos, exotic pictures of cars, the ever-present Ferraris in every marque he could find, a surf rider cracking a huge green wave with another beneath that riding a pipeline. There was a picture of Arnold Schwarzenegger next to a neatly cut-out bust of Beethoven, the two men representing two separate parts of Damon's fantasy. There were several girls cut from magazines, though surprisingly none from the usual *Penthouse* or *Playboy* pages or even ones taken from conventional calendar pin-ups. Each was of a girl he'd thought of as his ideal at the time and they ranged from sloe-eyed orientals to green-eyed blondes. The doors also contained graffiti, the signatures of his friends, phone numbers, dates with mysterious single words beside them such as, *Alfie. Firecrackers. Doomsday. Yuk!* and one which was all too obvious, *HSC trails!* which referred to his final year exams. Also in Damon's writing, these words which had obviously amused him at some time but now, I realise, may have made a lasting impression:

> "What are you famous for?" she asked
> "I am simply famous," he replied.

Instead of being a place for his clothes, the wardrobe had become a repository for his brief life, each phase carelessly pasted over the last so that now only glimpses of his childhood showed in a fading montage.

The wardrobe was the only untidy-looking part of Damon's room, which, unlike those of his brothers, he'd always kept surprisingly neat. Squared up on the walls were framed pictures, mostly his own, though some begged from elsewhere in the house. His bedspread was always without a single crease, squared and tucked in over his box frame bed in the manner of the beds in a military barracks. I'd once shown Damon how to make an army barracks bed and he'd done it this way ever since. Next to the bed stood a console which carried his precious stereo, dusted and spotless and, in a never-ending search for the perfect sound, always in the process of an update. Even the books in his bookshelf were neatly arranged and ranged from childhood to the present — though his reading, even when he was quite young, was pretty sophisticated and certainly eclectic and the titles probably weren't quite the usual chronicle of a boy's life to maturity. Damon painted the wardrobe on his return home with a single, thin coat of paint which had failed to fully conceal all the phases of his life that lay beneath it, so that stickers and pictures and cut-out memorabilia gazed through a milky whiteness, like memories returning as the ghosts of his childhood.

After the cottage and the months spent with Celeste, this room must have seemed small and childish, over-filled with the past, as though he'd been forcibly returned to be chained to memories from which he'd successfully escaped for a few short months. This was the room where he'd spent thousands of hours staring at the painted Southern Cross on the navy ceiling, unable to move from his bed. It had held him captive on countless sunlit days of play. He'd been cloistered in this small, neat room while the rest of the world had places to go and games to play, playful punches to throw, balls to catch and sixes to smash, tries to score and tackles to make, excursions to take and daily adventures to antici-pate. He'd been here alone in this small room when all the planned and delicious phantasmagoria of childhood had taken place for his brothers and which, he had learned, mostly never happened to him, because his very excitement at their prospect seemed to bring on yet another bleed.

But I felt none of this. Damon was home where he belonged and life would resume as it had always done. Celeste too had returned home, no doubt to an equally worried and now happy mother, to a warm and welcoming hearth.

I hadn't even thought to paint Damon's room and so attempt to wash from it some of the ghosts of his childhood. As far as I was concerned, the adventure was over and Damon, as his two brothers had done, must now comply with my need to have him go to university, before he would again be allowed to assume responsibility for his adult life.

Directly after a bleed is no time for a confrontation; a blood transfusion, no matter how often it is done, is a tricky business and one which requires great concentration. When it's over there is a sense of a job well done, like an athlete who has worked hard on a training run and has earned the rest that follows. When Damon was younger, this was the time Benita would read to him or we would sit and talk quietly, knowing that the pain was still there and would increase for several hours yet, but that we had at least collaborated with each other at the beginning of its end.

But this time I was not concerned with the usual sensibilities. I was guilty of allowing him to take the cottage in the first place and now, as a result, he'd caused his mother and myself a great deal of stress and he'd also let us down with his studies. I tidied away the used syringe and bottles, wrapping them neatly in a steri-pad. "Damon, I want to talk to you about university." It was a direct and aggressive opening.

Damon, as I had hoped, was taken by surprise. "University?"

"Yes. I believe you've been cutting classes and that you're unlikely to pass first year."

Damon was silent and I could see that he felt that my timing was lousy, that I'd broken the unwritten law between us that quiet and love always followed a blood transfusion. He picked at a piece of lint on his bed cover, not looking at me, then he sighed deeply. Damon was a master sigher and could put his entire disapproval into a single, huge sigh. He looked up at me at last. "Dad! I've just had a bleed!" He was demanding that I return to the unspoken post-bleed routine we'd followed all his life.

"No! We have to talk, now! You're back home, hopefully back into a decent routine and that includes university and proper study."

Damon looked down again, his fingers teasing the bedspread, looking for another piece of lint to pluck from it. "Dad, I don't like uni, it's a waste of time. It really is!" He looked up at me, his eyes pleading. "It's all bullshit, Dad. You don't learn a single thing you can use later!"

"That's what you think now, but you'll change your mind later in life. What you learn may not seem useful now, but it will be."

"How? An Arts degree? It's hopeless. Do you really think it's going to help me in life to know how to parse a sentence?" He paused, "Do you know how to parse a sentence, Dad?"

"No, I don't."

"There you are! You're the creative director of one of the world's largest advertising agencies. Not knowing how to parse a sentence hasn't exactly been a disadvantage, has it?"

Damon prided himself on his cross-examination technique; he'd take a single point and hammer it until he was sufficiently removed from the subject under discussion for his opponent to begin responding blindly to his questions, no longer sure of the original premise.

"Parsing a sentence is only a discipline in grammar, like five-finger exercises on the piano. Your degree teaches you to understand and to handle information, to collate, cross-reference and think; in other words to use the known to discover the unknown. That's the whole point of an education — it takes you up to the wire and gives you some idea of how to negotiate your way across No Man's Land." I was pretty pleased with this rather neat summary.

"Dad, I've read most of the books we're about to *discover* as our introduction to *literature!*" He pronounced the words, discover and literature, with a touch of sarcasm. "Some of them I'd read by the time I was fourteen. I don't need to parse them or write an essay about the neurosis and deeply hidden motive of the main protagonist. All that does is to take away the enjoyment of the original reading." He paused and looked up at me. "Except for the set works we've been given, I've hardly read a book since I've been at uni."

I looked at him, my right eyebrow slightly arched. "Perhaps you've been otherwise occupied?"

Damon understood immediately. "Dad, that's not fair! Celeste hasn't stopped me going to uni."

"Nevertheless, if you fail this year you're going to have to repeat and I'll see to it that you attend lectures, even if your mother has to drive you to them herself or you have to go on crutches or in a wheelchair." I moved a step forward so that I was directly above him. "I hope you understand what I'm saying?"

Damon was silent for a moment and then, without looking up at me, said quietly, "I've missed too many lectures, I don't have sufficient credits to pass now, even if I tried my hardest."

I rubbed my palms on the back of my pants. This was the capitulation I was seeking. Damon was back under my authority and now I spoke more gently. "Well, try anyway. That way it will be that much easier when you repeat next year." I turned to leave the room, knowing that he was upset and would prefer me to leave.

"Next year? Next year I could be dead." He said it softly, though loud enough for me to hear. His words stabbed deep, cutting through all those things within me which were securely knotted and lashed down so that they would never be allowed to emerge. It was as though all the years of frustration and hurt and humiliation had become focused by his self-pity. I turned to face him, my teeth clenched. "Don't let me *ever. And I mean ever!* Don't let me *ever* hear you talk like that!" I'd reached his side and now stood over him. *"You bloody coward!"* I screamed, spraying spittle down onto his face.

As I spat the words out, I saw his surprise and obvious confusion and realised immediately that he'd made the remark as any frustrated child might have done, not meaning it to be taken seriously, but simply as an immature desire to have the last word. It was a remark which had nothing whatsoever to do with his HIV status.

I brought my hands up to my face to cover my distress. "Jesus, Damon, I'm sorry, I'm terribly, terribly sorry!"

He looked up and the hurt expression left his rather nice face. He smiled up at me, then gave a little laugh, "That's okay, Dad. I'm going to beat it anyway. You'll see, it won't turn into full-blown AIDS. I promise."

15

Damon

From a paper given by Damon at a conference held at the
University of New South Wales on 23 November 1989. The title of
the conference was "Children and Adolescents with HIV/AIDS". It
was conducted under the auspices of the Department of Child and
Adult Psychiatry at the Prince of Wales Hospital.
Damon had just turned twenty-three.

Haemophilia is a very difficult disease to live with. It is painful, it is debilitating and it is devious. It strikes when you least expect it. Most people with haemophilia would agree that very few of their bleeding episodes, or "bleeds", are directly related to an actual incident such as a sprain or a fall. Rather, they most often seem to occur spontaneously, for no apparent reason.

This makes haemophilia a very frustrating disease to live with, as there seems almost no way to prevent bleeds. Of course one doesn't play rugby or get into fights, but even so, leading a normal, everyday existence can bring on the most massive and dreadfully painful bleeds.

However, there was always one thing about haemophilia, at least in my lifetime, that made it bearable. And that, of course, is that there is effective and relatively fast-acting treatment available. In my lifetime, the treatment of a bleed has advanced from the frozen plasma known as cryoprecipitate to concentrated *Factor VIII* which comes in powder form. *Factor VIII* is, of course, the clotting ingredient in our blood. It has reduced the size of a treatment from a 250 ml transfusion to about a 60 ml transfusion. The concentrate is also easy to store and transport and much more simple to administer.

So in most cases the worst a bleed would mean was a day or two off your feet or you'd be without the use of an arm or an elbow, a shoulder, knee or ankle, or sometimes all of them.

Of course, the most difficult part of haemophilia is not the actual time spent in pain through a bleed, but the subsequent arthritic damage caused to the joints. It is the latter which causes most severe haemophiliacs to limp or to lose the full range of movement in one or several joints. It also means that for many, by the time they are fourteen or fifteen, they are in constant pain to a greater or lesser degree.

Going through puberty with a body that always did look a little different did, of course, have its problems. Girls are naturally curious creatures and invariably there would come a time when you would have to explain why you limped or why you couldn't straighten your arm. Then would come the inevitable question, "Does that mean if you scratch yourself you will bleed to death?"

But a lifetime of learning how to explain your illness meant that these questions were explained easily enough and you were accepted as just another guy.

How things have changed.

For the first time haemophilia has become something to hide.

Because of constant media attention, many people are aware that the haemophilia community has been severely affected by the HIV virus. And because of the nature of the sickness and the immediate ignorance and the fear it inspires in people, there is a new kind of shame for haemophiliacs to endure. You don't want people to know you have AIDS because you fear rejection. Therefore, you don't want people to know you have haemophilia. So the easiest thing to do is to lie and to tell people you have something, like chronic arthritis. Now that's fine for people who are new acquaintances, but for all those people who already know you and know about haemophilia, this approach is of no use. So you tell them when they ask — and they do ask — that you were one of the lucky ones, that somehow you were spared. My heart still misses a beat when I tell that lie.

That, of course, is only to those whom you don't want to know. There are friends in whom you have enough confidence to tell the truth. It becomes virtually impossible not to anyway, if and when you actually begin to get ill. But telling friends and having them support you is one of the most vital ways of coping with this threat.

The point I am making is that for the haemophiliac it has never been difficult to discuss his disease, after all, it is very like having diabetes, nothing to be ashamed of. But suddenly we must make a choice among all our friends and decide which of them can be trusted with this new information. And it is a very difficult choice to make. Get it wrong and you have to face ignorance and idiocy. But get it right and you create an entire network of support that is vital to coping with a personal catastrophe.

The implications of living with haemophilia and HIV at the same time are immense. Without trying to sound too self-pitying, it is the haemophiliacs who have suffered more than any other group affected by AIDS. This is simply because we have always had to struggle to stay well anyway, and are usually in a constant state of pain, or at the least, discomfort. Then there are the days when you can't walk or the times when it is impossible to use one of your arms. Combine this with the added threat of AIDS and you have a life which, at times, is very difficult to live.

It seems that one of the most common problems caused by AIDS is not in itself a life-threatening condition, it is simply that you have this general feeling of enormous fatigue, a lack of energy. It is very important that the haemophiliac takes regular exercise, the best form of which is swimming. This is to ensure that as much mobility and flexibility as possible is retained against the crippling effects of joint damage. The will to exercise becomes greatly reduced when energy levels are depleted by HIV. In an indirect way, the presence of HIV in fact makes it a great deal harder to stay on top of the damage caused by the haemophilia itself.

The next problem is the treatment itself. For some, AZT (Azidiothymidine) is absolutely horrible stuff! It's side effects can be absolutely ghastly. For the past two years, since I have been on AZT, I have been chronically anaemic. In addition to the the lack of energy caused by the virus, AZT also takes its toll. There are days when even to get out of bed and face a new day becomes a tremendous struggle.

The anaemia caused by AZT is treatable with a pure blood transfusion, and let me tell you it is like cocaine must be. Suddenly you have energy again, life becomes far more bearable, but soon the haemoglobin drops again and you are left feeling fatigued and frustrated. There is also, of course, a limit to the frequency of whole blood transfusions, iron builds up in your system if they are too frequent, which is something to be much avoided. So the result is at least half of your life spent with little or no strength.

Apart from the anaemia, AZT can cause constant nausea in some people. I am one of them. Anti-nausea drugs do have some effect but are far from perfect. It has gotten to the stage where AZT makes me feel so awful that I take it only every second month. The improvement in the way I actually feel is so great that I am not looking forward to starting back on this toxic substance. However, I am grateful to AZT. It seems it has kept me relatively well, although I guess there is a chance I might have stayed well without it.

Of course, haemophiliacs are not the only ones who have to put up with the imperfections of AZT; however, combined with the pain of joint damage, there are times when, quite frankly, you feel like shit.

To be quite honest, the concept of dying at the age of twenty-two, or younger, is (virtually) impossible to accept. Certainly you are aware of the facts, of the statistics, but the truth of the matter is — and I have noticed this especially among young people with haemophilia — that deep down you believe that you can escape. You can defy the odds and be the exception to the rule.

Now the medical evidence may indicate otherwise, and doctors may tell you that you are living on borrowed time. But, with no disrespect intended to those of you from the medical community here today, from my life-long experience, I can firmly state that we would all be in a lot of trouble if we started believing everything doctors had to say.

I for one do not intend to die from this virus. I have developed an attitude which treats this disease as a chronic condition rather than a terminal one. Perhaps this is because I am accustomed to the concept of a chronic illness and have adopted this attitude as a defence mechanism. But I am firmly convinced that if the mind is strong in its defences against something as potent as AIDS then one's chances of surviving are far greater.

I said a moment ago that I had noticed that most people with haemophilia were sure that they could defeat this disease or, if not entirely defeat it, at least keep it at bay. This attitude, from my experience in hospital, is less common in gay people. I think this is probably because the concept of protracted illness is less alien to people with haemophilia. They have had to cope with severe disease all their lives and so have less trouble adjusting to the fact of this new condition, AIDS.

Illness is something to which we have to adjust. It is the success of such adjustment which is the measure of how well we cope with disease. If one person finds that adjustment easier to make than another, is it not logical to suppose that that person may find the actual disease less difficult to cope with?

The ability to adjust one's lifestyle and modes of behaviour successfully to take into account that one's body is fighting an invader, is the ability to self-cure. I am not talking about a spiritual approach to illness, or even a strictly psychological one. I am talking about a *total* attitude, a completely new way of looking at things.

It is not in any way a negative concept. To come to terms with reality and adapt yourself in the most effective way, utilising all that you know and all that you are learning, is the key to living the kind of life you want.

At least, it is the kind of life I want and that is a long and full one.

Thank you.

16

Mothra the Hoon, Sam the Drip and
Roger the Lodger.

Damon spent Christmas, 1985, with us and most of January, 1986, but by the time the university term was about to begin he'd moved in with Celeste and two other students sharing a small house in Pyrmont, an inner city suburb close to Sydney University. Celeste had enrolled to do architecture and I felt confident, that with both of them at university, Damon might knuckle down and start working and so I was persuaded that they should be together again. I admit that this must sound arrogant and dominating. In strictly legal terms, Damon was free to do as he wished. But I don't think Damon, or even Brett or Adam, would have considered leaving home without our permission to do so.

When Damon asked permission to live away from home again his logic as usual was compelling, he didn't speak of living with Celeste, only that the long periods of travel by bus to university would exhaust him and, even if I gave him a car as had been suggested (by him), there would be days when bleeds into his ankles would make it impossible to drive. It had become apparent to Benita and me that, despite his return home, he had no intention of relinquishing Celeste, nor she him. In the arrogant and presumptuous way parents allow themselves to make such decisions, we'd slowly become convinced that they were genuinely in love and seemed to need each other in a special sort of way.

It was as though they were less young lovers and more a practised family of two people and a couple of cats named Sam and Mothra. Sam was a loser. His nose dripped constantly, he sneezed a lot, he looked miserable and got in the way so that he was tripped over a lot. Mothra was evil, destined to be a feline hoon who ran the local alleyways with an iron claw. At six months, he was the local top cat and already had the scars to show for it. Both had generations of Kings Cross alley cat coursing through their veins and were genetically criminal archetypes.

Both had started as abandoned kittens and were the umpteenth litter of an old Maison le Guessly cat named Pandora. Celeste, in a fair-minded gesture, had taken Sam the runt and Mothra the spunk and carted them in a string bag to the cottage in Woollahra. They'd immediately rewarded her by starting a flea colony which bred in the fertile dust of the ancient front room carpet into Ghengis Khan-like hordes that invaded everything and seemed to be resistant to every known form of chemical warfare.

When the stay at the cottage ended Celeste took Mothra and Sam back with her to Maison le Guessly where Mothra immediately took off for the bright lights of the Cross to aggregate his bad habits and learn stand-over tactics. He only ever returned home to be sewn up.

On the other hand Sam's hay fever and dripping nose never allowed him to go further than a patch of sun on the pavement outside Maison le Guessly where he became the neighbourhood chronically ill cat, a sort of wheezing and sneezing cat bum, faking old age by walking on stiff legs, useless before he'd even fully grown up.

Celeste seldom spoke of her family or of her home life and, apart from learning that she didn't have a father and lived with her mother and grandmother, we knew little else about her. We simply presumed, with her Kambala school background, that she came from a traditional sort of home and that her reluctance to talk about her mother was just another part of her natural reserve.

She had become less shy in our company as she spent more time with Damon in our home and we discovered in her a young woman of intelligence, wit and charm, who was fully aware of what she was embarking upon with Damon. On the old subject of sexual congress between the two of them she became stubborn, she didn't deny that they acted no differently from any young couple living together. "We take all the necessary precautions, Bryce. It's my life, my decision." She said to me once and it was apparent that she felt very strongly about her rights in the matter and that, in her own quiet way, she was telling me to mind my own business.

However, in other things she began to confide in us and we soon realised that she was pretty miserable at home and guessed that she might have good cause to be. We were becoming less certain that she and Damon would not resume their relationship, but it was only after they were together again in a place of their own that I understood fully the special kind of hell she'd gone through on her return to Maison le Guessly from the cottage. I recall her talking about the incident:

"Leaving the cottage was just . . . it was awful, it was really awful! I didn't know where I was going to go. Suddenly the six months with Damon was ended. It was like a fairy tale, this little house we had together, and suddenly I had to go back to Maison le Guessly, to the Cross, to my mother and the mess.

"It was hugely awful, I returned to my childhood room, nothing had changed, around me everything was dirty and smelly. Mum was just ecstatic, I was back home and as far as she was concerned I was going to *stay*! To stay forever and never go away again."

I asked Celeste how she reconciled her mother's seeming disinterest in her during her childhood and adolescence with what now appeared to be fierce possessiveness.

"Because she saw my leaving as being a personal hurt to her. A personal fight against her as a person. She saw my leaving as being unfilial; she possessed me, I belonged to her like a chair or picture on the wall or anything else in the house. The house was hers and I was a part of the house and a part of her; she'd created a family to be her possession, they were to be with her until she died." She paused, thinking for a moment. "It's hard to explain. She couldn't waste anything in the house. We, my sister, brother and myself, were like a nest of mice in a corner of the kitchen, they belonged utterly to her regardless of whether she liked them or not."

Celeste looked up at me, her pretty face creased into a frown. "She's proud of us, but not like you're proud of Damon or Brett and Adam — she's proud because we come from *her*. She sees us as springing from her and everything we've done, my sister's achievements and my brother's achievements and my own, belongs to her, because *she* is so brilliant. To see me leave, *me*, a part of her personal property, leaving her, was just too much. It was as though I was stealing myself from her. So when I got back she was over the moon."

Celeste stopped and looked behind her, almost as though she were checking to see whether her mother was within earshot. "I couldn't tell her I planned to move out as soon as I possibly could. I lived at home for six weeks and they were probably the six worst weeks of my life. Apart from the fact that I was separated from Damon, I was back into dirt and chaos. My whole life seemed to fall apart in a matter of hours, I hated every moment, every second of being back."

Celeste was coming to be more and more loved by our family and we were beginning to realise that they were both better off together. Besides, there was simply no way we could legally or otherwise justify keeping them apart and now we no longer thought to do so. They seemed to need each other, to fit, as though each supplied the emotional parts missing in the other.

Damon, who'd had a secure and happy home life was outwardly confident and assured; inwardly, and despite his outward nonchalance, his insecurity over his somewhat misshapen body craved reassurance. Celeste seemed genuinely not to notice or care about those physical aspects over which he felt most troubled. She regarded Damon as perfect just the way he was.

For his part, Damon gave Celeste a sense of being wanted and loved and of being a part of himself and of his family. There was a calmness about them and they would seldom quarrel. It is a paradox that Celeste's first adult source of love and security should come from such a tenuous and dangerous liaison.

Before he ever asked me if he could leave home again Damon and Celeste had secretly been looking for a place to stay. The process opened their eyes to the real world and they were becoming increasingly dismayed as it got closer to the university term. Damon thought he could get a small living allowance from me and Celeste had qualified for Austudy, the away-from-home student living allowance of eighty-five dollars a week. Even the flea-pits and cockroach-infested bed-sits in Redfern were more than they could afford and, finally, they knew they would have to share with at least two other students if they wanted even their own bedroom.

The turn-of-the-century worker's cottage they finally discovered had absolutely no outward charm but it was freshly painted and clean. It opened directly on to a street in Pyrmont, near Sydney University and was located on an island sandwiched between two major freeways and a bypass. Once a part of a regular neighbourhood, together with half a dozen other cottages, a small iron foundry and a large tin shed which undertook motor repairs, it had become stranded in the spaghetti of the Western Freeway, trapped in a dusty pocket of land surrounded by concrete arteries leading to the inner city.

However, the rent the landlord was asking for it would be possible only if they shared it with two other people. Their new home contained two bedrooms on the ground floor and a tiny attic room. By six o'clock every morning the house trembled and shook so much from the heavy trucks thundering past that it became necessary to shout to be heard from one room to another. But it had a decent sort of a kitchen, a workable bathroom, a tree in the tiny backyard for Mothra and a patch of sun for Sam. In fact, had the house been situated anywhere beyond the cacophony of the heavy-duty dawn traffic, it would have been priced beyond their capacity to pay. The only member of the family who wasn't pleased with the new place was Mothra. He waited until dark and went over the back fence heading for the bright lights of Chinatown half a kilometre away. Sam, of course, stayed.

Simon Bartlett, "Bardy", who was studying music at the Conservatorium, moved into the attic room in which there was barely enough for a tiny desk and bed and in which he couldn't fully stand. He was large and easygoing, absolutely guaranteed trouble-free and useful around the place to boot. He could even cook in a manner of speaking with a single special dish named "Ki Si Bardy", a concoction they had at least once a week made from half a kilo of mince, a packet of instant Chinese noodles, rice and cabbage. While it was always met with loud groans, it was filling and really quite delicious, though the flatulence it caused lasted for two days.

Damon and Celeste shared the second-best room, and a ring-in by the name of Roger, who'd responded to an advertisement placed on the Arts Faculty notice board, was the fourth they needed. The rent was apportioned according to the size of the room and as Roger, or as he predictably became known "Roger the Lodger", was prepared to pay the largest rent, he got the front room where he lived a more or less separate life, sharing very little with the others

As always happens, they drew up a set of house rules. Everyone put twenty dollars in the kitty for food. They would share the chores and take turns to cook. But it soon became apparent that this didn't work with Roger the Lodger. His upbringing was quite different from that of the other three members of the tiny household. Doting parents supplied him with a colour TV, a tape player and an inexhaustible supply of good things to eat. These all stayed in his room where he played the TV and his rock tapes at full blast, as well as a guitar which, in his hands, gave this beautiful instrument a very bad name. Sometimes he would play all three together.

Damon would find his own music constantly disrupted by the cacophony blasting from Roger the Lodger's room and Bardy, who played a lovely trombone, was forced into the backyard to practise for his studies for the Conservatorium.

Celeste, after her early cottage experience, had emerged as a cook and knew all about keeping house and feeding hungry men so, in the eternal manner of three men and a woman, she became the major cook and, because of her obsession with tidiness, the proverbial house slave. She shopped at the nearby fish-market and they ate standard things which involved curries and mince-type things and vegetables. If Roger the Lodger didn't like the fare, which happened often enough, he'd prepare his own from his home-supplied hoard, never sharing a crumb with any of the others.

Damon, who could cook curry and spaghetti bolognese, make vegemite toast and boil water to make instant Chinese chicken-flavoured noodles from sachets, purchased incredibly cheaply in lots of a dozen from a shop in nearby Chinatown, acted as emergency cook when Celeste got the shits and refused to feed them. But it's difficult when a couple share a house with others, inevitably they demand higher standards than the rest and become very bossy. Celeste wanted her home kept clean and this often made her angry.

Basically they weren't really untidy, but Celeste, after her bout of housekeeping at Woollahra and her memories of Maison le Guessly, wasn't ever going to allow a mess about her again. She wanted to impose her law on the house and she was just a pain in the arse. They called her "Queen Celeste" when she'd get on her high horse if things weren't working properly, which in terms of domestic chores was most of the time.

Roger the Lodger appeared to have received no domestic training whatsoever and was practically incapable of turning on the kitchen tap. Even by the dispiriting standards of modern youth, he was disconcertingly useless around the place.

Before they decided to leave most of the cooking to Queen Celeste, on the first occasion it was Roger the Lodger's turn to cook the evening meal, he left early that morning for the supermarket where he bought a number sixteen frozen chicken practically the size of a turkey. He popped it, plastic stretch-wrap and all, into the oven, turned it up to high and left for the day to attend lectures.

Had it not been for Damon, who had been forced to return home from university with a bleed, a disaster might have occurred. He arrived to find a house billowing with smoke and the frantic *miaows* of Sam, who'd been mistakenly locked in by Roger the Lodger. When the windows had been opened and the house was cleared of smoke, Roger the Lodger's size sixteen chicken had been reduced to a lump of charcoal no bigger than a *poulette* and Sam's eyes watered permanently forever afterwards, causing him to wheeze, sneeze, sniff, drip, weep and to be loved all the more. Celeste was heartbroken when two weeks later he mistook a patch of sun on the freeway for the pavement outside Maison le Guessly and wore a rear set of heavy duty Mack truck tyres to his grave. Mothra didn't even bother to turn up for the funeral or even send a bunch of catnip, he had no time for losers.

Roger the Lodger, apart from being annoyingly *there*, had very little impact on their daily lives, though one amusing incident occurred on the first day they were together which caused Celeste to sometimes refer to him as "Bloody Roger".

The process of moving into the house had caused Damon to have a bad bleed in his knee. The house was a mess and the only space reasonably clear of clutter and suitable for a transfusion was the kitchen table. It had been a long hard day and Damon, hurting and somewhat irritable, was anxious to get the needle in and to get the transfusion completed with as little fuss as possible.

However, Roger had never seen anything like this before and huddled over Damon, his elbows on the table, hands cupped under his chin, chatting and asking irritating questions. Damon, annoyed at his intrusion and upset by his clumsy questions, though too polite to send him packing, worked to get going as quickly as possible.

"Did you know that some people faint at the sight of blood?" Roger said flippantly to Damon.

"Yes, I suppose," Damon replied, weary of Roger's vicarious interest in the transfusion. Ready at last and with the tourniquet in place and his veins pumped, he picked up the butterfly needle and inserted it skilfully into a vein in the crease of his right arm. A thin line of dark blood shot up the tube and Roger fainted, his head hitting the surface of the table with a clunk.

Roger the Lodger may have been the odd man out in the foursome, but it must be remembered that, unlike Bardy, he didn't arrive into the group as an old and beloved friend and, besides, he always paid his rent on time. Anyway, he was by no means the worst disruption in their lives. Celeste's mum took to phoning her at six in the morning to abuse her and become hysterical on the phone. "I know you're sleeping with all the boys in that house. You're a slut!" she'd scream, then she'd go on about Damon using Celeste's blood to stay alive. At the sound of her mother's voice on the phone Celeste became defenceless, a small child unable to withstand this verbal onslaught from her mother. She would tearfully deny the accusations, pleading with her mother to stop, somehow unable to retaliate, mesmerised by her mum's cruel, screaming voice, until she was so choked that her sobs would cause Damon to wake up.

Damon would grab the phone from Celeste and slam it down and then leave it off the hook.

"He'd take me in his arms and rock me and tell me how he loved me, until I felt better and I'd stopped weeping," Celeste once told me. "'What you need is a mug of my special memory-erasing Chinese noodles,' he'd say. Damon would struggle out of bed and hobble into the kitchen. He was always terribly stiff from arthritis in the early morning and walked with great difficulty. I'd hear him ouching and aahing as he put the kettle on, as though he were walking across a lawn full of bindi-eyes. Sometimes he'd be walking so lopsided and bent over that he'd spill half the noodles from the mug on the way back to the bedroom. He'd hand me the mug and always say the same thing, 'Here, babe, this is special Chinese forgetting medicine, drink it and you won't remember your mother even called and today can be perfect again.'"

Celeste looked up at me, her eyes brimming. "When I miss him terribly and it becomes unbearable to think of him gone, I make myself a mug of Damon's special forgetting Chinese noodles and go and sit in a corner and cry for a bit. Even now, Damon's noodles help a lot to stop the sadness."

Celeste's mum only visited once, arriving unexpectedly to confiscate Celeste's art books. The books were much loved by Celeste and besides, they were important references for her architectural studies but, on the principle that anything from Maison le Guessly belonged to her mother, they were taken away. She also took Adelaide.

Adelaide was a marble statue Celeste had discovered in the house as a small child and which she had kept ever since as her friend. Adelaide was perfect; in Celeste's imagination she lived in a beautiful Victorian house with yellow climbing roses growing under the eaves, she had the nicest clothes, bathed twice a day and always smelled of 4711 cologne and, when Celeste grew up, she wanted to be just like her. She'd been forced to leave Adelaide at home when she'd moved into the original cottage with Damon, but she'd missed having her around. Apart from the art books and personal clothes, Adelaide was the only other thing Celeste had taken from her room when she left home for the second time to be with Damon.

"They are all *my* things. The books and that statue, they belong to me!" Celeste's mother announced. "How dare you steal them? I've come to take them back!"

"I was panic-stricken," Celeste recalls. "I suppose it must seem silly, but Adelaide was so beautiful, she was made of white marble and wore a diaphanous gown with one perfect breast showing and she wore a garland of tiny, perfectly carved roses in her hair. She'd been with me since I was very little and she'd always stood on the window sill beside my bed. Every night of my life I'd talk to Adelaide and tell her all my secrets. She knew everything there was to know about me. Now, with my books gone and Adelaide taken from me, I felt violated. They were the only things I owned in the world and, suddenly, I didn't own them any more, they belonged to my mum. I pleaded with her to let me keep Adelaide. 'You can only have her if you come back,' she spat. 'The statue belongs to me like everything else. Even you!'

"I remember Damon coming up and putting his arm around me. 'Let her take them, you don't need them. We only need each other.' He said this directly to my mother and I expected her to go wild and accuse him of drinking my blood. My mum's a big woman and when she becomes hysterical she can be really formidable. She would have made mincemeat out of Damon. She tried to stare Damon down but couldn't, so she threw all my precious books into a big canvas bag she'd brought and put Adelaide under her arm and walked out of the house, leaving the front door open. That's when Sam walked on to the freeway and died. But we only discovered that later that afternoon when Roger the Lodger came in and said, 'There's a dead cat on the road. You should see how flat it is from being run over by trucks all day.'

"For a long time after my mother had left I could feel Damon's anger trembling as he held me, but he never said anything against her, he just held me and told me over and over again, 'It's all right, babe. Nothing matters, it's all right. You'll see. The only thing that matters is the two of us, you and me.' He'd keep saying this and then he'd get up and put on a really nice piece of music, Mozart or Vivaldi or something like that, and I'd suddenly feel terribly loved and protected."

The room Damon and Celeste shared was quite large and Celeste worked to make it as much like the attic in the cottage in Woollahra as possible. Damon set up his sound system and Celeste painted it white, so that it reminded them of their previous home as they lay in bed.

But it was the new bed that proved to be a major problem for Damon. A friend had loaned them a futon and Damon who was normally achy and stiff in the morning now found he would wake up in the most awful pain from sleeping on the futon which lay on bare floor boards. Even without the pain, waking up was a special kind of purgatory. Darling Harbour, the massive civil recreation complex, was being constructed less than half a kilometre down the road opposite Chinatown and, every morning at six, the cement trucks would begin the day shift, roaring past the front door.

Damon would wake up groaning, the floor he lay on would be vibrating and the house filled with the whine of passing trucks. He'd be stiff as a board with arthritis, exacerbated by lying on the hard futon. More and more he was cutting lectures as it became harder and harder for him to get started when, on top of the pain from his arthritis, the morning would often enough commence with a bad bleed which required a transfusion.

Celeste put this larger number of bleeds than normal down to the unforgiving futon, though it never occurred to either of them to ask us for a double bed. The subject of sleeping together had resulted in a sort of mutually agreed stand-off, and this might have made them hesitate to ask us for help in the sleeping department. I was unaware of Damon's sleep discomfort, for, while they came home to see us perhaps once a week, we respected their privacy and I'd only briefly visited their new home on one occasion when they'd invited me to do so. On that single visit, I am ashamed to admit, their need for a comfortable bed did not occur to me.

I think the need to be independent was very important to them, especially to Celeste, and they didn't want to ask me for anything they felt they could manage without. I'd paid the bond and the first month's rent and that was as far as they were prepared to go. I'm sure they feared, above all else, the prospect of having to come home again with their tails between their legs.

While I paid Damon a small allowance and Celeste received Austudy, it must have been difficult to make ends meet, but they were managing to eat quite well and have fun together and I know they were both rather proud of this achievement. Celeste also did four-hour phone shifts twice weekly at a research company and regular Saturday mornings at shopping malls asking questions. The company, Rhapshott International, became known as Ratshit International and she loathed the work, which meant making up to two hundred phone calls a night to get ten or so people to agree to co-operate and answer a questionnaire. It was boring and unrewarding work, but it earned eight dollars an hour or thirty-two dollars a shift and doubled Celeste's weekly income. Most people lasted about two months but Celeste lasted a year and did more than her share to keep the wolf from the door.

Towards the end of the first term of university Damon came to see me. He begged to be allowed to leave university and to get a job. He told me about the bleeding and the increased pain from arthritis and, with his considerable powers of persuasion, almost led me to believe that the bleeds where a psychological reaction to university. He also managed to get Benita on his side and this time I capitulated. We were learning more and more about AIDS and his latest tests had shown a slight decrease in his T-cell count. T-cells are the cells in our blood which normally fight infection. Without them, we have a deficient immune system. The point being that AIDS does not cause death, but requires over-use of the T-cell supply to fight it, thus allowing opportunistic infections to attack our systems and finally destroy us.

I had a sense of foreboding that the serious part of "The Virus" was about to begin, so I agreed that Damon could leave university and find a job — though not before cautioning him that interesting jobs that paid young people well and which required very little physical effort were not that easy to find, no matter how clever one was.

"I'll find one, Dad," he assured me excitedly, Damon the optimist instantly back into full stride. "With my first pay check we're going to move out to a quieter place where there are no cement trucks or Roger the Lodger and we're going to buy a big, new double bed to sleep in!"

True to form Damon landed precisely the job he wanted. It was with a company which dealt with the money market where he was to learn to manipulate currencies on the foreign exchange. It was precisely the way he'd imagined himself, buying and selling money, his nerve on the line, his brain now on active duty and his performance in front of his peers so awesomely impressive that his name was soon known in every international money market, where the *really* big boys spoke of him with growing respect.

The only problem was that while he was an expert at Chinese noodles he made a lousy cup of tea. As the tea boy, as well as working in the mail room and cleaning the computer screens and keyboards, he wasn't too impressive at all. Damon was in the real world at last and had come down to earth with a terrible bump.

17

Italian Genes, Fat Tyres and
Slim Pickings.

Damon started to make money and it was a big income too. Big when you put it against the money he and Celeste had been living on. He had so much he wanted to do and all of what he wanted seemed to involve money. It was *really* important for him to have a Ferrari and to get into what he called "fast living". He needed it for himself, for although he showed not the slightest sign of an inferiority complex, I think, in his mind, he'd postponed the active part of his childhood for when he was grown up. The games he could never play and the excursions he'd had to miss and the special treats, all would translate into doing grown-up kid things, fast cars, concerts, beautiful women, posh places and he'd have all the yuppie toys to go with these things.

He'd explain to Celeste, "It's got to be perfect. You'll

see, it will be. We'll have everything, I'll give you everything, we'll do everything!" Although he repeatedly stated
that he believed his HIV positive status would never
progress into full-blown AIDS, insisting that his "mind
power" would simply never allow it, he was aware that
arthritis was slowly wearing away at his joints, silting
them up, causing increasing immobility. I think he wanted
to do as much living as he could while he could still get
around in a fairly normal manner, before the aches and
pains become too prolonged and turned him prematurely into a cripple.

He came home to visit us, terribly excited after the first
week at work and clutching an extravagantly large bunch
of red roses for his mother. "Look, Mum, long stemmed
and perfect, every one is perfect. I'm on my way!" He
turned to me, "It's made for me, Dad, I mean the job."
He paused to take a breath, "It's about *money*!"

I laughed. Damon had inherited his attitude to money
from his mother, which was, simply, that money was a
commodity that should never be allowed to stay in one
spot for very long before it was converted into something
more exciting than a small rectangular-shaped piece of
paper. If their lives had depended on it, neither would
have been able to identify the historical face or any of
the motifs and hieroglyphics on the face of any given
Australian note; the colour was all that counted, it told
them everything they needed to know.

"Try and save some of it when you get it," I said
lamely.

Damon either didn't hear me, or perhaps the idea was
so alien it simply didn't register, instead he continued
excitedly, "When I went for the interview I sat in the

foyer and there was this screen, Dad." He pointed to a spot on the wall a couple of feet above my head. "Flashing on to it were the various currencies, yen, pounds sterling, Deutschmarks, Swiss francs and greenbacks," he paused to explain, "Greenbacks, that's U.S. dollars, Dad. I just sat and studied it and I knew I could do it. I could read the screen and calculate the fractions of a percentage point. It was like it was an instinct, it just happened inside my head without me having to think." Damon's eyes were shining. "Then a guy called Mr Cooper interviewed me. He's the boss. After a while I could see he knew I knew because he asked me where I'd learned about currencies. 'From sitting in the foyer for an hour, sir,' I said and he laughed and just said, 'Well then, you'd better start next Monday. I like people who like to be on time.'"

We all laughed. Damon, who lacked discipline, had no sense of time whatsoever and could just as easily have arrived an hour late as early.

It was very important to him that I approve of his first real job. He spoke of conquering the commercial world and then going back to university when he had something behind him. This wasn't simply to console me, I am certain that he meant it. Damon always meant everything he said, it was just that he was a lousy implementer of his intentions.

"Celeste tells me your bleeds have been very bad lately. How will you cope with the job?" I wanted to share in his enthusiasm and indeed I was pleased for him, but if he couldn't manage university because of the bleeds I didn't share his optimism about working full time. I guess I wanted to prepare him for the disappointment if he failed, if his body let him down as it had done so often before. I must have seemed a bit of a wet blanket, but Damon often needed to be dampened down a bit; all his life his character and enthusiasm and his personal charisma had kept his temporary jobs open for him when he failed to turn up because of another ubiquitous bleed. People were always willing to forgive Damon, not only because they understood his physical problems, but also because they found him a nice part of their lives. His personal charm enchanted all who knew him and Damon wasn't at all above exploiting this state of affairs.

But I knew that being unable to do the deliveries at Bernie Carlisle's chemist shop or not turning up at Woollahra Electronics where he sold only on commission or even arranging for the ever-obliging Toby to take his shift at Vaucluse Locksmiths was one thing. Holding down a high pressure job dealing in international currency was certain to be quite another.

"Dad, it's nothing. My bleeds are because of the futon! We've got this futon on the floor with only the floor boards under it and so it gives me bleeds. It's okay now, we're going to buy a proper bed. Celeste and I are going to Harvey Norman Discounts tomorrow, they've got this sale with two months before you have to pay and we're going to buy one with the right kind of mattress."

I was appalled, though I had no right to be, I'd been so concerned with the fact that they were sharing a bed that I'd simply never asked, or even thought to ask, about the kind of bed they were sleeping in. "Your bed has been giving you bleeds? Jesus, Damon, why didn't you tell me!"

Damon looked down at his shoes. "Dad, we couldn't

ask you to buy us a double bed, you know, well after . . .
all . . . the fuss." He looked up at me appealingly, not
wishing to spoil the moment and, I could see, anxious to
change the subject in case it should lead to an argument.
"Dad, my gear, it isn't the best. I'm going to need some
of your proper silk ties and some shirts and maybe some
of your other stuff? I've got to look successful, it's part of
the job, clients come in and things."

Ashamed of myself for not thinking about the bed they
slept in, I took him into the bedroom and opened my
wardrobe. He helped himself, taking an expensive double-
breasted blazer and two pairs of hand-tailored, grey flan-
nels, along with several business shirts, a pair of Italian
shoes and several silk ties. The ties were carefully picked
by his mother so they wouldn't seem too old for him.
Damon was ready for the corporate world and he was
going to start the way he intended to finish, looking like
the youngest Chairman of the Board in the history of
international finance.

Damon, who knew with a certainty, that he was born
to juggle numbers in his head, to buy and sell in fractions, wasn't born to make tea and run errands and be
the dogsbody around the place.

Almost at once he began to hate his menial job. The
need for him to serve as any sort of general factotum
hadn't entered his head. He expected his cadetship in
finance fractions would take a few days at the console
and an intelligent prod from a superior every once in a
while, but the rest would come as naturally as breathing.
At lunchtime and after work he'd grab a computer console and in the evenings he'd learn all about the business
of currencies. Very soon he felt he knew as much as the

operators who were "making a poultice". He was ready for the big time and was genuinely curious as to the reason why this wasn't recognised by everyone in the company.

After three weeks he went to see Mr Cooper, pointing out to him that, while it wasn't so much a matter of making tea or running errands that distressed him, it was the tremendous waste of a rather special human talent. There was a console to be manned and money to be made and he knew just the man to do it. Mr Cooper who, despite Damon's precocity, liked him, remained unimpressed. He told him he'd have to wait, that everyone had to do time as the office boy. He added, though not unkindly, that if Damon didn't start at the bottom he'd never know when he'd reached the top.

"How dumb is that?" Damon reported to me later.

"Not as dumb as you think," I replied, impressed with Cooper. There is a strong streak of puritanism in me which believes things shouldn't come too easily. Mr Cooper and I obviously shared a not dissimilar view of my youngest son.

"But, Dad, they're not very smart, *really* they're not. I know I could do it! I could be making them thousands instead of making them tea. It just isn't logical."

Damon's confidence was partly born of a too-sheltered life, where everyone else's job seemed easy from the vantage point of his own inexperience in doing almost anything which required a sustained effort. He was widely read because he'd been reading from a very young age with lots more time than most kids to do so. He'd done well at school, despite a mostly three-day school week, because he was naturally clever and widely read.

His brothers had learned to surf by working in the waves for endless hours and days and months. Children learn perseverance not only because they are made to persist by their elders, but naturally, at a young age, when they wish to master skills which interest them. Learning to ride a surf or a skate board or cricket or tennis is as much a lesson in the dynamics of life as any formal lessons in persistent application. Damon had no such experience in sustained effort. His brain was all he had and it wasn't practised in tenacity. His bleeds always meant that the sort of continuity of dull work which builds character in all of us was too often cut short for him. He could always walk away from a difficult task with a face-saving excuse. His intelligence was his only way of competing or besting his peers. Where other kids sorted out their differences with a wrestle on the lawn or a punch to the jaw or a race to a given point, Damon did so with his tongue and his mind. As a result, he was apt to judge his peers too quickly and often much too harshly.

I had no doubt that he'd tried on his contemporaries at work and that he'd found them intellectually inferior to himself. He explained that they smoked three packets of cigarettes a day, pulled their ties down to the second button on their shirts, loosened their collars and ran their hands through their hair, while they allowed cups of black coffee to grow cold. It was Damon's considered and rather arrogant conclusion that they ought to make a space for someone who was, at the very least, their equal. Damon knew he could feel the numbers screened on to the inside of his eyeballs and hear the fractions that added up to a profit as they danced off the tip of his tongue.

To show just how extremely bright he was, after a few weeks he too began to smoke. Damon, who had begged both his parents to give up smoking because he feared an untimely tobacco-related death in the family, who'd often lectured his brothers against taking it up, now smoked and pulled his tie away from his collar and affected all the mannerisms he'd so recently despised. He claimed, of course, that personal boredom was the cause. That the standing around making tea and coffee, doing the washing up and fetching cigarettes and sticky buns for the cognoscenti behind the consoles, whom he knew he could lick blind-folded with one intellectual arm behind his back, had started his smoking.

Damon was sure he'd been side-streamed in his first canoe when he was ready to meet the roaring rapids of life, well able to navigate his craft through the choppy waters of the money market. Being the best-dressed tea-boy in Australia was not the apprenticeship he regarded as suitable to someone who was soon destined to be a mercurial presence in an oak-panelled boardroom.

Though the frequency of his bleeds didn't lessen he somehow made it to work each day, often on crutches or wearing a sling. Damon was quite accustomed to being a bit of a physical spectacle. All his life he'd been known and accepted by everyone as a brain attached to a some-what wonky and unreliable body which wore leg braces, bandages, slings and used crutches as a natural extension of itself.

But the high pressure people who worked at shaving fractions of a decimal point from fluctuating international currencies were not the sort to allow for his physical afflictions. Theirs was a world where you either peed or got off the pot, where only the strongest and the most rapacious survived. Greed was good and an inflated ego and selfish disregard for others was the sign of a promising career. This was the greedy eighties and there wasn't any sympathy or understanding to spare for a superior little Cranbrook boy with a permanent limp, who came to work with his arm in a sling or on crutches and who took twice as long as he ought to make a simple cup of coffee or fetch a pack of cigarettes from the paper shop on the corner. Damon, however, despite no experience in tenacity, hung in and hung on, defending himself well against not infrequent complaints from the operators about the poor standard of the office housekeeping. Always optimistic, he was sure the day would soon come when he was called to the Faith, when he would flex his arthritic wrists and take his rightful place behind a console to begin his meteoric career, where he would immediately confound his contemporaries with a dazzling performance.

In anticipation of this Damon felt he couldn't wait any longer to buy his first car. This he knew couldn't be a Ferrari, but would nevertheless need to have a number of characteristics which would place it in the same genre. He and Celeste discussed the subject endlessly — perhaps an old Alfa Romeo with good lines. It was important that their first car be Italian so that in an aspirational sense it was correct and came with the right European sports car pedigree. He didn't mind if it was old, even very old, but it must have classic lines and be, he was forced to concede, rather cheap. The fact that any car that fitted these criteria might also occasionally break down never occurred to them.

They searched the *Sydney Morning Herald* classifieds every Wednesday and Saturday; but everything that qualified was well beyond their budget, which was more or less nothing, except the promise of a regular income from his new job. Damon, always confident in his formidable powers of persuasion, had as a deposit a father who, he was sure, could be made to part with the first few hundred.

One morning Celeste found the car they'd been looking for in the local Glebe newspaper:

Silver grey 1974 Fiat 124 Model CC sports car.
Immaculate condition, good mileage, needs min. work.
Fat tyres, fully imported, original Italian instrumentation.
$6000 o.n.o. Phone Bob 793-1800 after 5 p.m.

At five minutes to five Damon started to dial in order to keep any other hopefuls off the air; finally at a quarter past five someone on the other end picked up the receiver. "The Fiat, the 124. It hasn't gone, has it?" The voice assured him it hadn't gone and that he wouldn't sell until Damon arrived from work at 6 p.m.

When Damon and Celeste arrived they couldn't believe their eyes, a silver grey Fiat 124 stood in the driveway of a suburban house and at first glance it looked practically new. It stood low to the ground, surprisingly low, and was equipped with high performance fat tyres. A glance into the interior showed it had leather upholstery which, though somewhat worn with a long tear in one of the seams of the driver's bucket seat where a dirty strip of sponge rubber popped through, was still very presentable.

They ignored the faded patches on the dashboard, their eyes deliberately running over them quickly so they wouldn't see too clearly where the sun had cracked the vinyl and lifted the laminate. "Needs a good cut back to come up like new." He turned to Celeste. "What a car! Hey, babe!"

They knocked on the front door and soon a tall, good-looking, young guy with blond hair and blue eyes answered.

"Hi. You must be Damon?"

Damon tried his best to look non-committal and businesslike; he was still in his business clothes and hoped he looked older and not the sort to be easily conned. He introduced Celeste. The blond guy extended his hand, shaking both their hands. "Bob . . . Bob Glover." He was dressed in a clean pair of blue jeans and a white T-shirt. "You'll look good in the 124, Celeste," he smiled. Celeste felt a fleeting doubt, but brushed it aside, forcing a smile. Bob Glover stepped out of the doorway and they stepped aside to let him pass. "I suppose you'll want to give it a burl, eh?"

Damon nodded and they followed him to the car. Bob Glover opened the door and slid in behind the wheel leaving the door open. "Give her a bit of a pump and half an inch of choke," he pointed to the choke, pulling it gently, then he turned the ignition key. But nothing happened. He pushed the choke back in and grinned disarmingly. "Wog cars, they've all got their own little ways." He patted the dashboard. "Come on now, behave yourself." He pulled the choke out again slowly, as though he was measuring an exact dose of petrol into the carburettor, then he pumped the accelerator and turned the ignition key. The 124 coughed, hesitated for a moment, then caught and roared into life.

A slight smell of petrol perfumed the air, it was a heady mixture which brought Damon close to swooning. As he squeezed Celeste's hand he was instantly and profoundly in love. It wasn't a Ferrari but it was exactly the antecedent they were looking for. For six thousand dollars it was a truly remarkable buy. Only one small problem remained, between them they had sixty-two dollars and next week's pay coming in two days.

Bob Glover agreed to take fifty bucks as a holding deposit and, after a little hesitation, agreed that they could pay him a thousand dollars by the weekend, at which time they could take the car and he'd give them five months to pay off the remainder.

Damon presented the merits of the car carefully to me. He explained that a fully imported Fiat of this marque was a very rare find and one in this sort of condition practically impossible to obtain. He claimed that just from the sound of the engine it was obvious it had been lovingly owned and never stressed. I wasn't inclined to take this piece of lyrical description too seriously; it was Friday night and he needed the one thousand dollars to secure the car by nine o'clock the next morning. He was putting on the pressure.

"Damon, you know nothing about cars, I mean engines. Before you pay this guy you must have it inspected by the NRMA. It could look great and be a heap of crap. Some people put bananas in the diff. to make a problem car run smoothly." Like every male who's ever lived, I'd heard this piece of conventional wisdom and lost no time passing it on.

Damon's face clouded. "Dad, it isn't a bomb! It's in terrific shape. If I ask him for an NRMA inspection he'll sell it to someone else." His expression was pleading. "A car like that isn't hard to sell. He said he'd keep it only until tomorrow morning!"

"I don't know, Damon, you're buying it from some bloke in a backyard. You know nothing about him or the car's history and he's pressuring you."

"Dad! You're wrong. This guy, Bob, he works with disabled people, he's a really nice guy who has an MG he wants to fix; he doesn't make a lot of money and he needs the money to fix the MG. Dad, you can come out and see the car for yourself; it's got fat tyres, even you know they don't put fat tyres on a crap car!"

I looked at Damon steadily. "Come on, be sensible. Tell him you want an NRMA assessment. You'll have it by Monday or Tuesday and if the car's okay I'll go to the bank and get him cash." I smiled to encourage him. Damon burst into tears, "Dad, I want it. I want it more than anything! I know everything will be okay, I just know!" He sniffed, "I'll pay you back, Dad . . . it's . . . it's only a loan."

Damon was a bit spoilt, but he didn't bawl easily. In fact it was out of character that he would allow himself to be reduced to tears over anything. Ashamed, he crossed the room with his face averted and walked quickly into the garden.

Benita, who must have been listening, walked slowly in from the kitchen. "He said he'll pay you back. It's *only* a loan. If he makes a mistake that's his problem."

I snapped at Benita, "Ha! He pays back the way you pay back. Never!"

Benita pulled back, her lip curling. "Hey! Don't pick on me because you're feeling like a bastard!"

I sighed, trying not to sound angry, "*Ferchrissake!* I want to make sure the bloody car he buys is safe!"

"He's not stupid, he wouldn't buy an unsafe car!"

"Oh, yeah? He knows bugger-all about cars!"

"He wants *that* car. If he loses it because you want him to get a thing from the NRMA he'll never forgive you."

"Fuck it, Benita! When are we going to stop indulging the child!"

Benita looked at me, her face scornful. "I don't believe I heard that. Indulged! Jesus, what do you *mean* indulged?"

"I'm going crazy," I said, shaking my head, but I knew I'd lost. When it came to the crunch I was piss-weak.

The car, of course, was a disaster. Celeste is fond of talking about it as the single most stupid thing she and Damon ever did together. "It was unbelievable, that car broke down so many times it was dangerously traumatic! But the first fifteen minutes of owning it was marvellous. Suddenly, we owned a beautiful, new, second-hand car. Leaving Bob Glover's place the car was purring like a kitten and when Damon reached a longish straight bit on the road home he pushed down the accelerator and it roared like some angry beast. It was one of the happiest moments of my life. Damon behind the wheel of his own pedigree Italian Fiat 124 and me beside him. It was wonderful, just, well . . . wonderful!

"We drove home and parked in the lane behind the house and I ran in to fetch Bardy. When we returned Damon was still sitting behind the wheel with this grin on his face, he was as happy as I'd ever seen him. The sun was shining and you could hardly see the patches where the paint had faded on the bonnet, it was just a great, great-looking car.

" 'Jeez, Damon, it's great!' Bardy said, stopping a few paces away and placing his head on his shoulder so that he could sort of squint to take it all in at once. I laughed, happy to be a part of the moment. 'Get in,' Damon said, sort of matter-of-factly, frowning slightly so it wouldn't show how proud he was. I clicked the bucket seat on my side and climbed into the back seat leaving the front seat for Bardy. Damon turned on the ignition and nothing happened.

" 'Wog cars, they've all got their own temperament,' Damon said, then he patted the dashboard, 'Come on now, behave yourself.' He pulled the choke out about half an inch and pumped the petrol a couple of times, then switched on the ignition. Nothing happened. We'd had the car fifteen minutes and it had broken down already.

"There was a moment of terrible silence. 'It's the battery, the battery's flat,' Bardy said quickly, filling the awful void. 'My mum's car does that a lot.'

"We all climbed out and opened the bonnet and examined where the battery was. There was a lot of white stuff, like white powder, around the two terminals and the battery looked as though it had been in a long time. 'There, you see, it's the battery,' Bardy said convincingly, dabbing at the white stuff with a finger and holding it up for us to see.

"There was a place where they fixed cars further down the lane, not a proper garage, just a large tin shed where blokes in overalls worked on cars. 'I'll see if I can get one of those guys from the garage to help,' I said quickly. I wasn't game to look at Damon's bewildered face, so I began to run down the lane instead.

"It turned out to be the battery all right, the guy from the garage brought this little meter along with him and he placed it on the two terminals.

" 'It's rooted, your battery's rooted. Not just flat, there's bugger-all life left in it.' He turned the meter box towards us and pressed the button, the needle in the window didn't move, even a fraction of a centimetre. 'See, bugger-all.' He looked at Damon, 'Youse gunna have to get a new one, mate.'

" 'Can't you just charge it so it lasts a few days longer?' Damon asked.

" 'It's history, mate. It won't take a charge.' He looked into the engine, touching a few wires, tugging at bits and running his forefinger along the engine block until it was covered in oil, then he brought his finger to his nose and smelled it. He said nothing, just grunted, and then he tugged at the radiator hose which came away in his hand. He pushed it back on and tightened the loose bolt on the metal collar around the hose with his fingers. Finally, he took his head out of the engine and rubbed the top of his greasy hand under his nose. 'Where'd yer get this heap of I-talian shit?' he asked."

*   *   *

Roger the Lodger and the early morning traffic was a combination which was proving too much for Damon. With a little more money at their disposal, they decided to leave the house at Pyrmont and move to a small, newly renovated terrace house in Talfourd Street, Glebe, which they could share with two university friends. Glebe was the suburb in which they'd purchased the Fiat 124 and was even closer to university for Celeste, who could now walk to lectures in ten minutes.

The house was smaller than the one they'd vacated but it was somewhat better designed. Damon had been bringing stuff from home for some months and Samantha Lau and Andrew Sully, their new house mates, also had some stuff they'd scavenged from their homes so they were able to furnish the new place quite nicely. Samantha, known as Sam, and Andrew were pretty easygoing people and more or less allowed Celeste to be the boss. Celeste admits that she was pretty fierce about tidiness. "A bit of a pain, really." She'd promised herself that she'd never be reminded of the mess in Maison le Guessly. They were soon organised into an efficient and comfortable household. The chaos of most student digs was nowhere apparent, Celeste was making up for her childhood with a vengeance.

Almost immediately they'd moved in poverty struck again. They were rapidly falling behind in their payments for the car. They'd let the phone go, mostly because they couldn't afford it and because there was a public phone two minutes away on the corner, but also because Bob Glover's phone calls asking for his money were becoming too frequent and traumatic. Damon, in a bold move to get Bob Glover off his back, had been to see him to complain. Finally Glover admitted that the Fiat, like the people he looked after, was basically permanently disabled and that he'd never really been able to get it going properly himself. He agreed to drop the price by a thousand dollars, but only if they'd bring their payments up to date immediately.

Damon returned home and told Celeste the news.

They were two thousand dollars behind and Damon was still making tea, fetching cigarettes and sticky buns; his salary couldn't possibly cover what they owed even if the car never broke down again.

Damon decided he had no alternative but to sell his hi-fi gear, the joy of his life. He'd built it up over the years, matching each component for the ultimate in high fidelity. As sound gear it was a small masterpiece. They sold it for eighteen hundred dollars, about three thousand dollars less than had gone into it. Damon's tapes and records fetched another two hundred and fifty dollars, all of which went to bring them up to date with the payments on the Fiat 124.

The end came when, after the umpteenth repair and the usual assurances that their problems where finally over, they decided to take a trip to the Hunter Valley, a wine-growing area about a hundred and fifty kilometres from Sydney. Andrew Sully's parents had invited them to spend the weekend at their small vineyard near Branxton. They left on a Friday night and, although the traffic heading away for the weekend was pretty hectic, for once the car didn't overheat and they soon found themselves on the Newcastle Expressway purring along, happy as Larry. Then, about fifty kilometres out of town and for no apparent reason, they lost their headlights and had to pull over and sleep the night on the side of the expressway.

At first light they set off again and made it to the Sollys' small vineyard by breakfast. Later that day they decided to explore the district and to visit some of the bigger wineries. On the outskirts of a tiny hamlet, named Broke, the Fiat 124 hit a gigantic hole in the bitumen at some speed and responded by breaking down in a terrible clatter of metal parts, which appeared to be separating from each other as the car wobbled and bounced to a halt, hissing steam and smoke. The suspension collapsed and the chassis mysteriously separated from the bodywork. In this metallic shearing of parts, the conrod spat through the side of the engine and blasted the distributor off, the engine fell through its mounting and split the engine block, broke the radiator and caused all manner of internal combustion damage. It was the end of the road for the Fiat. The marque 124 CC, a genetically imperfect member of a great Italian family, had finally dropped dead. Adam, who sang and played guitar rather well, composed a song about the Fiat 124. I don't recall all the lyrics, but one verse went:

> Damon, who was broke,
> had a car that broke,
> in a place called Broke.

On the Monday following the final demise of the Fiat 124, Damon lost his job without ever having made it beyond the status of tea boy. He'd been having too many bleeds and too many days when he simply couldn't make it into work. His severance and holiday pay came to eight hundred dollars, which covered the cost of towing the car back to Sydney, where he sold it for spare parts for another seven hundred dollars. I added the remaining thirteen hundred to make the final payment to Bob Glover, the true friend to the disabled.

The first disastrous step to owning a Dino Ferrari was thankfully over.

Damon had no car, no music, no job and no immediate prospects.

He had also started to get night sweats.

18

*Dripping and Steaming and the Return
of the Prodigal Tom.*

The new house in Talfourd Street, though clean and neat, had been renovated using cheap gyprock internal walls; through them every sound travelled, almost as though they were made of Japanese rice paper. Sam and her boyfriend, Paul, who was also a great friend of Damon's from his school days, were having a really sexy affair. They'd developed a ritual which caused their love-making to be particularly noisy. They'd blow raspberries on each other's bellies. It would begin with a great baritonal, "Prrrrrrrrrrhph!" from Paul, followed after a bit of giggling by a much lighter soprano "Prrrrrrrph!" from Sam. This sequence would continue, growing louder and louder, the giggles growing to gales of laughter until the "Prrrrrrrrphs" became simultaneous and really urgent, this was a sure sign that the serious stuff was about to

280

begin. "Oh, God, another night of raspberry love!" Damon would groan, pulling the blankets up over his head.

Paul Green, Sam's boyfriend, along with Bardy, Toby, Andrew and Christopher were Damon's closest friends and had been so since prep school. Paul was at Sydney College of the Arts studying to be a photographer; Sam, who had just completed her nursing degree at university, had decided she wanted no more medical experience in her life and Andrew now attended Sydney University. Celeste, of course, was still doing her Bachelor of Science in Architecture. Already she was showing a great deal of talent working in ceramics and would later win the university art prize for her final-year work.

So the little house was filled with laughter and lively discussion by a group of talented young people who all got on very well together. There was no Roger the Lodger among them, although Celeste admits to having been a bit of a pain insisting that the house be run along orderly lines and kept really clean. The period spent in Talfourd Street, Glebe, was a very happy time for Damon.

Damon had reluctantly come to the realisation that working full time in the city was not going to be possible and he started to make new plans. He'd caught the computer bug while working for the money people and now decided to start on his own business at home as a desktop publisher. This meant he could work the hours that suited him, or rather those when he wasn't laid up with a bleed.

Gareth Powell, a famous journalist and travel writer who, at that time, produced several of the world's airline magazines, is a friend of mine and an expert on desktop publishing. He generously agreed to help Damon to learn the business. I financed an Apple Mac and a LaserWriter which Celeste purchased at a special rate through the Students Co-op at Sydney University. These two machines, basically a word processor and a printer, were the essential hardware required. Gareth, though enormously busy, was always generous with his time and his mind. He helped Damon with software and instructed him in the initial expertise on the computer required for desktop publishing. He also allowed him to use his own considerable facilities when Damon's somewhat limited operation wasn't adequate for some over-ambitious task he'd undertaken with his usual aplomb.

Damon proved to be a quick learner, a surprisingly accurate typist and apparently clever with computers. He was soon in business for himself turning out letterheads and pamphlets for local businesses, thesis papers for students, brochures and sales training manuals for small companies, in fact, just about anything his limited resources, or those borrowed late at night or on Sundays from Gareth Powell, enabled him to do.

Quite soon he had a small income and with it, as always with Damon, came an inflated ambition. He would become a major publisher and build a stable of magazines and perhaps even publish books, starting with his own. He told me about Richard Branson, the British multi-millionaire, who'd started a magazine at school, at the age of seventeen, in which he'd offered for sale discount records which he'd persuaded a local record shop to supply. The record orders started to snowball and Branson started Virgin Records. By his mid twenties, Virgin Records was one of the world's big music producers. This was a story tailor-made for Damon's imagination. He was in desktop publishing, but his first love was music; in his mind he could clearly see the way to greatness, a repeat performance of the Richard Branson story — but with one small variation. Damon wouldn't be content to let his publishing empire simply pave the way to a musical one, his own book would be a brilliant novel based on his life and would be his very first serious venture into publishing. Naturally, it would be a best-seller and so become the launching pad for the rest of his mega-empire. As usual, Damon was away and running before he'd properly learned how to tie his publishing shoelaces.

The first thing though was to get himself and Celeste back on their feet after the disastrous affair of the Fiat 124 and so he had to depend on local merchants and friends to give him their printing work before he branched out on his own. Unfortunately, the local butcher, estate agent and whoever else he could persuade that they needed the odd stationery requirement or advertising leaflet paid very little. But it *was* a real contribution to the household expenses and Damon became most anxious for Celeste to give up her telephone work at Ratshit International. Celeste, who was more acutely aware of how impecunious their life was, hung on to her job, though she hated it. She promised that she'd give up when Damon got a big order and the cheque actually arrived.

The heat of late summer finally slipped into autumn, a time in Sydney when the days are bright and cool and the humidity disappears altogether. These halcyon autumnal days are God's special gift to Sydney people and they coincided with the first three months spent in the Glebe house. They were to prove to be the last time Damon would have to contend only with his haemophilia; the last time, in Damon's strictly limited definition of physical well being, when he would be well.

The house was filled with laughter and fun. They'd put on instant plays, argue late into the night about music and life and then drink flagon wine and play chess until the early hours. Chess had always been Damon's way of getting even with his more active friends. He was a very good player in a houseful of pretty good players, the best after Damon being Sam, who lusted after Damon's chess scalp and who was good enough to win an occasional game. This would make her even more determined to best him. Damon was a natural player and the others all started getting into chess books and really learning games in an effort to beat him. But for the most part they were beaten by a player who played by instinct and who had, over the years, developed a depth of concentration which would allow him to out-think them consistently on the chess board.

Damon's jobs always seemed to be small ones and Celeste was forced to keep her spare-time job. With the loss of Damon's city job, their combined income was severely reduced and his desktop publishing career was still in its capital-intensive stage when it required reams of paper and the software Gareth Powell wasn't able to supply. With the extra money Celeste earned doing research questionnaires over the phone they only just managed to stay afloat. The others were no better off and so mostly they made their own fun. This was helpful for Damon, who was less and less able to go out for extended periods; a trip, even to the movies, would generally bring on a knee bleed.

Celeste, determined to be Young Housekeeper of the Decade, was learning about food and they would go to the nearby fish markets on Saturday and shop carefully at the adjacent fruit and vegetable stalls, so that, although the food they ate was plain, it was fresh and good and there was always enough to eat in the house.

The weather turned cold and Damon came home to visit us and to load up with blankets and a doona. We were surprised to see how much weight he'd lost in the the month or so since he'd last visited. Always rather skinny, he seemed to have lost almost half a stone and I took him through to the bathroom to weigh him. He saw the concerned look on my face as he stepped off the scales. "It's probably because we don't eat much meat, Dad. We have fish a couple of times a week, but mostly vegetables. I'm fine, I really am. I'm not having nearly as many bleeds since I left work [a fib] and I'm really very healthy." Damon had lost seven pounds, though he seemed quite well and despite my urging that he try to put on a little weight he continued to insist that he was healthy as anything and feeling exceedingly well.

"Have you been doing your swimming, Damon?" Benita asked. Swimming was the only exercise Damon could undertake with some safety and Benita was constantly at him to use the heated pool at the Royal Prince Alfred Hospital. It was where the Haemophilia Centre was located and very close to where Damon and Celeste now lived.

Damon would wake chronically stiff in the mornings, but with the cold weather he would take even longer each day to become mobile and Benita knew he needed to swim to keep his joints as flexible as possible and to keep his arthritis under some sort of control.

Damon was becoming noticeably more lopsided, with less movement in his wrists and elbows and his old limp rather more pronounced. This was the limp caused by the calliper he was forced to wear as a small child and the accident in the swimming pool, but it had become exacerbated when he'd reached puberty and his bad knee and elbow had started to give him a lot of trouble. He was growing rapidly during that period and one or both joints seemed to bleed every day so that it began to look as though he might eventually lose all movement in both. There was nothing we could do until he came out of puberty and his rate of growth began to slow down. At sixteen, in order to retain some fifty per cent of the movement and flexibility in both badly damaged joints, he'd had his bad knee and bad elbow fused. This was supposed to minimise the effect of the constant bleeding into them. In particular, these fused joints needed to be exercised regularly.

When he'd been at home, Benita had become remorseless about his swimming every day. So much so, that he'd grown to hate the pool. The constant nagging from his mother (The hated question: "Have you done your swimming?") was about the only thing that would occasionally reduce Damon to tears. It was hard on Benita too. She had no choice but to go on at him and would sometimes demand that I back her up. I'd do so, but in a half-hearted way, knowing how it bugged Damon. Whereupon Benita would burst into tears, "It's always me! I'm always the bad guy! He's your son too. Why don't you help a bit?" Damon's swimming was a source of constant aggravation to us all so now, when he came home, he would faithfully promise his mother he'd make the daily trip over to the hospital indoor pool, but, of course, he never did. Exercise, any exercise, was extremely painful for him and once away from a mother of Benita's determination, no matter how ultimately necessary swimming might be, it was asking too much of him to comply with her wishes.

Not long into winter Sam started to win at chess. Damon appeared distracted and his famous concentration seemed to be misfiring. The games were still hard fought but Sam, to her delight, was beating him more than she was losing. It wasn't as though Damon was losing interest; he hated to lose, particularly at chess and especially to Sam. At chess he was an extremely bad loser. Chess was his "get even" in life and he was supposed to win.

Then one winter's night Celeste woke in the early hours. She was bitterly cold and to her astonishment the sheet she lay on and her entire body were soaking wet.

Celeste tells what happened:

"Damon seemed to have some sort of flu, which was pretty unusual for him. Although he had bleeds and his arthritis bothered him a lot, he never got ill in the conventional sense, not even a cold. But he'd gone to bed saying he felt ratshit and was aching more than usual and he sounded sort of fluey and quite sick. He'd also lost a game of chess to Sam, the third in four nights and he was pretty cranky. I don't know how late it was, but we both woke up more or less at the same time and, despite the cold, we were dripping wet. I switched on the light and took the top sheet off Damon; not only was the sheet wet, but he was steaming. I looked at him and he was dripping, he was soaked, absolutely soaked, the undersheet was soaked; the mattress was soaked, everything was soaked and I was soaked too; from having been lying next to him, yet steam was coming off his body. It was weird.

"We looked at one another, confused, neither of us had the foggiest what it meant, we really didn't! I asked him if he was feeling ill? 'No, not really, not great, just like last night,' he replied. I felt his head, he had a slight fever, though not much, certainly not enough to cause this sweating. We were both very confused.

" 'It's a reaction from *Factor VIII*,' Damon said at last, though a little hopefully, trying to comfort me. *Factor VIII* was the stuff he used to inject into his veins to stop his bleeds and occasionally he'd get a bad batch which would cause a reaction.

" 'Damon you didn't have a transfusion last night,' I reminded him. Besides, I'd seen him have a *Factor VIII* reaction, he would break out in a sort of bright red rash all over his body and run a bit of a temperature, but it only lasted about an hour and wasn't at all like what was happening now.

"We got up, and I changed the bed linen. Damon had a shower and afterwards the sweating seemed to have stopped a little, so we went back to bed. A couple of hours later the same thing happened, we were absolutely and totally soaked again. By this time he'd sweated so much he was dehydrating and he complained of being thirsty. I remember he drank four glasses of water straight off.

"We were totally confused, the sweats came only at night and about three nights a week, though it didn't occur to us to ask anyone about them. It sounds funny now, but we thought it had something to do with our respective body temperatures and this persistent flu Damon seemed unable to get rid of. I am someone who feels the cold a lot so I'd smother myself in blankets and also the doona, whereas Damon would need only one blanket throughout winter. We tried to convince ourselves that the heat generated by my side of the bed was bringing on his peculiar sweats.

"I know this sounds unconvincing and I suppose we were both scared and didn't want to face up to the possibility of it being something else, the something else being 'you know what'. So we grabbed the first explanation we could find without questioning it too closely. I'd place towels under him before we went to bed at night and these would be soaked; he'd wake up and remove the towels and by the time the sheets and mattress were wet it was usually morning. I used to use a hair dryer on the mattress every morning and then, if there was any sun in the backyard, I'd get Andrew to help me and we'd air it and dry it out.

"It was quite awful, his whole body would be dripping and steaming and almost as soon as daylight came the thing would go away. It was weird, even spooky, and so uncomfortable. In fact, the sweats were the beginning of Damon never being comfortable again. He'd wake up cold and clammy and wet from sweating and scared, not knowing what was wrong or what to expect or why it was happening. After a couple of weeks we were both scared, although it never occurred to me that these night sweats were the first real sign of AIDS.

"No, I'm fibbing, it wasn't quite like that, I simply wouldn't allow my mind to suggest AIDS to me. I think Damon knew the night sweats were the beginning, but he was also too scared to say so, hoping that by ignoring them they'd go away. The night sweats lasted a couple of months and then as suddenly as they'd started they stopped. Damon was doing a lot of meditation. Only that's not what he called it, he simply said it was self-hypnosis, mind over matter, and when the night sweats stopped he was convinced he'd made this happen, he'd beaten them with his mind power in the same way he'd controlled some of the worst pain from his bleeds for so many years. Maybe he did beat the night sweats. Though every now and again he'd get another one; but they were sporadic and he felt he had them under control.

"During this period of night sweats the bleeds started to get much worse. It was mostly his bad knee again, the one which had been fused, it would bleed almost every day and he was in a bad way, unable to walk, even on crutches.

"For some reason we hadn't told Sam about Damon's HIV status. I don't know why, perhaps because she was a graduate nurse and might know too much or have a funny predisposition to people with HIV. We didn't want to know too much ourselves, anyway. Sam just thought Damon was having his usual bleeds and, as he never complained, no matter how bad a bleed was or how much pain he was undergoing, she still rushed home at night to challenge him to a game of chess. He'd always oblige her, not wanting to seem churlish, but more and more he was losing. Naturally, Sam thought his state of dismay was due to her triumph. It used to make me mad, really angry, but Damon forbade me to tell her ever."

* * *

AIDS education clinics were being conducted by the nearby Prince Alfred Hospital which the Haemophilia Centre wanted their patients to attend. The people attending at the clinics were very carefully described as being HIV positive and not as having AIDS and Denise at the Haemophilia Centre finally persuaded Damon to attend. Denise had been the sister in charge of the Haemophilia Centre for most of Damon's teens and, while he had little or no time for the medicos, he trusted her implicitly. Denise had always been wonderful to him and we all loved her very dearly, Damon simply couldn't refuse when she begged him to go to one of the HIV lectures.

At the first lecture, during question time, Damon mentioned the night sweats. He explained that he'd beaten them but that he was curious to know whether they had anything to do with his HIV status?

The doctor who ran the clinic looked steadily at him then said, "Damon, night sweats are one of the first signs that your HIV status has moved into the next phase."

"AIDS?" Damon asked, his voice steady, but his heart was thumping furiously.

The young doctor didn't answer directly, merely nodding his head in the affirmative and tapping the end of his pen against the surface of the desk where he sat.

Damon was suddenly furious. "Why didn't you tell

me before? Why don't you people tell us what to expect? That way I wouldn't have been so confused and worried sick!"

"Damon, I'm truly sorry." The doctor wasn't a lot older than Damon and seemed genuinely upset, "You haven't attended these sessions before, have you?" Then he added, looking around him at the half-dozen people in the room, "But, it's true, I haven't mentioned them, the night sweats." He looked down at his hands. "We simply don't know what to do. We know there is no known cure for AIDS, so to tell you months, perhaps even a couple of years before the night sweats begin, what you should expect is ... well," he met Damon's gaze, "it's likely to cause more anxiety than not knowing. I'm sorry if this has been a wrong judgment in your case."

He had a point. The AIDS virus is so insidious, it makes itself known in dozens of clever disguises, hiding behind common ailments such as pneumonia, skin rashes, herpes, shingles, thrush, bowel infections, cancer and other nasty ailments. During its initial stages it's very easy to kid yourself that you've caught some sort of wog going around and that, with the right treatment, you'll soon be well again. AIDS is a little like flicking a dab of icing off a freshly baked cake with your forefinger; then, the next time you pass, another; then breaking off a small piece. And as time goes by, each time you pass the cake, you sample it until slowly it loses its original new baked-shape and starts to look a little battered. More dabs follow, larger pieces are removed and it soon becomes obvious to everyone that the cake is being systemati-cally tampered with. That's how the AIDS virus works, a little bit of destruction at a time, then bigger bits, then finally the whole system begins to break down.

This early part of Damon's AIDS coincided with another event, the return of Tom into his life.

Tom was yet another chapter of Damon's life at Cranbrook, though a rather sad one. He came from a broken home with a mother who seemed to have very little control over him and not much interest and a father, an international television correspondent, who spent most of his time on assignments overseas.

Tom was a lonely child who would often come home to our place in the afternoons after school, along with some of the brighter kids at Cranbrook, to play Dungeons and Dragons and War Games and Damon regarded him as a real friend. He'd often stay over for supper and stay late, as though reluctant to leave for his own home.

"Hadn't you better be off home now?" Benita would ask.

Tom would shrug, "My mum works late. Can I stay a little longer, Mrs Courtenay?"

"Only if you call home every half an hour."

Tom would call home and hold the receiver up for Benita to hear that it wasn't being lifted at the other end. When eventually it was answered, Tom's mother always seemed quite cheerful and unconcerned, quite willing to let him stay with us and come home when he wished to do so.

This wasn't Benita's way of doing things and she compensated by always making Tom feel welcome. He was rather pale and never ate very much and she would worry about him and try to build him up, probing for details about his home life and horrified at his admission that, for the most part, he fed himself from the fridge or was given money to eat at McDonald's or Pizza Hut or get Chinese take-away.

Benita is a lousy cook by almost any standards and by Jewish standards she is outstandingly awful. But for years I'd been going to the Flemington markets at daybreak on a Saturday morning and the house was always supplied with fresh fruit and salads and the very best cuts of meat.

The week-day meals for the our kids seldom varied from rump steak and a tossed salad with the meal ending with loads of fresh fruit. What this diet lacked in originality it made up for by being balanced, although their diet probably contained too much meat. Perhaps not, they were growing, they were surfers and they seemed to need a high protein intake.

Once a week Benita made a spaghetti bolognese which, by all the known standards of this ubiquitous Australian stand-by meal, was atrocious, but which, for some unexplained reason, Brett, Adam and Damon simply adored. They loved the hard, burnt lumps of mince doused in a carelessly sloshed-together sauce of tomato, onions and capsicum. They even seemed to prefer the thick strands of glued-together spaghetti which sprawled, limp and broken, beneath this horrible mess. Benita's secret was to throw everything into a large pan at the same time, put it on a low heat and ignore it until supper time several hours later. By the time the meal was ready to serve, a deep crust of burn had developed over the bottom of the pan. This was then scraped out and served on spaghetti boiled for half an hour or so in a splash of tap water. Quite why this was the favourite meal was impossible to say as it was patently uneatable, that is, except by my children who would eat it with glazed-eyed ecstasy, holding out their plates for more. On weekends I'd take over the cooking because I enjoyed cooking and it did have the additional advantage of bringing a little variety into the family cuisine, though nothing I made, no matter how exotic, every earned the accolades reserved for Benita's all-time-rotten *spaghetti bolognese de la maison.*

Tom would often visit Damon after school when he was at home with a bleed and they became very good friends. We all liked him, he was always rather pale and very shy, but a nice boy with good manners and, quite frankly, we felt sorry and a little responsible for him.

Tom felt about motorbikes the way Damon felt about a Ferrari and, sometimes, on weekends he'd arrive wearing a black leather bikie jacket. I know Damon secretly cherished the idea of a jacket but couldn't admit to doing so, because Ferrari drivers didn't wear jackets with a silver skull and crossbones painted on the back.

One afternoon Damon arrived home from Cranbrook clearly distraught, he'd been away from school for a couple of days and, during this time, Tom and Jason, the son of a well-known Sydney academic, had broken into the computer room at Cranbrook and stolen four Apple Macintosh computers. The two boys had been seen and later identified by one of the gardeners and Mark Bishop, the headmaster, had instigated an inquiry at which both boys were to be represented by their parents. Tom and Jason were expelled from Cranbrook. Later Mark Bishop, the headmaster, told us that Damon had come to see him before the hearing and had admitted to knowing of the plot.

"I asked him if he'd actually involved himself," Mark Bishop said to me.

"No sir, I had a bleed that day," Damon replied.

"Well, would you have been with them if you hadn't had a bleed, Damon?" the headmaster then asked him.

"I don't know. Probably sir." Damon said, then added, "When you've got friends you have to stick by them."

Jason, a very clever boy, was accepted by another school and the incident faded into his childhood. But Tom never went back to school and started to hang around Kings Cross. Soon he was smoking pot and doing a fair bit of posing as a tough kid. Occasionally, he'd arrive late at night and tap on Damon's window and, unbeknownst to us, Damon would let him into his room to sleep on the carpet.

Now, almost four years later, Tom was back. He simply arrived at the house in Talfourd Street one afternoon on a Yamaha 750cc to visit, having traced Damon's whereabouts through a mutual friend. Soon Tom became a regular visitor to Talfourd Street and seemed to like being with them, saying very little but quietly enjoying the rowdy house. He also found Damon some hi-fi gear at a remarkably low cost through a contact he had in the Cross. The gear was obviously hot but Damon was much too anxious to have music back in his life to ask too many questions.

That first time Tom visited, Celeste was very quiet all afternoon and during the evening when he stayed for dinner. Later, after he'd gone and she was sitting with Damon as he lay on their bed, Damon asked her what she thought of Tom.

"He's okay," she said, dismissing the question with a shrug.

Damon then told her the story of Tom's expulsion from

Cranbrook. "You don't like him, do you, babe?"

Celeste, who has great difficulty hiding her feelings, frowned. "No, it's not that; it's not even his expulsion from Cranbrook, my sister was expelled from Sydney High, anyone can be!" She screwed up her pretty face in a quick grimace. "It's . . . well, I know his type. He's like Davo, he's from the Cross." She looked up at Damon, "I'll bet he doesn't work at a gear shop like he said." Then she added, "He ate nothing at dinner except a mouthful of pumpkin."

"He never ate much when he used to come home." Damon looked up at Celeste, "Tom wouldn't lie, I know that for sure. You know what he once did? When Mark Bishop, the headmaster at Cranbrook, asked him during the inquiry over the stolen computers whether I'd been an accomplice, or would have been had I not had a bleed? You know what he said? He said, 'Damon would never have agreed to do it. That's why we did it on a day when he had a bleed.'" Damon looked up at Celeste, "Why would he lie now?"

Celeste smiled, "You're probably right. It's me, I think I'm a bit drunk . . . I've had too much of that white wine Tom brought."

Tom would sometimes be away for weeks then suddenly emerge without an explanation and they soon gave up questioning him. He'd sold his motorbike and would arrive by taxi, often in the early hours of the morning, unannounced. He'd simply work one of the windows open and be asleep on the battered old lounge when someone happened to walk into the living room. Once he broke a window to get in and Damon told him he'd have to stop coming. Tom fished into the inside of his leather jacket and produced a hundred dollars which he threw on the lounge. "Fix the bloody window," he said and walked out.

Damon felt guilty for days. In all the years he'd known Tom I'd never even heard Damon raise his voice to him. Although Tom was hyperactive and just naturally jumpy, with Damon he was always calm. Now Damon knew he'd hurt him terribly. So when Tom arrived back a couple of weeks later Damon was quite glad to see him. It was during the day when he was alone at home. Nothing was said about the window and Tom seemed his old self. It was Celeste's birthday in two days' time, on the Friday, and they were going to have a surprise party for her. Damon hadn't told Celeste about Tom's hundred bucks. He'd simply paid for a pane of glass and some putty from the local hardware shop and Andrew had fixed the broken window. The remainder of the money he'd kept to fund the grand surprise party. An invitation to the party seemed a natural way to square things between the two friends and Tom promised to come.

On the morning of Celeste's birthday Damon woke feeling rotten, his knee was playing up again and he gave himself an early transfusion in the hope that he'd be okay by nightfall. Sam, Paul and Andrew were given shopping lists for food and grog which they could get on their way home from tech and uni and Damon had given them all that remained of Tom's money to buy the party stuff.

Celeste recalls going off to uni worried about Damon who seemed more distressed than usual and had almost forgotten to wish her happy birthday. Increasingly these days he seemed unwell, not his bleeds, which she was used to, but he simply felt unwell ("ratshit") and sometimes he seemed incapable of facing the day, as though a dreadful malaise had set in. He never complained and fought hard to overcome his feelings in front of her seldom giving in, but often, by the time she returned at night from university, he'd be drained and exhausted. He was much less the old cheerful Damon she loved and sometimes she felt she couldn't breathe with the anxiety she felt for him. It was as though her heart was being squeezed by a hand, not tightly, just sufficiently for her to feel that something was terribly wrong and slowly getting worse. Something over which neither of them had any control.

Damon had planned a special present for Celeste. It was a small, original ink drawing of two zebras, which rather cleverly appeared to share the same head, rather whimsical though splendidly and authentically drawn; a well-known artist friend of mine had given it to him as a child. It was a piece he dearly loved and it had always taken pride of place above his bed at home. Celeste had admired it greatly and it had travelled with them, always resuming the same spot over their bed. Somewhere along the line a bit of damp had crept into the cheap frame, warped the paper and slightly discoloured a part of the picture. Celeste wanted the painting re-framed properly but they never seemed to have the money. Now Damon had persuaded a local framer to take the painting in on the day of Celeste's birthday and while she was at uni to re-frame it so that he could give it to her when she returned. As payment, he had printed five hundred invitations to an upcoming art show to be held at the framer's premises.

Damon had somehow to get to the framer, which was about a kilometre away and rather further than he could comfortably walk on crutches with his bad knee. Damon's legs were getting worse and even on a good day a walk as far as this would be likely to bring on a bleed. But he'd given Sam all Tom's money to buy things and he hadn't any left to take a taxi. He spent the morning gathering his strength, cleaning the house as best he could and hoping the bleed in his knee would improve and that, generally speaking, he'd start feeling a bit better, but by early afternoon he could leave it no longer. It took him almost two hours to cover the kilometre or so to the framers and back and he was exhausted when he returned home.

In the meantime Sam and Paul had returned with the food and grog for the party and were busy getting things ready. Damon tried to help but they could plainly see that he wasn't well and both insisted he go and rest, Paul promising he'd get him up well before Celeste was due back.

Damon was exhausted and, despite the pain and his feeling awfully unwell, he fell asleep. He awoke in the dark with someone shaking him gently. He was groggy and felt ghastly and his knee hurt enormously.

"That you, Paul?" he asked.

"No, it's Tom. Paul sent me to wake you, the guests have all arrived and Celeste will be here soon."

"Thanks, Tom, will you switch on the light, please."

Tom switched on the light and Damon tried to rise from the bed but he was too stiff and sore. Tom hadn't seen him quite like this before. "What's wrong?" he asked, alarmed, "You look terrible."

"It's nothing, just a bleed in my knee and I'm stiff. Give me a hand, will you?" Tom helped Damon sit on the bed. "Can you get my crutches please, mate?"

Tom handed Damon the crutches which lay across the end of the bed and Damon rose unsteadily to his feet. "You'll have to help me a bit, just hang on to my arm until we get to the living room." Damon took a couple of steps forward than stopped, "Shit!" he groaned, then turned and took the two steps back to the bed and sat down heavily. He was panting slightly. "You go ahead, Tom, I'll be okay in a moment, I just need to get up a bit of strength."

Tom was clearly distressed, Damon had broken out in a sweat. "What's the matter? Are you okay? Can I do something. Do you need an aspirin?" he asked.

Damon grinned through his pain, it was more a grimace really. Then he gave a short laugh. "Aspirin makes my stomach-lining bleed. I've got some other stuff for pain, but I've run out."

"What is it?"

"Well, Endone. I should have gone to the hospital dispensary for more but I forgot."

"I'll be back," Tom said.

"You can't get them from a chemist, they're prescription only."

Tom laughed. "There's nothing I can't get," then he was gone.

He returned less than half an hour later. Celeste, later than she normally was, had not yet arrived. Tom went up to Damon's room and gave him the pain-killers. Then he fished into the pocket of his leather jacket and brought out a twist of silver paper, undid the tiny parcel very carefully and picked out two tiny pills. "Here, try these," he held the pills out to Damon.

"What are they?" Damon asked.

"Uppers! Amphetamines. I bought them from the guy who sold me the Endone, they're much better than grog. You'll have a good time."

Damon didn't think twice, Celeste would soon be home and he was feeling like death warmed up; the Endone would kill the pain, but he didn't feel like a party any more. Maybe Tom's pills would help cheer him up?

Tom returned with a glass of water and Damon took the two tiny pills, one purple, the other white. "It takes about fifteen minutes for them to work if they're going to. That's a good combo," Tom said.

It was almost eight-thirty when Celeste arrived and Damon met her at the door. He was smiling and seemed to be in a terrific mood. "Happy Birthday, babe!" he shouted in an exaggeratedly loud voice, not a bit like Damon's usual quiet though happy greeting. Celeste immediately suspected something, but before she could open her mouth, people popped up from everywhere and someone started to sing, "Happy Birthday to You . . . Happy Birthday to You!" Soon the room was filled with everyone taking up the song which was followed by three cheers and lots of laughter and the party was instantly under way.

Late, very late, in fact very early on Saturday morning, Damon and Celeste were finally alone in their bedroom. He gave her his present. Celeste was a bit smashed and very happy, it had been a great party and Damon had been wonderful all night. She unwrapped the parcel and when she saw the elegant new frame around the zebras she looked up at him; her mouth quivered and she fought to control her tears.

"It's yours now, babe. Not ours, *yours!* I'm giving it to you to keep for yourself, forever! Nobody can take it away from you, not even your mother!" Damon's eyes were shining and he was grinning like a chimpanzee.

Celeste fell into his arms sobbing. "I love you so much, so very much. Please don't ever leave me, Damon."

"I won't, babe. I promise. I'm going to live forever. We'll always be together. You'll see."

19

Teeth, T-cells, Squatting on a Building Site and a
Job at Dinky Di Pies.

Because of his arthritis, which got progressively worse
and caused more and more pain, Damon would have
great difficulty getting up in the morning and to compensate, he would stay up very late, working when the rest
of the house was asleep. Tom got to know this and took
to calling around well after midnight. By now it was
apparent that he was pretty well into everything, not
just the usual recreational pills, but massive doses of
codeine and Valium, in fact anything he could lay his
hands on.

He'd arrive totally zonked, staring glassy-eyed at
everything, his speech patterns making little sense and
after each flurry of words would come a high-pitched
nervous titter. Damon would switch on the television
and Tom would spend the night in front of it, the shim-

mering screen complementing the psychedelic storm happening in his confused head. Damon worked on, knowing his friend was safe as long as he stayed with him. Sometimes though, Tom would be okay and he'd bring over a joint and the two of them would sit quietly and smoke. I'd like to think that Damon's use of marijuana stems from this time when it would have been useful to him as a pain-killer, which was how it was later privately recommended to him by a caring medico.

"Dope", as it is commonly called, has the ability, not only of dulling pain, but seemingly also, of removing the body from the mind, so that awareness of one's physical self is greatly diminished. A great many people with AIDS have turned to it for some relief from their tormented physical presence, allowing themselves to drift into the cocoon-like euphoria which it seems to induce.

But I would be lying if I claimed that marijuana, or pot or dope or smoking a joint, was something Damon discovered after he was beginning to suffer from the effects of AIDS. After Tom was expelled from Cranbrook and started to hang around Kings Cross in a serious way, he'd occasionally knock on Damon's window late at night to be let in, and that was when he'd first introduced him to marijuana. Damon discovered how very effective it was for him as a pain-killer. He'd continued to use it during bad bleeds whenever he was able to get hold of it. I must be honest and say that it seems unlikely that he would simply have used pot in this way. Celeste testifies to the fact that they would smoke if it was offered casually, but even though marijuana wasn't very expensive by drug standards, it was usually well beyond their budget.

Tom was always welcomed at Talfourd Street even though they all knew he was a junkie. He never created a fuss and Damon was the sort of person who was pretty loyal to his friends. Tom was simply Tom, hyperactive, somewhat bent, hooked on pills, pale, often silent, but he was still Tom — harmless enough and in need of friends. He had a habit, which is not uncommon in some young Australian women, of ending every sentence with an interrogative inflection denoting doubt, as though expecting an immediate put-down after everything he said. It isn't a common characteristic in Australian men, but it was in Tom and it used to drive Damon insane. "Tom, you have my permission to have an opinion. Stop ending every sentence with a bloody invisible query!" But Tom couldn't help himself, he was lost even among his only friends, though the kids in Talfourd Street were much too nice and certainly too cool to want to judge him. Though Damon might smoke a joint if he could afford one or when he had a bad bleed, he would only take a pill when he faced a big social occasion such as a party.

Even writing this I feel the concern which drugs conjure up for many of my generation. I am quite aware of the double standard this indicates, I thought nothing of smoking five packs of cigarettes on a long day and consuming anything up to a dozen beers and probably a bottle of wine. I have, often enough in the past, arrived home sufficiently inebriated to cause distress to my family. Yet I was regarded as a social drinker, and wasn't thought to have the slightest problem with alcohol. I simply behaved like all upwardly mobile, young Australian executives of my generation. Provided I didn't beat my wife or abuse my kids, I was simply exercising my male rights and letting off a little steam after a hard day's work. The idea of being judged a drug addict or alcoholic never entered my mind or anyone else's.

I still grow slightly cold as Celeste points out in her matter-of-fact voice that pills were cheaper than grog, that one had a better time on them at a party and didn't suffer a hangover the next morning. She points out that "Ecstasy" (the "designer" drug) is so common at parties that it is almost unthinkable not to use to have a *really* good time. "I can feel a glass of wine inside me," she said, "two glasses and I can feel it in my head, it doesn't feel safe. Drugs, not all drugs, but some, are clean, you don't feel them harming you like grog." This is a new generation, with new habits; for around the cost of a six-pack of Foster's you can buy a tiny purple tablet that will keep you happy all night and leave you with a clear head in the morning.

Even so, Celeste has since changed her mind about drugs. "We didn't realise at the time that speed was addictive and, thank God, it never became so for us. But it's a bad drug, like heroin, if you get hooked. Now I realise that drugs are wrong, not only because of what they can do to you physically, but also because they're an illusion. Acid can be a big trap. It makes you think you're something you're not. You see colours in the sunset and you think, 'Wow! This is great!' and that's a good trip. But the colours are all there if you learn to look for them, you don't need acid, you just need to be sensitive to what's around you. Then you can take acid and have a bad trip, a very bad experience, when you sense how much everything is decaying around you, you have an acute sense of death and you're part of that decay. You get sucked into this line of thought and you can't get away from it. It lasts for hours and hours and it's quite horrible. When we had both had a bad trip, we stopped. But of course at that time we didn't see that drugs could be bad, they seemed so clean, so harmless, so anti our parents."

And so I have had to come to accept that Damon was using drugs on occasion. Damon, who would end his life with a daily cocktail of palliative drugs that would make a pusher think he'd passed out and woken in a drug-induced fantasy land, had found that chemical substances helped alleviate the pain and let him have a good time at a party. He smoked marijuana and on occasions he took pills. Or as Celeste would put it, perhaps kindly for my sake, "I've got to say this, Bryce. I think there has to be a huge generation gap here. Drugs in my generation, they're just like, well, for most people, they're just a part of life."

But Tom couldn't stop there, he was well past the recreational or curiosity stage and he was beginning to look more and more woebegone. He wouldn't eat at all, his face looked increasingly gaunt and the haunted look in his eyes was becoming more obvious. They'd dart about, going from one face to another, bright pinpoints, like a small arboreal animal looking, but not seeing, his whole body tense as a drawn bow.

Damon came upon Tom upstairs one evening using one of his transfusion syringes to give himself a fix. "Christ, Tom! How long have you being doing this?"

Tom, unabashed, continued to push the plunger home, then, as he felt the "rush" in his bloodstream, he looked up at Damon and grinned. "Want some?"

Damon shook his head, clearly very upset. "Tom, how long?"

Tom put the syringe down and released the tourniquet from his upper arm; now his hands hung loose at his side and he gave his hips and shoulders a little jiggle and his hands flapped at the wrists, as though he were trying to shake an invisible garment from his thin body. When he spoke his voice was casual. "Two years. I thought you knew . . ."

"Pills are one thing, mate. But this is heavy shit! You could die!"

Tom looked at Damon steadily, then shrugged, "That makes two of us."

Sudden tears welled up in Damon's eyes. Even to himself he'd never admitted the possibility of dying. When the terminal aspect of AIDS was mentioned at the one time he'd attended the HIV clinic he'd comforted himself with the thought that he'd be the one exception, The Mighty Damon.

The Mighty Damon was the name I'd given him as a small child to boost his sometimes frail ego and it had persisted for so long that it was now a part of his psyche. The spectre of approaching death, coming like this from Tom, snuck under his guard and hit home hard. For a moment he saw it all clearly, the Mighty Damon was going to die.

"I didn't create my situation," Damon said in a voice hardly above a whisper.

Tom shrugged. "What the fuck, life sucks anyway!"

It was almost as though now that his heroin addiction was in the open Tom felt that he'd been reclassified in

the eyes of his friend. That he was alienated, that something had snapped between them, a childhood trust
grown too brittle perhaps? A trust that had previously
included the milder addictions, but now had been splin-
tered by the greater demands of his heroin habit.

Though Damon told no one of Tom's heroin addiction,
not even Celeste, it became evident that Tom believed
that he had. In his paranoid state it was clear to him they
now all saw him differently at Talfourd Street. Things
started to go missing, half Damon's record collection
went first, a few days later it was the VCR, then Celeste's
camera and finally some money. All these robberies took
place over a period of two weeks. Nobody suspected
Tom, who still called around regularly. They speculated
that it was someone, probably a drug addict, who'd
found a key and so Paul changed the locks. When the
robberies continued they finally became suspicious and
confronted Tom, who protested, then seemed to lose his
temper and finally stormed out. The robberies promptly
stopped.

Damon was deeply hurt. Tom may have been a bad
guy, but that's not how he'd ever seen him. Tom had
been his friend for years, often sitting up with him all
night when he'd had a bad bleed. He felt sure that he
could have helped him and that, regardless, he should
stand by him. But Celeste was firm and put Damon
straight in no uncertain way. "Don't waste your time,
Damon. I know what we're dealing with here. When you
discovered Tom was on smack it was all over. You are
no longer his friend, you are now his victim. If you have
him back he'll only steal from us again."

Behind Celeste's gentleness there was also a realist,

this was a part of her past. With Davo she'd seen addicts before, he was one himself and she would later tell me how pleased she was that Tom had gone out of Damon's life.

Life went on, each day not a great deal different. Damon was becoming less and less mobile, less and less inclined to be with people. The house at Talfourd Street was too full of life, there was too much energy generated between its walls. Damon who believed so very much in his will to win through found it harder and harder to act as though nothing was wrong with him that hadn't always been wrong. He still firmly believed that his HIV status hadn't deteriorated, that it was the haemophilia and the constant bleeding into his bad knee that was creating the extra burden. For years he'd been told to expect the onset of arthritis and he knew it would get progressively worse. Publicly, he put his malaise down to this. Privately, who knows what he thought? But Damon wasn't going to give up easily, he wasn't that sort of person and he wasn't going to spell out his deeper anxiety to anyone, not even his beloved Celeste.

At that time, AIDS doctors were still allowing that not all HIV positive people would develop further. The statistics Damon would quote, repeated from his doctor, were that of each hundred people who tested HIV positive eighty would go on to stage two, but only forty-eight per cent of these would move on to the third stage and develop full-blown AIDS. I'm not sure whether this is still the case. These figures were seductive, it wasn't too hard to convince yourself that you would be one of the exceptions. Damon, with his positive attitude saw himself as a prime candidate for exclusion from the dead and the damned. He'd spent his life in the business of beating the odds and he felt certain that he would be a natural not to proceed on to stage two of his HIV infection.

He was having some trouble with his wisdom teeth, which had grown too big, causing them to become impacted. Impacted wisdom teeth were potentially very painful and our family dentist suggested they be removed. The problem was simple enough, too many teeth were trying to fit into the same mouth, but, in Damon's case, it wasn't quite as easy as this. He went to see the dental surgeon at the Haemophilia Centre who agreed that they would need to operate at some time. Just "when" was the immediate dilemma; ideally, the operation should take place over several months, one impacted tooth coming out at a time.

Tooth extraction, particularly a wisdom tooth, is a bleeding opportunity which is problematic with haemophiliacs. The tearing of the roots from the gum sets up a certain and deep bleed which is very difficult to stop. It becomes a question of "how bad?" Damon's potential to bleed was such that this single tooth extraction could, if an emergency were to occur, require the entire month's supply of blood from the state Blood Bank. This was an almost impossible request and it might be months before the Haemophilia Centre could actually "save" enough blood for the operation. This they would do by collecting as much extra blood as they could by over-ordering from the Blood Bank and asking for any excess which might occur. To collect sufficient blood product for four separate extractions over a period short of two years was simply not practical. Quite why this was so we were never told. Blood product does not noticeably deteriorate, there isn't a "use by" date specified. Damon's impacted wisdom teeth were not urgently required to come out. Benita and I queried the wisdom of an operation before it was strictly necessary.

Of course, there wasn't any precaution we could have taken against impacted wisdom teeth. But we were apprehensive about removing them before it was absolutely necessary, especially as the surgeon, in conjunction with Damon's own doctor, the haematologist at the Haemophilia Centre, had finally come to the conclusion that removing all four teeth at the same time would not require greatly more emergency blood than would a single tooth.

I recall questioning Damon's doctor about this. "Why do something now which isn't entirely necessary, doctor? Isn't it rather a big operation, four teeth at once?"

Damon's doctor, a haematologist and one of a series who'd been at the Haemophilia Centre but was fairly new to us, was a slightly built man with a nervous manner, which didn't inspire confidence. He'd always seemed awkward with me, although perhaps he was with everyone. To cover his nerves he was very precise, almost didactic, so that he appeared to be giving a series of instructions.

"Mr Courtenay, I'm going to do it now while Damon is still quite strong." He was tapping the point of his biro on the desk pad in front of him making a precise circle of tiny dots. I thought it curious that the desk pad should be fitted with blotting paper in this day and age and that he seemed to use a ballpoint pen for the purpose of tapping only, for he carried an expensive fountain pen clipped to the breast pocket of his white coat. He stopped tapping the biro and glanced up at me. "You do understand what I mean, don't you?"

"No, I'm not sure I do."

"Well, in two years' time, Damon may not be strong enough to have the operation."

"I see." It was all I could think to say.

"His T-cells are normal at the moment, well . . . almost normal. This may not be the case further down the line."

"T-cells?" I hadn't heard the term before.

He made no attempt to explain. "We want to operate while Damon's T-cell count is normal." His glance fell from mine back to the desk blotter and he started to stab at it with the ballpoint again.

What I hated most about him was his assumption that Damon's HIV status would inevitably change. "It may remain normal, doctor? I mean this T-cell thing, it could remain the same as it is? His HIV positive status may not advance."

Damon's doctor looked up at me again. "And *it* may and *they* may not?" He gave me a tiny grin, like someone who'd just made a clever chess move. "Do you really want to take that chance?"

There was very little more to say. At the Haemophilia Centre at Prince Alfred they began to hoard blood. Damon was convinced that he could contain the bleeding the surgeon feared with hypnosis. He argued that the spontaneous nature of his internal bleeds was not the same thing as a bleed sustained deliberately.

"I can't anticipate an internal bleed, I mean I can't prepare for it, it just happens out of the blue," he explained to the surgeon. "But this will be different, I can go into deep hypnosis if you'll simply give me a local anaesthetic and I'll control the bleeding while I'm under hypnosis."

The doctor wouldn't hear of it. "This is a huge operation, Damon. You're going to need a general anaesthetic. I wouldn't be prepared to operate otherwise. We're only going to get one crack at getting them out."

Damon had long since lost his respect for the medical profession and he persisted, despite what seemed like an intelligent prognosis from the surgeon. He'd read a great deal about the technique of medical hypnosis and was certain he could accomplish it. The surgeon, quite understandably, was not prepared to take his word for it. He wanted sufficient blood to cope with a massive bleed, should it occur, and he refused to give his blessing for Damon to attempt to use hypnosis. It was a stalemate and Damon wanted me to back him up and to insist that the surgeon allow him to proceed with hypnosis.

Naturally we were all terribly concerned, that is, all of us except Celeste. I found myself in an invidious position. I'd taught Damon how to control his pain through hypnosis as a small child and he'd developed great skill and confidence in his ability. My encouragement in the past meant that he now quite naturally expected my support against the wishes of the surgeon.

Benita, Brett and Adam were, of course, violently against hypnosis. Adam, ever the pragmatist, the man who dealt with facts, rushed for the text books in an attempt to prove how foolish the idea was. Despite some pretty convincing case histories, he remained far from convinced that his little brother had mastered hypnosis to the extent that it could inhibit his blood flow. In fact there was sufficient contrary evidence to leave him pretty sceptical about the possibility of hypnosis ever being able to achieve the task of inhibiting blood flow in severe situations, such as Damon might experience.

But Damon was adamant and he wouldn't budge. We comforted ourselves privately that there was quite a lot of time needed to collect sufficient blood and that, as the day of the operation drew closer, he would change his mind.

We should have known otherwise. I think in the end it became very important to Damon that the surgery take place under self-hypnosis. It was a kind of a test. If he pulled it off then he was in charge of his destiny, not only of his bleeding, but of *the other thing* as well. The *other thing* that wasn't going to happen to him because he had the inner strength, the power to put himself on the positive side of the HIV statistics.

In the meantime, the stay in Talfourd Street came to an end. In preparation for third year architecture Celeste wanted to go on a study tour to Italy. At first this seemed impossible as they were stony broke, but Damon badly wanted her to do it.

Benita and I were rebuilding our home in Vaucluse and living in a very pleasant, though quite modest apartment in nearby Rose Bay. The apartment had two very small extra bedrooms which contained, stacked from floor to ceiling, all the extra stuff from our old home. I was using one tiny corner of one of them to write my first book, a space no more than four or five feet square, walled in to a height of six feet by cardboard packing cases. We offered to put some stuff into storage to allow Celeste and Damon to live with us, but Damon refused.

I didn't blame him, it probably wouldn't have worked very well; they were used to their independence and personal freedom and returning to anxious and somewhat neurotic parents wasn't the world's best idea.

Neurotic may seem a strange word to use about oneself, but while I had my work during the day and the prospect of writing a book to keep me occupied in my spare time, Benita had the daily job of supervising the construction of our new home. This task was bringing Benita closer to a nervous breakdown every day. We were fighting constantly as things went from bad to worse. The house was costing nearly twice as much as we'd borrowed and the bank was asking difficult questions and wanting guarantees we couldn't give them. It was beginning to look as though we'd be forced to sell our family home when it was finally completed just to pay the bank the extra money we owed for its construction! The builder had gone bust and, besides, had proved himself incompetent and we'd been obliged to fire him and subcontract the remaining work to be done. Every day we'd be faced with subcontractors who'd not been paid by the deposed builder, even though we'd already paid him for the job they'd done. As I was away at work, Benita had the impossible job of trying to cope with a world falling apart around us. Every day brought more threats from irate tradesmen and she was emotionally and physically exhausted.

Somehow, with the somewhat dubious help of our architect, we'd reached a lock-up stage, the taps carried running hot and cold water and the showers worked. Damon suggested that they squat on the building site, that is, move in and act as caretakers. In this way, he explained they would prevent any pilfering. Celeste could get a job during the long university vacation which commenced in November and, without rent to pay, she would be able to save up her airfare and the expenses required for her trip which she'd planned for late January.

Benita got Celeste a job at the Dinky Di Pies in Rose Bay North. The shop opened at 7.30 a.m. and closed at 6 p.m. and paid eight dollars an hour; Celeste offered to work through her lunch hour to gain the extra eight dollars a day, an extra fifty-six dollars a week was not to be sneezed at. The work was hard, for she not only served behind the counter but carried heavy trays of cakes all day, worked at the ovens, made salads and helped with the constant job of cleaning up and preparing several smaller bakes which took place during the day.

The customers liked Celeste, and Xavier, the temperamental French pastry-cook-owner, who was notorious for his short temper and the even shorter tenures of his hired help, liked her too. Soon he raised her salary to ten dollars an hour and Celeste was in clover. Cathy and Jenny, Xavier's wife and sister-in-law, were very kind to Celeste and ensured that she always ate at the shop and took food home, so that with no rent and most of their food supplied Celeste was able to save furiously.

Damon's desktop publishing business was chugging, rather than roaring, along but he earned sufficient for their very small housekeeping needs. By mid January, Celeste had her return plane ticket to Rome and enough to live on for eight weeks if she was very careful. Which wouldn't be too hard, Celeste was an expert at being very careful with money.

Damon went into hospital just before Celeste was due to leave for Italy. The Haemophilia Centre at Prince Alfred called to say that they had collected sufficient blood and that the operation should take place immediately as both the theatre and the surgeon were available. The business of hypnosis was never really resolved. The hospital flatly refused to do the operation without a general anaesthetic and I eventually persuaded Damon that he must capitulate. We had already discussed the problem when the deadline was presented to us. Damon was pretty upset, he felt that once again the medical profession had ignored his wishes and had gone ahead in their usual high-handed manner.

For my part, though, I was filled with anxiety. I knew that what he wanted to attempt with hypnosis was possible; moreover, that the reason he wanted to do it this way was deeply important to how he would regard himself in the future. I felt like a hypocrite because, at the same time, I secretly agreed with the surgeon; his warning of the potential for massive post-operative trauma had hit home with me. The idea that Damon might expose himself foolishly to unnecessary pain and further suffering I found almost unbearable. In desperation I hit on a ploy.

"Damon, listen! Whether you have a general anaesthetic or a local one doesn't prevent you from controlling the bleeding by hypnosis."

"What do you mean?"

"Well, all you have to do is go into the operation in a state of hypnosis, go into the anaesthetic that way."

Damon looked doubtful. "I've never heard of anyone doing that, Dad. The idea is that you're always in a wakeful state, conscious of what's happening around you, able to control things."

"Hypnosis can hardly be called a waking state, can it?" I lied, "I mean, it's a different radio frequency, your brain is on a different frequency from plain ordinary wakefulness."

"Dad, that's bullshit, you know that! You're quite conscious of noise and what's going on around you in hypnosis. The same is not true of whatever brain frequency you're on when you're under anaesthetic. How can you control what you're unaware of?"

It was a good point, but I pressed on regardless. "Damon, you trust your mind, don't you? If your last conscious decision in hypnosis is to control your bleeding and the mind," I paused, searching for a word, "*blanks* out under anaesthetic, why wouldn't it retain this last conscious thought? Why wouldn't that work?" I looked at him appealing to him to accept my doubtful logic, "Surely it's worth trying?"

Damon looked at me, I could see he was totally unconvinced but, like me, he was grasping at straws. "Okay, I'll give it a go. It's a crazy idea, but I have no choice, do I?" He looked up and gave me a grin. "Thanks, Dad, for trying at least. About the brain retaining the last thought before you go under, that's a dead-set dad fact." Damon went into the operating theatre and just prior to receiving the anaesthetic he put himself into a deep trance, concentrating on preventing his bleeding excessively from the extractions-to-come.

He had, of course, received a fairly massive pre-operative transfusion of *Factor VIII*, designed as a first line of defence, should he begin to bleed profusely during and immediately after the operation. This transfusion would allow sufficient time for an even more massive transfusion of whole blood to be mounted should it be required.

Whether it was luck or hypnosis, Damon bled hardly at all; in fact, no more than might be expected in any normal dental operation when four large back teeth are removed. The surgeon professed himself amazed, but when I told him later that Damon was under hypnosis when he received the general anaesthetic, he was unimpressed.

"Just one of those circumstances, I dare say; for some reason he didn't bleed. We were lucky."

"Wouldn't you say it's rather strange that this 'luck' is the only such circumstance, the singular circumstance, in Damon's entire medical history, doctor?"

The surgeon looked at me and shrugged. "Have it your way, Mr Courtenay, I'm a doctor, not a witchdoctor. Your son didn't bleed, I'm grateful for that."

The important thing was that Damon believed that he'd controlled the bleeding, that his mind power had been effective and that he was still in control of his HIV destiny. We were to learn how these small signs were of the utmost importance to his, and our own, psychological welfare. We became experts at clutching at the thinnest of straws. A little further down the track, any sign, omen, nonsensical superstition, chance remark, was sufficient to lift our hearts and give us hope.

I recall an occasion when Ann Williams, the artist friend who had given Damon the pen and ink sketch of the two zebra, had visited and Damon had come over.

Ann was gentle and lovely and also deeply into Buddhism and psychic healing. She had watched him walking towards her and remarked that Damon had a wonderful aura about him, that it flared hugely about his person and was the colour of a great healing. Both Damon and I were pretty cynical about that sort of thing and I could see he was barely able to conceal his mirth. He loved Ann too much to offer a rebuttal and instead thanked her politely. The following day he asked me rather shyly, "Dad, do you think there is anything in the stuff Ann believes in?"

"You mean about you having an aura around you the colour of healing?"

"Well, yes, all that Buddhist stuff."

I thought for a moment. "I'm from Africa, I believe in everything nobody else believes in and disbelieve just about everything most people claim to be God's truth." It was a nonsense reply, but it was the best I could offer. For I, too, had later thought about what Ann had said and had secretly hoped that what she claimed to have seen might be mystically possible. After all, grasping at straws was better than learning the art of how to drown very well.

But all of this came later. When Damon went into his tooth operation, he was well by his own peculiar standards. He could still think of himself as unaffected by the HIV virus and boast that he hadn't budged from stage one of the viral infection. Anything that appeared to go wrong with him could conveniently be laid at the feet of his haemophilia and its ever-attendant arthritis.

Damon had hoped to be out of hospital to see Celeste off to Europe, but his face was still badly swollen and he was in considerable pain. The decision was correctly made to keep him in hospital under observation for three or four days at least. The operation appeared to have been a success and Celeste was certain in her own mind that Damon had arranged it in order that she could go without feeling guilty or worried about leaving him.

She never doubted that he would control his bleeding, whether under anaesthetic or not. But she'd naturally been concerned; four wisdom teeth in one sitting is a huge operation even on a healthy person and she would have been reluctant about leaving him if his prognosis were not good.

On 27 January, 1988, the day after Australia Day, when most of Australia was recovering from a celebratory hangover, Celeste, with her backpack filled with all the essentials — jeans, T-shirts, sleeping bag and lots of sketching pads and pencils — left for Italy and her big adventure. Damon was perhaps more excited than she was.

But unbeknownst to Celeste or any of us, Damon was about to face his first real AIDS-related crisis. The premature operation to remove his impacted wisdom teeth was to prove a terrible mistake. The two years his doctor said he couldn't afford to wait was to be about all the time he had left. This situation was brought about largely because of this unnecessary dental operation.

20

Food Poisoning of the Kneecap and the
Moment of Truth.

Damon needed no emergency blood during the operation for the removal of his four impacted wisdom teeth
and he required only the mandatory blood transfusion
when he returned to his hospital bed. This came as an
enormous surprise to Denise who, knowing Damon was
a classic haemophiliac, expected the worst and transfused
him with *Factor VIII* for several days before the operation.
Nonetheless, the almost complete lack of bleeding was
without precedent. Damon *always* bled, classic haemophiliacs always do, it was only a question of degree.
Denise had been concerned that she might not have
enough blood product saved up for the occasion.

I find it curious that with their quasi-scientific mind-
set, most doctors will give you a specific reason for almost
any medical outcome. They will tell you that the body is

essentially a piece of plumbing and that it contains no surprises, everything has a physico-mechanical explanation. Science explains all. So when something comes along to confound this glib prognosis, such as the fact that Damon, a classic haemophiliac and therefore a chronic bleeder, bled less during the operation than a normal patient might be expected to do, the surgeon simply regarded this as a coincidence. Not even a curious circumstance, simply something that happened on a wet Thursday morning.

The real irony of course was that they'd gone ahead with an operation on Damon which could easily have waited a further two years or more. Though there seems no doubt that eventually his wisdom teeth would need to be removed, he'd suffered no real inconvenience from them and the decision to proceed very nearly cost him his life and certainly moved his relatively benign HIV status on to full-blown AIDS. It was a case of a system which once in motion couldn't be stopped. The blood for such an operation had been collected, the surgeon was booked, the theatre came up and so the procedure took place.

Despite the comparative lack of bleeding the operation was very traumatic and Damon remained in hospital for two weeks before he was allowed to come home. During this period he lost considerable weight.

"It's to be expected," we told ourselves. "He can't eat much with his mutilated gums and badly swollen jaw."

He returned home and, while we were anxious that he come to live with us in the flat at Rose Bay, he insisted on going back to our still-not-completed house in Vaucluse so that he might be with Celeste for the last few days before she left for Europe. His recovery from the operation was remarkable and by the time Celeste left, though his mouth was still painful, he seemed almost his old self again. Celeste had confided in me that she wouldn't go if Damon wasn't better and now she left quite cheerfully, Damon, she knew, was well on his way to complete recovery.

After Celeste had left, Damon insisted he wanted to stay at the house in Hopetoun Avenue alone. Though this didn't please us overly much, Damon was neat in his ways and quite capable of looking after himself. After considerable nagging from Benita he agreed to take three meals a week with us in the Rose Bay flat.

The idea of his being on his own wasn't quite as stupid as it must seem. Benita would go up to the house in Vaucluse every day to supervise the workmen and would spend a good portion of the day on the job. As I've mentioned before, this was a traumatic time for us all and in particular for Benita. I was busy with my book and work and could only go to the site before work on weekdays and weekends. Benita needed to be on hand, often several times a day, for deliveries and for the detailed supervision that becomes essential, particularly when completing the hundreds of tiny details on a new house.

The good side of this was that she could monitor Damon's progress without appearing to do so and so we didn't feel too bad about him staying alone so soon after his operation. He needed rest and this way he remained largely undisturbed.

One of Damon's major reasons for wanting to stay at Vaucluse after Celeste had left was Mr Schmoo the cat. Mr Schmoo had turned up one day at the house in Talfourd Street and proclaimed it home and Celeste his mum.

Anyone with a heart less open than Celeste's would have recognised a professional cat bum in an instant. Mr Schmoo was no gentleman and he knew a good thing when he saw one. But Celeste adopted him with no questions asked and Mr Schmoo became family. When they'd moved from Talfourd Street to our near-complete house in Vaucluse Mr Schmoo, of course, had gone with them. Now with Celeste overseas Damon didn't like the idea of Celeste's cat being left alone. Mr Schmoo, he knew, couldn't come down to the Rose Bay flat because of Lana, our Weimaraner, who didn't take kindly to cats.

We need not have worried, Mr Schmoo was a cat for all seasons and would simply have moved on to his next meal ticket. In fact, Mr Schmoo is still in the neighbourhood with owner number six since Celeste's original adoption papers went through. How many surrogate families he'd attached himself to before he wandered into Celeste and Damon's life is, of course, unknown. He is definitely a cat for all seasons. I was signing books at a local bookstore recently when a young couple came up and said, "We've got Schmoo the cat."

"Ha!" I said. "For how long? You're his sixth owner that I know of."

"Oh no!" they chorused, looking quite indignant, "Mr Schmoo loves us and will never, never leave."

"He will!" I assured them.

Mr Schmoo was the proverbial fat cat and pretty beat up looking at that. He had a purr inside him like a tractor engine and you could hear him coming from a hundred feet. He must have had some sort of indefinable feline charisma because everyone who ever owned Mr Schmoo (Owned? That's really funny!) always spoke well of him, despite having been dropped without a backward miaow when something more suitable came along.

Now here was Damon alone in an incomplete house and doing it for the sake of Mr Schmoo, the cat bum! Taken together with Mothra and Sam, Celeste's taste in cats had to be severely questioned.

Damon seemed fine for a couple of days after Celeste's departure, but on the Thursday he wasn't well and seemed to be running a temperature. Benita tried to make him come home but he refused. His good knee was really bad again and we discovered that he hadn't really been fine at all. His knee had blown up on the morning of Celeste's departure and he'd given himself a massive transfusion and bluffed his way through the day despite being in considerable pain.

He'd kept transfusing himself every morning and again at night, but the knee had grown steadily worse. By Thursday, he was in a great deal of pain and Benita persuaded him to go to the Haemophilia Centre at Prince Alfred. He agreed on one condition: that he not be made to remain in hospital. Benita phoned me at work and I agreed she should give him the assurance, provided he wasn't putting himself in any serious danger.

When Denise was told how many transfusions he'd given himself she was concerned. Damon had given himself sufficient *Factor VIII* to stop almost any kind of internal bleed short of a major accident. Not only had the bleeding not stopped but it was located in his good knee and, on the third day, started up in his good elbow.

Every classic haemophiliac lives in dread of one thing; that he will become immune to *Factor VIII*. Damon had received huge doses of *Factor VIII* prior to the teeth operation and now he had added to this a further eight transfusions in four days. None of these seemed to have helped and this was cause for great concern, the real concern being that there was no medical routine to put into effect. Waiting and hoping was all that could be done.

Damon was in a lot of pain, but Denise agreed that being in hospital wasn't going to make things any better, they couldn't do any more for him than we could. Thankfully Damon readily agreed to stay at home with us. He was beginning to feel really unwell and was, I suspect, grateful to come home to be looked after. I'd previously removed the boxes out of the spare room when he'd had his teeth removed, fully expecting him to come home to us after the operation. This room was now ready for him. The boxes had been moved into the room next door, known by now as my cardboard kingdom. This additional load so filled the tiny room that the cardboard containers stood as high as the stately old-fashioned ceilings would allow, with only a narrow corridor leading from the door to a small bunker where my computer stood on a card table. My working view was of a solid wall of khaki cardboard no more than eighteen inches at any point from where I sat and stretching to the roof.

Outside my window was the full sweep of one of the most beautiful bays on earth, a seascape busy with water traffic — scurrying ferries, yachts with baggy spinnakers, schooners in full sail and the occasional oil tanker or cargo ship looking sedate and businesslike as it came or left via the main shipping channels in the harbour. But within my cardboard kingdom there was nothing to distract me, it was a marvellous way to write.

With a solemn promise that I'd personally feed Mr Schmoo a can of Snappy Tom sardines every morning when I went up to the house, Damon agreed that he'd stay with us. He was sick as hell and sweating profusely by the time we got him home and into bed. That night I awoke to hear him moving around in his room. I looked at my watch, it was two a.m. and I got up and walked quietly down the passage and knocked at the door. "May I come in?" I opened the door without waiting for his reply.

Damon's light was on and he was seated beside his bed with all his transfusion gear spread out on the table next to it. His hands were trembling as he was attempting to suck the clotting factor into a syringe. Then I saw that he was weeping quietly.

"Damon, are you all right?"

He looked up at me, his eyes glistening. "Dad, my knee hurts terribly."

"Can I help?" I pointed to the stuff on the table.

He handed me the syringe and I pulled the liquid slowly into it from the bottle. "It's useless, I know, but I've got to try," he said, then he looked at me and his eyes brimmed with tears. "Shit, Dad, it hurts worse than any time I can remember." I could see the beads of sweat forming on his forehead.

I put my hand to his head and it came away wet, then I inserted a thermometer under his tongue. "Damon, you've got a temperature." I looked at him and put my arm around him. "Perhaps we should take you into hospital, what do you say, eh?"

Damon pulled back and winced with the sudden pain of even this simple body movement. "No, Dad. Please no! I couldn't stand going back to hospital." He was wiping his eyes, using the back of his hand. "These days when I go into hospital, I think of death." I was deeply shocked. Damon, who'd been in hospital so often he simply regarded it as a part of his life, was suddenly frightened. Damon, who had faced every battle with wonderful courage, was panicking.

"We'll leave it until the morning," I said. "I think tomorrow we ought to make a decision. I don't believe you're getting well, fast enough."

Damon's eyes filled with tears again. "Dad, please don't take me to hospital, this transfusion will work, you'll see." He sounded like a little boy pleading and I felt a lump grow in my throat. I loved him so much and there was nothing I could do for him. The idea that he might have become immune to *Factor VIII* was too awful to contemplate. If he had and he survived, he'd be a hopeless cripple in a few months, his body consumed with arthritis. Before the discovery of cryoprecipitate (*Factor VIII*) classic haemophiliacs seldom made it to their teens.

I pointed at the butterfly needle he'd placed beside the syringe. "Come, I'll put that in for you."

Despite himself he sniffed and then smiled, a wan little smile. "Dad, you haven't put a needle in for two years."

I grinned, hiding my anxiety. "Watch me!" Then I added, "It's like riding a bicycle."

I pulled the tourniquet around his upper arm tight and

he began opening and closing his fist, pumping up the vein in the back of his hand. The beads of perspiration stood out on his forehead and his eyes were very bright. "It's something else," I said to myself. "It's not simply his knee. There's something else very wrong. Oh God, please help us help him!" My heart was beating fast and I fought to control myself, struggled not to show my concern. I was about to attempt to put a needle into a vein, something I hadn't done for a long, long time and my heart was pounding from the anxiety I felt. I looked down and my hands *were* trembling.

I messed up the first go but got the needle in on the second attempt. "Not bad," Damon sighed, trying to be flip but choking back his tears in the process. He covered his emotion by jerking the tourniquet from his arm, the velcro making a tearing sound as it released from his frail-looking arm. Damon had been so proud of that arm, it was fully developed and he'd sometimes flex the muscles and look at it; it was some arm compared to the other parts of his body. Now it too was frail-looking, the muscle tone gone, a small vulnerable arm to match everything about him. I had never seen my son like this before, crumpled, defeated.

I stayed up with him most of the night and by early morning, with the help of a couple of Valium, he drifted into a fitful sleep. On Friday morning he was no better and it was obvious he was still running a fever, though when Benita took his temperature, it proved to be slightly lower than when I'd taken it the night before.

I moved him into our bedroom, on to our double bed, where there was a little more air and where a cross breeze would sometimes pass through the window, across the bed and out of the bedroom door. It was one week into February and still hot as hell and we thought he'd be more comfortable in our room. Damon's knee was up like a balloon and Benita had propped it up on two pillows to bear the weight. It was too early to call his doctor at the Haemophilia Centre and I left for a work a bit bleary-eyed, leaving Benita to call the hospital.

At mid morning she called me to say that Damon seemed a little better and that his doctor had said simply to watch him, give him plenty of rest, lots of liquid, take his temperature every two hours and attempt another transfusion in twelve hours.

He told her he'd be away for the weekend and if things got any worse or Damon's temperature started to climb noticeably to take him into Emergency. Denise called soon after to say that she'd alerted Emergency so that, should he need to come in, he wouldn't have to wait around.

In fact, when I got home that evening Damon seemed about the same as I'd left him in the morning, though he was due for another transfusion and was plainly incapable of doing this himself. A transfusion was a procedure Benita hadn't ever performed and so they'd waited for me to return to attempt it. I botched it twice and was left with the prospect of getting the needle through a vein in what was known as his bad arm, the arm on which they'd fused the elbow and which over the years had become atrophied. The tiny vein in the seat of this permanently fused elbow was an entry point of desperate last resort. I'd just blown two perfectly good veins, one on the back of his good hand and another inside the elbow of his good arm and, now, all I had was this very suspect, tiny vein, hardly blue enough to see under the skin with the naked eye.

I could sense Damon was practically screaming with impatience, he was very sick and in great pain and the clumsiness of my two previous attempts was almost more than he could bear. Inwardly quaking, I attempted the new vein, lining the needle up, inserting it, straightening it along the vein and pushing. Thank Christ it seated home perfectly at the first attempt and I completed the procedure by connecting the syringe and pushing home the plunger with such care, lest I *blow* the vein, that it took me nearly twenty minutes to transfuse Damon.

The tension and the pain was too much for Benita and she started to sob. "It's okay, Mum. Don't cry, Dad got the needle in perfectly. It will be okay, you'll see." Damon himself was exhausted and his voice came in gasps, his lips were cracked with the fever he was running from the dreadful pain in his knee. I'd brought a large free-standing fan home from the office, which I placed in a corner of the room and which now swept cool air across the bed where he lay. That night Benita slept in Damon's room and I slept on the sofa in the living room.

On Saturday morning he was somewhat worse and the knee hadn't responded to the previous evening's transfusion. Damon was groaning and in ghastly pain. He seemed to be only semi-conscious and I decided we couldn't delay it any longer and that he must go into Emergency. But he was still adamant that he didn't want to go and begged me not to call the ambulance.

"Please, Dad, it's just a very, very bad bleed. They can't do anything we can't do here." He turned to Benita. "Please, Mum don't let Dad send me to hospital!" He was crying and the dark hair on his chest was matted with perspiration. "Please, Dad, I don't want to die in hospital!"

By Saturday night, his knee was so painful that he asked to have the fan turned off, just the effect of the draught of air crossing his knee was too much for him to bear. I took his temperature which had climbed slightly again, but he remained adamant that he wasn't going to hospital and we spent a torrid night as he got steadily worse. In the early hours of Sunday morning, I called the ambulance and half an hour later it arrived.

But this time simply touching Damon anywhere was painful and the knee was swollen to a size I'd never seen it before. The two ambulance paramedics, one an older man who took control, tried to move him on the bed and he screamed, his eyes panicked and wide with the dreadful pain caused by even the slightest movement. Even as a child I'd never seen Damon scream, but now he was panicked with pain. Damon who could take almost any amount of pain was in such terrible agony I thought he might die. It was dawn on a Sunday morning, Celeste would not call until Thursday, we had no forwarding address, she was staying in youth hostels and was on her way to Portugal. Oh, God, why hadn't we suggested she stay, not go away; she would have stayed and I could have made it up to her with another trip, some other time.

Benita began to weep quietly, turning her head away so the two men wouldn't see her. The ambulance men made the decision that there was no good way to move him, that they simply had to proceed, whatever the consequences. They were as gentle as it was possible to be but Damon's screams were awful and he bit completely through his bottom lip trying to control his agony as they lifted him on to the gurney and wheeled him towards the waiting ambulance. Outside, where the ambulance was parked, lights were coming on in the surrounding apartments as people wakened to his screams.

They placed him in the back of the ambulance, the younger of the two men staying with Damon. The driver turned to me, "I'm sorry, sir, but we can't give him morphine, not without a doctor seeing him first."

He said this apropos of nothing; I hadn't asked for a pain-killer, Damon had to be very careful what he took and I knew he wouldn't be capable of swallowing a Digesic in his present state. Besides, nothing we'd previously given him seemed to help in the least.

The two of them were nice blokes, salt of the earth types. "Has he got AIDS?" the older man asked suddenly. He looked upset. "I'm sorry, we have to ask you, sir, they'll want to know when we get him to Emergency."

"No, no, he hasn't. He's had his wisdom teeth out." I realised at once that this sounded ridiculous, what the hell did a tooth extraction have to do with his knee? "He's a haemophiliac, a bleeder," I added. "You should tell them that." I was confused, calm enough in appearance on the outside but inwardly churned up and in a state of panic. Had I left it too late? I now realised that Damon was dangerously ill. I should have insisted, called the ambulance on Friday night. "No, don't worry, I'll be following you to the hospital, I can tell them myself."

We spent all day at Royal Prince Alfred Hospital where Damon remained in Emergency. His doctor was away but Denise came in, even though it was her day off.

There wasn't much she could do, but she acted as a sort of go-between as we were not permitted to see Damon while they were taking tests. All she could tell us was that something more than the knee was wrong with Damon, but that the pathology tests so far hadn't revealed anything they could work on.

On Monday morning he was worse, but then later in the day he seemed to get worse again. His doctor, the biro-tapper, had returned and had been to see him and, for once, pronounced himself completely mystified. "He's very sick, we know that. Not just the knee. It's a massive infection, but we don't know *what* infection." Then the didactic bastard corrected himself, "We don't know *which* infection."

"How bad is it? I mean could it . . .?"

"Kill him? It's possible he'll die if he gets much worse, but he seems to have stabilised for the moment. (He sounded matter of fact.) We simply don't know what's wrong. He's very sick." Then he added, "There's really no point in your staying, there's no immediate danger. We'll notify you in plenty of time if things get worse."

We stayed of course and by mid afternoon a young doctor from pathology came over to see us. He looked tired and announced that they'd isolated the problem. "Damon has developed a *Salmonella* infection in his knee."

I'd once serviced a canned fish food account at the agency and I knew *Salmonella* was a kind of food poisoning; you got it from, among other things, bad tinned fish. Damon hadn't eaten any tinned fish; besides, what the young man was saying didn't make sense. "How the hell can you have *Salmonella* in the knee? It's a form of food poisoning isn't it, doctor?"

The young man nodded, "It sounds weird, I know." His hair hung over his forehead and he looked as though it needed a wash and a scrub up. His white coat was stained as though he'd used it to wipe his hands. He sighed and held one hand across his eyes for a moment then narrowed the thumb and forefinger down to pinch the bridge of his nose. It was as though he was trying to concentrate, trying to seem concerned for our sake. "That's why we couldn't isolate what was wrong, until we started to look for a similar case history in someone else who had AIDS."

I felt Benita stiffen beside me.

"We eventually found a case-history written up in America. You see a *Salmonella* infection goes to the place of least resistance. In this instance it entered through his mouth, through the cavities made by Damon's recent teeth extractions. From there, it found its way to the weakened knee and his elbow." Then he repeated, "It's certainly not typical, but that's the problem with AIDS, it lets in any opportunistic infection that happens to be about."

"AIDS? Damon is only HIV positive, doctor."

The young pathologist looked at me slightly bemused, he was too tired to attempt an apology. "Damon has AIDS, Mr Courtenay," he said simply; then he shrugged, "The operation to his teeth was unfortunate. It allowed a massive infection to enter his system. He's very, very sick and has very little resistance."

I held on to Benita's arm. She was biting back her tears and I could feel her body trembling against mine. "You'll have to excuse me," the pathologist said, then added as though it were an afterthought, "You can be sure we'll do everything we can to pull him through." He looked down at his feet, avoiding Benita's obvious distress, searching for something comforting to say to us. "At least we now know how to treat him, I think he's going to make it now," he said. He was young and a little gauche, he'd probably been working a double or triple shift, it wasn't his fault and he couldn't have known we didn't know that Damon had acquired full-blown AIDS. Nevertheless, and quite unreasonably, because he'd done his best and it wasn't good enough, I wanted to jump up and smash his teeth in. Somebody, somewhere had to take responsibility for what was happening to my boy! Hadn't he had enough? Why this? More pain, more suffering, with this time — no hope. Damon had full-blown AIDS. Damon was going to die!

I held Benita tightly as she began to sob and sob, taking in great gasps of air, as the very private person in her struggled to stop crying and kill the sound of her weeping and restore to privacy the distress which now overwhelmed her in this most public of all places, a lousy hospital corridor. It was the loneliest moment I'd faced since all those years ago, when I'd walked into the tiny room at the Children's Hospital to see my baby wearing a huge purple head, larger than his entire body. A purple head which blew tiny bubbles, against a backdrop of painted pixies dancing around a polka-dotted mushroom, all of them wearing floppy red Father Christmas caps and green felt boots that curled up at the toes.

It was, I knew, the beginning of the end of the journey we'd begun together so many years ago, when I'd pulled back Damon's blue baby blanket and witnessed his blood-soaked nappy on the terrible night of the day of his circumcision.

That evening a sign went up on the door of Damon's hospital room. The broken black circle on a yellow background. Beside it was a notice:

INFECTED AREA
Gloves, mask and gowns
<u>must</u> be worn at all times.

The word *must* had been pedantically underlined twice in red with a broad felt pen. In the corridor directly outside his room stood a two-sided sign, like a small sandwich board, propped up on its triangular base and positioned on the polished, grey vinyl floor so that it could be read by hospital personnel approaching from either direction. Its background was painted the same bright yellow as the sign on the door and on it appeared the broken black circle. In red lettering above the circle was printed:

DANGER
Infected Area

It was confirmed. Damon had full-blown AIDS. The machinery of his terrible infection was beginning to crank into life. Henceforth, Damon was a creature to be feared; untouchable, unclean, dangerous, somebody to be approached with great caution and only when wearing a face mask, gown and gloves. Henceforth, wherever he sat or lay, whatever he touched, became an infected area. Or so they were prepared to believe at the time when it was thought a sneeze or a cough might carry the deadly virus across a room, along the corridor and out into the innocent, unsuspecting world.

The ignorance about AIDS was monumental.

In some ways, it still is.

The nightmare had begun.

21

From Italy with Love and Anxiety.
The Mount Sinai Chicken Soup Affair
and Eyes of Christ.

Celeste had called for the first time on the Thursday from Rome and Damon was of course still home. He made no mention of his bad knee and even though he was plainly in pain, talked to her in an animated way for nearly half an hour.

As there wasn't a phone in the house at Vaucluse they'd agreed that Celeste would call the flat at Rose Bay every Thursday at 8 p.m. when Damon would be waiting. Her first call came after she'd been in Rome for nearly forty-eight hours and she was bubbling over with excitement, speaking excitedly to him about what she'd seen.

She gave him a blow-by-blow description of the Sistine Chapel which she'd seen that very afternoon, the Colosseum, the Pantheon and the Piazza della Rotunda, the dome of St Peter's and a walk along the banks of the Tiber with the chestnut trees coming into leaf. Her artist's eye and architectural training made the ancient buildings and their history truly come alive for him.

Damon hung on, sweat pouring from his brow and often biting back the pain, his face scrunched up. But when he spoke to her there wasn't the slightest hint that he wasn't terribly excited and loving every vicarious moment. There are times in your life when you look at your children and you're happy that you got it right. With Damon we've been blessed with a great many such moments, but none made me more proud of him than this first phone call from Celeste.

By the time Celeste phoned again, this time from Florence, Damon had been in hospital almost a week. In retrospect, we should have told her everything, but we didn't, merely saying that his knee and elbow, his *good* knee and *good* elbow, had blown up and that he needed special attention only the hospital could give him.

Celeste accepted this, Damon's bad knee and elbow gave him constant problems but the other side of his body, referred to as his good side, bled reasonably seldom and, in a physical sense, was developed and not atrophied. He depended on his good knee and elbow enormously when the bad side went down and he was forced to walk on crutches. Maintaining the good side in good shape was always a priority with him and Celeste quickly understood that special care would be needed to attend to a really bad bleed in both. Besides, she was enormously excited and perhaps a little distracted at what she'd seen in this wonderful Tuscan city and her final statement to me was, "Tell Damon 'the fingers of God' are real!"

"Fingers of God?"

"Yes, it's what we call those beams of light that come out of the clouds in Renaissance paintings. Tell him that I arrived here just after an afternoon storm and as the sun was setting the clouds were tipped with gold and 'the fingers of God' shot straight out of them and on to the Pitti Palace exactly like the paintings." She giggled in her infectious way. "We always thought they were rather funny, sort of spotlights created by Renaissance painters to show the peasants where to look for the crucifixion scene." There was a moment's silence then she added in a soft voice, "Tell him I think of him every minute and I miss him terribly and I cried when I saw 'the fingers of God' and he wasn't with me."

The phone calls came every week and Damon was still in hospital. After the fourth week, Celeste started to worry and wanted to come home. She was talking to Benita on the phone when she suddenly burst into tears. "Please, Benita, what's wrong? I know something's terribly wrong and I must come home!" Then she added, "I can't, because I can only return with the ticket I've got in another three weeks. Please, will Bryce send me a ticket and I'll pay him back!"

Benita was close to tears herself, but Damon had made her swear that she wouldn't tell Celeste anything. He knew that if she knew the full story she'd want to return immediately and he was determined that she should have a wonderful holiday.

"Talk to Bryce, see what he says," she said, then added, "Hold on, he's working on his book, I'll get him."

Benita stood at the door, at the entrance to my cardboard kingdom. "Darling, can you come here for a moment?" She seldom came into the room as the boxes towering above her gave her claustrophobia.

"I can't, I'm busy," I said, irritated at being disturbed again. I'd been out half an hour or so earlier to say hello to Celeste before Benita settled down to have a proper yak.

"Please, it's important!"

I sighed and made my way down the cardboard passage to the door. "Jesus! What?"

"Celeste is worried about Damon, she wants to come home."

"That's dumb!" I said.

"Will you talk to her?"

"What? Now?"

"Of course *now*. Celeste is waiting on the phone!"

"It's a *really* dumb idea," I said, irritated but walking down the passage to the phone. I picked up the receiver. "Celeste?" I said in a peremptory voice.

She didn't allow me to continue. "Bryce, I want to come home. I feel there's something *very* wrong with Damon." Her voice was urgent, she was speaking fast and I could hear she was close to tears. "My ticket won't let me leave Europe until the end of March, please can you send me another one. I'll pay you back as soon as I can?"

To cut a long story short I convinced her to stay in Europe. I used all the usual arguments — the trip of a lifetime; Australia's distance from Europe; things to learn; Damon's knee and elbow getting better by the day. I added that Damon would be furious if he thought she'd come back on his behalf. "There's nothing you can do for him," I said rather harshly, trying to make my point more forcibly.

Finally she seemed mollified. "Celeste, if things got bad with Damon you know we'd send you a ticket right away, but there's no indication that anything is likely to happen, he's just making a rather slow recovery, that's all."

Celeste told me later that she'd been reasonably satisfied after speaking to me but, the following night in her *pensione* in a small village outside Siena she'd wakened with a terrible fright in the middle of the night with my words, "There's nothing you can do for him", pounding in her ears. She became suddenly, unshakeably convinced that Damon was dead and that we were keeping the news of his death from her.

She caught the train next day to Rome where she persuaded the Alitalia people to let her fly out a week early, though her ticket wasn't valid. After they agreed she went into the Via Condotti and bought a beautiful outfit with the money she'd saved from the final week of her trip, then she phoned from Rome airport to say she was coming home. She paid a few lire to have a shower at the airport and got dolled up to the nines in her new outfit and boarded the plane for Sydney.

Later she told me, "I kept telling myself that if I arrived in Sydney and Damon wasn't there to meet me then he was definitely dead. But if he *was* there waiting for me, then I wanted to look perfectly stunning for him, the totally sophisticated Italian, the sort of woman he spoke of as being seated beside him in his red Ferrari when he made his first million."

She went on to explain how she felt on her arrival in Sydney: "I arrived home, having spent the last hour in the plane getting my make-up perfect and hoping the red in my eyes didn't show how exhausted I was. I came out of customs after what seemed like a hundred years and there was Adam. I looked to see if Damon was with him and, when I saw he wasn't, I felt the panic rise in me. It was an empty, burning feeling like acid vomit rising. I wanted suddenly to run away, to run back into the customs hall and up the ramp and back on the plane, which would somehow take off and fly me away, like a video tape rolling backwards, rewinding, cancelling out the action that had just taken place. All I could think was that Damon was dead and you'd sent Adam to break the news to me!

"I have always loved Adam. He is just a wonderful person and you can love him just for that. But he loved Damon terribly and was enormously protective of him and I loved him for this as well. I knew if something had happened to Damon, Adam would want to be the one to tell me. Adam took me in his arms and I started to cry. 'It's okay, really it's okay,' he kept saying.

"I didn't seem able to register whether this meant Damon was alive or that he was comforting me because Damon was dead. Adam seemed suddenly to understand my confusion because he said, 'It's okay, Celeste. Damon's in hospital, but he's waiting impatiently to see us.'

"I was exhausted from the journey; after all I'd been travelling non-stop for two and a half days and I hadn't slept much on the plane and I still wasn't entirely con- vinced. Perhaps I was hallucinating or something? 'You have to take me to him now, Adam! I have to see him right away!' I must have been shouting, though I was unaware of doing so.

"'Shhh, Celeste, I promise you he's okay, I *promise!*' Adam said, then added, 'We had trouble restraining him from coming to the airport.' Which I later found was untrue; although Damon would have wanted to come, he was still too weak to leave his bed.

"On the way Adam tried to prepare me for the shock. 'Damon has lost a lot of weight,' he cautioned, then he explained about the *Salmonella* in his good knee and elbow. 'It hasn't been good, he's been through a bit of a tough time.'

"'Why didn't you tell me! Why didn't Bryce or Benita tell me? It's not fair, I wailed.'"

"Adam was silent for a moment and when he continued his voice was suddenly shaky. 'We couldn't, Damon wouldn't let us . . .' I looked up and tears were streaming down his face. 'He's got AIDS,' he whispered. 'Shit, Celeste, my little brother's got AIDS!' He pulled the car suddenly to the side of the road and slammed on the brakes so that I shot forward in my seat belt. Then we held each other and wept and wept and wept.

"I rushed into Damon's hospital room, still not entirely convinced, the signs meant nothing to me. Now that I think about it, I'm not sure I even saw them. I just wanted to see Damon with my own eyes."

Damon spent another two weeks in hospital after Celeste's return and she seemed to spend almost all her time with him. Adam was living in a tiny flat above Dinky Di Pies where Celeste had worked and where she'd earned most of the money to go to Europe. The bakery's real name was Classic Catering, but everyone called it Dinky Di Pies, because that was what was written on the canvas awning overhanging the shop. Xavier, the owner, had agreed that Celeste could move in with Adam, though there was hardly room for two, but he agreed to them sharing until she could find a place to live.

She was due to start back at university for the third year of her degree in architecture but, with all the time she spent with Damon, it became almost impossible for her to look for a place of her own. Our house in Vaucluse was finally completed, though we were never to live in it. Benita and I had lived through two horrific years of building and felt that the house held nothing but trauma and heartache. The prospect of owning the home we'd dreamed of had been completely shattered. Coupled with the emotional impact of Damon's near death, our memories of that old and most happy of homes, were still poignant and of the new one, unbearable. We decided to sell. This meant it was no longer available to Celeste.

After nearly seven weeks in hospital Damon wanted out. Years of being in hospitals meant Damon knew his way around and, with the assurance gained over time, he was no longer a compliant patient. Instead he demanded to know the details of every bit of medication and how it would affect him and whether there would be any side effects. He'd long since lost his respect for the average medico and realised that he was largely responsible for his own body and its medication. So he'd often argue with a doctor before he agreed to take a treatment. And, sometimes, he'd even refuse to take medication if he felt it was wrongly prescribed.

In a busy public hospital with doctors changing all

the time and where interns are mostly on duty, cross-examinations and interrogations such as Damon would conduct were disruptive and often embarrassing to the senior nursing staff who, simply acting on instructions left by the physician, were often unable to answer his questions. Damon was usually better briefed than they were and they didn't take kindly to his arrogant and his often know-all manner. Damon knew better than to expect doctors to know everything and this was particularly true of interns. He would tell of one evening coming to Prince Alfred late because he had a bleed and had run out of blood product at home. He explained to the intern in Emergency that he would need to take him to the Haemophilia Centre for the AHF blood product required for a transfusion. The Haemophilia Centre was closed at night, but Damon was familiar with the procedure, while the intern obviously was not.

The intern looked at him suspiciously. "You claim you're a haemophiliac and you require a blood transfusion?"

"Well yes. AHF. You know the *Factor VIII* compound? I'll need to transfuse myself. It's stored at the Haemophilia Centre. You keep the keys here in Emergency."

"You seem to know a lot," the intern replied, then added, "But not enough!" With one eyebrow slightly arched he said, "Haemophiliacs receive medication for bleeding *orally*! Now just who are you and what do you want?"

Though Prince Alfred contained its own AIDS ward, Damon had not been placed in it, he'd come into hospital via Emergency and, with his infected knee, he'd simply been put in a private room in the general-medicine section. The staff in this area were not accustomed to treating AIDS patients and over-reacted somewhat to accepting him. Some of the nurses and cleaning staff simply refused to enter his room. In an incident, which I hasten to point out wasn't typical, two male nurses barged into his room gloved and gowned on the pretence of attending to him; then they simply stood by his bed and called him a "fucking poofta" and a "turd burglar" whereupon they left.

Fortunately Damon· was too sick to react, nor did he feel that their attitude was typical. He seemed to understand from the beginning the fear that AIDS gave to people, including hospital staff, who, unless they worked in an AIDS ward, really knew very little more about the virus than did the general public.

Those of the staff who were prepared to nurse him wore so much protective clothing that they looked as though they were entering the radioactive chamber of a nuclear reactor. It was a tiring and difficult time for everyone, though, of course, as is always the case, some of the hospital staff were quite wonderful. But they were not in the majority, the fear of AIDS, coupled with the ignorance of how it's spread, made everyone who came near Damon apprehensive and he couldn't help but feel their anxiety, which inevitably added to his overall resentment of the hospital environment.

In fairness, it must also be said that, toward the end of his stay, Damon was giving back as much as he was getting and he too wasn't being very co-operative. After seven weeks he'd had enough. He felt sure he was sufficiently well enough to leave and he wanted to get the hell out of the place. But the biro-tapper from the

Haemophilia Centre, who was nominally still the doctor in charge of Damon, was adamant that he remain in hospital for a further three weeks. The doctors at the Centre changed all the time and this one, whom we referred to as the biro-tapper, had no continuity with Damon. Furthermore, as Damon's *Salmonella* problem was outside his specialty, he was unable to give Damon a rational reason as a physician for a continued stay. Admittedly, Damon was being difficult and finally one morning the biro-stabber exclaimed in exasperation, "If you go now and get sick again you'll be wasting the taxpayers' money! I simply won't be responsible for such public waste!"

Damon was furious and called me at my office, informing me that he was signing himself out and could I come and fetch him. Worried that it might be the wrong move I phoned Denise. To my surprise she was on Damon's side. "Damon will get better sooner if he goes home," she said, then lowering her voice on the phone she mentioned the biro-tapper by name. "You see Damon's T-cell count is down, the doctor's just trying to cover his backside in case Damon catches another infection."

"What does that mean: his T-cell count is down?" I asked.

"Not a lot, we'll need to wait and see. It's no reason to keep him here anyway."

We all trusted Denise, she knew more about her haemophiliac patients than any of the doctors and we accepted her advice more readily than that of any of the physicians. The thing about Denise was that she seldom pulled her punches while, at the same time, she cared enormously for the haemophiliacs in her care. Damon loved her and she could make him undergo tedious exercise routines where even his mother wouldn't succeed.

"Denise, you'd tell me if there was something very wrong, wouldn't you?" Damon was one of the first of the haemophiliacs with an HIV positive status and I knew that Denise herself was on a learning curve.

"Bryce, I don't know. *We* don't know! The fact that his T-cell count is slightly further down may simply be due to the tooth operation and of course the subsequent *Salmonella* infection. In somebody like Damon, the tooth operation alone is a very traumatic experience. In fact, it's a pretty rotten thing for anyone to have to undergo. Add the *Salmonella* and we're very lucky we didn't lose him."

"What do his T-cells do?"

Again Denise was hesitant. "Precisely — they fight infection. They protect us from being infected."

"Infected from what?"

"Well, you see we all have an immune system and the T-cells are sort of the front-line fighters belonging to this system; without them we'd all catch just about everything going around. Diseases are always around in the air. Though some appear at certain times, most are always present, but our immune systems keep them from infecting us." She paused and then went on to explain, "Our T-cells fight them off — they're the soldiers that keep our blood protected."

"So, without them, we become easily infected?"

"Well yes, that's the general idea. That's how the *Salmonella* got into his system."

"And Damon's T-cells are down even further than before?"

"Yes, but we've got a lot of T-cells, losing a few more isn't a disaster." Denise's voice was deliberately casual.

"How many have we got? I mean the average person?"

"Well it varies; a healthy T-cell count can vary from five hundred to as many as two thousand."

"How many did Damon have?"

"Originally? Sixteen hundred."

"How many does he have to lose to be in danger, to be vulnerable?"

"Well, we don't like the count to go much below two hundred and fifty."

"And what is Damon's T-cell count at the moment?"

There was a pause on the other end, "Damon's count is precisely one hundred and ninety eight." It was the old, precise, no-punches-pulled Denise. Then she added, "They could build up again. Really we don't know." She sighed, "There is *so much* we don't know, Bryce."

My heart sank. After sixteen hundred, one hundred and ninety eight T-cells seemed like nothing. "But you think it's safe for him to come out of hospital?"

Denise sighed, "Bryce, where do you think the most opportunistic infections are likely to be found?"

"In a hospital?"

"Precisely! The sooner he's out of this place the better."

Damon returned home with us. He was still too unwell to live with Celeste who was about to start university again. Besides, even if Adam moved out of the tiny flat above the bakery, as he'd already offered to do, Damon would have found the narrow stairs up to the no-bathroom flat impossible to negotiate.

Our Rose Bay apartment wasn't big, but it was light and sunny and fronting a small, inner-harbour beach which, at low tide, became glorious flats with shallow puddles to splash through and soft sandreaches to walk along. It was an ideal place for him to recover his strength. I found him, once, sitting in his wheelchair on the front verandah, for in the first week home Damon lacked the strength to walk. He was looking at the shimmering bay where a small seaplane was coming into land, tears were running down his cheeks. I sat quietly beside him, saying nothing. "It's so wonderful to be alive, Dad," he said at last.

Fattening Damon up was our chief priority, he'd entered hospital weighing sixty-two kilos and returned home weighing just forty-two. We tried almost everything to tempt him, but he seemed to lack appetite and, despite a conscious desire to regain his strength, he ate like a bird. It was about this time that we noticed that oral thrush (*Candida*), a yellow fungus, was growing in his mouth. It wasn't bad and didn't seem to worry him overmuch, but nothing the chemist gave us to control it seemed to help very much. We'd manage to rinse it out, but by morning a fresh crop would grow.

Thrush is the eternal companion of AIDS and it would eventually build up in his mouth and throat and the lining of his stomach so that it had to be scraped off with a spatula and he could tolerate only soft custards and jelly.

Benita's friends loved Damon and the house was always full of fancy food, confectionery and cake and all manner of delicacies, which Damon rarely touched. Rose Abrams, a dear family friend, brought chicken soup. She would arrive with a large pot covered with a gingham dishcloth. "I've brought your Jewish penicillin, Damon!" she'd announce in a booming voice from the kitchen door. Rose's chicken soup was a concoction designed to look sickness straight in the eye and challenge it to mortal combat. It contained all sorts of magical properties, the greatest of them being Rose herself.

Once, I'd entered the kitchen to find her hovering over the stove with Damon seated at the kitchen table talking to her. "What a divine smell!" I said, sniffing at the air. Rose turned to face me, a large wooden spoon in her hand. "Funny you should say that, I mean about my soup being divine. Did you know that chicken soup is actually the official beverage of God? A present from Mrs Moses to the Almighty."

She said it deadpan and Damon and I laughed. Rose was a great storyteller. So Damon, who knew how to get her going, said, "The Mrs Moses of the Red-Sea-and-Wilderness Moses?"

"The same," Rose said casually, sipping daintily at the edge of the wooden spoon.

"Chicken soup isn't only Jewish, Rose," I added.

Rose turned to face us, her expression one of exaggerated shock. "What do you mean chicken soup isn't only Jewish? That stuff in a can, you call that chicken soup? That is stuff you wouldn't dignify by flushing down the toilet! A certain Mr Campbell, an American, who by the way is definitely not a Jew, puts that poultry slop in a tin! It's such awful crap that it's practically anti-semitic!"

She pointed to the pot on the stove, "Tell me, since when did you see anybody but a Jewish mother make chicken soup like that?" She leaned over the pot and

LEFT: Bryce and Benita Courtenay on their wedding day (2 October 1959)

BELOW: Damon at four months (February 1967)

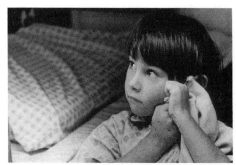

ABOVE: Damon at 3

BELOW: Damon tests the waters (aged 3, 1969)

LEFT: **Damon at 6**

LEFT: **(l to r) Brett
(14), Adam (12),
and Damon (9)**

ABOVE: **Bryce Courtenay and his three sons, (l to r) Adam (8), Damon (3) and Brett (6)**

LEFT: **Damon in a page from the *Cranbook Yearbook* 1984, the year Damon was diagnosed HIV positive**

ABOVE: Damon, Toby and Celeste in 'Maison le Guessly', King's Cross (early 1985)

ABOVE: The Fiat, Damon (reclining on the hood) and friends Andrew and Rebecca (Hunter Valley, 1987)

RIGHT: **Damon in Woollahra bedroom (1985)**

BELOW: **Damon and Celeste with Mr Schmoo (Talfourd St, 1987)**

ABOVE: **Damon and Celeste in Paris (October 1990)**

BELOW: **(l to r) Bryce, Celeste, Brett, Ann and Benita with puppy**

ABOVE: **Benita, Damon and Adam Courtenay in Rome (November 1990)**

LEFT: **Damon and Celeste**

lifted the lid again; steam rose up in a cloud and you almost expected a snatch of the Hallelujah chorus to accompany it, like opening the lid of an old-fashioned music box. Except, of course, it couldn't have been the Hallelujah chorus, because that wouldn't have been kosher. The soup smelled so good you could have inhaled the nourishment in it through your nostrils. "Divine is right!" Rose continued. "Chicken soup is definitely the official drink of God and is why Jews stay faithful to their wives and don't fool around with other women who are not nuptially theirs." She looked at us defiantly, prepared, it seemed, to be challenged, though I wasn't sure whether in defence of the lower rate of promiscuity among Jewish husbands or of God's choice of preferred drink. "You mean to tell me you don't *really* know the story of Moses and his wife's chicken soup?" she asked finally.

Damon glanced sideways at me; Rose's stories had a tendency to go on a bit and I could see he was wondering whether he had the stamina to cope and, just in case, he wanted me to hang around and share the load with him.

"I didn't read anywhere in the Bible where Moses had a wife." I grinned, nudging her on.

Rose sniffed and looked scornful as she pulled out a chair. "In *your* Bible maybe it doesn't mention this important fact. Do you think we're *meshuggeneh*? So crazy that we'd let a bachelor lead the children of Israel through the wilderness? Of course he had a wife! It stands to reason, doesn't it?" She pointed the wooden spoon at the pot of steaming soup. "When Moses climbed to the summit of Mount Sinai to talk to God he took along a large pot of his wife's chicken soup. The Lord tasted it and then polished off the lot and demanded to know the recipe."

Damon gave me a look which plainly said, "Oh God, she's away! No turning back now."

"Now Moses was in a bit of a dilemma," Rose continued. "He was a great leader, perhaps the greatest, but, believe me, he was no cook. He didn't know how to make chicken soup from prune juice and even if he was forced to *shlep* all the way back down the mountain to get the recipe from his wife, he wasn't at all sure she'd give it to him. She was descended directly from Abraham and so was her secret chicken soup recipe.

"'Lord, you're welcome to my humble table to drink chicken soup any time,' Moses said, preparing the Almighty for the bad news, 'but you must understand, a great chicken soup recipe is not something to be given away like a handful of salted pretzels.'

"God stroked His beard for a minute or two. 'Hmmm . . .' He said and the heavens rumbled. Then He smiled." Rose paused and looked at us, "When God smiles in a certain way, believe me it's time to say your prayers twice over!

"'Well then never mind. Have you brought your hammer and chisel?' Moses nodded, pleased that the Lord wasn't going to make a scene. God brought His hands on to His lap and looked towards the sky as though He were about to think up a commandment to dictate. 'Let's go to work then, we have three hundred and one commandments to write down before sunset.'

"Moses gasped, three hundred and one commandments! He knew better than to argue with God but he also knew trouble was not a big enough word for what he was suddenly in. A few commandments here or there the Children of Israel would accept, but three hundred and one? It was like asking them to accept the plague of locusts all over again, even worse, maybe to return to Egypt. With the heavy heart of a beaten man he picked up his hammer and chisel. 'Ready when you are, Lord,' he sighed."

Rose's voice took on a stentorian tone and she tucked her double chin into her ample breasts every time she gave God His lines. "'Okay, now this one is important, make sure you get it down right,' God paused, thinking about the exact words, then, in a voice of thunder, He began to dictate: 'Thou, nor thy wife, nor thy sons nor thy daughters nor thy manservants nor thy maidservants nor any person who shall dwell in thine house shall consume chicken soup.' God paused. 'Get that down, that's the first commandment.'

"Moses chiselled furiously, but his heart wasn't any longer in what he was doing, he thought seriously about handing in his resignation on the spot. He became dizzy with anxiety as he imagined a world where the Jews were unable to serve chicken soup at the family table. Imagine Friday night without chicken soup? If the idea wasn't so preposterous it would be funny! If it hadn't come from God Himself it would be declared an official sin against the Jewish people!

"'Only three hundred more to go, my son,' God purred, with only the slightest touch of irony in His voice.

"Moses bowed low so that his forehead rested on the ground at God's feet, 'Lord, can there be no compromise?'

"'A little negotiation perhaps? Why not? I am not an unreasonable God,' God said.

"'I could talk to my wife, I mean . . . about the recipe?'

"'I like it!' God said, brightening up, but as suddenly He frowned and the heavens filled with distant thunder. 'But a recipe for chicken soup? It's not such a big deal?' He scratched at the corner of His mouth and a couple of hundred rocks dislodged and rolled down the mountain. 'Hmm, I could cut maybe forty, fifty commandments, what do you say, Mo?'

"Moses had to think fast, 'Lord, this is not *just* chicken soup! For chicken soup, maybe forty, fifty commandments; but this soup, holy macaroni! This is a secret recipe! In my wife's family since before the time of Abraham's near sacrifice of Isaac. Such a prize should be worth a very large reduction in commandments; a very, very big reduction, if I may be so bold, Lord.'

"'So, how many commandments, total, did you have in mind?'

"Moses gulped, 'Nine would be nice, Lord,' he said, half swallowing the number so that if God felt insulted, he could retrieve it to sound like ninety."

Rose's voice became very deep. "God thought for a moment and a black cloud came from nowhere and covered the sun. 'Okay, I'm a fair man, or God, get Me the recipe for your wife's chicken soup and I'll make it only nine commandments and a few assorted rules for keeping kosher.' The cloud melted as quickly as it had appeared and the sun shone as fiercely as ever.

"Moses couldn't believe his good fortune and he picked up the tablet which contained the commandment regarding the banning of chicken soup and dashed it to the ground, where it broke into more than a thousand pieces. Then he took up his hammer and stone chisel and quickly fashioned a new tablet of stone, marking it with the number One. 'Ready when you are, Lord.'

"'Not so fast, young man! First you go get the recipe. I can promise you, no recipe and you'll be chipping stone until your arms are so worn down your fingers will be attached to your armpits!'"

Damon looked at me and laughed, Rose was a real case.

Rose continued, "So Moses set off back down the mountain, he was pretty pleased with himself, I can tell you! True, his wife had her difficult moments, but at heart she was soft as a matzo ball. Except for once when she'd caught him in bed with a temple girl, she'd never raised her voice to him. Getting the recipe wouldn't be a piece of cheesecake but, when he told her God demanded it, he felt sure she'd agree. Especially when he informed her of the part she'd inadvertently played in the reduction of three hundred onerous commandments down to a mere nine.

"The next morning as the sun rose gloriously over the desert, Moses was standing on the summit of Mount Sinai. Far below him he could see the Israelite tents, tiny white dots on the desert floor arranged in neat rows; from each rose a wisp of smoke into the sharp, clean air as ten thousand families prepared breakfast. They appeared to be a great disciplined army, a people of one accord, one determination, one destiny!

"'Fat hope!' he said to himself. 'Ten thousand tents, ten thousand different opinions, ten thousand leaders.' Sometimes being the so-called great Jewish leader didn't seem much fun at all and he often quite resented being *the* chosen person among the *chosen* people.

"In a sudden blinding flash accompanied by a crackle of electric blue and the sharp smell of gunpowder and chipped granite, God appeared.

"'Well?'

"Moses pressed his forehead against the earth, he trembled as he spoke, 'Lord, there has been a complication, a bit of a hitch . . .' he tried to push his forehead even further into the hard ground to emphasise his respect and deep regret.

"'No complications! No hitches!' God slammed His mighty fist against the top of the mountain causing the height of Mount Sinai to be lowered by several feet. 'Do you have the recipe, or what?' He demanded to know.

"'Well, yes, but . . .' Moses realised he'd be lucky to escape alive.

"'No buts. Hand it over, I may have all eternity, but I haven't got all day!'

"Moses raised his head slightly, he had to play his cards exactly right. God was a pretty impatient sort and didn't like to be thwarted. Moses knew he'd get only one crack at getting it right and even the wrong inflection on a single word of the proposition he was about to put to His Extreme Crankiness and it would be all over. He'd be consigned to Jewish history as Mo the schmuck, the one who got lost up the mountain and left his people wandering aimlessly in the desert!

"He wore an appropriately injured expression as he spoke, 'Well, yes, that's all very well for You, Lord. You haven't got a wife. I begged her, I threatened to beat her. Finally I did beat her!'

"'Well, good for you, Mo, now we have a wife-beater!'

"'Well, more a clip behind the ear, not a proper beating you understand, a light clip just so she knew who's the boss,' Moses quickly corrected.

"'Hand the recipe over then, we haven't got forever. Even chipping nine commandments will take all morning.'

"'Well, you see, Lord, it's . . . well, there's a condition.' Moses gulped, 'I cannot tell a lie, the recipe is missing a critical ingredient.'

"'Missing! Ingredient? What do you mean a missing ingredient?' God looked really mad and a whole heap of dark clouds appeared above His head and the top of Mount Sinai disappeared from view.

"'Well, Lord, you see, my wife wants a clause put in the contract. Well, not a clause really, more like an extra commandment.'

"'Clause? Contract? Commandment? Who said contract? WHO MAKES THE COMMANDMENTS AROUND HERE ANYWAY!'

"'That's what I told her,' Moses said quickly. 'But she wouldn't listen! She's got no respect. You know what she said?' The leader of the Israelites paused momentarily, 'She said, "No extra commandment, no secret ingredient!"' Moses spread his hands wide, 'What can you do? A woman is a woman, God created them. Who knows how a woman's mind works?'

"'You're right, not even Me. So? What is this secret ingredient?'

"Moses was practically whimpering as he spoke, 'Lord, You got to promise first? You've got to okay an extra commandment. Until You do this my lips are sealed. You've tasted my wife's chicken soup, which is absolutely heavenly, absolutely guaranteed perfect every time! Now it's for You to say, Lord.'

"Moses knew he was skating on thin ice, it was a cheeky approach, he hoped to hell he was playing his cards right; after all, this was *the* God of Wrath, the original tough guy, this was not some cheap trader to be haggled with over a worthless trinket in the bazaar. To his relief God seemed quite calm. The birds continued to sing in the nearby salt scrub and a chicken hawk gliding high above his head didn't tumble from the sky. Finally God said, 'Okay, I hear you, what's the extra commandment she wants?'

"Moses looked a bit abashed as he spoke, 'Understand, Lord, personally I recommend against it. As a matter of fact this commandment is going to hurt me more than it will hurt You.'

"'Well, that's a good, positive sign,' God said cheerfully.

"Moses coughed into his fist before he spoke. 'The tenth commandment my wife wants, Lord, is ... *Thou shalt not commit adultery?'*

"God smiled to himself, a surprisingly benign smile and instantly the sky became a brighter, nicer shade of blue. 'Hmm, a bit impractical, but not a bad concept — one man one wife — no hanky panky. Not bad, not bad at all!'

"'If You say so, Lord,' Moses replied in a dejected voice; he was trying to decide which he enjoyed more, chicken soup or adultery. It was a hard decision for a man with an Egyptian upbringing.

"'Okay, tell her we got a deal! But We can't make *no adultery* Number Ten, it's rather too lightweight for a tenth and final commandment, a bit impractical too. Let

Me see, yes, We'll make it Number Seven; buried towards the end like that it shouldn't prove too troublesome.' Pleased with Himself, the Almighty rubbed His hands at the thought of the chicken soup recipe He now owned and, at once, giant boulders commenced to crash and tumble down the slopes of Mount Sinai and roll several miles into the desert to create the Golan Heights.

"'Now, tell Me at once,' God demanded, 'What's the missing secret ingredient essential to your wife's chicken soup? Keep it simple, I'm no great cook!'

"Moses knew a momentous moment when he saw one and he modulated his voice to suit the powerful sentiment of his words.

'A JEWISH MOTHER'S LOVE.'"

Rose let the words hang there on their own for a moment, then she added, "That's what goes into *real* chicken soup, that's what makes the difference, that's what makes it positively divine. Believe me, that crap Mr Campbell makes is from the devil's own kitchen!" She looked up at Damon who was trying hard not to laugh.

"Rose, that's a terrible story!" Damon said at last.

Rose ignored us and her voice continued serious, "So now you know where the power comes from in my chicken soup, hey? You must have some every day, darling. You'll see, it will soon make you strong again."

Though the properties of Rose's chicken soup were undoubtedly divine and the love she brought to bear in its preparation was unquestionably efficacious, Damon's real penicillin was Celeste. At his insistence I'd gone through the boxes piled up in my cardboard kingdom until, some hours later, I found the one with the Italian art and another with travel books Benita had collected over the years.

At night Celeste would make him a couple of famous FES sandwiches (Fried Egg Sandwich) and they'd pore over the Italian books as she reconstructed every detail of her trip for him.

She'd tell him about Florence and its marvellous light and undoubtedly the best ice cream in the history of the whole world! Pistachio, Peach, Apricot, Wild Berry and the most scrumptious chocolate ice cream in the entire universe and a shop that sold chocolate in every colour imaginable, green and blue and pink, every colour more delicious than the last!

They'd look for "fingers of God" paintings and she'd repeat the story of the wonderment of light after the afternoon storm. She spoke of Venice and it came alive as she talked and he saw it's shimmering waterways and the way the ancient buildings seemed to float in light and dance in the hazy air. Every meal she'd taken was talked about precisely and Benita, who is no cook but knows all about Italian food from the eating end, would join them to talk about a particular dish, where it came from and what sort of wine Celeste would have been served to drink with it if she'd been able to afford wine.

In this way each day of Celeste's journey was recreated. Damon wanted to experience everything in his head, to be mentally holding Celeste's hand as she journeyed across Italy. It was marvellous penicillin. Celeste has the eye of an artist and besides, is very articulate, and so she would bring her trip alive for Damon who, in turn, had a wonderful memory and a head for facts. He made Celeste give him exact locations, the heights of the buildings, even the precise dimensions of the Gates of Paradise in the Duomo in Florence.

Celeste would come hurrying home from university each evening almost breathless with anticipation. She loved Damon so much, she wanted him to be his old self again and so, in her mind, she made him so. And in the process she convinced all of us that he was, that the old Damon had returned.

Until the *Salmonella*, the night sweats had been the only indication that Damon's HIV virus had progressed further. But the sweats had eventually passed and now the effects of the *Salmonella* seemed also to be fading. As the days went by Damon put on a little weight and we conned ourselves that he was soon looking more like his old self again.

With only one difference. His eyes. We couldn't escape Damon's eyes.

This difference is best explained in Celeste's own words for, as much as she tried to wind back the clock, Damon's eyes betrayed him and reminded us that things were not the same as they'd been.

"When Adam took me straight from the airport to the hospital and I walked into that awful room, I was terribly shocked to see what had happened to Damon. He looked like . . . he really looked like Jesus. Like the image of Jesus I'd seen all those times in all those churches. His beard had grown long and scraggly and his face was so thin. Damon had always had a sort of round face and now his cheeks were hollow and his face sharp, the skin seemed to be pulled tightly downwards so that you could almost see the shape of the skull underneath. His eyes looked, you know, his eyeballs had sunken. That was the look that started to happen, it's such an AIDS look. He'd aged, he'd grown a lot older, his hair had started to fall out, because of all the drugs he'd been given I should imagine.

"When he saw me he cried, we both cried, and I spent several hours at the hospital until I was almost fainting with exhaustion. I hadn't really slept, except in snatches, for four days. But it was so lovely, so lovely, being with him again, knowing he wasn't dead.

"But that first shock, that first look from his eyes has never left me. It's a look that comes and never goes away. It never again left Damon and, sometimes, I'd just start crying in the middle of a lecture at uni or when I was having a cup of coffee somewhere with a friend. I'd just start weeping when I thought of Damon's eyes. Damon's crucified Christ eyes."

22

---

*Where Pooled Blood led to Murder by Decree and Doctors
and Politicians Stood by with their Hands Firmly Clasped about
their Buttocks.*

Damon had, in a matter of weeks, actually grown physically older, his hair had started to fall out and his skin became strangely translucent. He walked tentatively, like an old man, each foot placed carefully forward as though he were afraid of losing his balance, his neck stiff and pushed slightly forward like a cartoon turtle walking on his hind legs, his shoulders hunched over as though he wore some great scarabaeus shell.

He wasn't happy with the way he'd been treated at Royal Prince Alfred Hospital and he was no longer willing to be under the general care of the biro-tapper. Damon particularly disliked this doctor and no doubt the feeling was mutual. This medico was from the old school, not accustomed to being questioned, whereas Damon's manner assumed that they were both on an equal basis.

This was not the way the biro-tapper saw his relationship with his patients and so their mutual physician-patient understanding had deteriorated considerably.

Damon felt that he would need to find proper care for himself elsewhere. While he loved and trusted Denise, she wasn't in control of his palliative care and, although the sister in charge of the Haemophilia Centre, she too had to follow instructions. Denise was to become an expert at caring for haemophiliacs with AIDS but, at this stage, she lacked the expertise to care for both conditions in one patient. Damon knew that things had changed for him. Haemophilia was now the secondary condition with which he would have to cope and all his energy would need to be concentrated on his AIDS. He would maintain contact with Denise for his haemophilia needs but would make alternative arrangements for the AIDS.

Damon was one of the earliest haemophiliacs to contract AIDS and eventually nearly one hundred of the state's haemophiliacs would become infected with HIV, a legacy from a seemingly uncaring medical system. When it became known in American medical journals as early as 1981 that a disease usually seen only in people with impaired immune systems was occurring in alarmingly increased numbers in homosexual men, nothing was done to stop gay people giving blood. There is clear evidence from the U.S. at the time which could have alerted the Australian authorities and the evidence is shown here.

In the 6 June 1981 and 3 July 1981 issues of *Morbidity and Mortality Weekly Report*, published by the Centers for Disease Control (CDC) in the USA, there was a front page report of the presence of Kaposi's Sarcoma (KS), a rare cancer usually found in elderly men, in twenty-six young homosexual males. In addition, an almost equally rare form of pneumonia, *Pneumocystis carinii* (PCP), had occurred over the past twenty months in fifteen homosexual men, two of whom had also suffered from KS.

Today we know that both these diseases are typical of AIDS but at that stage no such disease was known. However, in the final paragraph of the 3 July 1981 report, the following appeared: "Physicians should be alert for Kaposi's Sarcoma, PC pneumonia, and the opportunistic infections associated with immunosuppression in homosexual men."

These were the first early warning signs and we know they reached Australia only a week after the reports were issued. In the 28 August 1981 issue of *MMWR*, the leading article stated that an additional seventy cases of these two diseases had been discovered, the vast majority among young, white, homosexual men. Of the 108 cases now known, forty-three had already proved fatal. It was becoming increasingly clear that male homosexuals as a group were becoming infected with a causative agent, possibly a virus, and that any centre, anywhere in the world with a large homosexual community ought to be on the alert. Once again there is no doubt that this information was available to Australian centres of immunology as well as Australian sources of blood supply. The *first* really serious warning about possible blood contamination had been issued.

By December of 1982, it was becoming abundantly clear that AIDS, as this new disease was now named, was almost certainly being transmitted through blood. Again the *MMWR* issue of 20 December 1982 is quoted: "This report and continuing reports of AIDS among persons with haemophilia raise serious questions about the possible transmission of AIDS through blood and blood products. The Assistant Secretary of Health is convening an industry committee to address these questions."

The *MMWR* issue of 4 March 1983 summarised the report of the industry committee which included the National Gay Task Force, the National Haemophilia Foundation, the American Red Cross, the American Association of Blood Banks, the Council of Community Blood Centres and several other organisations. The report stated: "Blood products or blood appear responsible for AIDS among haemophilia patients who require clotting factor replacement." Further on in the same report the Public Health Service makes several recommendations, first, and most obvious, being that sexual contact should be avoided with persons known to have AIDS. The second recommendation reads: "As a temporary measure, members of groups at increased risk for AIDS should refrain from donating plasma and/or blood. This recommendation includes all individuals belonging to such groups, even though many individuals are not at risk of AIDS".

The National Haemophilia Foundation, a member of the industry committee, made a special recommendation: "The interim recommendation requesting that high-risk persons refrain from donating plasma and/or blood is especially important for donors whose plasma is recovered from plasmapheresis centres or other sources and pooled to make products that are not inactivated and may transmit infections such as hepatitis B. The clear intent of this recommendation is to eliminate plasma and blood potentially containing the putative AIDS agent from the supply."

The recommendations end by saying: "... the above recommendations are prudent measures that should reduce the risk of acquiring and transmitting AIDS."

I know that some readers may find the information above somewhat tedious to follow and some may even ask what has all this to do with Australia? After all, these findings come from the US and the same conditions might not have prevailed here.

In fact, this is precisely my point, the gay nexus between America and Australia was already well developed in 1981. New York, Los Angeles and San Francisco, the three major centres of the new infection, were linked with Sydney as the most desirable destinations for homosexuals from both countries. Special gay package tours from America to Australia, and the other way around, were well established and Australian health authorities, aware of this, kept a constant check on the migration of sexually transmitted diseases among this group. What I am saying is that what happened to gays in America was an *immediate* and urgent warning that Australia was likely to be next or, given the frequent travel and known promiscuity of gays travelling between both countries, the simultaneous manifestation of a new infection was never out of the question. The weekly reports through the American Centers for Disease Control *are* and *were* required reading among those people in this country whose task it is to be concerned with infectious disease.

This clear, you could say overwhelming, warning to Blood Banks, hospitals and health authorities should, as a matter of sound medical practice, have led to an immediate cessation of homosexuals donating blood.

Of course the vast majority of the blood given by the gay community would naturally have been uncontaminated and therefore a valuable source of supply. But as there was no way at that time of removing the virus from contaminated blood, health authorities should, as a matter of correct procedure, have declined all homosexual donors. But, of course, no such thing happened. Perhaps at a pinch, this can be understood in 1981 and 1982. After all it was early days, the AIDS virus was still a mysterious disease thought to be carried predominantly by homosexuals. At that stage no person in Australia had actually been diagnosed as having AIDS. In fact, Australia's first AIDS case was hospitalised in Sydney in late 1982.

But in 1983 this was no longer the case, the evidence was conclusive that HIV was carried through blood. The 1983 medical journals throughout the world reported that AIDS was spreading world-wide. In June that year, the Council for Europe recommended that doctors use caution in prescribing blood concentrates made from vast pools which might contain infected blood. This followed a warning by the National Haemophilia Foundation of America carried in an official report of the CDC, arguably the most prestigious medical authority in the world for infectious diseases, clearly stating that haemophiliacs *should not* be treated with plasma from pooled blood resources. However, the new product containing AHF (antihaemophilic factor), though prepared from large donor pools, came into common use during the 1980s, replacing the earlier cryoprecipitate. While a cryo transfusion exposes the haemophilia patient to a smaller donor pool, it is much less convenient than the freeze-dried, assayed AHF.

I must, as a matter of integrity, point out that one man did try to do something. In May 1983, Dr Gordon Archer, Director of the Blood Bank, made a public announcement that homosexuals would no longer be accepted as blood donors. It was his belief that AIDS was in the Australian blood supply and this step had to be taken in an attempt to control its spread.

When Dr Archer, on behalf of the NSW Blood Bank, issued the edict, the Sydney Blood Bank was picketed by gay activists. Leaflets were distributed to donors branding Dr Archer a bigot and anti-homosexual. The press and media had a field day and the rights of Australians to a blood supply free of AIDS were ignored in favour of gay civil rights.

The Australian Red Cross, fearing a backlash from gay activists, backed down and ignored Dr Archer's recommendation, so that gay donors were not seriously stopped from giving blood for the next two years. The Archer recommendation was simply overturned and a new policy announced allowing homosexuals to give blood providing they did not have "multiple partners". Of course there was no possible method, short of a signed affidavit, for the Blood Bank to determine whether a donor had one or a hundred partners. Nor did anyone institute a reasonable questionnaire or interview technique in an attempt to vet or isolate promiscuous bisexuals or homosexuals.

In this way the "civil rights" of homosexuals to give blood was given over the rights of patients in hospitals requiring blood or haemophiliacs whose very lives depended on it. The consequence of this backdown by the Australian Red Cross is that many, many Australians, my son Damon among them, have died and will continue to die. It is now generally regarded that this period of three years — 1983 to 1985 — when basically all the facts required to take responsible action were known, and nothing was done, was when most victims of medically acquired AIDS became infected.

So, in summary, this is what was known in Australia in March 1983:

- AIDS is in the Australian blood supply.
- AIDS is a disease largely carried in Australia by homosexuals.
- AIDS is transmitted by blood.
- AIDS has been transmitted in the U.S. through a blood transfusion.
- Haemophiliacs are directly exposed to and have AIDS through donor blood.

In fact, in June 1983, Professor Ian Gust wrote an editorial in the Australian Medical Journal in which he presented the Australian situation: "It is now recommended that individuals at risk should not donate blood. The risks to persons with haemophilia can only be covered by replacing pool Factor VIII (AHF) with single donor cryoprecipitate — a formidable exercise."

What all this means is that it was acknowledged that homosexuals who were most likely to carry HIV, should not be allowed to give blood, and that the only way a haemophiliac could be completely safe was to stop using AHF and return to transfusions of cryoprecipitate.

Yet no move was made to change back to cryoprecipitate and AHF, now known to carry HIV, continued to be issued as the *only* blood product available to Australia's haemophiliacs, who were told that it was completely safe and that no danger whatsoever existed for the user.

The knowledge that HIV was transported in blood was so widespread among the haemophiliac community in 1983 that I recall asking whether the use of AHF was safe and what was its potential for carrying HIV. It now transpires that we were not the only haemophiliac family to ask these questions and to seek reassurance from our health authorities. The point behind our questions was fundamental. If AHF was a risk we would have elected to continue to use cryoprecipitate. If necessary we would supply the blood for its manufacture from our families and friends whom we could reasonably assume to be outside the high-risk area and who, in any event, could easily be tested for AIDS before giving blood.

We had always been warned that cryoprecipitate, the previous transfusion product, could potentially carry hepatitis; though in the seventeen years of Damon's haemophilia we did not hear of a single haemophiliac who had contracted hepatitis through blood transfusion. The assurance that AHF was safe to this enormous degree from HIV was a major consolation. Even so, had we wanted to return to the older and more tedious method of transfusions we were not given a choice, cryoprecipitate had been withdrawn from the system and was simply no longer available.

We believed what we'd been told and embraced the new blood product for all it was worth. We were grateful and counted ourselves fortunate to be the recipients of such a marvellous medical advance as the multiple donor AHF. It meant a 60 ml transfusion using an easy-to-store powdered concentrate that was mixed in moments with distilled water, rather than a 250 ml bag of *Factor VIII* frozen plasma.

The government acted totally irresponsibly in not withdrawing AHF until it could be certain there was no contamination. That decision must surely stand as one of the most cold-blooded and uncaring in the history of our national health system.

Compounding this cynicism, in 1985, two years after a clear warning that it carried HIV, AHF blood product was finally subjected to heat treatment to make it safe; this had been developed in October in the previous year. For once the Australian medical system didn't lag behind. But untreated and therefore potentially still contaminated AHF, *already* in the fridges of Australian haemophiliacs, appears not to have been withdrawn from use. Certainly those supplies we carried in our own fridge were not returned. I contacted the Haemophilia Society of Australia which was unable to find a single family who were contacted by the health authorities and asked to return or destroy existing supplies of AHF.

Had the Blood Bank and government health authorities at the time allowed for reasoned debate within the community and released all the available information about AIDS, the matter might have been quite easily settled and a great many innocent lives saved.

I disagree fundamentally with the gay rights movement on the issue of compensation for people who acquired AIDS through receiving infected blood via blood transfusion. Their argument is that there is no distinction to be drawn between those contaminated by blood products and those infected by anal intercourse between two consenting males. Allowing that compassion for either group is not in question, there is a legal argument which we use in other areas of insurance against accident, where there is fault caused by neglect by a second party. The tragedy is that no accident insurance exists for medically acquired AIDS.

The Australian barrister, Mr Jack Rush, on 15 May 1992, at a conference organised by the Australian Doctors Fund states the legal argument:

"I would submit that the distinction is obvious. I give the following analogy. An accident in circumstances where the driver is injured as a consequence of driving his car off the road into a light pole will normally occur in circumstances where no one is at fault. On the other hand a person injured in a car as a result of someone else driving through a red light can look to the other driver for compensation. The injuries occurred as a consequence of someone else's negligence. Our law entitles the other person to claim compensation for injuries occurring as a consequence of the other driver's negligence.

"Thus the haemophiliac or the blood recipient who can show HIV infection as a consequence of the negligence, the want of reasonable care, from the Red Cross, the Commonwealth Serum Laboratory, a doctor or anyone else, has a right to compensation upon proving the case. Indeed the gay man who can show his infection is due to the negligence of someone else has the same rights.

"In this context to condemn these settlements and to equate a person who has contracted the AIDS virus as a consequence of the receipt of contaminated blood with a person who has contracted AIDS as a consequence of consensual anal intercourse is fallacious."

Of far greater interest to me is that compensation should be paid to rehabilitate families where a member has died from medically acquired AIDS. It costs a great deal both materially and psychologically, to care for someone with AIDS outside the medical system. The bread winners, these days mostly both parents, if a child is involved, or the remaining adult, if a husband or wife, must give up their jobs for at least the last two years in the AIDS cycle. Often, because they do not belong to a gay network or even if they do, they are afraid of admitting to AIDS in the family. The fear, not always ill founded, is that they may be forced to leave their neighbourhood or local school. Often, they are forced to mortgage their homes to keep on paying living costs and or supplying extra needed comfort to a family member with AIDS. In terms of mental welfare, other children or members of the family are often neglected or put under such severe pressure that they develop severe psychological problems. When it's all over, not just one life has been destroyed but, in many cases, the future of an entire family. It is for these people that compensation is necessary. In the case of a haemophiliac with AIDS there isn't even a life insurance policy to be collected, as they cannot be insured. My concern is for who is left behind. It is for this reason that I think reasonable compensation should be paid, as it has been elsewhere in the civilised world, by compassionate and caring societies.

I have been criticised in the gay media for stressing that Damon died of *medically acquired* AIDS, the imputation being that, by differentiating between *sexually* acquired and *medically* acquired AIDS, I am suggesting one victim of this terrible disease is *innocent* and another somehow *guilty*. This thought has never entered my head. While there is absolutely no question of *innocent* and *guilty* AIDS sufferers, there is clearly the question of a guilty medical system. By stressing that my son died of *medically acquired* AIDS I am pointing to the medical profession, the attendant politicians and those people in the health care bureaucracy, who allowed cost and the fear of upsetting what they regarded as a potentially powerful minority faction, to lead to the deaths of a small, unimportant and apparently expendable group.

No guilt can reasonably belong to the AIDS sufferer, patently HIV does not differentiate between the homosexual or heterosexual. The responsibility for Damon's death must be laid squarely at the feet of a myopic medical and health system and the men and women who made the critical decisions during this period. There is sufficient evidence to suggest that they knew what they were doing. If they didn't know, then the indictment is even greater, because it was their professional duty to know. Either way their actions perpetrated a form of institutionalised manslaughter for which, in the end, they must accept responsibility.

What clearly happened was that the collective conscience wasn't questioned, the moral decision was, in each instance, left to somebody else. In plain language, "I was only doing my job, following orders", remains the worst of both moral and institutional excuses.

Human lives should count more than balance sheets, but the introduction of AHF was clearly a monetary decision — it was cheaper to buy and cheaper to store. The introduction of the blood factor concentrate in a more convenient powder form was arbitrary, cynical and instituted without even superficial concern for the consequences which were, even then, apparent after the most casual perusal of the available facts by any half-competent haematologist. However, when you habitually think of people as a statistic and not as heart and mind, muscle, sinew and good red blood, as was done with the 260 known medically acquired, HIV-infected haemophiliacs in Australia, it is easy to sacrifice them for a better looking balance sheet. This is still the case today. In a statement made this year to the Standing Committee on Social Issues of the New South Wales Parliament a spokesperson for the Commonwealth Government said:

"The Commonwealth Government has made an assessment that, in general, health authorities were not responsible for medically acquired HIV and, on this basis, legal aid may soon cease to fund these cases."

Soon the problem will have disappeared altogether, as the last of the HIV-infected haemophiliacs and others with medically acquired AIDS die or the legal statute of limitations applies. Distraught, broken and mostly debt-ridden families will be left to cope for themselves in a nation whose politicians don't appear to give a damn and are more interested in covering their backsides than uncovering the truth.

Shame! Shame! Shame!

Beloved Australia, I am terribly ashamed of you. Ashamed that as a country we acted this way, ashamed that no one seems to care, ashamed of politicians who have ducked for cover, of doctors and other bureaucrats who have ignored the rights of individuals who died through lack of care or responsibility and who have wilfully confused evidence to prevent themselves from being indicted.

How shall I ever stop feeling bitter?

23

---

*Micro-organisms that Lurk on the Fringes of
Human Existence and a Lopsided Rabbit
named Cassidy.*

Damon stayed at Rose Bay for a month while Celeste
continued living above Dinky Di Pies which was reasonably close by. It was during this period that we all came
in contact for the first time with the AIDS network. CSN,
Community Support Network, consisted largely of vol-
unteers who were helping people with AIDS and most
of its helpers were men from within the gay community.

CSN sent us Tim Rigg a charming nurse who was
himself HIV positive and must have been in his early
forties. He was to become a close personal friend of
Damon and Celeste. Though he hadn't as yet shown any
outward symptoms of the virus, Tim was to prove an
important connection. He was an experienced nurse who,
finding himself to be HIV positive, switched to caring for
AIDS patients. For the first time Damon could talk to

someone who understood the disease and who had the emotional energy to explain it to him.

Tim was a realist, he didn't believe in the possibility of a cure for AIDS. "We are going to die, Damon. It's only a question of time," he would say without melancholy in his quiet, matter-of-fact voice. Somehow Tim's reconciled attitude bolstered Damon's determination to live. "There's always an exception, Tim. I'm going to be the exception, you'll see." In fact, Damon seemed as sure of his ultimate triumph as Tim was certain of his demise.

Based as it was, on opposing points of view, it was a strange friendship, but somehow it worked and the gentle and wise Tim was to remain a part of Celeste and Damon's lives to the very end. Celeste, in particular, came to regard him as a sort of uncle, an adult person who was able to explain Damon's condition to her as it slowly began to take over his life and, with it, her own. Through Tim they came in contact with a cross-section of the gay community and quickly learned that gay is not a finite description, rather, a state of mind, and that within it people differ in character, personality and style as much as heterosexuals.

While this must seem obvious, it isn't. Although homosexuals have lived among us for a thousand generations we still largely think of this sexual proclivity as a set of visible and behavioural characteristics which are manifestly different from our own, as different for instance as a zebra is from a donkey. Somehow heterosexuals don't see gay people simply as accountants and lawyers, doctors, shopkeepers, garbage collectors, van drivers in our society. Gay is not regarded, as it should be, as a description of a sexual proclivity, but is seen instead as a special breed of humankind. Our shame is that we try to make homosexuality into something it isn't, to turn our brothers and sisters into strangers and weirdos to be vilified by a far from straight, heterosexual community.

The two things society doesn't want to talk about are sexuality and dying and with AIDS we have both, so that the tendency is to ignore the disease or to ascribe it to someone who is *different* from yourself or your sons and daughters.

*　　*　　*

The *Salmonella* infection had caused massive damage to Damon's good knee and elbow and allowed his arthritis to attack both joints severely, causing irreversible damage. Suddenly his daily pain load got a lot worse. Now he was seldom, if ever, free of pain and some form of drug became essential, not just daily but several times during each day. The four-hour medication cycle had begun.

Constipation caused by mostly codeine-based drugs was a constant problem and this was followed by bouts of severe diarrhoea when he was forced to take an equally strong laxative. The cycle from severe constipation to acute diarrhoea was taxing his strength and inhibiting his recovery which was slower than he'd expected it to be. We wanted him to stay home with us until he was strong enough to manage safely on his own. But he greatly missed being with Celeste and she, him, and both were determined to get together at the earliest possible time.

This came about sooner than Benita and I had hoped when Xavier, the proprietor of Dinky Di Pies, won a place in the finals of a national meat pie competition conducted by a local radio station. The immediate demand created by the local pie freaks made him decide to expand his operation. In Australia, a reputation built around a meat pie is money in the bank! To do so Xavier needed the flat upstairs for storage and so Adam and Celeste were asked to move out.

After six weeks at home Damon felt he was well enough to live with Celeste again and the two weeks' notice from Dinky Di Pies meant that Celeste was forced to look for a new place. They set about finding accommodation together even though Damon was still walking on crutches, a form of getting around so familiar that at school he'd practically been able to do acrobatics.

Damon spent most of the day on the telephone lining up real estate agents and properties in the eastern suburbs to look at and, after uni each day, Celeste and Damon would take Benita's car and go looking at them. After living in Pyrmont and Glebe, Damon's homing instinct reasserted itself and he wanted to come back to the eastern suburbs, back to the familiar places of his childhood.

It was the usual problem of money, though even more so. The areas nearer home were more expensive and what they were invariably shown was too little for too much. Finally, in late April 1988, just as the colder weather was beginning to carry a bite, they found a lovely little apartment in Vaucluse right on the cliff face, with all its windows looking directly past the elegant South Head lighthouse and out to sea.

Damon loved it immediately; moreover it was within their budget. This seemed like a miracle for it contained a large bedroom, a lounge, a second smaller bedroom, which could become a workroom for Celeste, a small dining alcove and a large glassed-in balcony. They'd seen dozens of flats with less room, a poorer outlook and at a much higher price, this one now seemed too good to be true.

Damon wanted to put a deposit on it immediately, afraid that such a bargain might escape, but Steve, their landlord-to-be, confessed to them that it had a major drawback. At night, at five-second intervals, every room in the flat would blaze momentarily with light and then flick back to darkness as the lighthouse beam struck the windows. He mournfully pointed out that the last tenant had lasted only two weeks. Celeste would later claim that this spasmodic, nocturnal illumination led to the most amazing psychedelic dreams and that, always, within these dreams she'd hear Damon saying, "It's okay, we'll take it, we're not scared of the light."

Notwithstanding the news of the lighting effect, as far as they were both concerned the flat's only drawback was that it was one flight of stairs up from ground level. But Damon was sure he could manage the steps and, while climbing the stairs might prove to be hard work, the steps were fairly wide with a strong banister and he was certain he'd be able to negotiate them. In fact he was right, though sometimes this would be done slowly and painfully and even, on occasion, by pushing himself up backwards on his bottom, one step at a time. Being together again made up for everything and the effect of their few bits of familiar furniture around them and their posh double bed back in a bedroom of their own and in a lovely sunny flat did wonders for Damon's spirits.

Celeste was working again part time at Dinky Di Pies. They soon had enough money to paint the walls and cover the worn linoleum with cheap cotton dhurries and generally fix it up to be a warm and welcoming home of their own with nobody else to share the space. It soon became apparent that Damon couldn't walk more than a few feet at a time without having to stop and wait for the pain to pass. Both knees were now completely shot and he was forced on most days to use a cane. So as soon as he was strong enough to drive I gave him a second-hand, silver grey Mazda RX7 automatic. It was not quite a Ferrari but, nevertheless a very sporty little Japanese car which I'd bought from Alex Hamill, an old and trusted friend. I'd driven the car myself for a while, so knew it to be completely reliable and in immaculate condition. Perhaps I was more generous than many other parents can afford to be. But things don't alleviate pain or prevent the process of dying and, in the end, it's not the things but the love that counts. Love is everything whether you're rich or poor; it is the emotional capital that counts most.

They now had a place of their own and a set of reliable wheels. Only one thing was missing and so Celeste made the trip down to our Vaucluse house (which still hadn't been sold) and fetched Mr Schmoo.

On arrival, Mr Schmoo invited the landlord's cat into the park for a couple of rounds of paw-boxing which he won easily, seemingly with one paw tied behind his back. And so Mr Schmoo took up his accustomed position as the cat who wore the top hat and spats at the lighthouse flats. The whole family was together again and things were definitely looking up.

For the remainder of 1988 all seemed to go well. Going well was probably a relative term with someone as chronically ill as Damon. It meant he was more or less in control of a life of some small quality, one which was not totally dictated by his illness but which, nevertheless, kept him in constant pain. And so Damon and Celeste spent Damon's twenty-second year at the flat with the five-second special illumination effects and he regained much of his old enthusiasm for life. He set about his desktop publishing with a vengeance, determined once again to be the major provider.

Damon didn't like to think of himself as ill or sick and never spoke in such terms. At best he would admit to being unwell and referred to his AIDS condition as, "my thing" and to his arthritis condition as "it". A bleeding joint was simply called "a bleed". "It's not good today" was his response when he had a lot of arthritic pain or, when he had a bad bleed, he'd dismiss this by saying, "It's only a dumb bleed."

While Tim Rigg had done quite a lot to educate us, Celeste and Damon still didn't know a great deal about AIDS. In fact, in the less than five years the disease had been publicly around no one really seemed to know a great deal about it. We soon learned that a peculiar human aspect of this viral disease is that most of its victims seem not to want to know too much about it. One possible explanation is that AIDS is still largely a disease found in the homosexual community, which is, in a great many instances, a covert way of life. Often parents and relatives are unaware of the sexual proclivities of their loved ones and this leads to a hidden agenda. The gay community is, of necessity, well rehearsed in this double standard of behaviour which is often regarded as a primary condition of being a homosexual. Tim himself suffered at the hands of his own family who found his homosexuality difficult to accept and, in fact, were not to know of his AIDS condition until near the end when it became physically obvious that he was terminally ill.

While the Gay Liberation movement has come a long way in its fight for acceptance by the general public, at the ordinary mum-and-dad level, things haven't changed very much. It may be fine for someone else's son to be gay, but quite unacceptable in one's own child. So the attempt by gay men to live two separate lives, a straight one at home and a gay one beyond the garden gate, becomes impossible; they move away and are no longer seen by their families regularly. An occasional visit home isn't too difficult.

But with the advent of AIDS came a new problem. AIDS is a terminal condition which inevitably exposes its host and forces him to confront distraught and often unprepared families with the news of his dying. The personal guilt is often enormous for someone with AIDS who is close to a loving family. It seems to have had the curious effect of repressing the serious nature of the AIDS illness. Add to this the fact that most victims are normal young men with a healthy sense of immortality. The sudden knowledge that AIDS means certain death is an admission to be postponed as long as possible.

Doctors and nurses will tell you that fewer questions are asked by AIDS patients than by victims of almost any other disease. It is not that doctors won't talk about AIDS, but only that there still isn't a great body of understanding of the virus and there isn't a long-established protocol for the disease. The lack of knowledge, normally possessed by a community familiar with a disease for a long time, combined with the reluctance of HIV-infected people to talk becomes understandable.

While this is becoming less true as more people die of AIDS, the full range of first symptoms has taken some time to work out and may still not be fully documented. AIDS strikes in many different ways, simply because it disarms the body's immune system rendering it totally vulnerable. This opens the doors to just about anything that happens to be about. As one doctor put it to us, "AIDS is a thousand different, often unexpected diseases, wrapped in one package."

Damon though was different; because his HIV infection was medically acquired he had no experience of homosexual guilt and he wanted to know everything. Later, as his AIDS condition developed, he was to face prejudice from people who assumed he was a homosexual. This would sadden him greatly, not the thought of being wrongly identified, because I never heard him deny or defend himself, but rather because he discovered that the explicit judgments people made about him often affected the way they behaved towards him. Latent homophobia in the community was one of the reasons he wanted to write a book, to explain that AIDS was something which required compassion and understanding — not judgment, censure and condemnation.

Towards the end of his stay in hospital with the *Salmonella* infection in his knee, when he'd been placed in the general part of the hospital with AIDS infection warning signs outside the door of his room, Damon was visited by a member of a charismatic religious group "witnessing" for the Lord. I should add that what followed would not, I believe, have happened in an AIDS ward where the religious counsellors we encountered were non-judgmental and compassionate people doing a marvellous job. The woman visiting Damon implied that God was ready to forgive him and take him, despite his condition, as his born-again child. All he had to do in return was to repent and accept the Lord Jesus into his heart.

Damon, who had listened patiently to what turned out to be a rather long-winded oration, finally managed to halt the flow of God's messenger by asking her if he could ask questions. She immediately agreed. And, I suspect, in self-defence against the Niagara Falls of verbiage, he asked her whether she would try to answer his questions with a simple yes or no. Once again, the Lord's witness agreed readily. No doubt, in the witnessing business, questions mean progress on the path to salvation. A bit like a salesman closing a sale in a used car lot: when the prospect starts to ask questions you can begin to wind him in.

"Do you believe homosexuality is a sin?" Damon asked.

"Well, the Bible is quite specific about this, it says sodomy . . ."

"Please, a simple yes or no, ma'am."

The lady at his bedside paused momentarily, then made a little expostulating sound to thump home her conviction, "Yes!" she said.

"If it is a sin, then is AIDS God's punishment for this sin?"

"God's mercy and compassion is everlasting and His understanding . . ."

Again Damon cut her short, "Ma'am, please, just yes or no." Damon always fancied himself as a bit of a lawyer and secretly took pride in his logical and incisive mind.

"Well, yes! I have to say that I believe it is." She took another sharp breath, "As I was trying to say, the Bible is quite explicit about sodomy, it is a sin and, God says, 'The wages of sin is death!' "

"Well if sex between consenting adults is a sin for which God has sent AIDS as His terrible punishment, what do you think about sex between an adult male and a non-consenting child?"

The lady was clearly shocked at the question, but Damon rammed it home. "Particularly incest, sex between a father and his daughter. Would that not be an even worse sin in the eyes of God?"

The lady witnessing for the Lord, shocked at Damon's directness, failed to see the all-too-obvious trap, "Well yes, of course it's a sin! A terrible sin!"

"No, that wasn't my question, is it a *worse* sin? A *bigger* sin in the eyes of God?"

The lady paused, looking down at her hands, conscious now that she'd been led into a trap, finally she looked up, "Yes, I suppose so!" She appeared to be angry, she had lost control of the situation and was unable to find an apposite quote from the New Testament to cover her confusion, her training obviously hadn't covered incest.

"Well then, why doesn't God send a terrible disease down to infect the father rapist of the sexually assaulted child?" Damon asked.

The woman had already started to gather her tracts together and dipping into her handbag she produced a boiled lolly wrapped in a twist of cellophane and, first putting a tract down on the bedside unit, she placed the lolly on the tract. Then she tucked her Bible under her arm and left with the words, "Goodbye, Damon, I will pray to the Lord for you."

"Thank you," Damon said. "Thank you for coming." He was not being a smart arse, though he was probably feeling quite pleased with himself. As a mark, she was too easy and he could afford to be charitable.

The Lord's hospital witness wasn't quite through, she paused at the door, her lips pursed, " 'I am not mocked,' saith the Lord!" She turned and was gone, her heels making a squeaking sound on the rubber corridor as she retreated. Her first brush with AIDS no doubt confirmed her attitude towards homosexuals.

Damon understood completely that gay men, by being rejected by the community and sometimes *even* their families, carried an extra load of emotional pain. He wanted to make people understand that their rejection was cruel and senseless.

It is one of life's ironies that the terrible guilt some AIDS victims feel and the fear of the consequences, when they tell their family of their plight, is sometimes only in their imagination. Conventional wisdom suggests that in many cases the declaration of their HIV status leads to acceptance and compassion from family members, some of whom have been alienated from each other for years. Underneath everything, love is a powerful reconciling force.

For most parents and families the most traumatic issue

is not the fact that a son is gay, but that he is dying. Though sadly, in smaller communities, a loved one often cannot come home to die, because the dreadful reality is that the parents still have to live in a bigoted community after their son's death. The disapproval of a small community is likely to make the victim's relatives secondary victims of the disease. AIDS is proving to bring out the very best in families and the very worst in the community.

Bizarre as it may be, the biggest threat from AIDS may not be the homosexual community, but the heterosexual one. Despite growing evidence to the contrary, the heterosexual community seems confident that AIDS won't happen to them, that it will remain a gay disease. This naivete, no, plain stupidity, is terribly dangerous.

Casual homosexuality, "butt rustling" has always been a part of our social structure. That is, men who do not describe themselves as homosexual but who, several times a year, steal across the sexual border to indulge in a homosexual act. The pubs around Darlinghurst and Oxford Street attract these "butt rustlers"; the "meat market" in these so-called heterosexual pubs is alive and doing a roaring trade. Drunken football teams and Bucks nights as well as lone rangers often end up in places like this.

Liaisons are usually hasty and often take place when partners are drunk, so that sex usually occurs without a condom. These casual assignations are fraught with real infection opportunities that present problems far more difficult to confront than those posed by openly gay men. Both male partners in these casual acts of sex would, if they were confronted, vehemently deny being homosexual or even bisexual. The most common response in research is the reply, "When you're pissed you do lots of bloody stupid things." These outwardly heterosexual men won't disclose that they're having clandestine sex with a male occasionally or even frequently. If they become infected with HIV, this may not be discovered for years, during which time the infection is allowed to spread widely through the community, with the virus not only being passed to other males, but also to girlfriends, wives and children.

In fact the gay community has responded magnificently to AIDS education and has readily adopted the precautionary measures designed to lessen the long-term deaths in the AIDS pandemic. In Australia eighty-seven per cent of homosexuals take proper prophylactic precautions before sex, while the figure for single, heterosexual males is only fifty-seven per cent. In country towns and some working-class communities, the figure is considerably lower.

In the long term, AIDS may yet prove to be a predominantly heterosexual disease where ignorance, stupidity, bigotry and secrecy are the components which most often combine to cause the human immunodeficiency virus to be spread through the community.

* * *

Damon had survived the *Salmonella* infection which his doctors all agreed should have killed him and now the despair he had begun to feel when he'd entered hospital during the crisis had changed. He was once again adamant he could beat AIDS. He felt he'd seen the worst, faced death, and now was ready to conquer his affliction with the sheer force of his will.

Damon sincerely believed he could make his body grow new T-cells until his blood would once again contain the required number to fight off infection. He'd go to the Haemophilia Centre for a T-cell count convinced that there would be an increase in numbers; when this didn't happen he simply told himself that he hadn't given his mind sufficient time to do the required trick. After all, who knows how long it takes to generate a new T-cell?

This absolute conviction worried his friend Tim who had seen AIDS victims, buoyed by false hope and then suddenly confronted with the certainty of their death, give up and die in a matter of days. Tim thought of himself as "living with AIDS" rather than dying from it, a way of regarding this terrible disease which is both useful and positive. He insisted it was only a matter of time to their certain demise; that Damon should get on with living. Damon became all the more positive that, while the clock might be running out for Tim, it was only a matter of exerting the correct amount of willpower before he, Damon Courtenay, would be on the road to ultimate recovery.

Tim also persuaded Damon to look to the Prince Henry Hospital for his AIDS care. The AIDS section of this grand old hospital was in a separate part of the grounds, in a building named Marks Pavilion with a lovely view over Little Bay, a rugged aspect of heathland and rocky coastline seen from most of the windows. Here too, the nursing staff were sympathetic and highly trained and this was where Damon was to meet Rick Osborne, a senior nurse, who took a special liking to him and proved to be a wonderful friend through many of the difficult times to come.

Tim had been chosen as one of the experimental group to be placed on AZT, a drug which was showing some success in America in inhibiting the progression of AIDS. Through Tim, Damon applied for selection in the AZT trial and, to our joy, he was quickly accepted. This was definitely a step in the right direction; provided his health didn't deteriorate Damon was convinced he could fix what was already wrong with him.

The AZT treatment placed an extra burden on both Damon and Celeste; like everyone else on the test dosage it was largely a matter of guessing. This was a brand new drug which hadn't gone through the elaborate testing procedures common for a new drug. Those on it were the guinea pigs, doses varied from patient to patient and so effects of the drug differed widely.

Damon was required to take two tablets every four hours and he was given a beeper box which was loud enough to wake him up at night to take his AZT pills. He'd wake up too stiff from his arthritis to get out of bed and Celeste would have to get up to fetch him a glass of water and make him something to eat. In an attempt to lessen the toxicity of the drug, he was required to eat something solid prior to taking the medication. This meant that Celeste was sharing Damon's disrupted night and having to put in a full day of uni study the next day as well. Nonetheless, they both felt that it was worth it — even if he had to wake up every four hours for the remainder of his life, it was worth it.

It had soon become apparent that AZT didn't suit Damon, it made him feel sick and he had become anaemic. But at first his spirits remained high. AZT was going to halt his AIDS until someone found the cure; he told himself it just didn't matter how he felt, what his reaction was, it was worth it. The determination he showed during this period is remarkable. AZT is a highly toxic drug and it was to prove especially so for Damon. Yet he hung in and whenever he wasn't too sick he worked at his desktop publishing company which he'd called "The Desktop Pub". Damon's natural charm had earned him several regular customers and, if he wasn't exactly dependable, they seemed always to forgive him and to extend his deadlines. And, while he certainly wasn't making a fortune, he was paying his way.

Damon had also met a remarkable haemophiliac from America, a man in his early fifties named Conrad Masterton, who had been semi-crippled in his late twenties by constant bleeding into the knee joints and had only recently had artificial knees put in. "My stainless steel knees," he called them, although they were made of titanium. Conrad's knees proved to be quite miraculous, he was able to walk all day with regular small rests, the joints behind the knee cap seldom created a bleed and were infinitely better than the originals had ever been.

Damon talked to us of going to the States and having his own stainless steel knees put in. As always with him, he could see the instant and splendid result in his imagination. The freshly kneed Damon spoke of going on bush walks with Celeste and being endlessly mobile, practically the same as anyone else. AZT was going to get him so well that he'd be able to go over to America and have the operation before the end of the year.

In the meantime he decided he'd build himself a fish tank. Not the usual expanded goldfish bowl — Damon didn't think about crawling if he could walk in the fish-keeping business — he wanted an aquarium choked with piscean exotica. Conning me for the money to buy the tank he explained, "Fish in a tank are a lot like me. You see, Dad, aquarium fish are in the same situation as I am, they have to make the most of their immediate environment because it's just about all they've got. I'm going to build this great fish tank with all the fish mod cons, luxuriant weeds and rocks and grottoes, real habitats for big and baby fish." He looked up at me, "When you're aching and in pain and can't read a book or concentrate on anything else you can watch fish in a tank. I don't know why it helps but it does, the way they move their bodies you just can't imagine a fish in pain."

Celeste for once refused to accommodate him and allow the over-large fish tank into their tiny living room. So it had to go on to the glassed-in verandah leading from the main bedroom.

Like all Damon's projects the fish tank and the fish that lived in it were not without disaster. The first tank they bought from an advertisement in *The Trading Post* cost one hundred dollars. The guy who sold it to them explained that he was a truck driver, that things were going crook for the road-hauling business in New South Wales. "The big companies, mate, they play us off, one against the fucking other!" He was fed up and moving his rig to Perth to get into the wheat-hauling business. He must have been a relation of Bob the carer of cripples who sold Damon the Fiat 124, for he swore the tank had been running, "Like the bloody Taronga Park Zoo aquarium, mate!" He painted a mental picture of a tank swarming with tropical fish just two days before he'd put the ad in the paper. "Pity, if I'd 'a only known, I'd 'a sold youse the bloody lot cheap!" When Damon asked him who'd bought his magnificent collection, for a moment the truck driver looked bemused, then flicking the ash from his cigarette on the kitchen floor, he said, "Dunno, mate, some Jew bastard who come up from Kogarah!"

When they got home with the tank Damon, with Celeste and Adam doing all the heavy work, located it on the glassed-in balcony on the rusty stand ("Whack a bita Kill-rust on it, mate, be as good as gold!") which had come with it for an extra twenty-five bucks. The fish tank seemed to take hours to fill with Adam and Celeste carrying water from the bathroom in two small cooking pots Celeste owned. Finally it stood resplendent, filled with water, ready to be art-directed with weed and rock and shell, and then grandly occupied with what Damon saw as a major collection of fish, not dissimilar to a small, but not insignificant, corner of the Great Barrier Reef.

But alas, the rubber seals which had dried out from months, perhaps years, of lying in the truck driver's backyard in the sun burst open at two in the morning flooding the entire flat and leaking through the wooden floor boards to awaken Steve in the apartment below, by means of a steady drip landing on his chest as the water slowly destroyed the ceiling above him.

The next fish tank, just as big, but this time brand new and purchased at a cost of one hundred and ten dollars, complete with five-year warranty, was installed without mishap. After which Damon went shopping all over metropolitan Sydney for the world's truly exotic fish. He naturally avoided any of the mainstream commercial aquariums, on the basis that they'd be over-popular and frequented by mere amateurs and therefore would be unlikely to carry suitable stock for the true cognoscenti of the fish world. Instead, he would visit strange places with faded signs which told of once having been pet shops, their dusty windows still containing sun-faded pet food posters of kittens playing with a ball of wool, bursting packets of birdseed which rising damp had caused to grow and subsequently die in pathetic patches of faded straw. Some windows contained cans, their labels long since rusted off as well as old bottles of mange solution, which told of a time when it truly had been a dog's life in the local canine world. Inside, Damon would have deep and earnest conversations with old men in short grey coats who hovered over rows of fish tanks and who produced well thumbed books and ancient exotic fish catalogues and who talked of blood worms and fish influenza.

That was the thing about Damon, he could go from nought to one hundred in a matter of minutes when it came to gathering information. He had a knack of seeming to be an expert, when he knew practically nothing about a subject. It was the way he listened and asked questions and, with no effort, seemed to produce jargon in the correct context, which he'd only minutes before heard for the first time. He could also isolate the information he needed, gathering only what was important for him to know. In a matter of a few days he had an almost encyclopaedic knowledge of the most exotic tropical fish, while knowing practically nothing about aquarium fish in general or the more common and therefore hardy and likely to survive in an amateur fish tank variety.

Damon as usual wanted only *Ferrari* fish and his earnings from The Desktop Pub went straight into the fish tank. Unfortunately, like the high-octane performers they were, the beautiful specimens he brought home didn't always take kindly to their new environment. He was constantly fishing out dead piscean exotica which had only the previous day cost him double digit money and, of course, had come without a guarantee from the previous owner, who must have kept them alive and flipping just long enough for Damon to arrive and purchase them. Often he would discover that one expensive and rare fish was the natural sworn enemy of another equally expensive specimen and a fight to the death would ensue, until both fish ended belly-up in the tank. Once, he saw a whole school of baby Angel fish devoured in ten minutes by his latest multiple-finned, dance of the seven veils, Black Egyptian fish.

The nocturnal light from South Head Lighthouse flickering past the building at five-second intervals also seemed to affect the fish for, strangely, it would sometimes cause a fish to go stir-crazy and take an amazing and non-typical leap right out of the tank to where Mr Schmoo was waiting below to scoop it up.

But soon, despite a great many setbacks, Damon's fish tank settled down and added to his well being. It became a thing of beauty and wonderment to anyone who liked that sort of thing, which wasn't a lot of people.

The last two-thirds of 1988 was proving to be good for Damon, though Celeste recalls little things were starting to add up despite Damon's totally positive attitude. By early 1989 the AZT, that is, the drug intended to slow the progress of the AIDS, was proving to be enormously debilitating. While it seemed to be working well with Tim, it was causing Damon to become anaemic. Furthermore, the nausea it caused him was becoming very severe so that he was constantly on a strong anti-nausea pill, Maxolon.

This proved to be a twofold problem for Damon. He was growing paler and paler each day with less and less energy from the anaemia brought on by the AZT. As well, he suffered from a very rare reaction to the nausea pills which caused him, early in 1989, to throw a massive fit.

Adam was visiting at the time and Damon, in the middle of a sentence went suddenly rigid and seemed to throw himself at the floor. As Adam told it later, "He simply dropped like a stone and began to jerk, his body in a sort of foetal position jerking involuntarily, one leg kicking out, the other folded against his chest; his hands were turned inwards like the claws of a bird and his eyes were popping out. He was making a sort of gurgling noise as though he was fighting for breath or was choking or something. I was totally panicked and so was Celeste. We tried to hold him but he was too strong, the convulsive jerking just went on and on. I screamed to Celeste to call an ambulance and she rushed to get the phone book and then just stood there holding it, not knowing what to do. I couldn't think either. 'Look under "A",' I kept shouting, 'Celeste, look under "A"!' Which was of course stupid, but we were both paralysed by fear and couldn't think to look in the front of the phone book.

Celeste suddenly dropped the book and rushed out of the front door.

"I panicked, 'Don't leave me, don't leave me with Damon!' I cried. But she'd gone and I could hear her jumping the steps two at a time and then, through the open door, I heard her banging both fists against the landlord's door, yelling, 'Steve! Steve!' I stayed with Damon, who was still jerking and gurgling, and I tried to hold him, but he just kept fitting and I thought his eyes were going to pop out of his head and that he was going to die. 'Please God don't let my brother die!' I kept shouting.

"Celeste must have managed to explain it to Steve who called an ambulance which arrived soon afterwards.

"The ambulance took Damon to the Prince of Wales hospital and we followed in the Mazda. The ambulance men must have told the doctor in Emergency that Damon had AIDS, though I can't recall either of us telling them. This was the first time we realised that AIDS could be a bit of red herring. Damon was coming out and then fitting again every few minutes and, even when he was out of a fit, his entire body trembled as though a strong electric current was running through him or he was terribly cold. They started to make tests, giving him all the usual things to stop fits in AIDS patients, but these drugs all proved negative."

The doctors at Prince of Wales, who had no history of Damon, had been trying to contact Damon's palliative specialist only to discover that he didn't have one. Amazingly, they didn't ask Celeste about the drugs he'd been taking, assuming that Damon was gay and neither Celeste nor his brother would know about his medication. Finally, towards midnight, six and half hours after he'd started fitting, Celeste asked the doctor if he thought the fits could have been caused by any of the drugs Damon was taking. "Yes, of course," the doctor replied curtly, "that's why we've been trying to get hold of his palliative regimen."

"But I know them all," Celeste said.

The doctor looked astonished. "You mean you know the drugs he's on, their actual names? What about the dosages?"

"Of course!" Celeste named them, some eight or nine and the frequency and amounts Damon usually took. When she got to Maxolon the doctor jumped, "Anti-nausea? It's unusual for it to have side effects, but not unknown. It's worth a try!" In fact, Maxolon was the culprit. Damon's fit was not something brought about by AIDS at all, but because he was one of the very rare people who reacted badly to Maxolon.

Damon, however, persisted with AZT despite the problems, not the least being the anaemia. He reasoned that he could cope with the anaemia and the constant nausea if the end result was the retardation of AIDS itself. He'd get paler and frailer until all the energy seemed to have leaked out of him and his red blood cell count was down to seven or less, which seemed to occur over a period of about two weeks. When this stage arrived he'd go into hospital, returning to Denise at the Haemophilia Centre for a whole blood transfusion and staying at the Centre all day. He'd arrive home that night with rosy cheeks, full of energy, the miracle of the gift of blood he'd been given, a new Damon, seemingly even strong enough to ignore the profound effects the AZT treatment was having on him.

But then at breakfast one morning, without any warning, Damon started to have a problem breathing. He was suddenly gulping for breath, clasping his chest and finding it difficult to breathe. "I ... c ... can't ... bre ... eathe," he gasped, dropping the piece of toast he was holding.

Celeste wrapped a blanket around him, even though it was a bright and sunny March morning, bundled him into the car and drove to Prince Henry, where he was admitted immediately to Marks Pavilion, the AIDS section of the hospital, and was given oxygen.

This time his problem wasn't hard to diagnose, this was the first incident in Damon's overall prognosis that clearly fitted the AIDS pattern — he was suffering from *Pneumocystis carinii*. Millions of little organisms had filled his lungs and threatened to slowly suffocate him. *Pneumocystis carinii* caused a type of pneumonia so rare that most people in the medical profession hadn't heard of it. It is a microbe which can grow only when the immune system has been depleted, that is, when there are no longer sufficient numbers of T-cells to stop it from growing in its most preferred ecological niche, the human lung. Today, this rare infection, caused by one of the thousands of malevolent micro-organisms that perpetually lurk on the fringes of human existence, is one of the commonest signs that AIDS is starting to take effect. It is now so typical that it is usually referred to, simply, as AIDS-related pneumonia or PCP.

AIDS-related pneumonia brought Damon into Marks Pavilion, the AIDS ward at Prince Henry Hospital for the first time. Here he saw people who were much more sick than he was. Later he was to describe this first visit to me.

"They put an oxygen mask over me and I was soon able to breathe more freely and after a while I was able to look around. I was in a small room with a man in the bed opposite me, who looked like he belonged in a horror movie. His head was shaven and he was skeletal, his mouth sucked in, eyes deep in their sockets, he couldn't have weighed more than four stone. He looked about a hundred years old and I learned later he was twenty-five. He was just a bag of bones in a bag of old skin! It was a terrible shock, like seeing yourself dying, seeing where you could be going, looking further down the path. It was awful and what with my breathing and the pain in my lungs I became terribly depressed. This was the first time I'd thought of myself as someone in a group. Someone in a category, someone other people saw as dying, or in the process of dying, no longer an individual, not Damon Courtenay — just a terminal disease eating at me while I waited for the end to come."

In the beginning, AIDS-related pneumonia killed a great many people and, when it wasn't treated immediately, it still accounted for quite a few deaths. But Celeste had caught it early and Damon's treatment was swift and efficient; using very strong antibiotics it was arrested quickly. Nevertheless he was in hospital for nearly a month and it was not inconceivable that he might have died had it been left for a couple of days, as often happened. That's the very point about AIDS, *anything* can come along once the T-cell barrier is down, opportunistic infections exist around us in their tens of thousands and often death can occur swiftly and with little warning.

The AIDS block was divided into two sections. Downstairs was used for those patients, like Damon, who were in the early stages of the disease and still relatively strong. Upstairs, the advanced patients were nursed, some of these would not return home or would do so simply to die. Damon had arrived when the downstairs section had been full and they'd temporarily placed him upstairs, in a bed where a patient had died only an hour before. It was here that he'd seen for the first time how the disease ravaged its victims and he was never to completely recover from this initial shock.

Damon now knew that he was in very serious trouble, that the fight which lay ahead of him was going to be an horrendous one. He'd suffered the toxic effects of AZT, the dreadful months of nausea, the fitting caused by the Maxolon, which had occurred again on two subsequent occasions and none of this prevented his disease from progressing to PCP, the next stage of AIDS. He lay with the oxygen mask over his face, tears rolling down his cheeks when he heard a voice.

"Hello, Damon, I'm Rick Osborne, the senior nurse."

Damon looked up, hardly able to see through his tears. A small, slim man in his late thirties with a cheerful open face was looking down at him and smiling. "Hello," Damon said, his voice muffled in the mask. He tried to offer his hand, but seemed suddenly too tired and weak to lift it.

"I can't have you staying here, it's much too depressing," the chap named Rick said. "If you don't mind sharing a room downstairs I can squeeze you in, the guy in it leaves tomorrow and then it's all yours, I promise." He looked around in a conspiratorial way and then leaned over to whisper into Damon's ear. "Please don't worry, you're a long, long way from where he is. We'll have *you* better quite soon. You've got PCP, it's a sort of pneumonia, but we'll knock that on the head in no time!" He pulled himself away again and stood up, fussing a little and straightening the sheet around Damon's chest. "Now, what do you say we get the hell out of here, hey?"

Rick, like most of the male nurses in the AIDS section at Prince Henry, was gay himself, but he immediately understood that Damon was not and, was sensitive to the fact that coming into an AIDS ward without any previous warning must be a terrible shock to him. Most patients arrived knowing more or less what to expect from having visited friends in the past.

Rick was originally a kid from Crookwell, a small country town famous for cattle and potatoes. Although he'd long since lost many of his county ways, he still responded in an open and friendly manner and it was difficult not to be charmed by him. As he once explained to me, his family was no big deal, they owned a small holding. Although it wasn't much, his father wanted his only son to inherit it and to be another generation on the land, to hunt and ride and take over from him as he had done from his father. At eight he'd put a .22 rifle in Rick's hands and one early morning they'd gone hunting.

Rick recalled this incident with a wry grin. "It was early morning and a bit misty the way it is in the country, our boots were making a crunchy sound on the frosty grass as we walked across an open, well-cropped paddock. Suddenly my Dad was pointing and whispering,

'There, next to the burnt stump, a real big 'un!'

"I looked in the direction he was pointing and there was a rabbit seated on its hind legs both paws over its nose like something out of a Beatrix Potter book. He was a big Jack with a white chest and grey markings. My heart started to beat faster; I didn't want to kill him, but I was afraid of what my Dad would think. I lifted the rifle and fired, taking no aim at all. The rabbit jumped and started to run and then I heard my old man shout, 'Good shot, son!' He must not have seen the look of horror on my face for he clapped me on the back, pushing me forward. 'Quick, it's a leg shot. Don't let the bugger get to a burrow!'

"I'd wounded the rabbit, which had run a few feet and collapsed and then had started to drag itself away, its hind leg shattered. The push from my father had propelled me forward and I continued running towards the big Jack still clutching the rifle. When I got to where it lay, I remember there was a slick of blood on the short, frosty grass for several feet where the big Jack had dragged its smashed leg before finally collapsing. I wanted to be sick on the spot and fought back the need to gag. It was still alive, its bright eyes looking up at me. Suddenly I wasn't afraid any more and I knew just what to do; I put the rifle on the ground and bent down and picked the rabbit up and hugged it, not caring about the blood on my shirt or what my mum would say when we got home.

"Then I picked the rifle up and hooked the strap over my shoulder and set off to where my Dad was standing. I could feel the morning sun on my face and the rapid heartbeat of the small creature through my shirt. My Dad was standing with the sun directly behind him so that his face was in shadow and I couldn't see his expression.

"'Look what I've done,' I held the rabbit out in front of me not knowing what to expect. 'I've got to make it better, Dad.'

"As I drew closer I could now see the expression on my dad's face and he was smiling, a small smile just there at the corners of his mouth. 'You'll never make a killer, son,' he said gently. 'But that's all right, the world has enough of those already.'

"We took the big Jack home and my dad must have talked to Mum because she wasn't a bit cranky about my blood-stained shirt. I put a splint on the rabbit's shattered leg. It soon got better but I guess I was a lousy doctor, it always hopped sort of lopsided and funny and my mum named it Cassidy, after Hop-a-long Cassidy." Rick grinned. "Cassidy got very fat and became a family pet and stayed around the place for years, a tough knock-about sort of rabbit, who, if he'd been a bloke would have been a real larrikin.

"I think that very morning when I shot Cassidy was when I knew I was, well, you know, not like the other boys at school and that I wanted to be a nurse when I grew up. Though I must say, in fairness, my dad seemed to understand and he never gave me a hard time or made me feel he was disappointed in me because I wasn't tough or aggressive. We simply never went shooting again."

From the very first day Rick treated Damon as being different and special and they became great friends. Later he was to play a vital role in nursing him through the many crises he would face with AIDS. Rick Osborne was a gift from a generous God and, of all the many nurses who were kind and helpful to Damon and to whom we are enormously grateful, it is to Tim Rigg and Rick Osborne and, a little later in Damon's illness, Lindsay Haber, that we owe the greatest debt of gratitude. They, along with Denise at the Haemophilia Centre, whom we loved very dearly, were the angels in white, the selfless people who always gave more, much more, than could be reasonably expected of them.

This had always been true; from the very beginning, the male doctors in Damon's life were a decidedly mixed bag, some few were great but, for the most part, they were arrogant, often callous and unthinking and sometimes downright stupid. But the hundreds of angels in white or blue, the sisters and the nurses that filled his life were, with perhaps the exception of a dozen or so old harridans, wonderful, caring people, filled with laughter, commonsense and compassion.

As Damon grew a little better he became quite impressed with Prince Henry Hospital. At Marks Pavilion he had a breezy room looking out over Little Bay with its heathland and rocky coastline view where the sea rushed in to smash against the rocks and tear itself into creamy white foam. At times the spray, slow-motioning into a high white arc, became a paradoxical symbol; witnessed by the dying from their faraway windows, it was the epitome of life and energy and continuity. The AIDS block was clean and spacious with two television rooms, which always contained fresh flowers. The staff seemed casual and friendly, mostly greeting visitors after only one visit by their correct names. They had all volunteered to work in the AIDS section which was often harder work and longer hours than in many other parts of the great hospital complex.

This was even more commendable as their job placed them constantly in the presence of men who were dying. They would watch a young man, perhaps in his early twenties, come in for the first time, looking strong and full of life, and they would know that they would eventually be present when he had become a frail and broken little creature in for the last time to quietly die.

To be an AIDS nurse takes a great deal of character and inner strength and even the best of them can't maintain it for more than two or three years before they need to get away from the constant death around them. They have every right to be indifferent, to develop a protective, untouchable, emotional armour to survive, yet they do no such thing. Perhaps because most of the male nurses were in the gay community, they brought a kind of dedication and compassion to their job and, in the process, they have become a special breed of men who exemplify everything that is good about our society.

Damon preferred Prince Henry because the AIDS section was separate and completely away from the other wards. In any other hospital in which he'd been treated, he'd felt that people were looking at him, that the general staff saw him as a young homosexual with AIDS. And while Damon never thought of himself as particularly straight and I never ever heard him make a negative judgment of someone who had contracted AIDS in a different manner than he, he wasn't anxious to be thought of as gay. In a person like Damon this was somewhat strange, normally he wouldn't have given a thought to how strangers might perceive him. But I think his need to be seen as heterosexual came about because of his love for Celeste. He felt perhaps that if people saw him as gay it somehow depreciated their relationship. I have no doubt this was an over-reaction and not entirely logical, but it is understandable. Damon was very young and inexperienced, even in sex, and certainly he was unaccustomed to the ways and, in particular, to the casual sexual banter and conversation which epitomised many of the people in the gay community.

He had learned that he was HIV positive while still at school and at an age when a young man's sexual drive, particularly his sexual fantasy, is very active. The first thing Damon had to come to terms with was that he was sexually dangerous. Naturally, he would have been emotionally distraught at such a prospect and become very sensitive about his own sex life. Celeste was his anchor and his only sexual experience, their sex life would have been expressed in the most simple and predictable ways. It isn't difficult to understand that he didn't want this experience with a single female partner undervalued in any way.

It is difficult to write about the way some gay people talk among each other, without appearing to upset the sensibilities of the gay community. But Damon, who for reasons I've just explained, was very tentative about sex, was suddenly surrounded by gay patients who seemed to talk openly and often explicitly about sex. He was almost completely innocent in such matters and now found himself among people who were vastly more sexually experienced. Gay friends would visit patients and the conversation would sometimes be about liaisons and details of promiscuity of a type and description, so completely bizarre and explicit, that they were previously unimagined by someone like Damon.

Perhaps if he'd been well, he might have found some of these conversations funny or even educative. But now he found them somewhat traumatic and he was never able to understand how, when sex had been the cause of such a calamity as AIDS, it could continue to be a subject of such total preoccupation among some gay patients.

Damon simply didn't wish to be viewed by people as gay, as he felt he and Celeste had no such experience. He'd once confided to Tim, "You must know I don't care about anyone being gay, but I just don't want to be viewed that way myself." Tim, as usual, had shrugged the notion off. "Anyone seeing you with Celeste would instantly know you were straight as an arrow, Damon."

However, at Prince Henry, with its separate Marks Pavilion in which all the patients had AIDS, the manner of how he had contracted AIDS didn't matter in the least. Here they were all in the same boat. He began to see AIDS as a disease he had contracted and not as a homosexual disease he had contracted. His AIDS wasn't different, he himself was. This difference was brought about by not sharing many of the interests which the other patients had in common.

Marks Pavilion also had a downside. Damon was the only haemophiliac there. The other haemophiliacs with AIDS had very sensibly remained at Prince Alfred to be near the Haemophilia Centre. This meant that when Damon had a bleed while in hospital, he would need to treat it himself, as no real expertise among the Marks Pavilion staff existed to handle his peculiar blood product problem. This was seldom a huge disadvantage unless

Damon was unable to transfuse himself; he would have to rely on a nursing sister or a doctor, who didn't really understand his treatment or fully comprehend how painful and inconvenient a bad bleed could be.

Celeste would bring the AHF in from home and it would be stored in the drug fridge at the hospital where the squat round bottles sat like strangers, foreign medication, among all the well-used drugs that fought the opportunistic infections allowed in by AIDS.

The younger medical staff seemed to understand that Damon was an "accident" and so they were generally very considerate to him. This was something for which we were very grateful. Damon didn't always appeal to medical staff. The years spent in hospitals had made him cunning and his determination to look after his own body often meant that he wasn't a good, compliant and co-operative patient. He wanted to know everything and, I must say, the many younger doctors at Prince Henry bent over backwards to accommodate him, showing more patience with his demands than any we'd come across before. We could see that the medical profession was changing at last, that young medicos coming into the profession were temperamentally and emotionally much better adjusted and prepared for their jobs. They were better doctors all round and seemed to have none of the arrogance and insensitivity of many of their older peers.

With the help of Rick Osborne and the younger medical staff, Damon was quite often allocated a room when, strictly speaking, he was jumping the queue. Perhaps this was unfair, though I know it made an enormous difference to all of us. We could visit Damon without inhibiting the conversations of, for the most part, young gay visitors, who would want to talk freely to their patient friends in their own manner. We would tell ourselves that everyone benefited, though this may simply have been our way of justifying Damon's privileged treatment. Nevertheless, I confess, I was always grateful if Rick or the doctor had somehow managed to move him straight into a private room, when normally he should be expected to wait his turn.

If I appear to have made light of Damon's first stay in an AIDS ward, then I have given quite the wrong impression. AIDS-related pneumonia is extremely serious and he was very ill for several weeks and required constant oxygen to breathe. *Pneumocystis* is a killer: in some circles it's called "the merciful killer" because it often occurs as the first real crisis in the progression of AIDS. If it proves terminal, the victim dies in fairly good shape and doesn't have to suffer through the mental and physical deterioration which is the inevitable way of the disease.

Towards the end of Damon's first stay at Marks Pavilion an incident occurred which shocked and saddened him tremendously and might have been one of the causes of the deep malaise or depression he was to fall into not long after leaving hospital. In the room next door to his own was a young man called John (in most cases only first names are used in AIDS wards) who was also suffering from AIDS-related pneumonia. His entry into hospital had been delayed and he'd had a tremendous fight on his hands, but now seemed to be over the worst.

But, while he'd been in hospital nobody had visited him. Rick explained to Damon that John was in the navy and his friends were not in Sydney and that his parents lived in the country. Damon, who by this time was sufficiently well to be allowed out of bed for two or three hours every day, spent a lot of his time just sitting with John, who seemed to be making a very slow recovery and wasn't yet off the danger list. Damon has always been a sharing person and soon we were bringing what we could for John, when we visited Damon, which was precious little as he was still very ill.

Benita would visit Damon every morning and Celeste would go straight from university so that she saw him every afternoon, while I would leave work at about seven and take the evening shift. One evening, Damon confided in me that he'd sometimes wake up at night to hear John sobbing and delirious, shouting, "Mum and Dad please forgive me!" Damon explained that it was like hearing a terribly distraught little boy, first the sobs and then his plaintive wail to be forgiven.

"He says it over and over again, Dad, like he's heart-broken but doesn't know what he's done. We have to do something, nobody has visited him since he came in." I suggested that Damon try to find out where John's parents lived and, if it was a question of money we could help, maybe fly them up or down to Sydney and put them up in a hotel for a couple of nights.

Damon went to work, but without success; John shook his head, too ill or weak or simply not wanting to reply. Rick confided in Damon that John's prognosis wasn't good. "He doesn't have anything to live for; when this happens they often just give up," he observed.

Then one day John had a visitor, a young woman who was the sister of a shipmate and had received a letter from her brother on HMAS *Perth* asking her to visit John. She hadn't known John previously and of course she was shocked by what she saw. Their conversation was awkward, she was young and shy and quite unprepared for anything like this, so she didn't stay very long but promised to come back if she could get away from work again.

Damon, seeing that she was about to depart, left his bed and waited at the front desk of the hospital until she arrived; confronting her, he asked if she knew where John's parents lived. She didn't seem too sure. "In Blacktown or Bankstown, one of them. I know because my brother once told me, but I don't know which one now," she shrugged. "I can't remember nothing more."

That night Rick went home and got on the phone and called everyone in the book by the name of Baker and who was located in or near either suburb. Baker is a pretty common surname and after about four hours he finally located a family who had a son called John who was in the Australian navy and on HMAS *Perth*.

Bingo!

Rick explained to Damon that they had somehow to get John's permission to make the call to his family. "He's very ill and we can't just have his parents drop in on him," he explained.

"But why?" Damon asked. "Surely they'd want to see him, come what may?"

Rick explained that gay people often lived a life of which parents were oblivious and that John's guilt could be terrible. "Just because you're gay doesn't mean that you're not influenced by all the values your parents hold. The church, what friends would think, the relations, all that working-class crap. John's in the navy, his dad's probably proud as punch and thinks he's practically the captain by now, a real son of a gun!"

Damon went to work on John, but again this was to no avail and that night, when I visited, Damon was exhausted himself, needing more oxygen than usual. Quietly, between bouts with the oxygen mask, he explained what had happened. "Dad, Rick says John's getting worse and may not make it and he'll die without seeing his mum and dad or even having them give him a hug or saying goodbye!" Tears were running down Damon's cheeks. "It's not fair, he didn't do anything wrong!"

I held Damon's hand, feeling helpless, saying nothing, unable to think of anything to say. In the next room, we could hear the hissing sound of John's breathing apparatus and his heart monitor and, above it all, his laboured breath. "Dad, will you talk to him?" Damon asked finally.

I rose and walked the few feet through the connecting door, feeling a little panic-stricken and I am ashamed to say a bit foolish. John's room was in semi-darkness with only the small night light above his bed. His breathing was laboured and his chest was rising and falling as though each inward breath brought him pain. The room smelt of the peaches Benita had brought the previous day, which were in a paper bag on his bedside console, three hothouse peaches, a blush of pink on the downy skin, one halfway out of the brown paper packet. They'd been brought in the hope that they might tempt him to eat something. Now I noted that they remained in the half-open bag untouched.

I sat down beside John and took his hand. It was a surprisingly big hand even for a big lad. It was cool and slightly clammy to the touch, a hand that could have come from generations of people who'd worked hard for a living. A big, practical hand, I thought, probably like his father's. John's hand lay limp in my own and I had no idea whether he was fully conscious as his eyes remained closed as I entered the room and sat beside his bed. I cleared my throat. "Good evening, John." I paused for a second then continued, "John, if you can hear me just nod your head, just a little from side to side or, if you like, squeeze my hand. Don't try to talk, just a squeeze or nod of your head."

In the semi-darkness I thought I saw his head nod, almost imperceptibly, although his hand remained limp in my own. "John, please let me call your parents," I said gently. "No matter what's happened between you, as a parent of three sons I know they'd want to be with you now." I waited a few moments then added, "John, if you agree just squeeze my hand. Just a tiny squeeze."

I waited but his hand remained limp, inert in my own. "Please, just a tiny squeeze, or if you like, just nod your head again." But still there wasn't any life in his hand and no movement of his head. Finally, after sitting with John for a little while longer, I returned to Damon's room. I was disappointed but didn't know what else I could do, though I must confess I was pretty certain John had heard me and that I had failed.

At ten the following morning Damon called me at work from hospital, he was terribly excited. "Dad, John told Rick this morning it was okay, to call his parents!" Damon started to cough over the phone, the excitement too much for him. "They're coming this afternoon, his parents are coming this afternoon to see him," he gasped then added in a thin, chesty voice, "He's going to be all right, you'll see, he'll get better now!"

I arrived to see Damon that evening to find him in a great deal of distress.

"You came too late, Dad," he sobbed. For several minutes I could get nothing from him, just the same phrase, "You came too late!" Finally he managed to tell me what had happened.

John's parents, had arrived late in the afternoon. "They were, you know, just ordinary working-class people like everybody else. Rick met them as they came in and John's father wanted to know what the matter was, you know, why was his son so sick? Rick took them to the TV lounge and asked them to take a seat. John's mum sat down but his father remained standing. John's mum had not spoken a word since they'd entered the hospital, she'd just followed them to the TV lounge. Rick said she looked scared. Rick then explained to John's father that he was very ill, that John had a kind of special pneumonia."

"Why wasn't we told before?" John's father demanded to know.

"Well, I told you on the phone this morning." Rick replied.

"No, before. Why wasn't we told before?"

Rick cleared his throat. "We couldn't get your phone number until I phoned two days ago; it was just a punt," he explained, then added, "I'd already phoned dozens and dozens of numbers, maybe fifty Bakers until I got you."

"Why didn't you tell me then, on the bloody phone! You just asked those questions about the navy and his ship and hung up. We thought he'd deserted, jumped ship or somethin' real bad like that!"

"I'm sorry, Mr Baker." Rick smiled, trying to disarm the big man who towered above him. "You see we were very worried, John is very sick and we knew only that you lived somewhere in Bankstown or Blacktown but that's all. He was too sick to tell us how to contact you. I couldn't tell you before I had his permission to call you. I mean, we didn't know if you . . . you," Rick hesitated, clearing his throat, "know, knew about John?"

John's dad looked down at Rick, he was a tough-looking guy, big and rough, the sort of man you made a mental note not to annoy in the pub, and he was very angry. "Knew what? Knew bloody what!"

Rick looked at Mrs Baker for help, but she was seated with her hands in her lap not looking up. He talked directly to her, not looking at John's old man standing beside him. "Mrs Baker, your son has AIDS, he's very sick with a sort of pneumonia called PCP, he wants to see you." The woman gasped and looked up at her husband, clutching at her neck with both hands. John's dad looked at his wife. "You hear that, woman?" It was as though he was accusing her of something, blaming her for his son's predicament.

Damon was weeping again. "Dad they went in and stayed perhaps for twenty minutes. John's mum sat on one side of the room and his dad on the other as far away from him as they could get. They didn't touch him, they didn't even speak to him. John's mum just sat and looked into her hands. Maybe she was crying, I couldn't see from the way she held her head.

"I couldn't see his dad at all, I just knew where the chair was he was sitting on, it was about four feet from John's bed. All I could hear was John crying and him saying, 'Forgive me, Mum and Dad, *please* forgive me!' Just like at night. He was begging them. His voice was terribly laboured and I knew how hard it was for him to speak. He'd get it out and then lie panting and then get the oxygen mask up and he'd try to get enough air to say it again. He kept repeating it, over and over, begging his mum and dad to forgive him, until I thought he was going to die; but his parents didn't move, didn't say anything! His mum didn't even look up."

Damon stopped, too upset to continue. I was shocked myself and close to tears. "It's hard, darling. It's very hard for a man and woman like that to be confronted suddenly with something like this. Perhaps they don't know how sick John is. Rick says that, often, when people hear of their son's homosexuality and AIDS condition together for the first time their reaction is traumatic, just like John's parents today; but then they go home and think it out and come back the next day and they are soon reconciled. People like that just don't understand, they've been conditioned, often since childhood, to think homosexuality is a sin or a terrible disgrace."

Damon wiped his eyes and I wasn't sure he'd been listening to me because he continued, anxious to get his story over. "Then I heard John's dad say, 'Come, woman!' and John's mum got up and they walked out. They didn't even stop at the door to say goodbye."

Damon was howling again and I cradled him and rocked him and tried to comfort him. It was only then that I realised that John's breathing apparatus wasn't making its customary hissing noise and that the door to his adjoining room, which was usually open, was now shut.

"Is John all right?" I asked.

Damon stopped sniffing and looked up at me. "He's dead. He died an hour ago!"

The remainder of the story came out later. Immediately his parents had departed, Damon and Rick had gone in to see John in an attempt to comfort him. John hadn't said anything, he just lay exhausted, his breath coming in great heaves from behind the oxygen mask, tears just kept running down his dark stubbled cheeks, running along the edge of the oval oxygen mask on to his chin and down the front of his neck and into the V-top of his pyjama jacket. Big, silent tears that just seemed to squeeze out every couple of seconds.

Rick pulled up a chair and Damon did the same and they sat on either side of the bed and held one large hand each. There wasn't anything they could say, they just held John's hands. Finally Rick had to go because they were paging him to an urgent call and Damon was left alone with John.

After a while John seemed to be wanting to get his oxygen mask off but he couldn't seem to raise his free hand, getting it as far as his chest before it fell back to his side again. Damon leaned over and removed it and John lay panting, gasping for breath. "They ... they ... wouldn't even touch me!" A great moan rose up from his inside and then he started to cough and sort of choke and Damon held the oxygen mask over his mouth so he could breathe again.

Damon turned to me. "Dad, I told him that you'd be coming tonight, that you'd hug him, that you'd be his dad as much as he wanted." Damon looked up at me, his eyes swollen from crying, suddenly he buried his head into my chest. "But you got here too late," he sobbed.

24

When Home is a Lifesaver at Bondi Beach.

The thing about AIDS is its constant bombardment of the human body. A healthy human being may be likened to a country protected by its own army and well able to keep its borders safe from invasion. When HIV infiltrates, it is like a mole in a spy story, the virus lies dormant waiting for some incident to trigger it into action. While nobody knows what this silent signal is, it allows the alien HIV to subvert and neutralise the body's armed forces — the T-cells — until the country can no longer defend itself.

When this happens the mole comes out into the open as Acquired Immune Deficiency Syndrome. The entire human body now becomes an invasion zone, helpless against the weapons of invading infections, which have been waiting for an opportune moment. Man-made drugs are all that is left to fight the onslaught, but with no natural forces within the body to help them, drugs mostly have a temporary effect, they win a skirmish here and a minor battle there, but can do very little to halt the remorseless invasion of new diseases entering the body.

These battalions of infectious diseases lurk on the fringes of all human existence. They are microbes which are completely alien to the normal health-protected human body but now are given free access for attack by AIDS. When one type is defeated then another takes its place. The number of these diseases is seemingly without end and attacks are sudden and ferocious, each capable of creating a firestorm that leaves the area it attacks totally devastated.

So much happens to a human body when it can't fight back that it would be almost impossible to talk about each physical onslaught, each wave, each disaster as it struck Damon's frail and undefended body.

The *Candida* or thrush came early and stayed and built and built, the thick gelatinous substance caked his lips and grew inward, on the inside of his ravaged body, over the lining of his mouth, throat and gut; a deadly yellow fungus helping to undermine him from the inside out.

Damon left hospital after his bout of AIDS-related pneumonia and we noted, with an awful anxiety, that he'd developed a shuffle, the hunched-over walk of the very old and the very sick. His skin was stretched taut across his face and at times, where the once-plump padding of rude health had been wasted away, you could see the outline of the bony skull. His hairline had receded and thinned and his nice, soft, sticky-out hair now seemed patchy and unsubstantial, like a badly executed haircut, as if it were the result of an end-of-term dormitory prank.

Damon too had come to see himself differently. While he was still the kid who walked to the beat of a different drum, he now became aware that, despite his need to be different, he'd joined others who were different too, and with whom he had embarked on a Kafka-esque nightmare, a forced march into an uncertain and precarious future. No disease is so vilified. A terminally ill cancer patient is given love, compassion and caring by a generous society, no such blessing is afforded the victim of AIDS, who often suffers rejection and loathing all the way to the grave. AIDS is the first disease in modern times which society has pronounced unclean, as though a sin against God, and the journey to its end has become long and lonely and dreadful.

The incident with John Baker's parents and John's subsequent death affected Damon deeply. Sometimes Celeste would find him seated quietly with tears running down his cheeks. He'd look up at her and sniff and give her a wan smile. "It's not for me, babe, I know I'm loved. I'm crying for John Baker. Do you think, wherever he is, he's all right?"

Damon, who'd always thought of himself as an agnostic, was beginning to mention the possibility of *something* after death. He'd brought it up once or twice with me and, again, with Benita and, of course, with Celeste, who brought him the most comfort. She believed simply and easily that the human spirit is on a continuous journey; that life on the blue planet is only one of many. Her catechism required no deep indoctrination, it was direct and perfect: life is a river, eternal, ongoing and constant, moving through an ever-changing landscape. Damon's present view, his life on this earth, is simply the land-scape passed in his spiritual flowing.

The questions he was beginning to ask seemed to be an indication that Damon's positive outlook to his disease was starting to be undermined and that he was begin-ning to think of death. If not yet his own, then certainly the death he saw all around him.

The things he'd witnessed while in hospital and the increasingly heavy load of pain he carried every day were having an effect on his psyche. Moreover, he was back on AZT and the immediate effect on his weakened state was appalling. Yet he insisted. There had been several occasions when he'd stopped taking AZT when, in an attempt to lessen its toxic effect on him, the doctors had put him on it only during alternative months. Though this had greatly helped the quality of his life he now thought that perhaps the AIDS-related pneumonia, the PCP, had snuck in under the protective AZT curtain, when it had been lifted for a month at a time. While in hospital he had been taken off AZT altogether.

Despite the drug's harrowing effects, in an attempt to arrest the advance of his disease, Damon was determined to return to the nightmare of constant AZT use. It was a decision which took great courage, the long recovery from PCP had left him very weak and the constant pain from his bleeds and arthritis were all combining to bring him down. Yet he was prepared to suffer further if this was the price he had to pay to salvage his life.

He was now on an elaborate concoction of drugs with-out the necessary palliative co-ordination he should have had. Nobody instructed him in the *combined* use of the medication prescribed. He was left to sort things out for himself, to take what he thought was correct medication when he needed it and in the amounts which seemed to him to be appropriate at the time.

Any doctor reading this is unlikely to believe me, but Damon's palliative care, combined with his haemophilia and severe arthritis was virtually non-existent at this stage of his illness. While some attempt was made to check and co-ordinate the drugs he required for his AIDS condition, none was made to combine the medley of problems which affected his particular condition. This was perhaps brought about because Damon had moved about, using several hospitals during his life, and his records were scattered all over Sydney. Another explanation may be that palliative care is usually accorded only to people who are terminally ill. With most diseases this takes place over a relatively short period of time and for a specific condition. With AIDS the period is extended for two years and beyond, during which a whole number of different diseases are involved. The palliative care system had not yet learned to cope. For most of his adult life Damon, who was always on several drug routines administered by more than one doctor, was forced to make himself more or less responsible for his own drug regimen and often he got it wrong.

Perhaps, and it seems very likely, this self-administered drug cocktail was causing strange and difficult side effects of its own. Sometimes he'd suffer from acute constipation for days, then suddenly the effect would reverse and he'd undergo a bout of diarrhoea, which was equally severe and would continue for days leaving him dangerously dehydrated and weakened. It was all becoming too much and he started to become severely depressed.

Nothing seemed to be improving and his T-cell count was now down to zero — the last soldier had gone down fighting. There seemed little hope of halting the remorseless spread of the multiple infections invading his frail and totally vulnerable body, his only chance he told himself, was the AZT and that was making him so sick he finally doubted whether he could carry on much longer using it.

It must seem curious that Damon's slide into deep depression gave us all a shock. After all, why wouldn't, or shouldn't, he be depressed? Nothing was going right for him and the four-hourly doses of Endone, a powerful pain-killer, was about all that kept him from a daily crisis of pain which threatened to affect his sanity. But we'd known Damon in pain all his life, his pain threshold was incredibly high. Medical crisis wasn't new to him, always he'd faced it, bared his teeth, spat in its face, defied it and always he'd come out of it stronger than before. But now the flame that had always burned so fiercely and constantly within Damon was down to a flicker, its wick floating in the melted wax of his faltering resolve. Damon sat for hours alone, rocking, saying nothing, trying to avoid speaking to anyone except Celeste.

We, who loved him, were wrong to be shocked at his depression; we had no way of measuring his pain and we'd simply assumed that it was much like the pain he'd always had to bear, whereas it was much, much worse. We should have seen his depression coming and tried to do something about it sooner. Though, in retrospect, I'm not sure we would have known what to do. Everything was a new experience with AIDS; no well-trod carer-path existed, it was all a new, precarious and wildly unknown way, where we faltered and bumbled and stumbled on, always feeling inadequate to the task.

I called Professor Brent Waters, professor of psychiatry at the University of New South Wales. Brent was an old friend, whom I trusted, and his first task was to look at Damon's drugs and consult with Dr Roger Cole at Prince Henry Hospital, who had only recently become Damon's palliative care specialist. This single sensible act between the psychiatrist and the physician probably prolonged Damon's life. It certainly brought him a measure of relief he'd not felt for some time. Roger Cole, a delightful, quietly spoken Englishman, turned out to be one of the great medical finds in Damon's life. Not only was he good at his job, he was a wonderful and compassionate person and Damon grew as close to loving a doctor as I imagine he was ever likely to get.

Dr Cole, if you read this book, please know how very much we are in your debt. Damon loved you and we thank you for your honesty and compassion and love.

Roger Cole soon had Damon on a drug regimen that levelled out the peaks and valleys and, except for the continuing effects of the AZT, made his life a lot more tolerable. Dr Cole gave him Panadol with the Endone tablets making the total pain-killer potential greater in combination and enabling Damon to take less of the more harmful Endone. He gave him Senekot for his constipation and suddenly, in a dozen different ways Damon had a workable drug situation which made an enormous difference.

But mostly Roger Cole spoke to him, he explained exhaustively the effect of each drug and its side effects and its potential complications and the way he'd tried to design a path around them. He treated Damon like the intelligent person he was and never once tried to avoid an issue or failed to explain the potential consequences of his actions. Moreover, he would admit to his own fallibility, indicating when he was experimenting, hoping for a good result and, at the same time, making Damon aware of what was happening and seeking his co-operation. He made it seem like a partnership, with Damon very much the senior partner, whose advice was to be listened to and to be acted upon.

Damon asked Roger Cole about continuing with AZT and Cole, a man whom we were to learn was wise as well as a good physician, suggested that Damon call a family conference. He pointed out that he didn't believe a simple medical opinion would resolve the dilemma Damon faced.

"Damon, I don't know. *None* of us knows about AZT. There is no certainty that it will work or, for that matter, have any long-term inhibiting effect. You must discuss it as a family, I'm not at all sure this is a medical decision." Roger Cole was one of the few doctors we'd met who was prepared to question his divine right to make a judgment on purely medical grounds.

It had long since become apparent to all of us that this AZT experiment, this so-called potential inhibitor of AIDS, was actually making Damon sicker than the disease itself. We'd already persuaded his medicos to lessen the dosage, which they'd done, though I must add, with very little result. His nausea persisted and his anaemia seemed no better, his blood count seemed to be going down to six or seven at about the same rate.

However, the decision to cease taking the AZT was

nonetheless an awful dilemma. If AZT eventually proved to delay the onset of AIDS, we told ourselves, then perhaps it was worth it? Though I was beginning to doubt even this. The drug was so apparently toxic in Damon's system that the quality of his life was almost non-existent. Damon, we all felt, was slipping away from us inch by inch. The bits of the cake were beginning to break off.

As his family, we collectively fixed on Maxolon, the awful stuff he was taking to try and combat the constant nausea caused by AZT. We felt that taking AZT forced him to take the Maxolon and that he couldn't take a chance with it, though there was absolutely no guarantee that Maxolon would not cause him to fit again, as it had done on two further occasions. Next time, we told ourselves, he might throw a fit when nobody was around and might fall and harm himself, perhaps fatally. For instance, should he fall down the granite stairs leading up to the flat, he could easily strike his head or set up a massive internal bleed that could kill him in his present state of health.

While we saw Maxolon as the enemy, it is really a very mild anti-nausea drug; it was just that Damon was one of the very few people which it affected adversely and caused to fit.

So when Damon called a family conference to discuss his AZT problem, we came to it with a sense of great relief, happy that we could discuss our fears in the open. We realised, of course, that the final decision would be Damon's alone to make. I knew he'd listen to us carefully and when it was my turn to talk I made certain not to sound too compelling. Damon trusted my opinion, but I didn't want him to make a decision where he felt he was being influenced by my desire to see him safe from the potentially disastrous outcome of a sudden fit.

After hearing us all out he seemed to be thinking for a long time, then he sighed deeply, the entire burden of a potentially life-destroying decision on his frail shoulders. The apparent failure of AZT was a really big blow to Damon and Celeste, who had together formulated a quite specific plan of action. Their idea was that he'd stay on the drug AZT, until eventually someone found the cure for AIDS or some new drug came along with a less awesome effect on his system. They'd read about a new drug *ddI* which Roger claimed seemed as though it might have fewer side effects. It's introduction was some time off, anyway, perhaps even two years away. Therefore the decision to come off AZT and leave himself exposed to the ravages of AIDS, until this new drug came along, was like holding a gun to your head and being asked to pull the trigger without knowing if it was loaded.

Finally Damon spoke to us, "The AZT is supposed to stop my sickness going any further but in my present state it's not worth staying alive anyway." He looked up with some relief, his eyes travelling directly to Celeste. "What do you say, babe? Let's stop right now, today!" He laughed softly; we hadn't heard that wonderful laugh, it seemed, for months. "You can get a good night's sleep for a change and I can stop throwing up and looking like the ghost of Christmas past." Celeste did what all of us wanted to do, she laughed and cried at the same time, hugging and kissing him. Somehow, we knew we'd helped him to make a very courageous decision. Celeste's tears were in case we were wrong and her laughter was to celebrate Damon's return to us, even if it wasn't to be forever.

"I think you've made the correct decision, Damon," was all Dr Roger Cole said when Damon telephoned to tell him.

"But what about your medical decision, Roger?" Damon asked.

"Damon, I've told you I don't know how much time you've got, but my job is to enhance the quality of whatever amount of life you've got. The decision you've made is the correct one, medicine doesn't come into it."

It seemed such a shame, AZT, which appeared to be working so well for Tim, who was convinced he was going to die but who looked so well, had reaped havoc on Damon, who was so determined to live and was so very ill. Sometimes God seems to play a really shitty game of snakes and ladders. But the constant upping and downing of his anaemia, the effects of everything he'd been through, not the least being the ongoing cocktail of drugs he'd been subject to without proper supervision before the advent of Roger Cole, had caused him to reach a point where Damon could no longer raise his spirit. The uplift in his psyche we'd hoped for when he came off AZT didn't eventuate. He tried, I have *never* seen anyone try as hard, but the black cloud that settled above his head seemed filled to bursting with his despair.

Celeste woke up early on her twenty-second birthday weeping; Damon had been very low for some days, finding a dark corner and silently rocking for hours, he'd also been in a lot of pain and hadn't once mentioned her upcoming birthday. It was all so different from the year before, when we'd vacated our flat for the night and handed it over to them for her twenty-first birthday party. Damon had almost completely recovered from the *Salmonella* in his knee and was really well. Celeste recalls that I made a speech about hope and the anticipation of life which had "... made everybody positive about their lives!"

It was the happiest of days and I recall we'd toasted them and all their friends with half a dozen bottles of French champagne, whereupon we'd left for a hotel where Benita and I had booked in for the night. Celeste's friends at Dinky Di Pies had donated an absolutely huge, at least three-foot-high, *croquembouche*, an elaborate cake built of a pyramid of golf ball-sized eclairs glazed in caramel. It was a generous token of their love of Celeste and added greatly to the glamour of the occasion.

Damon had given Celeste a single antique pearl suspended on a silver chain which Benita had found for him; it wasn't very expensive but quite lovely, a sort of engagement ring when you're not having an engagement, and Celeste loved it and it was seldom to leave her neck. Damon had actually managed the deposit, promising to pay the remainder at some future time when he was less strapped for funds. We all knew that would probably be never, though one never doubted Damon, his intention and even his conviction, was always totally genuine. It was the first big birthday party Celeste had ever had and with all her friends, some of them from all the way back to Woollahra Primary School and others from her architecture class at uni, as well as all Damon's friends, Toby, Christopher, Bardy, Paul and Tillo, the party raged all night and was a simply splendid affair. Later Celeste declared it to be one of the happiest days and nights in her life.

Now, a year later, she lay weeping in her bed just after dawn, with the flash of the light from South Head lighthouse sweeping the pale dawn out of the early morning bedroom every five or so seconds.

Celeste wept quietly, not wishing to wake Damon who slept beside her, she had never despaired of him getting well again, of finally beating AIDS — but she couldn't believe that he'd forget her birthday. Damon, even in the most terrible pain, would always think of something comforting to say to her when she was distressed. She now told herself that her best birthday present would simply be his remembering it, that this would be a sure sign that things were going to be all right.

At breakfast Damon ate nothing and, apart from a brief initial greeting, he sat slumped over the table staring into his cup of coffee while Celeste tried to make casual chat, fussing over him and being nice. Finally he looked up and gave her a small part of his old grin. Her heart began to race, he *hadn't* forgotten after all.

"I haven't got you a birthday present, babe. I'm truly sorry." His eyes welled and he sniffed and, using both hands, he knuckled away the tears. "I think I've had enough, will you help me to kill myself," he said quietly.

Celeste talked to him for several hours, afraid to leave him on his own. While Damon's despair was palpable, he was not the melodramatic sort, no matter how he felt he would not have wanted to create a fuss. He hated a fuss. He didn't want undue attention, quite the opposite, he was much too depressed to want to impress or make any sort of dramatic gesture. Damon overcame the urge to kill himself, because he was too great a lover of life to want to end it. If he had thought that he was making life unbearable for Celeste he might have done something drastic. Now she let him know that she couldn't be without him, that she loved him beyond her own life. Nevertheless, depression is not something we control with our willpower alone and he continued to sink lower and lower.

In a desperate effort to do something to better his condition, I suggested that Benita take him with Celeste to the tropical island of Vanuatu, where I'd not long before bought a small house with the advance from my first book. The idea was that we would spend part of our retirement there in about five years' time and I would do some writing. Now I made the excuse that the house needed repairs and Benita should visit the agent and set these in motion. In fact, all we hoped for was that the promise of sunshine, a relaxed atmosphere and the cheerful ways of the staff at the local hotel might snap Damon out of his depression.

The trip proved to be a dismal failure. Damon tried his best but, as Brent Waters explained, depression of this sort is seldom something you can snap out of. This sort of depression is an illness and even with careful treatment the person takes time to recover. He agreed that the trip might start this period of recovery and was worth a try. But I think privately he realised that it was more important for us to seem to be doing something and that Damon would come to less harm in a changed environment than he might if he stayed at home, where he was more likely to have the courage to act in a drastic and desperate manner.

In Celeste's words: "Damon was in his shell, it was like he'd gone somewhere. Damon wasn't in, he wasn't inside his own skin. It was a terribly sad time, an awful time, I still cry when I think about it."

Celeste has also talked to me about the changing relationship between them. How their respective roles had reversed. I recall how she spoke quietly, almost as though she was reluctant to accept the new role forced upon her by Damon's illness but, at the same time, she would do anything required to keep their relationship intact. This is how she put it:

"When we first met, I was very quiet and introspective, because all the time as I grew up I was to learn that the best way to cope was to be the one who didn't say anything, to be quiet. So I'd just sit there in a shell. At school I was really very quiet because if I piped up and made a sound then people would ask questions about me, where I lived, and things like that, things I was ashamed of. And so I was very quiet when I met Damon."

She looked up and smiled indulgently. "Damon was a big mouth, he could talk, he became my ego. It was like that for a long time, Damon was my ego, I didn't need to say much. But as he became more and more incapable of looking after us both I had to take on a far more masculine role. I had to maintain the feminine side of course, but I had to, well, I also had to make *all* the decisions. I was making lots and lots of decisions about his health, about me, about money, about my university, things like that. So suddenly I had to become more aggressive and I came out of this new role a totally different person. I felt like I was Damon inside me, the old Damon; I had to take on his personality, his certainty about everything."

Celeste looked somewhat bemused. "I mean it was really quite weird. For instance Damon was a great banterer, he'd sit down and have a conversation with friends and it would be full of clever wit and I'd be the one who just sat with him and his quick mind was enough for both of us.

"But as he got sicker and sicker and before his friends really realised how far he'd gone and that he was no longer capable or had the strength to keep up his end, to win against them as he'd mostly done before, I'd filled in, I'd suddenly be the one doing the bantering. So suddenly his characteristics came out in me." She laughed. "You know, it was quite a long time before anyone noticed."

Celeste has a charming way of tossing her head so that her hair flips to one side and then she fingers it back again like a little girl. "But what was really scary is that being both caring and 'feminine' and also 'masculine' assertive was really tough. I found it really hard. But when I had to do it I realised that Damon had taught me how. I'd watched how he did things and I was able to bring this out in me. Now he was so depressed that he required me to make almost all the decisions, even to help him when he decided to kill himself."

She brushed away a tear, her voice down to a whisper. "He was even dependent on me for that!"

After she'd spent most of her birthday quietly talking to Damon, trying to build his courage and lessen his despair, Celeste called Brent Waters. Damon liked Brent who, like Roger Cole, was without medical pretension.

Damon had always been careful with his health, questioning doctors' opinions and the medication they prescribed for him. But now, perhaps understandably, he had become obsessed with his health. AIDS is such a contradictory disease that he'd become quite confused; whereas he'd always had an opinion about his condition, now he didn't know what to expect. Brent talked to him at great length, explaining his depression, not flinching from telling him where it might lead and always discussing what he was giving him in the form of drug therapy and why he thought it might work.

The problem for Brent was that he wasn't simply treating a serious case of depression, there were medical multiples which were being treated with drugs that might affect the ones he was prescribing. In fact, the drugs themselves might have been causing the depression. Furthermore, the depression might have been an early sign of HIV infection of the brain itself which, in turn, was causing early signs of dementia and depression. While he worked closely with Roger Cole, they were often in No Man's Land, in new and unknown territory, hoping to hell they'd got it right.

His bowel problems continued, first severe constipation and then overflow diarrhoea. Overflow diarrhoea occurs when the faeces grows harder and harder until they are very nearly the hardness of cement and completely clog the bowel. Codeine, the major ingredient in most effective pain-killers, is the prime cause of this and an effective way to cure it is to go off pain-killers for a sufficiently prolonged period, so that the waste matter in the bowel can soften enough to pass through. In Damon's case this was not practical. He needed strong pain-killers simply to survive and, when the faeces were so hard that he hadn't passed any waste for ten days or more, the pressure on the internal walls of the bowel would become so great that liquid, unable to penetrate the faecal matter, would force itself between the rock hard waste and the wall of the bowel. This overflow diarrhoea is extremely painful. It is also very unpredictable so that Damon made sure he was never very far away from a toilet. And even then he'd sometimes have an *accident*. Life was becoming daily more miserable, undignified and dependent and Damon, who had always been in control, was now severely depressed. His control over his personal circumstances was so limited that he didn't even know when he was going to shit his pants.

Slowly and with a great deal of patience from Brent Waters, his depression evened out. One Sunday morning, while Brent and I were on a run along the coast from Bondi to Coogee beach he explained to me that Damon, battling to cope with the immediate circumstances of his life had lost his sense of continuity.

"You mean he can't see the wood for the trees?" I replied.

"Well, yes. His fear has become greater than his hopes. Somehow, we must redress the balance, help him see a little beyond his immediate problems. We have to try to help him set goals or even a single goal, beyond simply surviving each day."

"Have you explained this to Damon?"

"Well, I've tried, but he can't see beyond his hopelessness and the belief that he is just a burden to everyone, especially Celeste."

"Is there any specific reason why we shouldn't push

it? I mean at least help him set some goals?"

"None whatsoever, but he will be the last one to see the obvious, to understand this imbalance or lack of perspective. It is something you will have to work at. Help plant the notion of a future beyond the immediate, with care and tact, so that he can readily grasp and act on it."

"So, it's worth a try?"

"Bryce, Damon is severely depressed. I will do *my* thing with the antidepressant drugs and *you* will need to help him find things worth living for."

Whether we in fact succeeded in giving Damon back a sense of the future or a more immediate and positive goal, I'm not sure. Certainly Damon's depression seemed to lift a little, until one day he told Benita that he wanted a house, a proper home, which he and Celeste would own with a garden and a dog and Mr Schmoo, of course.

Damon was completely possessed with this idea. He had a goal again and, as usual, he had a grand plan to go with it. He wanted the house to be his ultimate gift to Celeste so that if something happened to her she'd be safe and secure. In fact he would sometimes stop in mid sentence and look at me and say, "Dad, you will look after Celeste always, promise me." He now felt that he *really* could write a book, a book about what it was like to have AIDS. Naturally, he expected it to be a best-seller which would pay for the house. But the book was more than this and I recall him talking to me about it.

"Dad, can't you see? Before, when I wanted to write a book, I didn't really have anything to write about, now I have. Can't you see, I *have* to write this book to tell people, ordinary people like John Baker's parents, about

AIDS. It will be a positive book and will tell people how to deal with their illness. It's a very important book to write and I know it will sell lots." He paused breathless. "It will be easy to pay you back for our house."

It may sound unduly indulgent that we should have entertained the idea of buying a home for Damon and Celeste, when they'd done nothing to earn it and had no way of helping to pay for it. But we were clutching at straws and the idea that a home and dog of their own might bring Damon back to us, allow him to come completely out of the severe and dangerous depression, which over the months, we felt was slowly killing him, wasn't a straw to be ignored. We grabbed it with both hands. In fact I didn't even think about it. I delighted in the fact that the old Damon had returned and the surest sign of this was that he had put together one of his phantasmagorical plans which would allow him, in his mind anyway, to borrow the money for a home with an absolutely clear conscience.

Celeste once perfectly summed up the way Damon thought. "He always looked for an answer, he'd think of something, a golden thing in the air, and he'd hold it and say, 'This is it! This is going to make me a million dollars!' or 'This is going to make me well again!' "

It was what Brent had talked about, a focus for Damon beyond the tyranny of his illness. As far as Benita and I were concerned if, by owning a home of his own, he was finally able to slough off his depression, it would be the biggest bargain of our lives. Just to see my son's eyes filled with hope, enthusiasm and anticipation, just to have the mighty Damon back with us, was worth a king's ransom.

Our new house in Vaucluse had finally been sold without our ever spending a single night under its beautiful Belgian slate roof. It had been Benita's dream, a perfect Mediterranean house, cool and shady in summer and cunningly trapping the sun in winter, the ceilings were high and the rooms spacious and welcoming with the garden coming in from almost anywhere you stood. But by the time it was completed it was lost to us, it had become a dream which an incompetent builder had managed to snatch away from us. It had become the nightmare house we no longer wished to call our own or ever desired to live in. How fortunate this turned out to be. We paid the bank the money we owed on it and we paid cash for a small terrace house in Woollahra for ourselves. There was still sufficient money over to put a deposit on a home for Damon and Celeste. If we'd stayed in our big, new house with far too many rooms in it anyway, we might not have been in a position to help them.

I think also that in wanting a home of his own Damon might have been trying to recapture the time when he and Celeste had lived in the cottage in Woollahra with Sam and Mothra, their cats of ill fame. It had been an especially happy time for them both when life had seemed endless and every moment was sweetened with their love for each other.

Now, as they set about looking for a place, Damon seemed to change for the better, to improve a little more each day. He was still taking the antidepressants Brent had prescribed but now they seemed to be effective. He even put on a few pounds in weight. The whole "home of our own" thing was turning out to be a miracle.

One afternoon they drove into a small side street in

Bondi and Damon became immediately enthusiastic. "This is the sort of street, babe!" He wound down the window of the Mazda and sniffed. "What a nice street, lots of trees and, look!" He pointed, "Small kids!" He turned to Celeste, "We could live here, babe!"

The house they'd come to see was a semi-detached cottage, old and run-down and Damon loved it immediately. Celeste recalls the moment. "We walked into this silly, little, semi-detached house which I thought, 'Oh no, it's dark and old', you know. It didn't do anything to me. It smelled a little like Maison le Guessly, old carpet, damp rot, mice poop and cats' wee. I was in third-year architecture and was supposed to be able to see potential in a place and I thought, 'This is hopeless!' It was so drab, so yucky. But Damon said, 'No, this is it. I love this house!' It was the first real decision he'd made in months and it was the old Damon speaking and I became very excited. Suddenly I loved the house too — it was the house that was going to make Damon better!"

It was amazing; as soon as they moved in and settled, Damon became his old self again, he got all his power back. He was still in a lot of pain and his T-cell count remained at zero, his bowels still blocked or overflowed and the *Candida* was here to stay, but now he thought in terms of waiting for the new *ddI* drug to come out; his single daily health aim was to keep himself well in his own limited terms until it did. After that, it would be all the way to a complete recovery. Damon's personality was so infectious that I felt a surge of hope. I wanted so badly to believe that he'd live, and, now, I felt that he was back in control of his life and I told myself that anything was possible.

It was wonderful, he and Celeste loved the new place and it *was* almost a repeat of their first love in the Woollahra cottage. Celeste scrubbed and cleaned and polished, disinfected, painted, cooked and invited friends over. They had an ancient enamel bathtub in the bathroom, just like the Woollahra cottage, with a shower over it fitted with a copper shower nozzle, which Celeste burnished until it shone like the sun itself.

They played music all day and Celeste seemed to be constantly singing. She was so alive and pretty and Damon was such a mess, but they only had eyes for each other and Celeste saw Damon simply as the handsomest and most clever person in the world.

Brent Waters pronounced Damon's depression well and truly over and soon after took him off antidepressants, he didn't need them any more. The mighty Damon was back to normal, he'd regained his mightiness as well as a twelve-week-old doberman puppy named Lucy.

25

Damon

Book Attempt No 7.

I have started writing this book about six times. I never seem to get past about page four before things seem to peter out. They reckon that seven is a lucky number. Let's find out.

Lucy is my dog. I shouldn't say my dog, I should say our dog. I live with Celeste. We share our lives together in every conceivable way. We live in the same house, we eat the same dinners, usually prepared by Celeste, I must admit, and we own the same dog. Lucy.

The thing about Lucy is that it has never failed to amaze me how much sheer energy a creature can have. Lucy is a six-month-old doberman and regards life as a never-ending blast of power to be expressed in the most manic and total way possible. If human beings lived like

Lucy, they would probably have a life span of about fifteen years. But I'll tell you one thing. They would get a hell of a lot of things done.

This is actually really fun, writing this stuff. I am in reality totally exhausted, probably due to the fact that I am very tired. I mean, how the hell can you get away with writing a statement like that. But I just did, and who the hell can or would give a damn about it. They might even get a bit of a chuckle.

On to the next paragraph. Rather a strange book this, don't you think? Did you actually go out and pay for the pleasure of owning a copy. Could be the best investment you have made today. Could be the only investment you have made today. Actually I am going to try to say a few things that might be of some interest to you. Or if not to you then maybe to somebody else. But if you think about it logically, that somebody else is you anyway, so it doesn't really matter.

Seven is going to be a lucky number.

I have only been writing for about twenty minutes. I am going to stop pretty soon, because I am running out of petrol and the filling station is known affectionately as the bedroom. Twenty minutes doesn't seem like much of an effort, but I think they may be the most important twenty minutes I have ever spent. They may be the twenty minutes, probably twenty-five by now, that save my life.

I should mention, I suppose, that I am very sick. Actually, I am about as sick as you get. I have AIDS. I guess that has put a bit of a downer on things. But you see, that is what I am going to talk about. Not about

AIDS, well, not just about AIDS anyway, but about what being really sick is all about.

How it affects your body. How it affects your relationships. But most importantly of all, how it affects the person you are. The person you were. And the person you are going to be.

Presumptuous perhaps, but isn't that what they call artistic licence?

I am twenty-three years old. It is a very young age to have to come to terms with the concept of dying. But in some ways it gives me rather an advantage over those who are my age. My friends are concerned with getting their lives established, beginning to build their careers. I wish them nothing but good luck. But I would be lying if I did not tell you that I feel angry at myself, at my illness, not to be joining them in the standard path of building a life, a normal life, which involves going to work every day, going to a club or a dancing venue or simply enjoying each other's company in the most ordinary ways possible. But what is normal? My normality is to sit behind this word processor and try to explain to you the way I feel. I don't know if this book is written for you or for me. I suppose in reality it is for both of us.

My real dream is that you will find it interesting enough to sit down and read it from cover to cover and say at the end. Yes, I actually gained something from that. It has changed the way I think about things. There are people out there who are living lives that revolve around things that are not the things which one would usually consider the norm. They are things, they are events, that happen to only a very few of us. And what I am trying to do is express them in a way that may make you think that what you have, the life you lead, is special, because you have one thing in common. Well, most of you anyway. You have your health. Please never take that for granted, because it is the greatest gift that will ever be given to you as a person. It allows you to choose the path you take in life. There are no limitations to what you can achieve if you have your health. There is nothing you can not do. Never forget that. If that is all you get out of reading this book, then I have achieved my aim. Good Lord. It is only page two.

Onwards.

What does disease mean? A real disease, not a cold or a flu, that clears up in a week or two and becomes something that is soon forgotten. But a disease such as haemophilia or AIDS that confines and defines the way you live and dominates your existence to change the person that you are forever, however long your existence may be.

One of the major concepts that I have had to come to terms with is whether an illness such as AIDS has more effect on you physically or if the real damage is done to who you are, the way you think and the fundamental conceptions you have about life. And death.

When I was first diagnosed as being antibody-positive to HIV, I found it very difficult to come to terms with the fact that this was in fact something very serious indeed. I felt well, I looked well and I truly believed myself to be well. The nature of this illness is that it can sit in the body for a very long period of time, not making its presence known for years on end. Thus it is very easy to believe that it is simply not there, or if it is, it is never going to affect your life in any discernible way. And indeed, for the first three years after my diagnosis, I may as well not have had the thing at all. It didn't affect me in any way, and to a great extent I simply ignored the fact that there it was, waiting for an opportunity to strike. That opportunity eventually presented itself three years later, 1988 to be exact. Then I knew. This was going to change my life.

Perhaps now is the time for a little background. I was born with an illness called haemophilia, a disease that prevents the blood from clotting from the most minor of internal injuries. For instance, a very small internal blood vessel may burst and in the normal course of events a part of the blood known simply as *Factor VIII*, will clot that burst vessel and the bleeding will progress no further. In the haemophiliac, however, that *Factor VIII* is either grossly reduced or nonexistent, so the bleeding will continue unabated until a large amount of blood has collected into the site where the bleeding has occurred. This means that unless the *Factor VIII* is artificially introduced via an intravenous transfusion, the bleeding will continue unabated, with the consequence of immense damage to the surrounding tissue, whether that be a joint or a muscle.

In my case, most of the bleeding has occurred within the site of joints, resulting in severe joint damage that has caused loss of movement and flexibility in the affected joints and, of course, a great deal of pain and immobility whilst the bleeding is actually happening. Fortunately, the treatment of replacing the missing *Factor VIII*, inserted via an intravenous injection taking about twenty minutes, is an effective and relatively fast-acting treatment. However, the irony of the entire situation is that the medicine that without doubt has saved my life countless times over also became the substance that may end it far too early.

I am the youngest of three sons. The chances of contracting haemophilia from a carrier, in this disease the mother, are exactly fifty-fifty.

I was born in 1966. In regards to the treatment of haemophilia, that was rather good timing. It was in that year that the technology to isolate *Factor VIII* from the rest of the blood was developed. This meant that no longer was it necessary to be given a full-blood transfusion for every bleeding episode, a process that took literally hours and hours. Instead, only the *Factor VIII* itself could now be transfused, massively simplifying treatment.

For the first few years of my life we were not wealthy people, but we always ate well, had nice clothes and lived in a nice house. We wanted for nothing and we were always surrounded by love. Illness aside, I had the happiest of childhoods.

Bitterness, anger and frustration. These are some of the emotions that I want to discuss. But there is a lot more.

Other people are sick, they suffer too much and they die too young, their lives unfulfilled. I would like to think that I have never felt sorry for myself as such. Where I feel sorrow lies in the concepts of injury, pain and suffering. Not just how they apply to me, but how they apply to the world in general.

Is there something intrinsically wrong with the way the human mind works?

26

Benita

The Day Damon Died.

A Prize from Queen Alexandra.
The Ceiling of the Sistine Chapel from a Library Book.
Words that Turn to Ice and Tinkle like Crystal
as They Fall to the Deck of an English Battleship.

I can't get past the day Damon died. When I was in
London last, I would find myself walking down the
Kings Road in Chelsea and I'd get flashes of seeing him
and helping him around. He was terribly ill, walking so
very slowly, like a frail, little, old man, afraid to cross the
road, confused by the traffic, clinging to my elbow, yet,
throughout, he seemed to be preserving what was left
of him for everybody. He wanted us all to have a wonderful time.

This Christmas just past, when there was one place
missing at our table, Damon's place, I recalled the Christmas before in England. By some miracle Damon was a

little better on Christmas Eve and declared that he'd like to go to a Christmas Eve service. Wren's glorious Royal Hospital Chapel, built by Charles II in the seventeenth century as a home for veteran soldiers, was only a couple of squares from where we were living and we decided we'd all walk.

We rugged Damon up to within an inch of his life, for while the walk would normally take no more than ten minutes, it would be a journey of at least half an hour for Damon.

Outside it was a cold, crisp evening, the BBC evening news had earlier suggested the possibility of snow. How wonderful that would have been, snow falling as we made our way to the beautiful hospital chapel. Celeste, Adam and Bryce walked ahead to secure seats and I walked behind with Damon.

I was with my beautiful son in my beloved Chelsea, where Bryce and I had met thirty-six years earlier on a not dissimilar night, a stone's throw from where I was now walking with the youngest of our three sons. Damon talked slowly, his breath frosting in the air. "You're happy here, aren't you Mum? I'm glad we're going to church this Christmas."

The two sentences didn't relate — yet they did — Damon was comforting me, telling me he knew how much I loved England, while at the same time quietly signalling that he was going to die. That this would be our last Christmas together.

On Christmas Day Bryce cooked an enormous turkey. A French turkey which everyone thought rather funny, a turkey somehow seems such an un-Frenchlike bird; goose, duck, quail, pheasant, yes, but not turkey.

We'd decorated the flat in Chelsea and put sparklies and decorations on the rather forlorn-looking ficus plant in the corner of the room, we'd placed a straw angel at its very top and tucked our presents under it. Bryce is the world's greatest parcel wrapper, a wizard with fancy paper and brightly coloured ribbon; he'd found a ribbon shop in the Kings Road which sold French grosgrain among other delightful bunting and he was in heaven, our gifts truly looked wonderful and they gave the forlorn little tree quite its finest moment.

The table groaned with goodies, all the traditional English fare. I'd bought the most enormous scarlet bonbon crackers from Harrods as well as proper Christmas napkins. Silver gleamed and crystal sparkled and we toasted each other in French champagne in fragile, tall-stemmed glasses.

Damon rose about noon and Celeste bathed and dressed him. When he emerged from their room about an hour later he seemed to be in good spirits. The turkey, browned to perfection and brought to the table by Bryce who carved it with aplomb and a great deal of immodesty, turned out to be superb and we laughed a lot and had a perfectly splendid time. If only Brett and Ann had been with us it would have been total bliss. When, at four o'clock, Damon was too exhausted to remain on his feet he went back to bed declaring it the nicest Christmas he could remember.

Christmas in Chelsea with Damon is the last happy picture of him that I carry in my mind. I sometimes think it must be the only one. Damon, his dark, hollow eyes and tiny, pale face under a ludicrously bright red Father Christmas cap. I cling to this single sharp image, my mind, desperate to hold it, to keep it focused, because all the other good times in his life, the other pictures, seem somehow to have been rubbed away.

But even this last happy moment starts to fade almost as soon as I recall it, replaced in my mind by that last day, the day of his death.

I see that husk, that little, tiny husk on the bed fighting for breath. I find it so difficult to think beyond those last images. Particularly that last day, it has stuck in my mind and it won't go away — the very fragile little stick creature, aged and so emptied of life that it seemed he might snap at the merest touch.

He was such a beautiful little boy, he had such a charming way. From the very beginning he was an enchanting child. And now I can only see the death in him. I can't see the life. His body was so tiny, like a child's skeleton, a Belsen survivor. I can't get that image out of my mind. My mind is stained through with the images of that last day, saturated with them, the huge, open bedsore at the base of his spine, it seems to haunt me, of all the images that particular one, that purple and bloody wound the size of large man's fist, haunts me.

When we were in London together, although he slept most of the day and I knew he was terribly sick, knew he was dying, we were still sharing things. There was still a whisper of the old Damon left, the little boy and later the young man who loved to see and hear new things.

Celeste and I took him around the British Museum in a wheelchair. We have a picture of Damon and Celeste taken standing within the Assyrian Transept, the great gateway figures built by a civilisation that had every assurance of lasting forever but, instead, only the mammoth basalt figures made it through the corrosion of time to the present. The rock that had existed before they came was still there long after they'd gone, the beautiful chipping and scratching they'd made upon its surface the only sign of where this arrogant and proud civilisation had once dreamed of its immortality. I try to tell myself that nothing lasts as long as we want it to, that all the preening and vainglory of man can be swept away in a moment by an earthquake or a flash flood or worn away by a persistent dry wind and a few seasons of stubborn drought.

Nothing ever happens the way we plan it, neither the monuments we build to our arrogance or the careful building of a single life; great civilisations are swept away in the flick of a mare's tail and a life disappears in the a blinking of a cat's eye.

Damon was and wasn't again so quickly that nothing remains but the hurt and the grief. They possess my memory and everything else is rubbed out as though with a child's dirty eraser.

He looked so frail in that photograph, yet he could still get excited, still share things with us. We'd take him to other places, the Tate, the Queen's Gallery, in a wheelchair to see the Chelsea pensioners and the little Physic Garden in Swan Walk, the old apothecaries' garden in England. A cheerful gardener picked aromatic herbs and we crushed them and held them for Damon to smell.

When Damon had been on AZT, the drug which made him so terribly nauseated, he'd lost his sense of smell and taste and since recovering it he'd wanted to smell everything. He loved the Chelsea Physic Garden. "We'll plant some of these great-smelling herbs when we get home, babe," he said to Celeste. "You could learn to cook things with them and our food would always smell beautiful." Poor Damon, his thrush was so bad he could only eat soft, bland things, yoghurt and jelly, nothing spicy or the least bit tasty.

Perhaps he was doing it for all of us? Going along, shunting what energy he had left into one final terminus to make us happy; but I genuinely think he was trying to stay alive, using up the very last bit of life in him, the last drop. It was so courageous, so beautiful, and he was emptying so fast.

That was the last sharing of Damon between us. After that there was nothing more, what was left belonged to Celeste. He came back home with Celeste alone. Bryce was forced to remain in London for a further three weeks to complete his novel *Tandia*, which was behind deadline, and we returned the morning after he completed writing the last page and we delivered it on the way to the airport to Laura Longrigg, his editor.

When we arrived home it was all over, the Damon I knew was completely gone, there was nothing left, it was just agony seeing him, agony every day. I know Celeste felt that I didn't stay with him long enough when I visited every day, but I *couldn't*. What I felt was total despair and total hatred. I *couldn't* show that to him, I *couldn't* show him that side. The grief in me would hold me like a vice, like a giant hand squeezing me and the hate and anger would grow within me and become so tight that I felt I was about to vomit up its putrefaction. I had to leave him or he would have seen my hate and known my utter desperation. For hours after, I would be shaking from the effect of this anger, this awful, terrible despair.

I didn't know where to direct the hatred, at the forces, whomever or whatever they were? I didn't know. I just felt absolute hatred, I still do. And despair! And disgust! I want revenge. Damon was murdered.

If any civilised government were to round up several hundred people in a minority group and make them dig their own graves, then shoot them in the back of the head, that would remain an act of murder which would go down in the nation's history as a terrible crime against its people.

But not in Australia. In Australia we have a history of getting away with things. We hunted the original Australians and murdered them. Now we've done it again with haemophiliacs and other medically acquired AIDS victims. Again there is no retribution. No questions have been asked, there is no thought of punishment.

The most superficial inquiry into the behaviour of the people involved with blood in the medical and health system will prove that these medically acquired AIDS deaths could have been largely avoided. I want the people who made those decisions brought to trial. We can't get our sons and daughters, our husbands and wives back, but the people who allowed them to die must be punished.

I admit, I felt despair about Damon all his life though I knew I couldn't do anything about it. I think I eventually got over the guilt of having carried the haemophilia gene, but my despair returned with his AIDS. This time somebody else was guilty, a cowardly medical system, and this time they took away my hope and infected me with hate and anger which I have to live with, perhaps for the remainder of my life.

And now they deny responsibility. These anonymous cowards disgust me, the doctors and the administrators who act so piously took two years to do what they knew all along they had to do.

Two years!

I want somebody to admit those two years, those despicable, cowardly two years that killed my darling boy who was so bright, so alive, so terribly unique as a human being.

Can you imagine if the sixty haemophiliacs who have died had been the sons of the doctors, politicians and bureaucrats who made this decision not to stop gays giving blood and to introduce AHF? Do you think they would have acted in the way they have and swept the whole thing under the carpet?

* * *

I spent my life knowing I had a very special child, though one who would suffer abnormal pain from the day he was born. There were complications as I went into labour. "Nothing," the gynaecologist assured me, "too unusual." My baby hadn't turned around fully and he seemed to think the baby (we didn't know the sex, but we hoped for a girl) would turn at the moment of birth. But that didn't happen and Damon's birth was very prolonged and, at one stage, they were forced to use forceps to deliver him.

Damon was born with bad bruising all along his back, big, ugly purple blotches which made me cry. This bruising surprised the doctor as it couldn't have been from the forceps, the bruises were too well progressed and the ones caused by the forceps would appear some days later. Obviously the bruising wasn't from any part of the birth process.

Damon seemed very pale and so they decided that he needed a blood transfusion, the first of over two and a half thousand he would undergo in his lifetime. This was a fortunate decision as this first blood saved my baby's life and we had cause, from the very beginning, to be grateful to some anonymous donor.

Brett and Adam had been such easy births. Bryce would say rather crudely that they'd popped out like a wet pumpkin pip squeezed between thumb and fore-finger. I was very upset that they took Damon from me for the first four days, I missed holding him terribly. God gave me a rapturous fecundity and ample breasts and I'd been expressing for days before the birth and had loads of milk ready to make him the strong, quiet, contented baby the others had been.

When I was allowed up to see him, he was in a humidi-crib with a horrific looking tube in his skull where they were feeding him with an intravenous drip. My breasts ached to feed him, he seemed so perfect, so utterly mine and I wanted my baby on my breast where all my other children had grown so strong and well.

Though I have to add that we weren't unduly worried; Crown Street Hospital was considered one of the best pre- and post-natal hospitals in the world and our gynae-cologist was quick to assure us that bruising at birth wasn't unusual, that it had probably happened when the baby was coming through the birth canal.

Which was, of course, nonsense; but at the time it

seemed like an adequate explanation. We didn't know then that a bruise of this hue was at least two days old. I felt completely secure that I was in good hands, knowing that if anything was going to go wrong this was the place I wanted to be.

After eight days we were allowed to bring him home. I remember he had a tiny bandage on his finger. Not a plaster, a bandage. I asked why this was and the sister had laughed, "We took a blood sample. It's routine, but he seemed to bleed a bit. Take it off when you get home." It seemed so silly, cute almost, a neat little bandage on his tiny finger, the bow tying it bigger than his hand. At home Bryce removed it and a drop of blood grew suddenly on the point of the finger. We thought little of it and Bryce wiped it away and put a little pressure on the finger and it stopped after a while.

Damon was home at last and it was all we wanted, our third little boy with his birth bruising now almost faded. He was still a little pale and seemed a very quiet baby, though he was gaining weight rapidly and seemed happy enough. He seldom cried and seemed to sleep a lot. Brett and Adam would stand beside the cot while he slept and they'd prod him lightly or stroke his tiny hand. Sometimes I'd find Adam with his cheek against his baby brother's, as though Damon were a teddy bear and Adam was taking comfort from the feel of him.

The two brothers would always remain very close and, just before Damon died, Adam held him and put his cheek against his own and wept. "It's nothing, Adam," Damon whispered, "Don't cry."

The incident concerning Damon's circumcision has already been told by Bryce, though I'm still not sure whether it was simply a fortuitous circumstance that we rushed home or Bryce's prescience. I'm not even sure he was not drunk, though I don't think so. Bryce can be a bit strange sometimes when the African part of him makes its presence felt. Not voodoo strange or anything like that, but he can get pretty deep into himself and sometimes claims he can see things. Maybe it's just another part of his famous dad facts?

All I remember was that Damon was taken from Crown Street, where we'd taken him on the night of his circumcision bleed, and transferred to the Children's Hospital at Camperdown where Sir Seymour Plutta, who became known to us all as Splutter Grunt, was in charge.

Damon remained in hospital for two weeks during which time we were told nothing. Christmas was approaching and I can remember how difficult it was coping with Brett and Adam's excitement at the advent of Christmas with my baby in hospital. It was during this period that I started to worry that Damon was a haemophiliac.

We'd visit the hospital every day where my tiny baby lay with no nappy on, his penis covered in bits of gauze through which the blood had leaked and dried. Sir Splutter Grunt had instructed that his legs be tied in the open position to either side of his crib so that they wouldn't rub the place on his tiny little penis where the circumcision had been.

I looked at him with his legs tied and the bloody gauze strips on his tummy and I wanted to cry, it looked exactly as though he was being tortured in some mediaeval torture chamber. It was horrible and I couldn't understand why the wound didn't seem to heal. After a few days I really began to worry, they'd change the gauze twice a day and soon fresh blood would seep through to the outside surface.

Not that I knew much about it, but my family two generations back had come from Russia and I'd been intrigued by this all my life. When Damon was declared a haemophiliac I immediately identified with the Russian Tsar Nicholas and his wife, Alexandra, whose son had been a haemophiliac.

I knew that haemophilia was carried by the female and was passed on only to males, though that's about all I did know. Where I'd learned this I don't recall. Now I began to think that Damon might also be a haemophiliac and that I might have given it to him, I might be a carrier.

I kept this thought to myself at first but finally confided in Bryce mentioning the Russian tsar's son. I recall he heaped a fair amount of scorn on the idea. He knew that I was inordinately proud of my Russian ancestry and prone to flights of fancy in this regard. "Christ, the story your nana told me was of her mother fleeing a pogrom and walking across Russia and most of Europe with a large frypan on her back and precious little else! Thank God for the frypan, but it hardly suggests you were Russian royalty, does it?"

Bryce loved my nana's fried fish which she prepared every Friday in the large and ancient frying pan which she claimed was the same one her mother had carted on foot across Russia, when she was fleeing from Jewish persecution. "If this thing, this haemo ... whatever, is hereditary, carried by the female and passed on to the male, then if it was in your mother's family, Victor would have been a haemophiliac, or in your dad's family, then he would have been one. How do you explain that?"

Bryce can be annoyingly logical at times. Victor was my younger brother. But by far the most compelling argument was when Bryce asked flatly why Brett or Adam were not haemophiliacs. "How the hell could you be a carrier with two healthy sons?" I derived some comfort from this, although I'm not sure, logic or not, that I was entirely convinced.

Damon came home the day before Christmas and, while I'd been lactating a lot and my breasts were very sore from carrying milk I couldn't use and couldn't totally get rid of, it wasn't too late to put him back on the breast. He was the best Christmas present I could have had. Damon with the sticky-up hair seemed none the worse for wear. In a remarkably short time, he put on the weight he'd lost in hospital and seemed the most contented baby in the world.

In early January we received a call from the Children's Hospital and an appointment was made for us to see Sir Splutter Grunt. By this time Damon was back to normal, eating well, sleeping through the night and not waking for a three o'clock feed and his skin was rosy pink with no sign of any bruising. The fears I'd had earlier were almost completely dispelled.

The interview with the head of the Children's Hospital has been told elsewhere in this book, but I still grow angry when I think of the exchange between this pompous and patronising little man and myself. He seemed to be toying with us and when I asked him, "Is he a haemophiliac, doctor," the surprise on his face was almost comic.

"How did you know?" he asked, obviously amazed that a lay person would even know how to pronounce the word.

Angry, I asked him when they'd discovered Damon's haemophilia? "Oh," he said casually. "We've known for a while now but I didn't want to spoil your Christmas by telling you earlier."

He then went on to explain entirely insensitively that Damon, *if* he lived, would not do so to an advanced age. "Your child won't make old bones, arthritis will get him," was the way I seem to remember he put it.

This most senior doctor in the Children's Hospital seemed quite oblivious to my shock at this news. What this cranky old man was really saying, was that my youngest child was a sufficiently interesting medical specimen to merit his superior attention and how fortunate this was for us.

I recall breaking down and weeping in the car going home, this was as much from anger, humiliation and hatred for this horrible little man as it was from the knowledge that all was not well with my beautiful, chubby, breast-fed, little baby.

We did have some nice doctors, Dr Robertson, who was the paediatric specialist in charge of Damon as a child up to the age of about ten or eleven was a very conservative man, but not a bad one. As it transpired he also made several unfortunate medical judgments, the knee calliper being one of them, resisting home transfusion another; but I do believe he cared a great deal for Damon's welfare.

I remember when we decided that Damon must transfer to the Haemophilia Centre at the neighbouring Prince

Alfred Hospital. They had built a specialist haemophilia unit and the facilities were vastly superior to the Children's Hospital. Robertson had been very upset. Damon was his patient and, as a classic haemophiliac, a special one and he belonged to the Children's Hospital and not to the institution up the road. The two institutions disliked each other and I don't think Damon's ultimate welfare came into it at all.

Damon's purple head was another instance where the imperious medical attitude overruled any consideration for his parents. Bryce was allowed to visit Damon but I was forbidden to do so. Today such an idea would be preposterous but, at that time, Sir Splutter Grunt and his cohorts, probably Robertson as well, simply decided that as a woman I wasn't up to seeing my child in such a distressing situation. They didn't ask me, they *told Bryce*! They told him that his wife was *forbidden* to see her baby. Can you imagine how that hurt me? How awful it was to be denied access to my child because *they* thought I'd panic at the sight of him? How bloody presumptuous!

I am still angry about that. It's all a part of the anger which I don't believe I will ever overcome. The anger that started so early with Damon and still lasts after he is dead.

We are supposed to forgive, but I'm not a Christian, I can't commend Damon's life to God and walk away and forgive everyone. Somebody should pay, somebody should be brought to account or it will all be repeated again and again.

Bryce has tried repeatedly to build me into this book, to show my part and to have readers hear my voice; but it hasn't been easy and, if he hasn't totally succeeded, that's largely my fault. Perhaps years from now if I ever grow less angry, less sorrowful and I am able to distance myself from Damon's life, I may be able to recall the sort of detail a book like this requires. But I can't now. It's a blur, everything is a blur. I can't remember the simplest things, the nicest memories of his childhood. The wonderful little boy he was. It's all blurred.

Bryce says it's the anger, I must get it out of my system. But how do you do that? He feels by talking it out to him in this book my anger might be lessened, I may be able to come to terms with it. But he doesn't understand, even though I've told him on so many occasions, when a mother has a child who needs to be cared for right up to his teenage years, a child who is never quite well, never entirely out of danger, you *can't* remember anything. It's like pain, or childbirth, you have to expunge it from your mind, you have to erase memories, otherwise they become unbearable. I can't remember — the nice parts and the horrible parts are all jumbled up. Damon's horrible death has made everything one, long, incomprehensible nightmare.

Sometimes you remember bits and pieces and they all hurt, like the small room off a corrugated iron workshop at Prince Alfred, where they'd hang the prosthetic limbs and callipers with deformed boots attached to them, and you'd wait for your little boy to be fitted. I remember the smell of the new leather and the sudden, sharp, burning light of a welding torch in the workshop where they were making the substitute limbs for broken, hurting, malformed people.

I remember, also, the swimming pool where Damon would have to swim, the water was tepid, smelled sharply of chlorine and Dettol and was a dirty green, almost khaki colour. A nurse once explained that it had to be so highly chlorinated because old people often became incontinent in the warm water. The pool was made of concrete with no tiles and the paint had peeled off in great black patches, which Damon used to refer to as maps of the world, always trying to find one which resembled the shape of Australia.

People, old people with arms and legs missing, would be pumping up and down on kick-boards, gasping like porpoises. They'd get out by pulling themselves clumsily up on to the edge or being hoisted out on a sort of sling and hoist arrangement, some of them being no more than pink and bluish-white torsos. It was like a scene from Lourdes, all stumps and pink flesh and scar tissue and my darling child had to swim up and down for an hour, three times a week, in this human soup. We'd sit for hours in a large fibro shed, a temporary shed that had stood ever since the war, it had a corrugated iron roof and it was unbelievably hot in the summer and we'd sit waiting, Damon and I and dozens of cripples and amputees and kids who'd been maimed in car accidents or in a fire.

I remember the coffee and tea machines, the slots for the paper cups were sticky with coffee powder or melted sugar and the whole contraption was disgusting. But it fascinated Damon, so I'd be forced to have four or five repulsive cups of tea with powdered milk just to keep him amused.

A string of doctors in white coats would come around and handle Damon like a medical specimen. The rheumatologist, the haematologist, the orthopaedic doctor, the physiotherapist and an assortment of interns and unknowns, gawping and prodding at his bruises.

Once a middle-aged doctor, whom we'd not seen before, came over and started examining Damon without a word to us, carefully checking his bruises. Finally he stood up and faced me, his expression tight-lipped. "Are you this child's mother?" he asked. I nodded my head. "I have every reason to believe that this child has been physically abused!" he said. I just knew the various doctors had very little idea of what to do about his bleeds or his mangled knee or his haemophilia. They hardly said anything which was in the least enlightening or useful and they almost always ended an examination by patting Damon's iron calliper. "You'll need this a little longer," they'd say sagely.

It was a litany, a medical mumble, when they didn't know what to do or say but needed a conclusion to their pathetic examination. "You'll need this a little longer" was like an exit line is some macabre stage play. The horrible calliper, which was causing the problem with his knee all the time, which should never have been placed on his leg in the first place, became the point of reference for all of them, the only thing they could think to grab onto before making their escape to the next grotesquery.

I'm sorry if that sounds harsh but that's how I felt; the doctors needed the callipers more than Damon did! When we'd arrive for this awful ritual Damon would look up at me and laugh. "You'll need this a little longer," he'd say, patting his calliper as we made our way to the chairs against the wall.

These are the memories that come first, not the nice ones, not the wonderful, cuddly ones, the powdered baby bottoms, the delightful first steps, baby skin that smelled of caramel, the tiny, perfect fingers and toes, none of these. My mind is filled with purple and yellow and green bruises and callipers and needles, thousands and thousands of syringes and needles and bandages and bottles and pills and tubes, all of them piled on top of each other like a mountain of assorted garbage, the detritus of my son's short life.

Except for a brief period before he started to crawl I never saw Damon completely whole. He was always covered in bruises in various stages of maturity, dark purple, green and yellow bruises, often in the most unexpected places.

Even Damon's first steps were fraught with anxiety, we'd hope he wouldn't get a bleed when he was just learning to toddle. My heart would be in my mouth every time he stretched his hands out and ran towards me in that wonderful, off-balance way toddlers affect, knowing they are about to be swept up in your arms and covered in kisses.

So you blot them out, you throw these memories out of your life. You hope only that your child will grow up and be all right and manage to live a normal life. That tomorrow will be better than today.

I was terribly proud of Damon, he had such a wonderful spirit, he took all the pain and the mismanagement and the inconvenience and the lack of the things other little boys took for granted without ever complaining. I often thought it was a miracle that we'd somehow managed to bring up a child who was, I think, unique. But then, at eighteen, when his life seemed to be normalising as a young adult and his brains could compete and become more important in the scheme of things than his emasculated body, he had a bleed, just a normal, every-day bleed which required a normal, everyday transfusion.

It was probably a bright sunny afternoon when he would have taken the stuff out of the fridge just as he'd done any one of a thousand times before. He'd have carefully pulled the life-giving liquid into a syringe and then transfused himself. Only this time, instead of saving his life, it killed him. The arteries and veins that carried his lifeblood became the rivers of death.

All I seem to remember that was positive about his childhood is the books. I don't mean his childhood wasn't positive, we were and he was always the world's great optimist. It's just that my memory won't focus, it's smudged with the horror of what happened and it refuses to recall the detail of the good times.

But I do clearly remember the books. We had a wonderful children's library and we spent what cash we had on books for the kids. I recall with great joy the hours with Damon on my knee or cuddled on my lap as I'd read to him. He'd suck his thumb and hold his Blanky, the blue baby blanket that was finally reduced to a six-inch square of faded wool, against his cheek and we'd disappear into a story world. The world of Maurice Sendak's *Where The Wild Things Are*, with its fiercesomely funny and superbly imaginative creatures, took possession of us. We'd find ourselves inside John Birningham's beautifully illustrated books, being shown around London's streets and places of importance by a most dignified and respectable draft horse who had made it to the very top, all the way to becoming the Drum Horse in the Queen's Household Cavalry. You could hear the clop,

clop, clop on the cobblestones of his majestically shod feet. We learned gentleness from his kind, polite ways with all the people, big and small, humble and important, who lived on the route where he worked.

By the time he was seven, Damon actually knew several of the poems of Edward Lear off by heart. This was the early seventies and some wonderful children's books were coming out of England and France. The Enid Blyton and Beatrix Potter nexus was broken at last, there was a renaissance in children's literature where some of the really good illustrators and graphic artists of the day became involved with truly imaginative children's writing. Young literature, emerging from the doldrums of the fifties and sixties, took a giant leap forward for children. We made the most of the revolution, revelling in the new order without having to deny the old and wonderful world of children's classics.

Books are therefore among the best memories remaining of the past, the hours spent inside their covers with Damon have remained untouched by the tragedy of his early adult life. They are as nice a memory as I can still carry. He loved books so very much and later, I think, they made much that was unbearable about Damon's life, tolerable for him and for me.

It's funny how reading seems to have been so important. My mother, a rather eccentric lady, to put it mildly, and one who couldn't be placed in the usual nana childminding capacity, as she never did help in that way, or in most of the other roles nanas usually fill, nevertheless was kind and fed my three boys on a constant diet of English comics which in my mind have become an agglomeration of one giant *Whizzer* and *Chips*. Without fail, every Saturday, she'd arrive with all the traditional English comics. So dedicated was she in this regard, that she still continued to deliver them when the kids were in their late teens and almost a decade after they'd given up reading them.

"Mum, they don't need the comics you bring any more, they've grown out of them." The point was that they were really quite expensive and she existed on a pension so that the comics represented quite a sacrifice on her part. I wanted her to use the money for herself to put on to another of the fifty or so lay-bys she would maintain at any given time.

"Nonsense," she'd retort. "You used to read them, Victor got them." She'd look vague. "That's right, I still get them for him." And she probably did, even though Victor was in his early thirties. My mother, once she got an idea into her head, was pretty hard to shift.

At first I got pretty upset that my mother wouldn't do any of the things grandmothers are supposed to do. There were times when I would have given an arm and a leg just for a few hours away on my own. Because I never knew how Damon would wake up, or whether I'd get a call from school to pick him up around mid morning because of a bleed, it was nearly impossible to make plans, to have a normal life, to meet a girlfriend for lunch or take the afternoon off to visit the Art Gallery or go to a movie matinee.

I used to think it terribly unfair that my mother wouldn't baby-sit or child mind even for a couple of hours at a time and, I must admit, there were occasions when I felt pretty bitter about this. But Damon always welcomed her as though she were a special treat, even though she'd never stay longer than a few minutes. Huffing down the front path, yelling her arrival, with eight or ten assorted parcels in four string bags filled with shopping.

My mother went shopping every day of her life and Bryce once estimated that she must have walked at least six miles each day weighed down by parcels. He'd remark, "She's the fittest old lady in Australia, when the time comes for her to die they're going to have to take her heart out, place it on the pavement and beat it to silence with a stick!"

"Cooeee! Comics! All your favourites!" she'd yell coming down the garden path at the same time every Saturday morning. Damon would meet her at the front door and take the bundle of paper from her. "Gee thanks, nana!" he'd say, seeing it as the special Saturday event it was. Aware of how important the Saturday morning routine was to the old lady, Damon continued welcoming her at the front door, years after all the boys had given up reading comics. At sixteen, he gave the arrival of the comics the same welcome he'd given them as a six-year-old, knowing that my mother was well beyond redemption and that to refuse her gift of love would be hurtful while serving no useful purpose.

Damon would drop the comics off at Cranbrook Prep. on his way to school on Monday and, in the process, he became a big hero with the small kids who'd be waiting in anticipation at the gate. And so, I suppose, his nana's comics continued to bring him pleasure.

During the war, when I was little, my mother used to take me to town to the then famous New South Wales Bookstall Library, where I'd sit in a huge old leather club chair, and I'd be given all the English magazines to read, *Tatler*, *Town & Country*, the *London Illustrated News* and *Punch*.

These wonderful magazines continued to exist throughout the war, though sometimes they were months out of date and so also did the English comics. There was *Girls' Own* and *Girls' Crystal* which I loved with every breath in my body. It was during this time that the English comic as a part of childhood was born in my mother's heart. With the birth of her grandchildren she saw it as her absolute duty to continue what, in her mind, had become a very important family tradition.

I feel quite sure that my consequent love of Britain and the things of England, which has been so much a part of my life, was born at this time. When at twenty, like so many of my generation, I sailed on the P&O liner *Arcadia* for London for the mandatory two-year working visit to Britain I had already acquired a knowledge of the English nation and its history and culture which, I now realise, was well beyond what most Australians knew and which I still maintain with a fierce loyalty and unabashed love.

My father was English, an East End cockney Jew, who had been orphaned almost at birth and had been brought up in a home for boys. At eleven, he'd been sent to the Royal Navy cadet-training ship, HMS *Conway*. As I saw it, in the tradition of Drake and Raleigh, he had seen the world and fought for his King and country as a fourteen-year-old, able-bodied seaman in the Royal Navy during the First World War. My dad's career was a bit hazy in my mind, some bright, burnished bits fixed in my imagination and, from these, I constructed his naval career. For, while he wasn't a quiet man, the conversation in our family was largely dominated by my mother and her parents, who lived with us; so he didn't talk much about his past. The past in our house was a subject almost totally owned by my mother's side of the family.

As I grew a little older I came to understand that my mother came from a good background, in fact, a mon-eyed background, and that she'd married somewhat beneath her. My grandpa, having "lost his fortune" had brought us all down to what seemed to be vaguely suggested as my dad's level.

I was later to learn that the loss of the big house with maids and the considerable fortune came about through gambling. Though my grandpa had been a big gambler, what had finally brought the family undone was my uncle Benny, my mother's brother. Completely indulged as a young man, he had finally "gone bad", taking my grandpa's fortune down with him and having to leave the country for reasons that remained unspoken and unclear. I remember him only as a worldly, sophisticated, delightful and generous uncle who, with his wife, Aunty Sarah, a huge, very plain women, ran a prominent Syd-ney restaurant and indulged me hopelessly.

Nevertheless, despite all this, my mother's side remained the respectable one. Perhaps this was by default as my dad's side was practically nonexistent. While he had two brothers and a sister in London, they'd all been raised in separate orphanages and so they shared no common background and no continuity or the inevitable mythology that goes with being a family.

All my dad had as a claim to fame was that his dad, before disaster had struck, had owned a Gentleman's Smoking Shop and had become known as the "Snuff

King of London". Quite what this disaster was, which had torn the family apart, never became clear. Daddy was always pretty silent on the subject of his early life, which I now imagine must have been very hard in an orphanage in Edwardian England.

But I didn't see it this way as a child, with the lack of hard information I substituted stuff of my own. As I accumulated information from the English magazines, comics and children's books with which my mother force-fed me on visits to the Bookstall Library, I compiled a complete and satisfactory background for my dad. What I didn't know about my daddy's background I filled in from the things I read, taking the bits and pieces he gave me from time to time and fitting them into the landscape I had imagined of his life.

For instance, at the age of eight he'd won a prize for art which had been presented to him by Queen Alexandra, no doubt on a visit to the orphanage. But in my eyes this amounted practically to being a famous artist patronised by royalty and so I began to study English artists, Whistler and Constable and Turner, hoping that some day I might stumble across an early Jack Solomons. He'd also been middle-weight boxing champion of the Royal Navy Mediterranean Fleet and, while stationed at Gibraltar, had won a medal in the fleet marathon. Most importantly, he had visited *Archangel* in an English warship supporting the Tsar and the "Whites" during the Russian revolution in 1917, firing at the wooden onion-domed churches where the "Reds" had taken refuge.

It was here where the incident of the famous frozen words occurred. In telling the story of the Reds hidden in onion-domed churches, my daddy had mentioned that the temperature was well below zero and that the words froze in your mouth. I'd immediately imagined As and Bs and Qs and Zs, in fact all the letters of the alphabet, emerging from the sailors' lips, formed in ice and tinkling like crystal as they fell to the steel deck of the great, grey battleship and shattered into tiny shards. I think it might have been this incident in *Archangel* which caused me to become interested in Russia so that, among other things, I knew about Tsar Nicholas's son being a haemophiliac.

By such strange devices are we conditioned and moulded. I know that, in turn, I passed on my love of England and Europe and its culture to my children and, in particular, to Damon. I would spend hours reading to him or telling him of Renaissance art or showing him the works of the great English artists. I'd take him on imagined trips, travelling through the pages of books where we'd visit all the famous places, so that he became familiar with the Tate and the National Gallery and the Louvre and the Vatican. We'd examine the ceiling of the Sistine Chapel in an art book borrowed from the Woollahra Library and I'd talk of Michelangelo or of Titian and Raphael, Cellini or, even earlier, Botticelli and his Birth of Venus, of how they all painted under the patronage of the Popes, Doges and constantly squabbling, noble families, Roman, Venetian and Florentine. We'd spend months caught up in the intrigues of the Renaissance court and in the machinations of the Borgia, the Medici and the Borghese families who produced popes, kings, generals and alliances at the drop of a pair of silk or velvet pantaloons. We'd visit Greece and Rome and the ancient Assyrian and Byzantine empires and we had a good knowledge of the world of the ancient Egyptians through the pages of the ever-present books.

When finally, in the months before his death, we visited the British Museum, Damon seemed almost to know the layout and where to expect to find the various empires. It was the same for the Pitti Palace in Florence, the Parthenon in Rome and a dozen, different, great, architectural and cultural shrines on the Continent.

And so all Damon's life, we built up an expectation of Europe and the Grand Tour we would surely make together when he'd finished studying medicine at university.

When Celeste went to Italy just after Damon's wisdom teeth were extracted and a week before he went into hospital with *Salmonella*, he was already well-informed. He was eager when she returned to know more, to hear her first-hand version of Europe and its endless treasures and to store up more detail and titillate his imagination for the time when he would travel to the other side of the world to see the European world for himself.

And so, in a sense, it had all begun with English comics and my dad's art prize from the hands of Queen Alexandra herself. From such tiny beginnings and with the help of my own, rather scatty mother, I'd fed my own mind and then, later, the minds of my children. So, in the process, I was able to indulge my own love for art and for England and, a finger's breadth away from it on the map, the Europe and Russia of my semitic forefathers.

This is what I remember most about the good side of bringing up this beautiful child. He was passionate to know more, excited at the idea of belonging to a continuity of culture and tradition and the ongoing process of beauty. He was always astonished by what man had achieved or might yet achieve.

Bryce is an amazingly positive person who doesn't take kindly to the idea of defeat and I have no doubt he passed some of this sense of one's own worth to Damon. But I often think that the knowledge of Damon's own continuity and the astonishing achievement of his particular Anglo-Judaeo-European lineage also gave him a sense of destiny, the feeling that, despite his physical handicap, he was an important part of the universal process of creativity and that there *was* a reason for his having been created.

It was little enough to give him and, in the giving, I gained immeasurably in return. But now, with his life gone out of my own, it has become Damon's gift to me, Damon with his bruises and his sticky-up hair and his bright eyes and his calliper that gave him a sort of stiff leaning-to-one-side walk.

Will the grieving for him never stop?

27

The Mighty Damon kicks the Door in.
A Nightmare Brush with the CIA.
The Great Boxing Day Escape.

AIDS is a series of severe shocks. No sooner has the victim recovered from one disease when another takes it place. It is as though the various diseases are competing to see which can do the most damage in the shortest possible time. AIDS is about watching the pieces fall off. The body slowly disintegrates, things that worked yesterday don't work today. There seems to be little warning, diseases come in the night and are full-blown by the morning. Tongues don't work, bowels don't work, bladders don't work, ears don't work, lungs don't work, joints don't work, even eyelashes fall out! One night you get into bed with perfectly good eyelashes and in the morning they're not there, scattered like puppy hairs across your pillow. Later, even eyes, no longer able to hide behind a curtain of dark lashes, are blinded, perhaps to shut out the last of what's left of the shitty world.

But of all these disasters the attack on the mind is the worst. One day you begin to sense that your mind is not working as well as it should, but this happens more slowly, this creeps up on you so that you are not aware of what's happening and you become bemused at the everyday world around you.

The first time I sensed anything was wrong was in mid November, 1989, when Damon came up the hill to our apartment from Bondi. The ten-minute walk would normally have taken a lot longer than this for Damon had he attempted it at all. "Dad, I made it here in ten minutes. Good eh?" Damon announced as I opened the door to him.

He was barefoot and wore an old pair of shorts and a very dirty T-shirt. His hair, what was left of it, was tufted and greasy and his nails were black with grime. On his wrist was a metal and leather bracelet about two inches wide, simply a band of metal wrapped around a leather strap. It seemed huge, even gross on his fragile arm, more like an impediment than an amulet. This too was strange; Damon usually wore a copper bracelet because of rheumatism or arthritis. Now he'd replaced this with the wide, cheap-looking, metal bracelet of nondescript design.

"Christ, what happened to you?" I asked.

Damon, because he was so aware of his body, always wore long pants and a long-sleeved shirt; walking barefoot simply wasn't possible, his feet were deformed from the years of bleeding and he wore orthotics in his shoes just to get around. Now he seemed to be walking, though admittedly slightly lopsidedly but with comparative ease.

He stuck out a reed-like arm, flexed it and made a muscle. "Feel that!"

"Damon, what's the matter?" I put my thumb and forefinger around his tiny arm and pressed the ball of my thumb into the top of his right biceps, there was barely any resistance. Damon was still the proverbial 125-pound weakling who gets sand kicked into his face by the bully on the beach.

"I'm cured, Dad!" He took a step backwards and, raising his hands in the accepted Bruce Lee fighting stance, he chopped into the wooden panel of the front door. Then, to my astonishment he suddenly leapt up and kicked, driving the ball of his left foot into the same part of the door.

I grabbed him. "Damon stop it!" I was deeply shocked, what he'd just done would put him in hospital with a severe bleed for days and probably put the hand and leg out of use for several weeks. Besides, what I'd just witnessed was, for him anyway, physically quite impossible.

Damon chuckled. "See, I'm healed!" He spread his hands and shrugged his shoulders. "Simple. I don't have AIDS any more and I don't have haemophilia and I walked here in ten minutes." He took a hurried breath, like a little boy who can't get the words out fast enough. "And I feel wonderful!" His eyes shone. "I can't do it properly yet, but tomorrow I'm going to run."

"Run?" I must have shown my bewilderment.

He smiled and put one hand on my shoulder. "Dad, do you remember the last time I ran, I mean really ran, I was five. I remember I was playing with Brett and Adam and we had a scuffle and I fell into the swimming pool when it was being built." Damon put his head on his shoulder and smiled. "That was the last time." I recalled the incident which had eventually led to the calliper on his left leg and his bad knee which had, years later, been attacked by the *Salmonella*. That initial fall into the empty pool had meant weeks in hospital, the kick he'd just given the door had been hard enough to put him back for several days. While some bleeding is problematic, a severe bump such as this would always result in a bad bleed.

He took his hand from my shoulder and slapped both hands against his quadriceps and jumped up and down, running on the spot. "Now I'm going to do it all the time again!" He was grinning and didn't seem the least bit affected by the punch or the kick he'd delivered to the door. "I could run with you? I mean when I'm properly fit, of course — ten kilometres, I've always wanted to do that."

I decided to ignore the way he was dressed or even to mention the absence of his shoes. Instead I rather stupidly asked him if he'd like me to make him a "Dad Sandwich" which is how this famous culinary treat which involved bread and about a dozen other ingredients was known to my sons and all their friends. I am an expert avoider of the too-difficult moment, offering to make food is a great way to escape having to face it. Though now the offer was ridiculous, Damon, with his terrible oral thrush, couldn't possibly have eaten a Dad Sandwich and I immediately felt stupid, but Damon wasn't in the least upset.

"Thanks, Dad, tomorrow maybe. That's when *they* are going to cure my mouth and throat."

I'd followed him on to the large terrace which leads

out from our lounge room and which we'd turned into a small but very pretty garden about fifty feet up from the ground level. He lifted himself into one of the brick garden troughs raised about eighteen inches from the terrace floor and which acted as both garden and wall along three sides. Damon flapped his arms balancing on the far edge of the trough and looking down said, "I can fly if I want to, you know!" He looked at me mischievously, a small boy again. "I really can, Dad!"

"Jesus, Damon, get down!" Damon normally had trouble balancing his lopsided little body on a flat carpet, let alone on a five-inch-wide brick ledge overlooking a fifty-foot drop. Merely waving his arms around, as he was now doing, could be sufficient to cause him to lose his balance and plunge to his death. He turned, took a step towards me and jumped back on to the terrace. The jump was a bit clumsy and I needed to grab his arm to steady him, but it was nevertheless miraculous. Almost as much a miracle for Damon, then, as if he'd actually flapped his arms, taken off and flown away.

The whole scenario was awesome and very frightening and I could feel my heart thumping and my throat constrict. Damon simply *couldn't* do any of the things he'd done in the space of the past few minutes. He'd never been able to, he never would be able to, but he *was!*

The Bondi cottage had been wonderful for him and within a couple of weeks had completely lifted his depression and he also seemed to be going through a period when he seemed relatively well. But I was suddenly aware that something else was about to occur that we couldn't possibly understand. I had seen him do enough in these few minutes to put himself into hospital with a series of bleeds which, given his present physical condition, could quite easily set him back for months. And yet he seemed unharmed. He hadn't flinched as he'd slammed both the side of his hand and the ball of his foot into the door, nor had he as much as grunted when he'd jumped from the terrace wall.

Thank God Benita wasn't home. She is not the calmest person on earth, and while we didn't know at the time, she'd developed a severe heart condition; I was certain that had she witnessed Damon's performance she would have been overcome with a panic attack.

"Good, eh?" Damon asked again, plainly in high spirits.

"Damon, are you on drugs, LSD or something?"

"No Dad, I swear!" he looked genuinely shocked.

"Hypnosis? Are you in a hypnotic trance? If you are, then tell me and I'll help to get you out of it!"

It was all I could think to say though I couldn't believe Damon would be this stupid. Hypnosis can alter a state of physical awareness and even allow a demonstration of physical strength impossible to imagine in a normal waking state. The aftermath, in Damon's case, would be much too severe. I told myself he would never do anything as stupid as to put himself so deeply into hypnosis.

Besides, if it were hypnosis, it was doubtful that he could induce such a deep trance in himself without co-operation from someone else. People can be persuaded under hypnosis to do some remarkable things, but the pattern for what had taken place with Damon in the past minutes was completely beyond anything I understood.

"Dad, you don't understand. I'm cured!" He stopped and put his hands on his hips like a small child, clicking his tongue he added, "Well, parts of me are! *They* are still working on the other parts."

I thought I'd heard the word "they" on the first occasion but I hadn't been absolutely sure, now it was unmistakable. I knew with a sudden certainty that Damon was not fully in control of his mind.

I am an African first and foremost, I have seen people possessed by evil spirits. Rationally I'll tell you that's nonsense, of course, but I have learned that few things in this world are wrought by logic alone; now I was certain Damon was being controlled by someone or something else.

"Do you mind if I smoke, Dad?" he asked, following me into the living room.

"Smoke? Are you smoking again?" It was a surprise to me, he'd given up when he'd had the AIDS-related pneumonia.

"No, not cigarettes." He reached into the back pocket of his dirty shorts and produced what looked like a packet of cigarettes. "These." The packet was of an unusual design and from it he withdrew a long, chocolate brown cylinder, slightly thinner and about half as long again as a normal cigarette. "They're special cigarettes, they have special qualities made particularly for me." Then, as though reading my thoughts, he said, "Not dope, Dad!" He pushed the long, slim cigarette carefully into the corner of his mouth, first using a dirty fingernail to pick away at the thrush formed on the inside of his lips.

It was then that I saw how dirty his hands were. The dirt not only covered the back of his hand but it ran into the creases between his fingers. Damon who'd wanted to be a doctor and who washed his hands a dozen times or more each day. It seemed impossible.

"I'm *not* going to light my cigarette without a match." He looked up at me before reaching into the same back pocket of his shorts and producing what looked like a genuine Zippo lighter. Well, at least the old Damon was still under there somewhere, if he couldn't have a solid gold Dunhill I knew it would have to be a genuine American Zippo.

"I could light it, you know, spontaneously, just with my mind." He flicked the lighter open with his thumb and lit the thin brown cigarette, letting it hang expertly at the corner of his mouth, squinting through the rising smoke. "But you've seen enough today."

Celeste arrived soon afterwards, calling "Hello everybody!" as she came through the front door which had remained ajar.

"I'm just telling Dad about my cure, babe!" Damon shouted happily. "He's pretty impressed, I showed him my karate kick!"

"That's good, Damon," she replied, her voice controlled and matter-of-fact, then she added, "But we really ought to be going home, Christopher's coming over for lunch. Remember?"

"Okay then, Dad, I've got to go," he said cheerfully. He walked over and rested a hand on both my shoulders. "Pleased, eh? It's good isn't it? I'm almost cured. I told you my mind could do it, *now* do you believe me?"

Damon was looking directly into my eyes, his own were still sunk deep into his skull, though the whites were clean and clear around the lovely hazel of his pupils; this was strange for they seemed to have regained their depth and colour and had lost the dark, dead, soaked-raisin appearance they'd taken on with his AIDS condition. I didn't know what to say. If I agreed with him, would I then be driving him further into the fantasy world he was clearly living in? Or if I objected and called his bluff, would I damage his fragile ego and plunge him back into depression?

"I don't know, Damon. I just don't know, it's all rather a lot to take in all at once."

Damon smiled and gave me a hug, it was the old killer smile and little boy hug I hadn't felt for years. "I know, I know," he said, pressing his fingers into my shoulders. "I love you, Dad. I really love you such a lot; now that I'm better I'm going to show you, I'm going back to uni to become a doctor."

"That's good," I said softly, not sure what else to say.

I walked with them to the front door and when Damon was not looking I cupped my fist to my ear and mimed, "Call me!" Celeste nodded, almost imperceptibly, afraid Damon might see her. It was clear that whatever was wrong with him, Celeste was prepared to go along with it. Celeste called several hours later to say that Damon had been acting strangely for some time, but that the change in him had been gradual, hardly perceptible at first.

"It was a very gradual high, that started to get higher and higher. Remember how depressed he was? Then we came here to Bondi and, almost immediately, he became happy and much more cheerful. He felt that he had everything to look forward to, this house was his dream and he was *really* happy! We both were, it was like the Woollahra cottage all over again, only better. Damon was back to the old Damon again, it had been a long time since he'd been well and happy, a very long time.

"It started when we were painting the house. He was helping, except he couldn't climb up the ladder and things, but he was *really* helping. Mixing and stirring the paint and doing lots of other things. And, gradually, he just got higher and higher and higher and he started having trouble sleeping at night. He'd be on the computer a lot and he was talking a lot about what he wanted to achieve and I noticed that he wanted to have people around him a lot. Damon liked people, but he also liked to be alone; but now he didn't, he wanted people around him all of the time."

Celeste paused on the phone. "There's something I have to say which I don't think you're going to like."

"Say it," I said, sure that I could cope, that another shock wouldn't make all that much difference to my already traumatised system.

"Well, Damon's been on drugs, on Ecstasy."

"But Damon hasn't taken any non-prescription drugs for a long time?"

"Ecstasy is different. Well, for Damon."

"Why?" I asked, trying to sound casual. "You've just said, he was happy with the move and having his own house?" Recreational drugs frightened me.

"I don't know," Celeste explained, "it's a new drug. Someone told him that it was a cross between Speed and LSD, it keeps you in an elevated sense of consciousness and you feel as though nothing can harm you."

"How would he have gotten hold of it?" I asked, not at all happy with what Celeste was saying but trying not to show my annoyance. It was one thing to blame AIDS, but if Damon's present condition was the result of taking drugs I wasn't sure I knew how to react.

"Oh, Bryce, it's very easy to get. You can get it anywhere. It's new, there's plenty of it around." Celeste's voice was casual and I found myself further irritated.

"For Christ's sake, Celeste! Damon's paranoid about the stuff they give him in hospital, he questions everything! Why would he put an unknown drug into his body? I mean that's super stupid!"

Celeste sighed. "That's Damon being *sick*, being unwell, I mean in hospital around doctors. Damon *better* sees himself no different from anybody else. Ecstasy's a new drug taken by just about everybody we know." Celeste paused, "I've taken it, though only once."

"Well?"

Celeste sounded a little exasperated. "It's okay, it was good! But I didn't need it." She paused. "Damon does, I mean did."

"And what now?" I was trying not to sound shocked, even though I felt like giving her a lecture on the spot. Celeste seemed not to notice the exasperation in my voice.

"Damon had Ecstasy and had a good time, Bryce! It's a party drug and when he takes it he's happy again." She sighed a deep sigh, as though she was trying to teach a backward child. "He had it once and it worked and so he's had it again; it makes him happy, makes him have fun. But with Damon it's more than that, it's also making him not feel pain, it's making him feel strong and letting him have confidence in his body. He says it makes him feel sexy and well and fit." She paused. "All of those things!"

"I asked him this morning if he was on drugs and he denied it. He gave a damn good imitation of appearing to be shocked at the question."

"Well yes, he would! He isn't, he hasn't had Ecstasy since he started to get on a high. He's not on drugs, I mean, you know, that sort, like Ecstasy, non-medical ones." Celeste adopted a slightly patronising manner. "Bryce, it's not the way you think, he *needed* it at that time when he was coming out of his depression." Celeste paused again. "He wasn't addicted or anything, he just took it maybe three or four times, I only told you because it was after taking Ecstasy that he started to get on this high."

"What are you trying to say? The drug, this Ecstasy and not his AIDS, brought on the high?"

"I don't know, maybe it was a combination? I told Brent Waters, he says maybe." Celeste then added, "Maybe, you know, Ecstasy was a catalyst."

"When was all this? When did he start behaving strangely?" I hated the idea that Damon might have brought this dreadful thing upon himself. It seemed so bloody stupid after all he'd been through.

"At the beginning of this month, about two weeks ago," Celeste said.

As she spoke I recalled my secretary, Cathy, having come into my office a week or so previously to ask whether she could, on Damon's behalf, send flowers to a lady called Denise at Prince Alfred Hospital. I was busy and I simply nodded my agreement, Damon was given to such thoughtful gestures, it was one of his more disarming characteristics. Denise, I imagined, must have done something very nice for him and, as usual, he was broke. With Damon the gesture was always more important than his ability to pay for it, but I excused his presumption by reasoning that we owed Denise a great deal anyway.

A little later Cathy came back, her expression puzzled. She waited until I was off the phone and then said, "It's none of my business, Bryce, but what did this Denise do that earned her six-dozen, long-stemmed, yellow roses?"

Damon's favourite flowers were yellow roses, but even for Damon this was somewhat grand and I had intended asking him about it. Now I mentioned the roses to Celeste, who laughed, "I'm sorry I didn't know about the roses, but I've cancelled the BMW!"

"What!" I yelled.

"Damon wants to trade in the Mazda on a new BMW, the salesman has been coming around for days and he's already had a test drive. I told him that you'd definitely said 'No' to the BMW and he's going to see you about it, to try and convince you that his cure for AIDS will make him so much money, he'll be able to pay you back immediately."

"Have you called Brent?" I asked.

"Yes, but Damon doesn't want to see him. Brent said not to force it yet, that it sounds like a mild mania. He said if it got any worse to call him, as we may have to *make* him take treatment. But it's not easy, Damon has to agree to see him and also agree to go on Lithium, that's the drug they might possibly use for this condition."

"I'll come down immediately," I said.

Celeste's voice grew suddenly tremulous and I thought for a moment she was going to cry. "No, please don't," she said softly, "Robert says there's *nothing* wrong with him, that sometimes AIDS makes you go a bit funny and imagine things. He keeps telling me Damon is all right! It would be embarrassing if you confronted Damon or upset him in front of Robert."

Robert was the Uncle Robert of Damon's childhood, a great friend of the family, who'd known us for all of Damon's life and of whom Damon was very fond. Robert, who was gay, had moved to the United States some three years earlier to open a native art gallery in New York and he and his friend, Philip Burgos, had arrived for a visit. Damon had been most anxious to have him stay in his new Bondi house.

"Robert insists it's nothing to worry about, but I don't believe him, Damon's completely off the air!" Celeste started to sob. "He thinks that stupid bracelet Robert gave him has magical powers, that it's some sort of transmitter from the space probe, Gemini, which warns him if the CIA are near!"

"Celeste! We have to do something, he could hurt himself. He's going to have a terrible bleed in his hand and foot from the karate chops he inflicted on the front door."

"That's the problem, Bryce, he isn't having bleeds! He's been doing that for several days, saying he's been taught by Bruce Lee, the guy in the Chinese movies, and the amazing thing is he hasn't had a bleed anywhere since he started to act strangely. If he had a bad bleed maybe he'd come out of it, he'd realise he wasn't cured!" Now she sobbed openly.

"Darling, are you sure I couldn't help? Can't I speak to him? He looks a mess, how long has he been in those clothes?"

Celeste controlled her tears, sniffing over the phone, "He won't wash or change, he says he's in his fighting clothes, that he must be like this, the dirt is his disguise. They know everything about him and they'd know he'd never be dirty!"

"There *must* be something we can do? Call me when he returns home and I'll come down and bring him up here, now that I know the full story I'll try to make some sense out of all of this."

"Please, Bryce, can you leave it until Robert and Philip leave?" Celeste begged, "Damon is so proud of having them in his own home and he seems much better when they are around, he loves acting as head of the household. Perhaps you can try to talk to him when they've gone?"

Benita and I tried as little as possible to interfere in Celeste and Damon's personal lives and I had decided not to mention Damon's latest problem to Benita who was out shopping. "Okay, but can you get Robert to ring me at work tomorrow?" I asked.

Robert and his friend, Philip, were coming to dinner the following evening and I wanted to talk to him before they did so. Robert is Dutch and, while a loving and loyal friend, he is not known for his tact; he might just say something that could alert or upset Benita before I was ready to tell her about Damon. Though tell her what? I wasn't quite sure.

I called Brent Waters and was fortunate enough to find him at home. "Brent, sorry to call you at home, mate." I paused, "It's about Damon."

"No, don't be silly, I'm glad you called," Brent said, "You know don't you, I've already spoken to Celeste?"

"He's taken a drug the kids call Ecstasy, it seems to have triggered something."

"Bryce, who the hell knows, it could have started the whole thing off, but mania of this sort is also one of the complications of AIDS."

"Mania? What does that mean?" I asked.

"Well, I can't tell unless I examine him and it's unlikely he'll let me do that. You see he feels totally in control. But the symptoms Celeste talks about are fairly typical of hypomania and he's paranoid as well. Sometimes when people come down from mania, they complain bitterly that life was much more pleasant when they were under its influence. They could be right, of course, but the real problem is the consequences of the mad things they do — extravagant purchases, indiscreet remarks, midnight phone calls — they can do a lot of damage."

"Brent, we could even take our chances on that, but he isn't normal, I mean, a normal person. He's a haemophiliac, he can't go around trying to chop doors in half!"

Brent sighed, "The only way I could treat him against his will is to schedule him and I can't do that yet."

"Schedule? What does that mean?"

"Admitting him into a psychiatric institution against his will because his judgment is so far gone that he is a danger to himself or someone else."

"You mean Celeste? Of course, we'd hate that, but there's no sign of him being violent. It's the other thing; he talks about having a cure, being given a cure for AIDS!"

"Well, it sounds as if his judgment is pretty bad now, but I don't want to do this thing, Bryce, and I don't think we have to yet. I don't think it's so bad yet that he has to be incarcerated to protect him from himself."

"What if he hurts himself, I mean *really* badly. Are there not private places he can go to, to be looked after?"

"Bryce, I can't schedule him yet." Brent cleared his throat, "We must somehow get him to co-operate. The treatment is dead simple. If it's what I think it is and I can get him on to a program of Lithium and tranquillisers, he'll be okay in a matter of days."

"Lithium. It will fix him?"

"With tranquillisers, if we start them now we'll settle him almost immediately; but he may have to take the Lithium indefinitely or for quite a while anyway to stop the mania coming back."

"Would that be bad for him?"

"Well, normally, no! People who suffer from hypo-mania or severe depression are everywhere — judges, politicians, doctors, accountants. They stay on Lithium and they're perfectly normal, it's simple maintenance, a bit like insulin with a diabetic."

"I'll try to persuade him. I'm sure I can get through to him, he'll listen to me."

"I haven't fully answered your question," Brent persisted, "Damon is on so many drugs, by adding other fairly strong, mind-altering drugs like Lithium and tranquillisers they may interfere with each other." He sighed, "But there really isn't a lot of choice."

"He's always listened to me," I said, still confident that, when the chips were down, I was the one who would be able to get through to Damon.

"I hope so," Brent Waters sounded doubtful, "But don't bet on it, Bryce. Damon, as you know, won't take anything when he doesn't know its side effects. He's fed up with doctors and medication, besides, he won't be anxious to alter his present situation, he's feeling in control for the first time in his life. He isn't having bleeds, he feels strong, brilliant."

"He took Ecstasy?" I protested.

"It's not quite the same thing, he probably wouldn't see a recreational drug in the same light."

"Brent, he's trying to kick doors down with his bare feet! He won't last long doing that!"

"Yes, Celeste told me, that's part of him feeling himself invincible. I doubt whether he'll do it again to the door. Has he?"

"Well, no, I don't think so. But I saw him do it and, by some miracle, he didn't get a massive bleed. It's hard to understand, it should have put him in hospital."

"Yes, it's curious, but not uncommon. Hypomania of this kind is something we can treat relatively easily, but that doesn't mean we understand it all that well, or its effects on the brain. A high threshold for pain is not unusual, though. I've never seen it in a haemophiliac before, I don't know why he didn't bleed. Some things we just have to accept."

"Brent, if, as you say, he's so happy with his hypomania, what about the CIA? He thinks he's being followed and he's obviously scared. He's becoming obsessed!"

"Yes, that's the real worry. It could cause him problems with the people he has to deal with, authorities and the like. He could start calling the police, foreign embassies, the prime minister."

"Shit! What will we do?"

Brent attempted to comfort me again, "They're pretty used to crank calls, he's not the only person with hypomania or an assortment of other psychiatric problems on the streets. Let's see how it develops. In the meantime cancel all his credit cards, if he has any, or bank accounts. Is the car or the house in his name?"

"No, I hadn't thought to change the car over as I pay the insurance, the petrol, the same with the house."

"Well, let's hope it's temporary, Bryce, and that he'll let me examine him soon. I've already suggested on the phone to him that he come and see me but, of course, he refused. In his own mind he's never been better in his life. It's difficult, we can't force him."

"I'll get him to take the Lithium," I said, sounding definite again.

"Yes, well, I wish you would and soon! I'd like to examine him and organise treatment for him as soon as possible." Brent's voice took on a tone of urgency, "Try hard. Next week I leave for Canada, I'll be away until mid January."

I didn't know how to break the news of Damon's hypomania to Benita. I felt it might be best to say nothing for the time being. I'm one of those people who believes that when in doubt, say nothing. It's a philosophy which usually gets me into a lot of trouble with my wife.

Because Damon, upon arriving at Bondi and the new house, had come out of his depression so well we'd made a point of leaving the two of them largely to themselves. Once a week we'd drop in, or Damon and Celeste would come up for dinner or lunch or simply to see us, just as he'd done the previous day. We told ourselves that they had their own lives to lead and we trusted Celeste to call us if anything was needed or Damon was unwell or she needed help to get him to hospital. She's a very independently minded young woman and, even this, she usually managed on her own.

When Benita arrived home, careful to keep my voice matter-of-fact, I said, "Damon came up, he sends his love."

"How is he?" she asked, equally casually.

"In good spirits, he was on top of the world."

It wasn't a lie and Benita accepted my reply at face value. "That's nice. David Jones was a horror story, but their Christmas decorations are up and they look nice."

I waited another hour or so when we were sitting on the terrace having a cup of tea. With Robert and his friend coming to dinner the next Monday evening, I thought it best to tell her I was just a bit worried about Damon's general demeanour and had spoken to Brent Waters about him.

I left out most of what Brent had said to me, saying only that Brent thought he was possibly suffering from a slightly manic condition and that it could be fixed fairly easily with a drug called Lithium.

Benita is not easily fooled and she became immediately worried, "What do you mean, slightly manic condition?" she demanded. It was a mistake. I secretly backhanded myself. I have learned over the years not to try to explain too much; with Benita it just gets you further into the poo. I feigned annoyance at her over-reaction. "For Christ's sake, he's okay! There's nothing to worry about. Ask Robert when you see him, he'll tell you."

I should have known better than to trust a Dutchman in a matter requiring any sort of subtlety.

"Benita, it's just one of those things," Robert replied

when Benita broached the question of Damon's behaviour.

I groaned inwardly. Bloody Robert, subtle as a meat axe!

"What's just one of those things?" Benita snorted, immediately suspicious. We'd reached the coffee stage of the meal and I'd just poured Robert and Philip a glass of cognac. Between the two of them, they'd already consumed a bottle of Chardonnay followed by a good red, with Benita drinking a single glass from the white wine, not touching the red.

Robert was very relaxed and he waved his arms in a melodramatic gesture, "There's nothing wrong with Damon. I mean, my dear, you should see some of them, some of my friends in the States!" He rolled his eyes, and gave a series of Robert bellows which so amused the kids when they were young, a sort of deep nasal snort followed by a loud braying sound you could hear at a hundred feet. "They've gone quite looney! It attacks the brain, you know?" He brought the brandy balloon to his lips, his face buried in the interior of the glass as he threw back his head and quaffed. Finally withdrawing the balloon, he added, "Damon's fine, my dear, there's nothing wrong with him. If he's acting a bit weird it's just the excitement of his new house, that's all."

As usual, Robert had put his bloody, great, Netherlandish foot in it.

Benita pouted her disapproval, dabbing at her mouth with her napkin before placing it on the table beside her. "Damon doesn't *act* weird, Robert!" She rose from the table and shot an angry look at me and in a cold voice announced, "Excuse me, I think I'll call, Celeste." I knew it was all over. Celeste was no match for Benita.

I'd called Celeste after I'd spoken to Brent Waters and now I knew, under my wife's remorseless interrogation, she'd repeat Brent's comments back to Benita, who'd immediately see it as some sort of conspiracy between us to keep her from knowing about her son. If there was one thing Benita couldn't abide, it was being kept in the dark about anything. Years of doctors and medical crap had made her particularly wary and sensitive about Damon. Benita retired to the bedroom to phone Celeste. Robert was a sufficiently old friend for me to suggest that he and Philip drink up their brandy fairly hastily, fold up their tents and slip silently into the night, that is, if they didn't want to share in the wrath which was soon to descend upon me.

"But he is *all* right, Bryce, Robert assured me. Robert, as with so many Dutch people, spoke Australian with only the slightest accent. "The same thing happened to me when I had the operation on my brain. I heard voices and acted in a funny way," Robert's eyes opened wide and he shrugged his shoulders, "That was supposed to be AIDS related." He shrugged again, "Look at me, Bryce, that was four bloody years ago!"

"Christ, Robert, the AIDS virus must have had just sufficient time to destroy the part of your brain where you store your bloody tact! I think you two really ought to go." I could hear Benita from the bedroom, her voice raised, and I could imagine the verbal hiding Celeste was taking.

The two weeks that followed were hell for us, though not for Damon. For, while he was becoming more and more convinced that he was being pursued by the CIA for the secret formulae he held for curing AIDS he now thought of himself as fully in control of this situation. In his mind he had power, enormous power, to defeat his enemies.

Celeste recalls how he had a fantastic time, "He was paranoid, sure, but at the same time he was elated, high on himself all the time! What's more he had a task, a duty entrusted to him as a great leader to save mankind, or at least the world's AIDS sufferers from being exterminated."

According to one of Damon's main conspiracy theories, it seemed the Americans didn't want him to give the world this AIDS cure. In fact, they didn't want a cure at all. It was they who had first isolated the AIDS virus in a laboratory and who were spreading it around the world, first by means of a smallpox vaccination serum they'd developed for Africa and Haiti, then through the blood systems of homosexuals and drug users who shared needles among each other. AIDS was a disease invented by the CIA for its own evil purposes. In Damon's eyes it was all a giant conspiracy. The CIA wanted to control the world and to do so they needed to first kill off all the people they didn't want, the "useless people" like the people in Africa and other Third World countries, as well as the blacks and the gays in America.

"They want to get rid of all of them, Dad!" Damon would look into my eyes pleading to be believed, "I am all that is standing between them. I have the cure!"

"What about the Russians and Chinese?" I asked cruelly.

"I suppose they'll come next, I don't know," Damon said earnestly, "I don't think they've got AIDS yet."

Celeste told of yet another conspiracy theory he held

at the time. The reason Damon believed he had AIDS was because there had been "a scientific experiment" and in Damon's particular case it had backfired. The experiment was to create a super race of children who would rule the world. He justified this theory to her one morning by saying, "All of our friends are exceptional people, don't you agree, Celeste?"

"Well yes, they are exceptional people," Celeste said, not wishing to cause any fuss.

"We're exceptional people, too, aren't we?" Damon continued.

"Hmm? We're all right," Celeste mumbled.

"No, we're not! You know we're exceptional!" Damon pressed the point then looked up and explained how all of them were a part of this experiment, which had backfired, and that he was the weakest link, so he was the one with the haemophilia and now the AIDS. At one point in this discussion he'd leaned closer to Celeste, "You know how you don't know who your father was? It's because Bryce is your father, too. Really! We're brother and sister and I'm the leader of us all!"

Damon saw himself as the leader of an army, who had people whom he pronounced as his generals. Some of these were Toby, Bardy, Paul, Christopher and Andrew Sully; the neighbour next door, Geoff Pash, was yet another. Celeste laughed, recalling, "I was in there somewhere, too, but I don't think I got general. Concubine, maybe? Damon always thought it was enough just to be loved by him. To be with him. I mean he had a tremendous ego, one that went way over the top sometimes. But it was one of the things his friends liked about him, he was so confident, so certain and always outrageous."

She thought for a moment, "You know, I once mentioned to Toby that Damon had the potential for hypomania, I mean, all on his own. He was always so certain and thought out of the square, the things he came up with were so outrageous they'd often shock people who didn't know him well."

Damon's army was the army of righteousness pitted against the CIA, the dark forces of evil. He had been given the cure for AIDS because he was the one with whom the experiment had backfired. Celeste recalls how he told her that they'd just gone too far with the experiment to create a super race of children, which had resulted in his haemophilia and AIDS. His most superior brain, because of the advanced stage of the experiment, benefited the most. That's why he'd been given the cure for AIDS. That was also why he'd always been destined to be the leader.

During this intense period somewhere along the line his hypomania became mania, a rather more serious and intense condition. Damon came up with several other conspiracy theories, all of them bizarre, but some of them quite plausible if you were inclined to believe such things, as many people are.

Damon took to carrying one of those loud beepers old ladies are encouraged to carry in their handbags, which set off a terrible racket if you're suddenly attacked. The brand name of this pocket alarm was *Gemini*. He held it up to me one morning, looking directly into my eyes, "See, Dad, it's the same name as the space probe, Gemini. My people have got a satellite that protects me, this is my warning system when I'm in danger." He looked over his shoulder momentarily then back at me, "I just activate it and *they* take care of things."

He refused also to remove Uncle Robert's bracelet even when he bathed. It may seem like a contradiction that even though he felt empowered, the general of a vast army, he was also scared and constantly felt that he was going to be personally attacked before he could do what he'd been created to do. Brent Waters explains that this kind of contradiction is not unusual. Damon also claimed that he was waiting to be told to whom he must take his AIDS cure. That he could trust no one, not even his best friends; the hospital system was also corrupt and was in the pay of the CIA, though some people within it were to be trusted. He must wait to be told who these people were. The bracelet would tell him and the buzzer was his protection; in his own mind, both were his only protection.

As Christmas approached, Damon became more paranoid and, with it, secretive. We were terribly worried; Brent had left for Canada after calling to say he'd given Damon's case notes to a colleague, a psychiatrist whom he'd briefed. He was confident the man could be trusted to handle Damon competently. However, we didn't know this psychiatrist. I suppose we should have met him, but we hadn't, so we were reluctant to call on him, unless it became a real emergency and Damon looked as though he could do himself or someone else a real harm. Again, Celeste bore most of the brunt and tells the events that followed best.

"About a week before Christmas, the worst of all the things that happened before Christmas, happened — the worst because it was really saddening. Damon was up all night again, I'd wake up every now and again and have a look to see what he was doing and he'd be on the Apple. On one occasion, I woke to hear him talking very loudly on the telephone, it would have been three in the morning.

"I got up and walked down the passage into the front room, 'What are you doing?' I asked.

"'I'm trying to phone the police,' he said loudly. He was very angry and kept slamming the receiver back down into its cradle, cursing it and everything else. It was this slamming and cursing which had wakened me.

"He turned around and said, 'I have to go to the hospital! I just have to go to the hospital!'

"'Why, have you got a bad bleed?' I asked. The Mazda was away being repaired, which was very lucky, Damon was in no state to drive.

"'No! I have to cure the people there. It's time, I have to go. Now!'

"By this time I was pretty used to his phone calls at all hours of the night. After trying to persuade him to come to bed I eventually gave up. He was dressed in shorts and T-shirt and was barefoot and I knew he was too afraid to leave the house on his own, especially at night. That was when they would get him. I think I might even have reminded him of this, using his fear. I didn't care, I was too tired, I would have used anything I could."

I nodded at Celeste; we'd been at the receiving end of several of Damon's three a.m. phone calls and we'd learned going down to see him was pointless, there was nothing you could do for him.

"Anyway," Celeste continued, "I went back to bed and he must have called a cab. I didn't wake up for this, but

I learned later that he'd persuaded the cab to take him to the automatic teller at Bondi to get money out so that he could get to the hospital. Why, when he was dressed like that, the cab agreed, I don't know. Though I suppose cabs are used to picking up some pretty strange people. The automatic teller wouldn't respond to his cash card because our bank account had nothing in it. He'd cleaned it out long ago and I hadn't put any back in, because of what Brent had said to you and, also, we had to have some money!

"The cab driver swore at him and drove off and Damon had to walk home in the early hours from the beach front, which must have been really scary for him. After that, was when the really sad business started.

"Damon came back home and went to the Apple Mac and printed himself a set of cards stating that he was a doctor. These he scattered around the house for anyone to see. Then he got dressed in his best suit and put on a pair of Ray-Ban reflectors. It was weird, wearing those Ray-Ban reflectors in the middle of the night, like one of the Blues Brothers. He'd found a small basket in the kitchen and he started to collect things he was going to take to the hospital, this was his medical kit and in it was shampoo, my tampons, Panadol . . . all manner of very strange things, tubes, syringes . . . you know, just things! He was pacing up and down carrying the basket over his arm, when I woke up and came out.

"I was astonished; he'd never looked as though he was going to leave the house before, that was why I'd felt safe enough to go back to bed, he was always too frightened. Of course, I hadn't realised that he'd already been out in the cab and walked back home from the beach.

He seemed to be deep in thought, pacing the hallway. 'Damon, why are you all dressed up?' I was suddenly very wide awake.

"He didn't look up, I doubt if he could have seen me with his Ray-Bans on. 'Hello, babe,' he said almost absently. Then suddenly he exclaimed, 'That's it! The fish food!' He hurried over to the bottom of the sink where we kept the fish food. I don't suppose he could have seen anything inside because of his stupid glasses. 'Where's the fish food?' he shouted urgently. I walked over and took the packet of fish food from the shelf in front of him and handed it to him.

" 'Jesus! Thank Christ!' he said, clutching the fish food to his chest (we still had the fish from the flat), and then he put this packet of fish food into the basket and started to pace up and down again. Finally, he decided he didn't need the basket, he just took the fish food out and put it into his jacket pocket. That was what he was going to use to cure the people.

"He said to me at the time, sounding perfectly rational, that it wasn't the fish food that was going to cure the people with AIDS, the fish food was just that people needed to think that they were having something. He said it was the placebo, he'd give them a bit of fish food and that would make them feel better, but that the cure was in his hands.

"He was totally convinced that if he could get to the hospital he could cure people. He didn't ask me for help or money, I think he knew I wouldn't give it to him or go with him. He called the ambulance and explained to them that he was a doctor and had to get to the hospital. But they just thought 'This guy's a looney' and hung up on him. The police were the same, they wouldn't have anything to do with him. After this, he was raging mad, running around the house in his Ray-Bans, falling over things and he really looked mad. I didn't know what to do, I was truly frightened; it was the first time he'd really looked as though he was insane. Then suddenly, he stopped and sat down and began to cry. 'What's wrong? What's wrong with me!' he wept. I took him, I remember it was just getting light, and I led him to our bedroom and put him to bed and he fell asleep still weeping.

"That was the worst, the worst night, that was the saddest moment of all, because I realised Damon, the Damon I loved so terribly much, wasn't going to get better unless he had treatment. I was losing him. I crept into bed beside him and took him in my arms and then I cried, too, until I must have fallen asleep."

Celeste was in a state of total exhaustion, she was hardly sleeping at night as Damon required constant attention. I tried to persuade him to let me bring a nurse into the house. Tim Rigg had left CSN because his own health was now too frail to cope. Damon had made him an honorary general in his army. I called a private nursing place and they told me they could supply a trained-psychiatric male nurse for eight hundred dollars per twenty-four hour shift. I would happily have paid, but Damon clearly couldn't have coped. "That's just what they're waiting for. Who do you think the nurse would be?" Damon shouted at me when I brought it up again.

"Who?" I asked, annoyed, tired of arguing, tired of pretending he was all right.

"Dad, you know!"

"No! I don't! Damon, you tell me."

"Them! The CIA!"

"Oh, for Christ's sake!"

Tears welled in his eyes, "Dad, you don't understand. They're looking for me, they want to eliminate me."

Celeste didn't allow me to persist, there wasn't the slightest doubt that Damon believed the CIA was out to get him.

We did manage to get Dr Phil Jones, his doctor at Prince Henry, to prescribe a strong sedative to make him sleep at night. Phil Jones is a sensitive and capable doctor, whom Damon liked and who understood the situation. Celeste put it into his drink and for a few nights he slept and she was able to get some rest. But even this had an unfortunate outcome. It was an abnormally wet December and we discovered, to our dismay, that the cottage had been built on a sandstone quarry and that the basement filled with water after sustained rain. One morning several days before Christmas, Celeste woke to find it had risen above the floorboards. She called a plumber who placed an underwater pump in the basement with an ordinary garden hose pushed through a window to pump the water into the street. There were several thousands of gallons of water in the cellar and, as the weather forecast promised rain until beyond Christmas, it was decided to run the pump day and night for several days in an attempt to empty the underground supply. However, the pump was not allowed to be run at night, Damon insisted on the windows being locked at nightfall. As most of the rain seemed to fall at night, Celeste would wait until the sedative had taken effect and he was asleep, when she'd sneak out to the front room and switch the pump on again, opening the window and pushing the hose through it. A flooded Christmas was more than she could have coped with.

On the second night of Damon's sedation and one when it was raining, Celeste woke to find the figure of a man bending over her. In her half-wakened state she thought it was Damon going about his usual nocturnal manner, but then she realised that he was asleep, breathing fitfully beside her. Celeste screamed and the man fled through the house and Damon somehow woke, though still in a drugged state from the sedative. Celeste sat on the bed hugging her knees, terrified and hysterical. Damon, unaware that he was on sleeping pills, thought that he'd been deliberately drugged and that the intruder was a CIA agent who'd come to kill him. He clung to Celeste and she to him, neither quite sure who was protecting whom.

It was probably this more than anything else that brought the two of them to their senses. It was not long before dawn when the incident had occurred and with more light Celeste calmed down sufficiently to call the police. By the time the police arrived it was quite light and most of Damon's sedation had worn off, though Celeste made him promise that he'd let her do all the talking. But of course, this didn't happen and, after a few minutes, the two police constables were glancing meaningfully at each other. They took the details, such as they were; ignoring Damon they asked Celeste to establish what had been stolen. This turned out to be nothing, the man must have been a drug addict looking for money or drugs and that's why he'd come into the bedroom. There was no bathroom cabinet and Celeste, fearing Damon would find the sedatives the hospital had given her for him, had hid them behind a detergent pack in the out-side laundry. To the intruder, the bedroom would have seemed the most likely place to look for either money or pills.

They were stony-broke as usual and while there were heaps of drugs in the house, kept in a box under the kitchen sink, they were not of the kind an addict would instantly recognise as useful. They had no video recorder to steal, the record-player was being repaired and the TV, an old one given to them by us, would have been too cumbersome for one man to move. The window the man had come through was, of course, the one left open for the hose but, as the hose was still stuck through it pumping water, to the police officers present it was hardly convincing evidence of a "break and entry". They left, no doubt deciding that clearly Damon was a case (one look at him said it all, he looked like an addict himself) and the girl was clearly the hysterical type. As far as they were concerned, it was an open and shut nut case.

Later, after the police had gone they discovered where the man had calmly sat in the lounge room smoking a cigarette. He'd also found the box of Damon's bleed stuff under the kitchen sink. And there was another contain-ing Damon's medications which Celeste, knowing they contained no drugs of addiction, hadn't thought to men-tion to the police. He'd taken the box containing the bleed stuff into the lounge room and had gone through it, afterwards pushing the contents into a corner of the old settee and casually covering them with a couple of cushions.

Celeste knew it would be pointless recalling the police,

they wouldn't believe her anyway, so she used this evidence to try to convince Damon that it *was* an addict looking for money or drugs and not the CIA.

But Damon, seeing the swabs, a couple of butterfly needles and syringes and other gear used for bleeds in the corner of the settee, cleverly countered by saying that CIA agents weren't stupid and that scattering the contents of his bleed box was simply a cautionary plan. If the agent had been caught he would have admitted to being a drug addict and used his drug dependency as his reason for breaking in, the whereabouts of the box of Damon's medication would then seem to be clear evidence of his addiction.

"See!" Damon pointed to the various scattered items revealed under the cushions, "He took almost all the syringes and needles! That's very clever. If they'd caught him, they wouldn't find any drugs on him just the syringes and needles which we couldn't positively prove belonged to us anyway. He'd be clean and with a perfect alibi. The police don't give drug addicts a hard time unless they find them with drugs in their possession."

It was true, the thief had taken all but half a dozen of Damon's syringes and packets of butterfly needles as well as the tourniquet he used for his transfusions.

The intrusion occurred three days before Christmas and the fact that the intruder had not taken any of the Christmas presents Celeste had made and lovingly wrapped and placed in front of the fireplace was further proof to her that a drug addict was involved; and just as convincing to Damon that the CIA wanted it to look this way.

The three days leading up to Christmas were very

difficult — Damon's mania became a lot worse, he locked all the doors and windows, despite the December heat and the tremendous humidity from the recent rains, and he spent most of the time patrolling the house with his beeper in his hand. Celeste was made to sit by the phone so that when the beeper went off she could quickly phone the police. Though Damon wasn't completely sure that they, too, weren't a part of the conspiracy.

Brett was home from Malaysia for Christmas, but Adam had left for England in late October, so the family wasn't complete for the first Christmas ever. We cooked a large leg of lamb and a sirloin of beef for Brett, Celeste and myself as well as a small turkey to last over the holidays and because Benita doesn't eat red meat. Christmas has always been a cold meal for us and this would be the first when Brett and Adam wouldn't squabble over who was to get the lamb bone to chew. Benita also ordered a superb salmon mousse from David Jones's food department. Damon loved smoked salmon and the mousse was soft enough for him to swallow in relative comfort.

Damon tried hard to be relaxed and seem to enjoy it when we played "Biggest Memories" where everyone tells of his or her biggest childhood or family memory. Celeste added some new material with her biggest memory, which was the story of the sudden explosion, in busy traffic, and subsequent demise of Daddy's precious 1956 Peugeot, an event which resulted in the family never again going out together as one unit. It was very funny, while at the same time a rather sad story, much like Celeste's life.

Damon, with his family around him, felt reasonably safe and, though he was very quiet, seemed to be enjoying himself. Brett amused us all and I can remember Damon cracking up at a story Brett told of one of his exploits in Malaysia. He was laughing, as we all were, when he started to cough and, a little later, to shake violently, unable to control his coughing. We thought he might have another fit, then he went scarlet and seemed to be fighting for breath, as Celeste rushed to take him in her arms, urging him to try to throw up as he was beginning to heave. But quite suddenly he was okay again. "That was very funny, Brett," he said, gasping for breath and wiping his mouth with a napkin. But we'd all been shocked, his frail little body had looked as though it might collapse entirely from the coughing and violent shaking and I think we knew that it wasn't only his head that was wonky, but also how very physically vulnerable and ill our darling Damon really was.

Damon and I were seated at the far end of the room, slightly away from the others, and Celeste was lying on the carpet fast asleep. It was a not unusual Christmas Day, very humid, with late afternoon clouds gathering over the Harbour, so that it looked like rain again that night. But for Damon's sickness, it was an Australian Christmas afternoon like any other, too much of everything and the quiet that comes after the family hullabaloo at the table.

"Dad, is there something wrong with me?" Damon suddenly asked, though quietly so that I alone could hear.

"Why do you ask?" I said, my heart suddenly beating faster.

"I think there is, but I'm not sure. Is it something wrong with my brain?"

I put my arms around him. "Damon, you've been hearing things, acting rather strangely; your mother and I would like you to see a doctor."

I could feel him stiffen in my arms, "Dad, I'm well. I haven't had a bad bleed for nearly a month. That's an all time record!"

"Damon," I said gently, "this thing you have, funny things happen. I know you haven't had any bad bleeds but we think something else may be wrong."

"Does Celeste think so?" His voice was tentative.

"Celeste would like very much for you to see a doctor, Damon."

"She's very tired you know, Dad. She has to be on her guard all the time because we're in danger."

I looked down at the sleeping Celeste, she had her head cupped inside her left arm and she looked very young and vulnerable and beautiful. "You could give her a rest by going into hospital for a few days, just to let them give you a thorough examination. We're all a bit worried, even Brent. Before he went away, he left the name of a colleague just in case."

Damon said nothing more that afternoon but the next day, Boxing Day, Celeste called early to say that Damon wanted to see the doctor Brent had recommended at the Prince of Wales hospital, the teaching hospital where he worked. I called the hospital to be told that this doctor was away over the Christmas break and that there was no psychiatrist available to see Damon.

Celeste called a little later to say Damon was becoming severely depressed one moment and losing his temper the next, that his mood swings were getting pretty wild.

"I've given him a sedative but it doesn't seem to be helping," she added.

"We'll have to get something to calm him down," I said, "Perhaps Roger Cole? I'll try to call him at Prince Henry."

I called and was told that Dr Roger Cole was away on holidays and that they had no phone number. "You mean he's taking today off. Surely you must have a number where we can reach him?"

"No, Doctor Cole is on holidays, he's gone down the coast somewhere. We have no authority to call him." The voice on the other end of the phone sounded final, "In fact we don't have a number."

"Please! Don't hang up," I pleaded, "Can you put me through to the Marks Pavilion?" The phone clicked immediately, the speaker at the other end anxious to get rid of me. After ringing for what seemed ages, someone answered at the other end.

"Good morning, this is Bryce Courtenay, Damon Courtenay's father," I explained, sure that the voice on the other end would know Damon.

"Yes, Mr Courtenay." The voice was tentative and one I didn't recognise, it also obviously didn't know who Damon was.

"You must be new?" I asked.

"Well yes, fairly. We haven't met." The nurse gave his name and we introduced ourselves to each other formally over the phone. His name, I seem to recall, was Alex.

"Is there a doctor I can speak to, Alex? Is Phil Jones available?"

"Well no, not really, only interns are on duty today

and they've already done their round, they won't be back until this evening. Doctor Jones isn't rostered for the Christmas break. Doctor Morgan was in an hour ago but he won't be coming back until evening."

"Is Rick Osborne on duty?" I asked, knowing he would help if he could.

"No, but hang on, I'll look at the roster." I heard the receiver being put down and then shortly afterwards taken up again, "Rick comes on this evening."

"I have to get hold of a psychiatrist or at least a doctor who can prescribe something for my son Damon, who is having some pretty bad mood swings and could be psychotic."

The nurse was trying to be nice but I could feel his impatience, "Well, we can't do anything here, I mean I can't give him anything unless his palliative specialist sees him. This isn't a psychiatric ward you know."

I sighed, "Yes, I've already tried to contact Roger Cole."

"Oh, you can't do that, he's on holidays."

"Yes, yes, I know," I said again wearily.

"Well, there's nothing I can do, Mr Courtenay!"

"Can you put me back to admissions, please?"

I got another lady this time, who was even less helpful than the first, and I was told there was nobody who could see Damon. "It's the holidays, Boxing Day is always the worst. There's really no one who can see your son, Mr Courtenay. We aren't taking any admissions in the Psychiatric Ward over the holidays. Perhaps you should try another hospital."

Throughout all this Benita had been standing beside me on the phone butting in, showing impatience as people are apt to do in an emergency, making suggestions with the benefit of only hearing half the conversation. When you're overanxious yourself you get very annoyed at this constant butting in and, more than once, I felt the urge to cup the phone and shout at Benita to go away. Now I came away from the phone thoroughly disenchanted, not knowing what to do next. There was nobody out there the least bit interested in helping us.

"We must call Shirley, John is Professor of Surgery at Prince of Wales. If she talks to him he may be able to pull some strings," Benita said as I put the phone down.

"What the hell can he do?" I exploded, "He's a goddamn brain surgeon!"

"He'd know someone to call!" Benita, surprised and upset by my outburst, shouted back.

"Well then *you* bloody call her!" I stormed out of the room. I'd been on the phone for nearly two hours and all I was getting was a monumental brush-off.

Shirley Ham is a dear family friend and also a physiotherapist who had her own practice in Rose Bay and who had treated Damon privately for most of his life. Damon loved her, in fact we all loved her a great deal. She was divorced from her husband, John, a professor of surgery at University of New South Wales.

I could hear Benita talking on the phone, explaining in a too-loud voice what had happened and asking Shirley if she would call John to see if he could help.

I heard her put the phone down and call, "Bryce?"

I walked quickly from the bedroom into the bathroom and turned on the tap and started to splash cold water on to my face from the running tap in an attempt to hide my anger and frustration. I knew Benita wasn't to blame, that she was just as anxious and fraught as I was, but I was close to shouting at her again and the cold water seemed to help. She came into the bathroom, "Shirley's going to call John Ham."

I pretended not to hear, splashing more water, "Uh?" I reached for a towel, burying my face in it.

"Shirley's going to call John Ham. If she can get him he'll call here. Will you take the call, please?"

"Jesus! What can *he* do!"

She burst into tears, "I don't know! But it's worth a try, isn't it?"

There didn't seem to be anything to say. She was right, of course, but I wasn't about to admit it. An hour or so later, John Ham phoned. He was extremely nice and I explained Damon's situation and how I'd been trying to contact his palliative specialist, as there didn't seem to be any psychiatric doctors around.

"It's the worst time of the year, Bryce," John Ham explained, "Hospitals are staffed by interns and a psychiatrist, outside a major institution, would be very hard to find. You're quite right, your son probably needs calming down. Who is Damon's palliative man?"

I explained that we'd already tried to contact Roger Cole, who was somewhere out of town and the hospital was reluctant, or simply unable, to give us a number to call.

"Leave it to me. I'll see what I can do." Just hearing him offer to help had a calming effect on me.

I turned to Benita, "Well, he's going to try. He seemed to imply that any doctor could be reached in an emergency."

"Oh, that's great," she said, her voice conciliatory.

"I'm sorry, darling. It's just that all the voices on the

other end of the phone don't seem in the least interested in helping. It's the bloody holidays and *they* have to work and it's giving them the shits! It seems every doctor in the world gets the bloody Christmas holidays off." To our surprise Roger Cole called within half an hour from somewhere on the South Coast. I apologised for "flushing him out" and he listened carefully as I told him about Damon and then he promised to call back. Which he did in twenty minutes or so.

"I've spoken to Doctor Springsteen, she's a psychiatrist at Prince Henry, rather young it seems and doubling up on everything else over the holidays. She has to take Casualty this afternoon, but she'll see Damon if you take him in. But call her first, call her immediately when I hang up. It may be some time before you get through, the hospital's on skeleton."

"Thank you, Roger. I can't tell you what a relief this is."

Roger Cole cleared his throat, "Bryce, don't thank me, there may be a problem."

"Problem?"

"The AIDS set-up isn't equipped to take a psychiatric patient — they may refuse — the nurses are not trained in psychiatric care. It's the holidays — they're short staffed. But I've asked Dr Springsteen to admit Damon, she knows they all know him and he has no past history of violence." He laughed softly, "I can't even *imagine* Damon being violent."

"If they won't take him, what about the psychiatric ward at the hospital?" I asked.

Roger Cole paused for what seemed like a long time, "Bryce, I don't know how to say this, but we have difficulty with their staff."

"Uh? I don't understand, Roger."

"Damon's got AIDS. They won't admit it openly, but they won't take anyone with AIDS into their ward."

"Thank you for telling me, Roger, we're beginning to learn a lot of things about being unclean!"

"I'm sorry, Bryce. I really am." His voice was kind and we knew him as a kind, caring man. He cleared his throat, "I don't know Dr Springsteen, but she seems quite competent, I'm sure she'll be able to help. I've asked her to put Damon into the Marks Pavilion. To admit him simply as an AIDS patient."

I wrote the name down on the pad next to the phone, memorising it at the same time by calling to mind the singer, Bruce Springsteen.

"Thanks, Roger, for everything, I'm truly grateful."

"No please, Bryce, understand, it's not an instruction. I can't order Dr Springsteen to admit Damon. If she thinks he is likely to be violent or she examines him and she's not happy . . ." he didn't finish the sentence. "Well anyway, I'm sure things will be all right. I've told her what Damon's medication is, that is, as much as I can remember, and I've authorised her to have my file on him sent up from the Marks Pavilion. I've also suggested what she might prescribe if he needs calming down." He paused, "Doctor Helen Springsteen," he repeated a third time, "call her as soon as you can."

I called Prince Henry again and asked for Dr Springsteen. I'm sure the phone rang for twenty minutes before finally a terse voice answered, "Yes!"

"Doctor Springsteen?"

"Yes?"

"My name is Bryce Courtenay, Doctor Roger Cole called you about my son, Damon."

"Yes?" again nothing more. I was not prepared to be charitable, another doctor was obviously learning the off-hand manners of her profession.

"Will you see him please, doctor?"

At last the voice committed itself to a whole sentence, "I'm the only one on duty today and I have to do several wards as well as Casualty, do you think it can wait?"

I was surprised. It wasn't what I'd expected. "You mean until later today?"

"No, until after the Christmas break. He hasn't shown any violent tendencies, has he?"

"Well no, but he seems to be getting more and more paranoid, we feel he should be in hospital."

There was a pause at the other end of the phone before she finally answered, "You said he has AIDS? We don't really have a place in the psychiatric ward."

I made no mention of the fact that Roger Cole had suggested he be admitted to the Marks Pavilion as an AIDS patient. "Perhaps they'll take him at the Marks Pavilion?" I suggested, not letting on that Roger Cole had told me about the psychiatric ward at Prince Henry. "I really think someone should see him, examine him. After that we'd prefer him to go into the Marks Pavilion, they know him there." Then I added, "I really don't think we can cope much longer, doctor." This last statement came out as a plea and I hated myself for having to be seen to beg, but I wasn't going to let her off the hook. "Please don't make me beg you, doctor," I said.

"He's not violent?"

"No, doctor."

"Bring him to Casualty this afternoon, I'll try to see him," she sounded worn out. But I didn't care, it was a breakthrough; all in all I'd been on the phone for four hours. I wanted Damon examined and then perhaps he'd agree to go on Lithium. Brent Waters had said that once he was on Lithium he'd soon be back to normal.

Lithium, the word sounded like music, like a glissando on the piano. Lithium, you could make a pretend sentence out of it. "And then when the heat became unbearable and men became maddened by it, slitting their own throats, Lithium, the soft, cool wind first mentioned by the Roman General Marcus Aurelias in his famous Confessions, would blow over the Sahara from the snow-capped Atlas mountains and cool things down again." Lithium, judges and professors used it regularly to keep them calm. Lithium would bring my boy back to me again.

Brett arrived home from early morning fishing at The Gap. I'd heard him get up at dawn. He'd caught two large tailor and a nice-sized bream and, when I told him Damon had agreed to go to hospital, he offered to accompany me. I was grateful, Brett has a nice calmness about him and it always seemed to help Damon to have one of his brothers with him.

It was a stinking hot day, oppressively humid from all the rain, and we arrived at Casualty to find the place full of the day-after-Christmas walking wounded. Bandaged heads and puffed-up faces, black eyes, broken noses, cut lips, dislocated shoulders and multiple lacerations on every body part imaginable. The place seemed filled with men holding their heads in their hands, nursing hangovers and featuring broken bits of their bodies. Some were seated beside the wives and children they'd battered while they'd been in a drunken stupor. In one corner, a family of eight was huddled with every member, except the baby, carrying some evidence of having been severely beaten up.

"Christ! The place looks like there's been a bomb attack somewhere!" I exclaimed to the lady behind the glass partition waiting to take Damon's particulars.

"Welcome to Boxing Day!" she said in a droll voice, "The rest of the world gets Carols by Candlelight," she pointed her ballpoint into the room, "We get carnage by daylight!"

I filled in the forms and we were asked to wait. After an hour Damon was getting pretty fidgety. He'd pace up and down with his hands behind his back. Then he'd sit down, but after a minute or so he'd be up again, pacing the length of the Emergency lounge. Finally he sat next to me again, "Dad, this is a trap, I know it's a trap, let's go home."

I went up to the lady behind the glass panel, "How much longer for Dr Springsteen, ma'am?"

She looked up, there was no recognition that she'd seen me and shared her sardonic humour with me an hour previously. "The doctor's busy, you'll just have to wait!" Her response was automatic, she'd said it a thousand times before and I'm not sure she even heard herself pronouncing the words. "The doctor's busy you'll have to wait" was an automatic response. Without a further glance at me she returned to her paperwork.

"Yes, but . . . I mean we've . . ."

She glanced up, but still there was no change of expression, "We're very busy, there're only two doctors, two interns, on duty." She pronounced the word "interns" with a sniff, showing her disapproval.

"Dr Springsteen is an intern?" I asked, surprised.

She shot a glance up at me, her lips pulled to one side in a disparaging pout, "Well, anyway she's very young!" Then she resumed her paperwork.

"How long do you think? An hour?"

She sighed heavily, looking up, "There are at least fifteen patients in front of you, some have been waiting since early this morning."

I put Damon in the car and we went for a long drive down to La Perouse, while Brett remained behind to keep our place. I pulled the car up beside the monument to the French sea captain and explorer, La Perouse, who had landed on Australian soil before Captain Cook. "This is where it all began, even before Captain Cook. Just think, if La Perouse had thought Australia was worth having for la belle France we might have all been French, Damon."

"Mum would have liked that," Damon said and for a while we talked, until I was finally able to persuade him to return to Emergency to see Dr Springsteen.

We returned an hour or so later and were required to wait another two hours, during which time Damon became very upset and, on three occasions, he attempted to barge into the room where we'd observed Dr Springsteen was seeing patients who'd arrived before us. Brett was able to hold him in his arms, gently, without seeming to harm him, but so that he was unable to move. Each time he'd hold his little brother and laugh, trying to make light of the incident, chiding Damon softly, "Don't worry, it will soon be your turn, Damon."

I was grateful for Brett's calm as he rocked Damon gently in his arms, he seemed so much more in control than I was. It was then that I noticed that the red T-shirt he was wearing was clinging to his body, soaked with sweat from the nervous tension he, too, felt.

Finally, late in the afternoon Dr Springsteen saw Damon. By this time he was thoroughly overwrought and I was terrified she'd declare him violent and refuse to take him into the Marks Pavilion, the AIDS ward.

I'd packed a set of my pyjamas and some underclothes, toothbrush and paste and my slippers and put them into the boot of the car, before we'd picked Damon up at Bondi to take him out to Prince Henry. He'd agreed to see the doctor, but Celeste had called just prior to our leaving to fetch him to say that he now didn't want to be put into hospital. Obviously, she couldn't pack an overnight bag without raising his suspicions and so I'd packed one of my own, hoping to persuade him to stay once we'd seen the doctor.

Dr Springsteen was a small, slightly dumpy-looking woman, perhaps in her late twenties, it was difficult to tell, for she wore no make-up and her henna red hair was untidily bobbed. Her legs were solid, pricked with fine red hair, and ended in a pair of leather sandals. I wondered vaguely why natural redheads so often dye quite attractive hair an unattractive henna red. She wore her white coat unbuttoned to show a shapeless, floral cotton dress underneath. In appearance she looked more like one of those young would-be writers you see around the Harold Park Hotel in Glebe than she did a specialist in psychiatry.

Perhaps I paint too harsh a picture of Dr Springsteen.

Why I should be concerned about her looks at all poses a question. I think perhaps it was because we'd been focused on her for several hours so that, unseen, she had become an object of unconscious speculation, someone on whom a great deal depended. In truth she was not altogether plain but looked harassed and was obviously dog-tired from a long and frustrating day. I was momentarily able to stem my own preoccupation to feel sorry for her, "I guess it's been a long day for you, too," I said, trying to be pleasant.

"Dad!" Damon said, "Let's get on with it!" he looked directly at Dr Springsteen, "What's your name? Are you an intern?" He glared at the young doctor, "Are you a proper doctor, a psychiatrist?"

I laughed nervously, "It's been a long one for us, too," I said.

"Sit down, Damon. I'm sorry you've had to wait. No, I'm not an intern. Yes, I'm a proper doctor. What can I do for you?" She hadn't raised her voice but there was no doubt that she got through to Damon who immediately sat down. "Well?" she asked again, looking directly at him.

"You can't help me, you're not the one I have to see."

The young doctor smiled, she had a nice smile, "Well, I'm afraid I'm all there is at the moment, Damon." I was beginning to admire this young woman. She'd obviously had a very difficult day but she was still coping admirably.

"What do you know about AIDS?" Damon asked.

"Not very much, it's not my area," Dr Springsteen answered truthfully.

"Well then I'm wasting my time. You're not the person I have to give my cure for AIDS to!"

"That's good, but while you're here I'd like to examine you. Will you help me?"

"No, I don't think so!" Damon said.

Doctor Springsteen was writing as she talked, "Take your shoes off. You'll be more comfortable, Damon."

Damon was clearly surprised, "Only if I can hold them. You can't take them away!"

Dr Springsteen examined Damon and asked him a number of questions; some he answered with his normal quick intelligence and with others he was evasive, plainly suspicious of her motives. At one stage he folded his arms across his chest, his shoes hugged to his breast, "I don't want to be interrogated any more!" he said and clammed up completely.

We waited in silence until finally the young doctor rose and asked Damon to follow her into a small examination room, asking me to wait. To my surprise, Damon rose and padded into the tiny room in his stockinged feet, though still clutching his shoes to his chest. Brett had remained outside in the lounge area when we'd been called in and I went out to explain to him that we'd be some time. I returned to the little office and, after a few minutes, I could hear Damon talking and in about half an hour Dr Springsteen came out, closed the door to the examination room, leaving Damon within. She sat down and wrote for some time, ignoring my presence. Finally she said, "I'm pretty certain Damon is manic. I think we ought to try and keep him here, though we can't really care for him. A few days probably won't matter as long as we keep him sedated. I don't *think* he's likely to become violent."

"Can he be placed in the AIDS section? He knows the nurses, he has friends there."

My voice must have betrayed my anxiety for she gave me a reassuring smile, "Well, I can suggest it, but it's really up to them. If they object to having a psychiatric patient, we may have to transfer him to another hospital. What about a private hospital?"

"Well, yes, but I'd rather he stayed here. I'm sure they won't object."

She looked at me and I noticed for the first time that she had very nice blue eyes. "You must realise that I have to admit him, I mean, not as an AIDS patient, but as a psychiatric one and that, if he tries to escape, I mean leaves the hospital without medical authority, that we will have to schedule him?"

"Schedule? You mean declare him insane?"

"Well, yes, that's not a word we like to use and it's not as easy as that. We will be forced to call the police and they will arrest him and take him to Rozelle Psychiatric Hospital."

I must have remained silent for longer than it seemed to me, for she added, "It's the law."

"I'll explain that to him," I said softly.

"Yes, you can try."

"He's not been violent and I think he'd be afraid to leave a protected environment," I said.

"We can't tell. His condition is subject to violent mood swings. These, I anticipate, will get worse and he may become completely irrational, not responsible for what he does. If he thinks something is wrong, he may become very angry, very agitated."

"Well, he's been more or less all right up to now, even though somewhat irrational at times, hearing voices, a bit paranoid, but underneath it all he's still Damon, my son. I don't think he'll ever change that, Doctor."

But with Dr Springsteen's warning I was becoming increasingly anxious. After all these hours in the chaos of Casualty I became suddenly worried about having brought him in. In my anxiety for my son I'd entirely forgotten about my earlier plea to her to hospitalise him. "Perhaps we *should* take him home and see if we can get through the holidays?" I said.

I was prepared to try very hard once more to get Damon to agree to stay up the hill with us, to persuade him that staying with us was the only alternative to the hospital.

Celeste simply had to have a few days' break away from him; but now I felt guilty that this was the real reason we wanted Damon in hospital and that we, Benita and I, hadn't tried hard enough. I decided I could call work and tell them I was not coming back until after the first week in January and we'd send Celeste away somewhere and force Damon to stay with us at home.

"That would be nice, but I don't think so," Dr Springsteen said. "I think you were right to bring him in." She reached for the phone and called the Marks Pavilion to alert them that we were coming down and asked at the same time, for a single room. "One away from the entrance and where the patient can be easily observed," she instructed.

The voice at the other end must have objected to her request, for the red-headed doctor sighed, "Well then, whatever you've got." She put down the phone and looked up wearily. "I've given him a sedative." She rose, "But they don't always help," then she took a step backwards, turned and opened the door to the small examination room.

Damon was sitting on the edge of the examination bed, his bony shoulders hunched and showing through his sweat shirt; he looked very small and thin and lost but he still clutched his shoes. "You have to stay for a few days, Damon," I said.

"Yes, I know," he said quietly. "Dad can you help me with my shoes?" I took the shoes from him and squatting down worked them on to his misshapen feet, "Can you have Celeste bring some stuff? My pyjamas and toothbrush and my Walkman," he asked, as I was tying a shoelace.

"I brought a pair of my summer ones, and a toothbrush and toothpaste." I tried to smile, "You know, I thought, just in case." I stood up, ready to help him from the examination couch.

Damon looked up at me, it was a terribly sad look and I felt as though I'd betrayed him utterly. "I thought you might change your mind and want to stay," I said feebly, trying to cover my shame. "I'll bring your Walkman tomorrow morning."

A tear ran down his cheek and he quickly wiped it away with the back of his hand and sniffed, he seemed about five years old; then he shrugged his shoulders and stood up and followed me. "I'm sorry, Damon, I'm truly sorry," I said, suddenly wanting to have a good howl myself.

"It's okay, Dad." He took my hand and clung on tightly; then, in a voice hardly above a whisper, he said, "I know there's something wrong with me, but I don't know what it is."

We joined Brett in the waiting room and walked together towards the car for the short drive within the grounds to the Mark Pavilion. It was the beginning of the worst eight days of our collective lives.

28

You're not Allowed to Smoke in Bedlam.

We were met at Marks Pavilion, the AIDS building at Prince Henry, without the usual friendly welcome. The nurses on duty were not staff we knew and it seemed they'd been informed of Damon's mania and were not at all pleased at having a "manic" on their hands. Not that they could be blamed, hypomania manifests itself in violent mood swings and none of the AIDS staff were trained to look after psychiatric patients. They were also aware and, no doubt resentful, that the psychiatric ward at Prince Henry would refuse to take Damon because he had AIDS.

Brett and I had arrived home and he'd showered and changed and gone out with friends for the evening. It had been a horrible and very sad day. We were all exhausted and grateful that Damon would be in more practical hands for a few days, with people who would look after him and start the process of getting him better. What we meant, of course, was that we were all off the hook for the rest of the holidays and that, as soon as the new year commenced, we could have Damon treated by the right people. We had all learned a bitter lesson, that to be ill over a period of extended holidays is a disaster in itself.

But most of all Damon's stay in hospital meant Celeste could have a rest. Normally pale, she seemed even more so, with dark rings around her eyes and, while she was holding herself together admirably, not surprisingly, she'd been close to hysteria on more than one occasion and we were becoming increasingly worried for both her physical and mental well being.

It is an enormous tribute to Celeste's character and the strength of her love for Damon that she didn't break down or simply collapse from total exhaustion. Most people her age would have lacked the personality and guts to stick it out and would long since have walked away. Celeste, by an increment of at least a hundred over Benita and me, desperately needed a break from Damon, who for some weeks now had wanted her constantly at his side.

When I called Celeste to tell her that Damon had been admitted she gave a great sigh, then she started to giggle. Somehow she managed to restrain her hysteria and instead became tremulous, then she broke down completely and wept. It wasn't a cry, in the sense that people "have a good cry" to get something out of their system, it was a wail she seemed unable to control and which came from deep within her somewhere. It wasn't the sound of a young girl weeping, but of a woman with a terrible sadness which she could longer contain.

"Shall I come down? Or Benita?" I kept asking awkwardly into the sounds made by her distress. She would gulp and sniff, trying to control her tears, then in a plaintive small child's voice she'd say, "No!" Finally she managed to talk, "Please don't come down, Bryce. Please! I'm all right."

Celeste, exhausted beyond endurance, simply wanted to be left alone and, belatedly, I understood her need. She didn't want me or Benita or Damon. For the moment she needed to be rid of us all more than anything else in her life.

Celeste had hardly been off the phone a few minutes, when Damon rang her from the hospital. He sounded perfectly normal, totally sane, and he wanted her to go over and see him. "I've called Toby, he's coming too," Damon said, his voice excited. "Please come, babe? It will be so nice, the old threesome together again." Celeste, of course, should not have gone, but she couldn't refuse Damon. She'd borrowed Benita's car earlier in the day and hadn't yet returned it. I guess she thought, now that he was safe in hospital, another hour or so with Damon couldn't do too much more to her exhaustion.

She called Toby to ask him how Damon had been when he called. "He sounded fine," Toby replied, "In fact, just like the old Damon, his voice didn't have that weird quality of conspiracy he's been using these days."

Celeste was rather glad of Toby's company. Of all Damon's friends, he and Christopher Molnar had been the most involved with Damon over the weeks of his mania and both had been very supportive, often coming over to be with Damon and keep him occupied, so that she could get away for a few hours on her own before Damon would begin to miss her again and become agitated. Celeste arranged to pick up Toby in half an hour, enough time for her to change her dress, splash cold water over her swollen eyes and comb her hair.

They drove into the hospital, stopping at the hospital gates to pay the dollar parking fee. They hadn't travelled more than a quarter of the distance to the Marks Pavilion when they saw Damon storming up the road towards them, actually running and swinging his small overnight bag around his head. He was several hundred yards from the Marks Pavilion and not where they would have expected to find him. He kept looking behind him, as though he were expecting to be followed, and it was clear even from a distance that he was running away. Running wasn't something Damon could do very well and, even from a distance, Celeste could see from the way he swung the bag about his head that he was in a state of great agitation.

"Shit, what now?" Toby said and Celeste stopped the car as they drew nearer to Damon. Then she jumped out of the car and ran towards him, "What's wrong! What are you doing, Damon?" she asked, trying to hold him, to stop him running.

"Get out of my way!" Damon screamed, his face inches from her own. He shrugged off her embrace and continued to run towards the car. "They're following me, they're following me!" He opened the car door and jumped into the driver's seat.

"No, Damon, don't!" Celeste screamed, running up to the car.

Damon slammed the driver's door shut and turned on the ignition, seemingly not aware of Toby seated beside him. "Jump in we're leaving, we've got no time," he yelled frantically at Celeste. With the engine running, it was no time to argue and Celeste jumped into the back of the car. Toby had his arm on Damon's, "Don't be a bloody fool, Damon, you can't possibly drive!" he said, trying to stay calm.

Damon shrugged his arm away and put his foot down on the petrol so that the car lurched forward then he slammed on the brakes, so that Celeste, who hadn't yet fastened her seat belt, was hurled backwards then forwards, knocking Damon forward as she grabbed frantically on to the back of the driver's seat. Damon swore, then straightened up and pushed the automatic into reverse and did a U-turn, hurling Celeste back into the rear seat again as they took off, tyres squealing.

They drove back out through the hospital gates and past a startled gateman, waving his hands in an attempt to stop them, and hurtled on to the major four-lane highway running past the hospital which, by some miracle, was free of traffic from both directions.

Celeste best describes what happened next.

"Driving down Anzac Parade Damon had his foot down flat. Both Toby and I were screaming at him to slow down, but nothing seemed to help. He was going as fast as the Citroën would allow while constantly looking behind him. I don't mean into the rear mirror, but screwing around and looking out of the back window. He was fearful, very, very scared and seeing him like this I momentarily lost my own fear. 'Please Damon, you shouldn't drive, let Toby drive,' I said, surprised at the calmness in my voice and massaging the back of his shoulders.

" 'No time, no time to change!' Damon said, looking back through the rear view mirror. Each time he did this, the car moved across a lane. Toby also seemed to understand that shouting at Damon wouldn't help. He leaned slightly towards Damon and in a calm voice said, 'Damon, you wouldn't want me to drive if I were this angry, now would you?' Almost immediately Damon took his foot off the accelerator. Toby's appeal to Damon's sense worked, because Damon didn't like bad drivers. Damon realised that he was driving irrationally, that he was very, very angry, perhaps even that an accident might prevent his escape.

"Toby pushed his advantage, 'I'll drive very fast, but I'm not angry, so I'm not going to have an accident.' Damon agreed with this, stopped and Toby got out of the car. He ran around the front of the car and jumped into the driver's seat and Damon simply moved over for him. The immediate crisis over, another presented itself: we had to convince Damon, while at the same time attempting to calm him down, not to go back to Bondi but to come to Bennelong Crescent, to you and Benita.

"I remember we said, 'Damon, let's go to Bellevue Hill, let's not go down to Bondi. Why don't we go and have a coffee with Benita and Bryce?' And Damon just said, 'Why? I want to go home!'

" 'No, no, I feel like some real coffee, Benita makes great coffee. We don't have any real coffee at home, only Nescafe.'

"We weren't thinking very straight, we didn't think to point out that *they*, whoever Damon thought was following us, would obviously go straight to Bondi. Instead we persisted with the silly business of having coffee at your place.

"'We'll stop on the way then and get some coffee,' Damon said, sounding the most logical of us all.

"Of course, I couldn't talk to Toby, but I knew that we didn't know how to deal with Damon's escape. You'd earlier told me what the consequences were if he ran away and I was scared. We simply had to get Damon to your place so that you could take charge of things. He was constantly looking behind through the rear window and this, in a sense, distracted him and so Toby drove on to the apartment. Damon was furious, he didn't want to see you, I suppose he saw you as a part of the conspiracy against him. It was Toby who made him leave the car by suddenly coming up with the obvious argument about the people chasing him logically going directly to Bondi.

"We took him to your flat, walked him down the steps and pressed the door bell."

* * *

Seemingly minutes before they arrived the phone rang and I picked it up. It was Dr Springsteen.

"Mr Damon Courtenay has left the hospital without permission, do you know where he is?"

I was shocked beyond words but finally managed, "When? How?"

The young, red-headed doctor sighed, "He had an altercation with some of the staff at the Marks Pavilion and stormed out. They had no instructions to restrain him." She paused momentarily, "Are you sure you don't know where he is?"

I had recovered enough to sense her question was loaded, "Yes, of course! Why?"

"The gate men reported he left at great speed in a car with two other people. They saw him get into the car and drive away."

"Damon? He doesn't have a car. His car is being repaired." I hadn't thought about Celeste having Benita's car or that the two people for that matter could be Celeste and one of Damon's friends. Celeste hadn't long been off the phone to me and I couldn't conceive of her visiting Damon in her present state. I was also sure Celeste wouldn't conspire to help him escape, it simply didn't make any sense. "If he turns up you *must* report it to us at once!" Springsteen said, I could feel she was angry. The way people are angry when their judgment has been wrong or their confidence has been betrayed.

I went cold, I remembered what she'd said about Damon leaving the hospital without permission. "Please, Dr Springsteen, if he comes here couldn't we just bring him back?"

"I don't know. But you *must* call if you know where he is. You understand, don't you, Mr Courtenay?"

"Yes," I said, "but Doctor, please promise . . ." She had rung off.

When the door bell rang Benita and I, alerted as we were, didn't know what to expect. Damon stood with his hands on his hips, defiant, obviously angry, while behind him stood Celeste and Toby. Neither looked up at first.

"Christ! What happened, Damon. Why did you leave the hospital?"

Damon glared at me, then pushed past Benita and myself and stormed into the apartment.

Celeste looked up, "You know?"

I nodded and turned quickly to follow Damon.

"Come in," I heard Benita say to Celeste and Toby.

Damon was in the living room seated on the Persian rug, he had stripped off his shirt and pulled off his shoes and stood up as I came upon him. Immediately his baggy pants fell halfway down his hips, though this didn't seem to concern him. He stood facing me, chopping at the air and leaping up in mock karate kicks, sniffing through his nose. "They won't get me! No, they won't!" he yelled, punching the air and practising a kick.

"Steady on, Damon, nothing is going to get you!"

The others had entered. "Would you like a Coke or a coffee, darling," Benita asked.

Damon stopped and swung around to face his mother, "They're not going to get me, Mum! I can defend myself you know!" He turned suddenly and made for the terrace and jumped on to one of the garden beds and stood on the brick wall looking down. "If they come, I'm going to jump! They're not going to take me!"

We'd never seen him quite like this. It was very frightening. I pulled him from the garden bed and led him indoors. Celeste quietly locked the door to the balcony and withdrew the key and then, moments later, I heard her closing and locking the bars outside the front door.

Benita took Damon and led him to a couch.

I left and went into the bedroom, it was one of the most awful moments of my life. Had I known the consequences of the phone call I was about to make, there is no way on earth I would have made it.

I dialled and, when the switch at the other end answered, I identified myself and was immediately put through to Dr Springsteen. She answered with the by now familiar "Yes?"

"Damon's here, he arrived home a few minutes ago."

"Can you keep him there?"

"Yes, I think so, though he's very agitated."

This time the young doctor sounded slightly more conciliatory when she spoke, "Mr Courtenay, I explained to you what would happen. I've had to schedule Damon. It's the law. I have no choice. I have notified the police."

"Oh, no!" I groaned, but Springsteen's voice cut in.

"If you try to prevent him being arrested, you are committing a crime. Please hold him until the police arrive." There was a moment's silence, "I'm sorry, Mr Courtenay, I am only doing my duty. I am only obeying the law. I hope Damon will be all right."

"What will they do?" I managed to say.

"He'll have to go to Rozelle Psychiatric Hospital under police escort."

"Doctor, please! I'll take him. Don't do that, please!!"

"I have no choice, Mr Courtenay. It's out of our hands. I'm truly sorry." I heard the receiver being replaced at the other end.

Benita, who'd come to the bedroom door, now entered. "The police are on their way, they have to arrest him," I said softly.

"Can't we just take him back?"

I shook my head, wanting to cry, "It's the law. She's, the doctor I told you about, she's scheduled him; he's officially insane!"

Benita burst into tears and I could feel an unbearable

lump in my throat as I fought back my tears. My darling boy, my beautiful Damon, old black and blue balloon head, my youngest son, the mighty Damon was *officially* insane. They were going to put him in the looney bin!

I held Benita and led her into the bathroom. When I could talk again, I made her dry her tears, "We have to be there with him when they come."

We were all sitting around in the living room with Damon walking up and down, but starting to grow a little more calm, when the door bell went. It has a loud peremptory "Dong-dong!" sound and now it seemed to fill all the space around us, as though we were sitting in the interior of a bell tower. We all jumped, startled. Damon's body froze and his right hand shot up in front of his face in the chopping motion karate players assume, the other held slightly lower. He looked at us, his eyes wild. "Who is it?"

I rose and walked towards him and tried to put my arm around his shoulder, but he moved away, keeping his distance. "Damon, it's the police. I had to call the hospital and tell them you were here."

Damon gave me a look of such hatred that I still have nightmares about it. I wake with the look etched into my consciousness. I tell myself that when the look goes, perhaps, things might start to get better.

I spread my hands, "Damon, I'm sorry, I'm terribly sorry."

"You betrayed me," he howled. "I knew you'd betray me."

The doorbell sounded again as Benita and Celeste moved towards Damon, who turned and rushed for the terrace door, trying to open it.

I ran to the front door and opened it. Outside stood two policemen, both very young. "Mr Courtenay?" one of them asked.

I nodded and went to open the outer door, a set of burglar-proof bars. I'd forgotten that Celeste had locked it. "Just a moment, I'll get the key." I turned and ran back into the hall, but the key wasn't where we kept it. "The key!" I yelled.

Damon now stood in the centre of the living room, "The police! The fucking police! You called the fucking police!" he screamed. Celeste put her hands into her jeans and threw the keys at me. She was bawling but still in control.

I rushed back to the front door and fumbled with the keys opening the door, "Is he violent?" one of the young constables asked.

"No, no, he's not very strong. He can't harm you."

They walked in and I turned to see Damon standing at the door of my study at the end of the hall. He looked like a little trapped animal with his back to my study door, his hands up in his pathetic karate defence, which couldn't possibly have fooled anyone, least of all the two, young police officers.

"Watch out! I can kill with these," he said, bringing his hands up closer to his face.

The two police officers moved towards him and Damon turned and, opening the door, darted into my study.

My study had a door leading into it from the hallway and another leading out into the living room. Damon emerged moments later carrying Brett's spear gun, which he'd left standing in a corner from his early morning fishing. A spear is loaded into the gun by pulling back a heavy rubber loop, which required a display of strength quite beyond Damon. As it was, it was no more harmful in Damon's hands than a heavy stick would have been. Now Damon held it pointed at the two policemen. "You bastards! Come!"

One of the policeman said, "Shit! He's got a weapon."

"Don't do anything," I yelled. Then walking towards Damon I held my hand out, "Give it to me, darling," I said. Our eyes met and locked; for a moment, just a fraction of a moment, I thought Damon was going to spear me, then he sighed and handed the gun to me. He was defeated, beaten, the look of despair in his eyes was awful.

But at the moment he handed me the spear gun, the two policemen jumped him, one of them grabbing his bad arm and forcing it behind his back.

Benita screamed, I think we all did. "Stop it! Stop it, he's a haemophiliac. You'll hurt him!" Celeste screamed.

The young constable took no notice at Damon's own scream of pain; his tiny, permanently bent arm, its elbow fused, was being forced higher up his back, until the shoulder joint looked as though it might pop.

"You bastard! Don't hurt him, please don't hurt him," Benita screamed.

Celeste rushed up to the policemen, "Stop it! Stop it! He's a *bleeder*, he'll bleed internally to *death*!"

The word "bleeder" or perhaps "death" seemed to get through. Damon was on his knees, forced to the ground by the two strong men, and the policeman forcing his arm upward released his grip. It was obvious that Damon was unable to defend himself. The useless arm fell to

Damon's side and his face was contorted with pain as he lay on the carpet weeping.

The older of the policemen took the handcuffs from his belt. Suddenly Benita was beside him, her face inches from the policeman's, "Don't! Don't put those on my son!" She wasn't crying, it was an order, and the policeman stepped back momentarily, not quite sure what to do. "He resisted arrest with a weapon. He's dangerous, madam."

"Oh, Christ, look at him," I pointed to Damon who lay on his side weeping. "Does he look dangerous?" The other policeman was now sitting on Damon's hip, holding him down, though there was no resistance coming from the broken little figure on the floor.

The policeman returned the handcuffs to his belt and the officer pinning Damon to the ground rose. Damon continued to lie, groaning with pain, but trying hard to stop, to overcome it, gulping and trying to stifle his moans. Mucus ran down his nostrils and lips and chin and his mouth was half-open showing the yellow-crusted *Candida* that flaked the inside of his lips. I knelt down and, pulling my shirt tail out, wiped his face.

Celeste and Toby tried to get him to his feet and managed to pull him into a standing position, though he seemed too weak to stand on his own and he clung to them both. Finally, with Toby and Celeste holding him on either side he stood, his head bowed.

"We have to take him to Rozelle Psychiatric Hospital," the older of the two officers said. The younger one was looking a bit foolish, he'd over-reacted and I think he knew it.

"I'll take him," I said, "I'll follow you."

"I'm afraid not, sir. The detainee has to come with us, he's under arrest."

"May I come in the police car with you?" I asked.

"We're in a wagon. You can't travel with him in the back, it's against the law."

"Where will you take him?"

"Admissions, it's in the main building," and he named a street.

I stepped over to Damon, "It's all right, darling, I'll come with you. I'll be there waiting before you get there." Damon, still weeping didn't look at me.

The two policemen took him by either arm and walked him out of the apartment. "Don't come!" I instructed the others, who'd followed to the door. I followed the policemen who almost carried Damon up the steps, though he was making no effort to resist. In the driveway was a paddy wagon, its blue roof light still turning. One of the policemen unlocked the back of the wagon, while the other held Damon. He swung the rear doors to the paddy wagon open and then came back to Damon, so that they once again stood on either side of him.

"Get in," the older policeman said and pushed at the back of Damon's bad leg to force him to step up into the wagon. The leg, of course, didn't bend at the knee and it must have seemed as though Damon was resisting them, trying to prop his leg against the van so they couldn't get him inside. Both officers lifted him bodily and flung him into the wagon. He landed on his shoulder and slid down the van floor between the seats, banging his head against the back of the driver's partition. They slammed the doors shut behind him.

"You bastards!" I yelled, "You didn't have to do that!"

The older of the two officers turned to me, "We've had enough trouble with him already, sir. We could charge him with resisting arrest and threatening a police officer with a deadly weapon. Count yourself very lucky, sir!"

They got into the van, reversed into the roadway and were gone. It was nine-thirty on Boxing Day evening and everything in my life had suddenly gone wrong.

I'd forgotten my car keys and now rushed inside to collect them, intending to follow the police paddy wagon so that I got to Rozelle at the same time as they did. I knew more or less where the asylum was. While Rozelle is called a psychiatric hospital, it's really Sydney's oldest and most famous insane asylum, though for some years now, large sections of it have been unused and only the central core is maintained for psychiatric cases. By the time I'd fetched my keys and backed the car out of the garage, the paddy wagon had long gone. I drove as fast as I was able to catch up with it though I was not sure of the route they'd taken. Also, I wasn't certain of the street on which the admission centre had been placed and had depended on them to lead me to it.

I never did find the police wagon and I arrived at Rozelle and entered by the wrong gate, so that I had to retrace my way and drive to the opposite side of the grounds to come to the admission centre. I parked in a No Parking zone outside and walked into a large, white building.

It was just past ten p.m. and there was no one at the reception desk. I looked about for a bell or a buzzer but couldn't find one. I called out and waited, but nobody came. Finally, I opened a door and, stepping in, found myself in a long, polished corridor. I walked past several empty rooms until I found one in which a very large man sat at a small table. The man had his hair slicked straight back with oil and looked to be in his late forties. He wore a white jacket and sweat shirt and was eating an uncut sandwich which he held in both hands, tearing at the bread with his teeth, his head slightly to one side in case some of the contents spilled out. His hands were so big the sandwich looked lost in them and I noticed he had an elaborate tattoo on the back of his right hand. In front of him was an enamel mug of tea or coffee, the contents still steaming. He can't have been seated very long.

"Excuse me, are you a doctor?" I felt instinctively he wasn't, but I asked anyway.

"No," he said, his mouth full.

"There's no one at the reception desk?" I jerked my head back in the direction I'd come.

"No," he said again, then swallowed and wiped his mouth with the back of his hand. "She's gone off, only night staff here now. It's holidays, we're on skeleton."

"Perhaps you can help? Do you know if the police have been?" It was a badly phrased question.

"You mean made a delivery?" I must have looked confused and he repeated, "Brought somebody in?"

"Yes. My son."

"Courtenay? That the name?"

"Yes, yes, Damon Courtenay."

He lifted the mug and took a careful sip, looking at me over the rim. "Bastards!" he said, putting the cup down again. "They radioed to say they wanted a strait-jacket, bringing in a violent case." He took another large bite of the sandwich and continued with a mouthful of bread,

"They do that so if the customer or his family make a charge of being manhandled by the cops they can prove they needed a jacket to restrain him on arrival here." He swallowed, "It's all bullshit, mate. We met the wagon with your son and, because they'd demanded it, we had to unload him from the wagon and put a restraining jacket on him. Poor little bugger, he was in a mess, real upset, but harmless. He told me his arm was hurting real bad and please to be careful."

The attendant or whatever he was held what was left of the sandwich, just a couple of crusts, between his thumb and forefinger, tossed them into the wastepaper basket and dusted his hands, "Bloody cops! They really like to get in among our kind, our patients, and have a go."

"Do you think I can see him?"

"Sure, mate. We just left him with the doctor, he'll be a while." He looked up at me, "It's none of my business but you look buggered. Your boy will be okay for a while, would you like a cuppa?"

It was the first time all day I wasn't getting the run-around, somebody in an institution was actually going out of his way to help. "Thanks, but do you think I could see the doctor, I mean, with Damon. He's hypomanic, I'm sure I could help with his details?"

He was sipping at the mug of tea as I spoke and now he almost choked, putting it down quickly, "No, I don't think so, mate. Not this doctor, she's a 'slope', no worse! She's Indonesian and hasn't a bloody clue. She's crazy; she'll mess about with him for a bit and then we'll go and get him and take him to a ward."

I grew alarmed, "What do you mean, crazy?"

"I mean she doesn't know what the fuck she's doing. She's Indonesian, she doesn't speak-so-good-the-English," he mimicked, then rolled his eyes, "If she's a psychiatric doctor then my arsehole is one of the crown jewels!"

"Still, I'd like to be with him. He's a haemophiliac, she has to know about that."

"Haemo . . .?"

"A bleeder, that's why his arm was sore. The police twisted it behind his back, he's going to need a massive blood transfusion."

"Bastards," he said automatically, then looked alarmed, "He wasn't bleeding when we got him, I swear there wasn't any blood!"

"It's internal bruising. Bruising is internal bleeding. He'll be in a lot of trouble if he doesn't get a blood transfusion. I have to explain it to her and then go home and get the stuff he needs."

"What tonight?" He looked amazed, "He's going to need a blood transfusion tonight?"

"Well yes. The police nearly put his shoulder out and he was handled very roughly in the paddy wagon, he'll be bleeding in a lot of places." I paused, "It's very dangerous for him," I added, hoping to impress on him the need to be taken to Damon right away.

"Right! Shit, eh? I'll take you through." He rose and came to the door, allowing me to go ahead of him. We walked down the corridor and turned left and went down a flight of stairs. At the bottom of the stairs, he stopped, "I don't know how you'll go with this doctor, mate. I mean with the transfusion."

We continued down another corridor to a door at the end and he opened it. We seemed to have entered a small dispensary with an examination couch against one wall, beside which stood a low table. A door on the opposite wall was closed and the attendant opened it without knocking.

"Come in, mate," he said, looking back at me and holding the door open. Turning his head to look into the room, he announced, "This is Damon's father." I entered and he stood at the door, not entering, and leaving me standing within a small office barely large enough to take a desk and chair and another upright chair in front of the desk on which Damon sat, wrapped in a cream canvas strait-jacket. Behind the desk sat an overweight Asian woman, who looked up as I entered. With me added the room was crowded.

"You are Mr Courtenay?" the woman behind the desk asked me.

"Yeah, the patient's father," the attendant answered for me from the open door.

"Yes, Doctor," I said and then looked down at Damon, pointing to the strait-jacket, "Surely, Doctor, this isn't necessary. My son isn't violent."

"Hello, Dad," Damon said, his voice small but in control.

The woman looked momentarily confused, then she began to pat the papers scattered over her untidy desk with the flat of her free hand, as though looking for something, "Ah!" She picked up a piece of paper and waved it at me, "Police report. Patient violent!" she said triumphantly.

"Doctor, my son is a haemophiliac, he's already been severely manhandled by the police," I pointed at the strait-jacket, "that thing is going to given him a bad bleed. You must take it off at once!"

To my astonishment she leaned forward, looking up at me as though she was impatiently explaining something to a child who was bothering her, "No, not haemophee, hypomania!" she tapped the paper on the desk in front of her with her pen.

"No, you don't understand. He is *also* a haemophiliac, a *bleeder!*" Without being aware of it I had raised my voice.

"It's no use, Dad." Damon's voice was resigned, "She doesn't know what a haemophiliac is."

"But that's not possible!" I exclaimed.

"Well she doesn't. I've been trying to tell her I need a blood transfusion, but she thinks I'm crazy."

I couldn't believe that a medical practitioner wouldn't know what a haemophiliac was.

"Perhaps there were no haemophiliacs in Indonesia, or they died when they were babies?" Damon said.

"He has a blood disease, Doctor! He has to have a transfusion, a *blood* transfusion tonight, it's very important!"

"No transfusion. We cannot here. No, no tonight ... no blood!"

"Not here, *you* don't have to give him a transfusion. I, me," I tapped myself on the chest, "*I* will give him transfusion. I go home and get blood, bring it here!" I suddenly realised I was mimicking her and as suddenly knew how futile all this was; if she didn't know what a haemophiliac was, then nothing I would say could convince her that Damon needed a blood transfusion.

The Indonesian doctor looked up and smiled brightly, "Ah! You also, you are a Doctor?"

"No," I said, shaking my head. "My son has blood transfusions at home, we keep the blood compound AHF at home in the fridge. Please Doctor, can you remove that restraining jacket from my son, it's doing him a lot of harm!"

"Okay," she said, scowling again, "I finish now. We take off." She lifted the phone and dialled three digits, "Frank? Also Hans, you come now." She put the receiver down.

I was already trying to work the main buckle loose on the strait-jacket when she replaced the receiver, "No, no! Not for you! They will do!"

"Are you hurting a lot, Damon," I asked, placing my hand on his shoulder. He winced and I apologised, hurriedly removing it.

"I'm in for a really bad bleed in my shoulder, Dad. How long will I have to stay here?" Damon didn't sound in the least manic and I thought what an incredible fuck-up the whole day had been; one, long, disastrous screw-up after another by all concerned and mostly by me.

"I don't know, darling. At least until the morning. I can't get you out tonight."

"You can bring the AHF and bleed stuff in the morning then. I'll be all right."

I knew he wouldn't be, that the night would be spent in incredible pain and by morning he'd be in a serious condition. "I'll try again, when we've got this thing off you. Maybe I can get someone to call her and explain, maybe another Doctor."

Damon glanced at his watch, "It's a quarter to eleven, Dad."

Just then the door opened and the attendant I'd spoken to and who'd brought me along to the doctor appeared; behind him came another man, a blond, almost as big. The first must be Frank and the second, Hans, who looked Dutch.

"Frank, can you take Damon's strait-jacket off. He's got a bad arm, it will cause a bleed."

Frank winked at me and walked over to Damon. I had to step aside to make space for him in the small office and Hans backed out of the door to let me stand where he'd been standing. "What do you say, Doctor?" He didn't wait for her to agree before he began to undo the ties on the jacket.

"Ja, is okay," the fat little woman said, "I tol' already. Frank we give pills in dispensary."

Frank nodded, pulling the straps away and then helping Damon out of the canvas jacket.

Damon got to his feet unsteadily and I hurried over to take him by the elbow, careful to take his good arm. Frank followed and we led him into the dispensary. "Have a lie-down, mate," Frank said to Damon, indicating the examination couch. Damon sat on the edge of the couch, the hand of his good arm clutching his shoulder where the police had torn it when they'd locked his arm behind his back.

"I'll ask for some pain-killers, shall I?" I suggested.

Damon was suddenly rigid, "Dad, they mustn't give me any pills! You mustn't let them give me any drugs!" His eyes had grown wide, "Please Dad. No!"

The doctor was standing behind a small counter, in

front of her on the counter were three bottles, each filled with capsules. She put a couple from each into tiny plastic containers. I walked over to her and noticed that, standing up, she was very overweight and was breathing heavily, as though just standing up was an exertion. Her skin, too, lacked the smoothness of most Asians and was lightly pock-marked. All in all she was rather a mess. "Please, Doctor, Damon won't take a drug of any sort unless he knows what it is."

She gave me a distasteful look, "He doctor also?"

"No."

She tapped her forefinger lightly against her breast, "I doctor. I give drugs."

I turned to Frank, "Damon won't take the pills. He has to know what they are first."

Frank looked embarrassed, then looked down and appeared to be wiping gently at the tattoo on the back of his hand with the pad of his forefinger, as though he were testing to see whether it might wipe off. "I'm sorry, but I can't help you there, mate. If she says he's got to have the pills, he's got to have the pills. Can't do nothing about that."

"I won't take them. No way!" Damon said, shaking his head, then pulling his feet up and pushing himself into the corner of the examination couch, as though he was prepared to do battle like a small cornered animal.

"Well, maybe we can just find out what they are?" I suggested.

"I know what they bloody are, mate!" Frank said, "Don't we, Hans?"

Hans who had said nothing up to this point nodded, "Pills, ja, we know, for sure!"

Damon was beginning to shake, it was clear he was becoming agitated.

"Now hang on. My son has a right to know what she's giving him!" I said, directing my question to Frank and then looking at the fat Indonesian doctor. "What are you giving him, Doctor?"

"Sedatives. I give sedatives," she said, not prepared to explain any further.

Frank looked up at me and jerked his head, indicating that I should come outside with him. I walked out of the office into the corridor and the big man put a hand on my shoulder, standing uncomfortably close and looking into my eyes. "They're pills to flatten him out, the main one's Mellaril, takes the fight out of him. She gives them to all the patients, it's all she bloody knows!" Frank grinned, nodding his head towards the dispensary door. "Flatten them, then they don't give her no trouble."

"Frank, are you a nurse? You also have to be responsible!"

"Me? A nurse? No way! I'm a ward orderly. Me job specification says I'm a cleaner." He looked at me, his expression sympathetic, "I'm sorry, Mr Courtenay, your son *has* to take them pills. It's more than me job's worth. I," he pointed towards the door, "we have to do what she says, medicine wise, or me job's on the line."

We returned to the dispensary and the doctor looked up. Her expression showed not the slightest curiosity as to where we might have been or what we might have said. She looked flatly at Frank, "Frank," she said pushing the three small plastic containers towards the edge of the counter. "You give medication now."

"I won't take them!" Damon said in a frightened but determined voice.

"You must take!" the doctor said, "Frank, Hans, you give patient now."

Frank walked over to the counter and placed the three small plastic containers on his left hand, "I'm sorry, mate. They're only sedatives, they'll make you sleep like a baby tonight."

"Damon won't take them, he won't take drugs he doesn't know about," I said.

"He must take!" the doctor said and then she turned and went into her office closing the door behind her. Hans went over to a surgical tap and, not bothering to use his elbow, turned it on and filled a plastic cup with water, then placed it on a small table beside the examination couch and stood beside Frank. The two men towered over us. Damon cradled in my arms looked like a tiny, frightened, simian creature, its eyes large and overbright.

"C'mon, mate, one way or another you've got to take these. They won't harm ya, just flatten you a bit."

I felt totally inadequate, Damon was getting more and more worked up and was beginning to tremble. I feared another outburst should they try to force the pills on to him. Maybe he *should* take them, maybe he needs a strong sedative to calm him down, I thought. Something to get him to sleep.

"Here, let me try," I said to Frank, holding my hands out for the pills.

"I won't Dad. I'm not taking those pills. They're trying to drug me, make me confess!"

Hans's huge hand suddenly shot out and grabbed

Damon by the lower jaw; with his thumb on one side and two fingers on the other he forced his mouth open. Frank quickly fed the pills into his mouth, one by one, whereupon Hans clamped his free hand over Damon's mouth while Frank held him pinned against the wall.

It had all happened so quickly that I'd barely had time to react but when I did it was a stupid response, "You can't force him! You can't force him, you bastards! He has rights just like anyone else!"

"Not here he hasn't. He's sick! He's not right in the nut, mate!"

Damon's eyes were nearly popping out of his head, he would have to swallow the pills or he was going to pass out. Quite unexpectedly, I heard my voice say, "Watch out for your hand, he has AIDS!"

The reaction was instant, both men jumped backwards in horror and Damon spat the capsules in his mouth on to the couch and the dispensary floor.

"Jesus! Why didn't you fucking tell us?" Frank shouted at me.

"You jumped him. It wouldn't have come up otherwise!" I shouted back.

Damon was choking, holding his throat, trying to dry spit the last capsule which stuck to his tongue. Finally, he picked it off his tongue and threw the tiny, coloured capsule to the floor, where it bounced a couple of times and came to rest near my foot.

"You bastards! You bloody bastards! Leave me alone!" Damon wailed, "Leave me alone!" Then he stopped and, bringing his hands up to cover his face, he began to weep. "Please, Dad, make them leave me alone," he said in a little boy's voice. "Please, Dad, don't let them hurt me any more!"

I moved over to the couch again and sat next to him. I took him in my arms and he put his head against my chest. I wanted to cry myself. Hans was at the sink frantically scrubbing his hands and swearing to himself. "It's okay, Hans, nothing will happen. You can't catch AIDS that way," I said, my immediate concern for Damon making me calm again.

"Is that true?" Frank asked furiously, stabbing a finger at me. "Is that fucking true?" The finger stayed poised, pointing at me, waiting for my reply.

I held on to Damon, "Yes, it's true! There's nothing to worry about."

Frank relaxed, his shoulders visibly dropping, though he still wasn't happy, "We can make you leave, you know."

"Frank, I'm sorry." I didn't want to be made to leave the hospital.

The door opened and the Indonesian doctor stood looking at us. She wore no discernible expression and it was as though she'd heard absolutely nothing, although she plainly would have heard the shouting going on. She had the canvas strait-jacket we'd removed in her office draped over her right arm. If she saw the three or four brightly coloured capsules lying on the polished floor in front of the examination couch where Damon had spat them then she chose to ignore them.

"Frank, Hans, you take to Ward 4." She repeated, "Take patient Ward 4." She held out her arm over which the jacket was draped and in her left hand she held a piece of paper, which turned out to be the authority to admit Damon to the ward.

Frank moved over and took the canvas jacket and the note, carelessly stuffing the note into the top pocket of his white jacket. He took three or four steps over to where I was sitting holding Damon. "He's got to wear this again," he indicated the strait-jacket, "We're taking him to Ward 4."

"Ward 4?"

"It's a high security ward, they can give him his stuff there," he kicked at one of the capsules on the floor, missed and had a second go, missing again and scraping the sole of his shoe along the rubber flooring. "This stuff's shit, anyway," he said. Then he looked at Damon and held up the strait-jacket and smiled, "You gunna co-operate, mate?" It wasn't said in a threatening way but almost as though he were saying, "You gunna have a cuppa tea, mate?" It was becoming obvious that Frank was more of a professional than I'd given him credit for being.

Damon nodded, sniffing, and pulled away from me, offering Frank his arms. Frank slipped one arm into the jacket sleeve, it was almost twice the length of a normal sleeve, then he followed with the other; then he pulled the rest of the canvas jacket around Damon's torso and Damon turned so that his back was facing the big man who tied the jacket tightly behind his back. Then he crossed Damon's arms over his chest and brought the sleeves back behind him and tied them behind his back. His movements were quick and efficient and he wasn't unduly rough and seemed to have completely recovered his composure.

"I'm sorry, Frank," I said, "but Damon's had about enough for one day." I don't know why I apologised to this man, perhaps for his initial politeness and later the sense of conspiracy he shared with me over the doctor. Perhaps it was out of simple weakness and I felt guilty that Damon hadn't co-operated and taken the pills.

"It's cool, I wouldn'a taken them things either," he said in an undertone, "They're shit!" Then he added, "But round here it's all shit."

A phone on the dispensary counter rang and Hans went over and answered it. "Ja, okay, we coming now," he said into the mouthpiece.

Without waiting for Hans to confirm the call Frank said, "We have to take Damon by car, the ward is several minutes drive. You can come if you like." He turned and nodded at Hans who came to stand beside Damon on the side opposite to Frank. "We're gunna help you up, mate," Frank said taking Damon by the elbow. Hans did the same and they lifted him to his feet. "It's not far to walk to the car. You okay, mate?"

There was a car waiting for us at what looked like a back door opening out to some sort of courtyard. "We sit in the back with Damon," Frank said, indicating with a nod that I should sit in the front.

I climbed into the front seat and said good evening to the driver who returned my greeting. "Ward 4, thanks mate," Frank instructed.

"Righto!" the driver said and drove off, the car's lights flaring and catching and momentarily silvering the foliage of the tall trees that grew everywhere in the grounds. This would be an easy place from which to escape, I thought, there are no outside lights whatsoever.

"My dad drives a Porsche," Damon said suddenly. He sounded about nine years old and seemed not to realise I was in the car. "He's very rich and he bought me a Mazda RX7. He knows the Prime Minister, you know?" When no reaction to this statement came from his escorts, he added, "You realise don't you, that you're all going to get into a lot of trouble when he tells him what you did to me?"

"Damon, I'm here!" I said, embarrassed.

"It's okay, mate," Frank said, whether to me or to Damon I wasn't sure, "We'll soon be there."

Damon seemed not to have heard me. "How many cylinders is this car?" he asked the driver in the same ingenuous voice.

"Four. It's amazing what the Japs can do with four cylinders these days."

"It's not as fast as my Mazda. That's four too!"

"Yeah, you're right. The Japs are getting the hang of sports cars, that Mazda RX7, it can move all right. Great looking car too!" the driver added.

"Much better than this one!" Damon replied.

The driver laughed in the darkness, "You're right. These are just cheap transport, nuthin more."

"Not so bloody cheap either!" Frank said.

At the sound of Frank's voice Damon lapsed into silence. The car slowed suddenly and we drove through an open gateway set in a high wall and into a huge, inner courtyard, its three sides composed of a sandstone building a couple of storeys high. Except for a dim light at each corner and one over a doorway on the far side, directly opposite the gate we'd entered, the courtyard was in blackness, the illumination only managing to throw pools of triangular light into each corner and light the doorway in the centre. Though the words "Insane Asylum" are old-fashioned, they were what came immediately to my mind. This was exactly how such a place would look. We had arrived at Ward 4. No place in any psychiatric institution in Australia is quite like Rozelle's Ward 4. It has the big reputation for being tough.

Frank rang a buzzer and we waited and, after what seemed like a couple of minutes, the door was opened and two men stood facing us, one wearing a nurses uniform and the other, another very big man, dressed like Frank in a white jacket. Frank didn't appear to know them and handed over the piece of paper the doctor had given him. "This is Damon Courtenay," he turned to face me, "and his father."

"May I come in with Damon," I asked the male nurse.

"Sure," he said, smiling, "For a few minutes anyway," he glanced at his watch, "It's late, almost midnight, the ward is asleep."

"Righto, we'll be off then, Mr Courtenay," Frank said.

"Thanks, Frank," I turned to Hans, "Thanks, Hans." I watched momentarily as they returned to the car and I wondered, briefly, how I would find my way back to the admission centre.

"Come with me, Damon," the nurse said and indicating the strait-jacket smiled, "We'll take that thing off when we get upstairs." He raised his eyebrows in disapproval, "I'm sure you don't need it. It's part of the procedure, that's all." It was a clever introduction to their relationship, he was trying to assess Damon's state of mind, while at the same time initiating the seemingly light-hearted jollying, which we were to learn was very much a part of keeping the tension down among the psychiatric patients.

Damon hadn't said a word since he'd stepped from the car and now he didn't react to the reassuring tone. The nurse seemed not to expect a reaction and turned and began to climb a set of narrow and rather steep cement stairs which led directly upward and to the right of the door. The big orderly nudged Damon, indicating that he should follow next and, as Damon did so, he stepped behind him so that Damon was positioned between the two men. Damon's bad leg normally made it difficult for him to climb stairs, now in the strait-jacket, unable to place his hand against the wall to steady himself, it made it more so and the orderly supported him by holding him under both elbows from behind and urging him up with encouraging grunts.

These are not bad men, I thought. Damon's going to be okay.

At the top of the stairs, which I seem to remember turned sharply left at one stage, we entered a long corridor lit from the ceiling by a series of naked bulbs set into those old-fashioned light shades we used to call Chinese coolie hats when I was a child. They threw sufficient light to light the corridor quite well, while at the same time making it seem just short of being well lit. The polished rubber flooring kicked back a strip of dull light down the centre of the corridor and the whole feeling was very old-fashioned and institutional. I can't remember clearly but, if you told me the walls were apple green and the ceilings cream, I would probably agree. The feeling, anyway, was depressing and the squeak of our feet on the rubber floor added to the feeling of loneliness and isolation from ordinary outside things.

We passed through a set of double doors into what seemed like a small hall with a central space and a number of doors, about four on either side, which I immediately realised were cells not much wider than the doors themselves. At the end of the hall was a set of double doors and, in one corner, a glass office with a small desk and a swivel chair and also a couple of upright chairs. The desk was pretty untidy, covered with papers, as though it belonged to several people, none of whom were responsible for its upkeep. The phone rang and the nurse picked it up. "Yes, he's arrived. Yes." He seemed to be listening, "Yes, okay, I understand." While he was on the phone, the orderly asked us to sit down and he immediately started to untie Damon's strait-jacket, his strong hands pulling at the ties as though they were nothing.

The nurse put down the receiver and, turning to the swivel chair at the desk, he spun it so that the back rest faced Damon, then he sat astride the chair with his elbows leaning on the back rest. His attitude was deliberately casual and he waited until the orderly had removed the strait-jacket and Damon's hands were free. Damon shook his arms momentarily, then crossed them and started to rub the circulation back into both his upper arms.

"I'm Sister Johnson," the nurse said, using the term now without gender in Australian hospitals, the title merely denoting a nurse of senior status. "This is Bruce," he added, not following with Bruce's surname. He extended his hand to Damon, who ignored it and continued massaging his arms. Sister Johnson hesitated fractionally before turning the swivel chair slightly and extending his hand to me.

I felt immediately more confident. In our long experience of hospitals the nursing sisters were, with few exceptions, salt of the earth types much more important than the doctors, generally very professional in their care and certainly truly caring of the patients' welfare.

"Hello, Sister," I said, extending my hand and shaking his; turning, I did the same to Bruce, "Hello, Bruce." Bruce had placed the strait-jacket over his right arm and now he hurriedly changed it over to his left and extended his huge hand. If anything he was even bigger than either Frank or Hans.

"He'll be okay," he said nodding down at Damon.

Damon still hadn't spoken and I was beginning to worry that he was building up a head of steam. Damon was a naturally polite person and it would normally have been impossible for him to ignore a greeting of this kind.

Sister Johnson swung the swivel chair back again to face Damon. "We're going to give you something to help you to sleep," he said quietly.

"What?" Damon scowled, looking up at Sister Johnson.

"Mellaril. I admit it's a strong sedative, but it will help you."

"You mean it will help you," Damon shot back.

"Yes, that too," Sister Johnson admitted readily.

"Is that what they tried to give me before?"

Sister Johnson smiled, "You guessed what that phone call was all about. No flies on you, Damon." He paused, then added in a quiet voice, "Yes, that and one or two other things, but we'll keep it strictly to the Mellaril, okay?"

"I don't want any pills!" Damon protested.

"Please, Damon, do it for me?" Bruce said unexpectedly.

We were both taken by surprise and Damon and I looked up at the big man, "I've had a shit of a day, I don't want to be up with you all night," Bruce said, shrugging his broad shoulders and smiling. "I got pissed Christmas Day, I feel bloody terrible."

It was ingenious and brilliantly timed and I realised that the two men worked in tandem. Later, we would come to know Ward 4 as an isolated and dangerous place, an atmosphere of enormous tension and frenetic movement, with a feeling of constant and overwhelming crisis. During the day it was filled with screams, sudden frantic yells and violent outbreaks. The orderlies, such as Bruce, were all young and strong and seemed impervious to tension, they seemed only to be present when needed, though they were in truth constantly around. They never raised their voices and used a technique of jollying and good humour to contain the patients and, in a curious way, to look after the inmates' dignity, no matter how crazy a patient appeared at the time. It would be easy to make these men seem brutal, but it would be quite unfair — they did a remarkable job under the circumstances. Though this didn't make Ward 4 any less a nightmare.

Now Damon looked up at the big orderly, his eyes suddenly cunning, "What if I don't take this Mellaril?" he asked.

Sister Johnson laughed, taking the pressure off Bruce. "Then we'd have to give you an injection which we'd prefer not to do."

Damon grinned, his face again showing cunning, "You

can't do that! I'm a haemophiliac, it will make me bleed!"
It was the same small boy's voice he'd used in the car
coming over.

Sister Johnson looked quickly up at me and I nodded
my head, confirming.

"My dad's going to report you all to the Prime Minister!" Damon added, looking smug, "I can make a lot of
trouble for you."

"Please don't, I've had a shit of a day, Damon. You're
not going to make me sit up with you all night just
because you don't want to take a little pill are you? Know
any good jokes?" Bruce said, grinning down at Damon.

"Only if you let me have a cigarette! I'll only take the
Mellaril if you let me have a cigarette."

I sighed inwardly, the two men had neatly averted
another crisis.

Sister Johnson smiled, shaking his head slowly, "I'm
sorry, Damon, there's no smoking in this ward. We would,
Bruce and me, but we can't, it's strictly no smoking,
mate."

Damon's mood swing was so sudden it took us all
completely by surprise.

"I want a fucking cigarette! That's all I want, a fucking
cigarette! You can't stop me, you fucking bastards, you
can't stop me. I WANT A CIGARETTE!" He screamed
this at the top of his voice and then started to wail,
"I-WANT-A-FUCKING-CIGARETTE!" He was on his feet
looking around for the door of the office, where Bruce
stood calmly, his arms folded.

"Now mate, you can have a smoko in the morning, no
cigarette tonight."

Damon ran at him his fists flailing the air, "ALL I

WANT IS A CIGARETTE! WHY CAN'T I HAVE A CIGARETTE!"

The walls seemed to come alive and people began to chant, "I want a cigarette! I want a cigarette!" The chant seemed to come from everywhere, "I want a cigarette! I want a cigarette!" The chanting continued and someone started to scream. Then a voice seemed to rise above the rest, "GIVE HIM A FUCKING CIGARETTE YOU BASTARDS!" it shouted through the walls, "HOW THE FUCK AM I SUPPOSED TO SLEEP!"

I looked around startled and realised that the doors I'd passed contained patients and that the wall beyond the office must hold a ward of some sort because most of the noise was coming from that direction.

"Jesus!" Sister Johnson said. He shot from the chair and reached over the desk to remove a key from a rack on the wall, then he moved towards Bruce who backed out of the door, taking Damon in a bear hug against his chest, his legs off the ground. Sister Johnson brushed hurriedly past them and crossed the corridor, he stopped two doors down from the small office and quickly opened up.

I'd followed them both out, more as a reaction than with any sense of purpose. Panic-stricken by Damon's unexpected outburst I shouted, "STOP IT, DAMON! BLOODY STOP IT!" I'd momentarily lost all sense of my son's predicament, I only wanted him to stop shouting. To stop using foul language. I wanted it all to stop, to go away, to never have happened in the first place! I was burning with shame at his behaviour.

Damon was kicking his legs in the air, struggling frantically, still yelling, "I want a fucking cigarette!" Voices from elsewhere continued chanting and banging on the walls and doors. Damon's struggle was pointless, Bruce held him in his enormous hug, the expression on the orderly's face unchanged, he was completely in control. He glanced at me and winked. The wink was obscene coming at that moment, but it had the instant effect of stopping me in my tracks and silencing me. I suddenly felt tremendously, overpoweringly, ashamed of myself. I thought I would break down, my knees cave in on the spot, then I had the impulse to turn and run. I began to shake and I wasn't sure I was going to be able to control my bladder.

Sister Johnson turned the door knob and the door swung open to reveal the tiny lighted cell. It seemed to contain only a low bed made up army style, the blankets pulled tight. Bruce carried Damon across the corridor, moving backwards so that Damon couldn't try to prevent them entering the cell by placing his feet on either side of the door.

Sister Johnson held the door, which opened outwards, Bruce stopped just short of the door and seemed to lift Damon higher and then toss him into the air, flipping him around at the same time, much as a child might a rag doll, so that when he caught him again, he was holding him horizontally in his arms, like a small, indignant child carried in his father's arms. He moved through the door quickly and, bending down low, placed Damon on the bed.

All this seemed to be happening quite naturally and without haste, as though Damon wasn't sobbing and struggling, the task merely routine. I now realise that young men such as Bruce are there because of their enormous strength and the fact that they are impervious to stress, that an incident such as this is a daily, perhaps an hourly, routine for them. Bruce was simply doing his job very well without exercising the luxury of an over-sensitive imagination. He wasn't making judgments but, like any other job, was just getting through his shift. Bruce stepped backwards out of the tiny room and Sister Johnson closed the cell door immediately, locking it. I could hear Damon sobbing violently, "All I want is a cigarette. Please!" He sounded like a heartbroken child.

I was standing helpless in the centre of the corridor, this time Damon was truly off my hands for the holidays. I felt suddenly terribly heartsick, so overcome that I started to weep deep down where no sound comes from, where no tears exist at all, just a terrible ache that seems as though it is going to break through your chest leaving a hole the size of a football. All around me the walls were chanting, "I want a cigarette! I want a fucking cigarette!" Somewhere a woman started to wail, a baying, keening sound like a trapped animal.

I felt Sister Johnson's hand on my shoulder and his voice close to my ear, "I'm sorry, Mr Courtenay, but you can't stay. You have to go now." He had his hand hard against my back and was moving me down the corridor, along the passageway with the Chinese coolie hat lights. I realised vaguely that Bruce was also at my side, gripping me by the elbow and that we were going down the stairs. Bruce pushed forward as we approached the bottom of the stairs and started to unlatch the door, a fairly lengthy business of locks and chains. It swung open suddenly allowing a puff of cool air into the stairwell from the dark courtyard beyond.

"You can come and see him tomorrow. Don't worry, he'll be all right." Sister Johnson patted me lightly on the back, "He'll be okay. You'll see." His voice was firm and I was suddenly conscious that they were *making* me leave. The sound of the patients chanting upstairs could no longer be heard.

"I can't leave him, not now! Not while he's like that!" I stupidly pointed in an upward direction to the top of the stairs, panic gripping me again.

"Tomorrow, Mr Courtenay. You can come back tomorrow," Bruce said, pushing me firmly and not too gently through the door and quickly pulling it shut again. I heard him latching it, the scratching of chain on steel and then the sound of their footsteps hurrying back up the cement stairs.

I stood outside in the courtyard; above me the midnight stars shone — not many — Rozelle is too close to the city lights for the stars to burn through. There were only a few, a few mangey stars in a dark heaven in which I was certain no God lived whom I knew or cared about.

29

Damon Takes Charge of the Mad House.

I arrived at Ward 4 around mid morning the following day, bringing with me five bottles of AHF and Damon's transfusion gear. I was certain he would be in agony, in a really bad way from the hammering he had taken at the hands of the police. To my surprise, he had only one small bleed in his thumb and while his shoulder, where they'd forced his arm up behind his back, was stiff the flesh around it wasn't hot to the touch, as it would have been if there had been a severe bleed in progress.

The bleeds, which had occurred during the five weeks since he'd become manic, were all relatively small ones and none of them had transpired from the deliberate and often severe knocks he'd taken. The mind is a truly strange mechanism but, since his childhood, we'd known that bleed followed bump as surely as night followed day. Now Damon's bleeding pattern had mysteriously changed, he'd become largely impervious to the big bumps and severe battering which should have put him into hospital, while the regular little spontaneous bleeds, the "domestic bleeds", thumbs, ankle, wrist, big toe, the odd finger, continued as ever before. Just why and how his mania should prevent the more serious bleeding occurrences remains a huge and still unresolved puzzlement.

This time I wasn't taken upstairs to Ward 4, but to what seemed to be a recreational centre where some fifteen or so patients, all fully dressed, though some rather strangely so, sat around or paced up and down or stared vacantly at a television set with the sound turned down too low for anyone to hear easily.

The people in the room all seemed to be alone, no patient seemed aware of the others; even though some sat in groups, they were not communicating with each other. It was as though they'd been placed in position, props in a stage setting who had been told not to move a muscle or blink an eye until further directed.

The severely mentally ill, we are told, experience awesome loneliness and, certainly, each person in the room seemed trapped in a world of their own. The thought that this might happen to Damon filled me with trepidation. His deep depression earlier in the year had caused him to be withdrawn and silent for long periods. These moods were sad enough, but the look in the eyes of the people in this room told of a deeper, more lonely withdrawal, a nightmare world in which they were permanently trapped. It seemed unlikely that these people would ever return to the world of laughter. Somehow I must get Damon away from this place fast; insanity is not infectious but, nonetheless, human beings are conditioned by their environment and Damon was just manic enough to be influenced by his. Whatever it was going to take, I determined not to rest until I had him safely away.

There were no outsiders present in the recreational centre other than myself. I'd phoned to ask if I could come earlier to give Damon a transfusion. Benita and Celeste were to follow later during visiting hours, when we were to have a talk with the psychiatrist on duty.

Damon seemed in remarkably good spirits and appeared to have forgotten or forgiven the incidents of the night before. I didn't bring these up and he didn't mention them, it was almost as though he'd accepted the routine and had decided to co-operate. I imagined he'd been tranquillised, though he didn't seem unduly zonked and I transfused him quickly, whereupon he offered to show me around.

I was astonished that he appeared to know everyone in the room. Damon couldn't have been awake more than three or four hours, yet, after he'd introduced me to the orderly in the room, another large man whose name was Steve, he took me to meet each of the patients, all of whom he seemed to know by their first name.

The people in the room were, well, *different*, they had the dishevelled and confused look I'd observed before in the severely mentally ill and almost all had teeth missing. Damon introduced me to each one in turn, "Dad this is Les, my new friend. Les, this is my dad."

"Hi, Les," I'd say, or Jim or Anna or whomever I was meeting. My first attempt to shake hands was met with a blank look, whereupon Les, pulling his top lip under his lower, slowly moved his head from side to side, like a small child.

Steve, observing, moved quietly over. "We don't shake hands here, Mr Courtenay, you never know what might happen," he said *sotto voce*. But mostly the person to whom I was introduced giggled, or appeared not to see me at all, each eye darting in a different direction; in the case of a lady named Anna, she buried her face in her hands and began to weep in a fearful manner, averting her head as though she was expecting a violent slap.

"It's all right, Anna, it's not your husband, it's only my dad," Damon said in a matter-of-fact voice as though he and the woman were old and familiar friends. Anna stopped crying immediately and peeked at us shyly through her fingers, the nails of which, I recall, were painted cobalt blue.

Damon seemed completely in charge of the situation and, after introducing me to everyone present, ushered me into a small interview room where we sat down. His eyes became excited as he spoke, "Dad, I've got good news!"

My heart skipped a beat, maybe they're going to let him come home?

"Tell me."

Damon grinned, "They're putting me in charge!" He paused, waiting for my congratulations, looking terribly pleased with himself.

"You mean here?" I pointed out of the doorway into the recreation room beyond.

"No, no, the whole place! I'm to have my own house

in the grounds and a special person just to look after me and they're going to let me run things."

"Does that mean you're coming out of Ward 4?" I asked, trying not to show my confusion.

"Sure, Ward 4 is for the real nut cases and people who are violent." He leaned closer to me and half-whispered, "This is where I'm going to do my work, I'm going to cure people with AIDS from here," He looked up and smiled broadly, "Don't you see? This is the hospital *they* were telling me to come to all the time!"

He must have noted my bemused look. "It's true, Dad! This place is half-closed down, more than half, but it's really a proper hospital. All they have to do is clean it up a bit and put in beds. It's perfect for what I want!" He continued, "It's all a part of our plan. They're going to move all the psychiatric patients out and they're giving it to me to run for people coming in for my AIDS cure!" Then, as though to prove his statement beyond doubt, "This afternoon they're going to show me my new house. You can come any time to see me, day or night." He straightened up in his chair thrusting out his chest like a small boy, "From now on I make the rules."

Benita and Celeste arrived shortly before eleven o'clock when we had an appointment with the psychiatrist. The interview took place without Damon, though in the same room as Damon had taken me into earlier. The psychiatrist was young and not a dissimilar type to Dr Springsteen, though taller and with long, dark hair, which she wore braided into a single plait falling over her left breast and tied with a rubber band. She, too, wore a cotton dress and sandals and she, too, was of the school of hirsute legs and armpits. Initially uncommunicative, she looked up briefly when we entered and asked us to sit down. She returned to writing on a clipboard which rested on her lap and on which appeared to be several sheets of paper, perhaps a questionnaire or admission form, as we'd completed no paperwork the previous evening.

I waited a few moments, allowing her to continue to write, but when this seemed to become an awkwardly long time I cleared my throat and said, "Doctor, this is my wife and this is Celeste. My name is Bryce Courtenay."

The young psychiatrist looked up, "Oh, yes," she said and then added, "I'm Doctor . . . it." she mumbled her name which I missed entirely. Assuming the others had heard it (which they hadn't) I didn't ask her to repeat it. She crossed her legs and placed her biro in one of those little, silver expandable ring holders you sometimes see fitted to clipboards, then she folded her hands over the board. "Damon came in last night, about ten thirty, is that right?" she looked directly at me.

"Yes, Doctor." I cleared my throat, "Before we start, I'd like to complain about the way he was treated when he came in."

The young women looked startled, "It was Boxing Day, we're on skeleton during the holidays!" It was the same familiar refrain and it confirmed, once again, that to need medical attention over the Christmas holidays wasn't very bright. She asked quickly, "Who was the doctor in charge?"

"I wasn't given a name. She was as Asian lady, Indonesian, I was told. It's about *her* that I want mostly to complain."

The young doctor started to flick through the pages of

the clipboard, then stopped and scanned one towards the end and ran the point of the biro down to a scrawled signature, then looked up relieved, "She's not a psychiatrist!" She didn't give us the name of the doctor who'd admitted Damon the previous evening. Then she added, "You'll have to complain to the hospital board." It was plain that as far as she was concerned she was absolved of any further responsibility, for she concluded quite amicably, "I'm not sure how you do that. Perhaps they can tell you at admissions." She looked at her watch and then withdrew the biro from the clipboard. "I'd like to ask you a few quèstions, please," she said, assuming control again.

When we got to a section in the questionnaire or admission document or whatever which inquired whether the patient had a past medical history or present illness, I stated that Damon had AIDS and I was about to add, haemophilia, when she interrupted me, "Yes, it's in the police report and also in his ward report."

She placed the clipboard down on the floor beside her chair and looked up at us nervously. It was obvious that she was pretty new in the job and that the question of dealing with an issue such as AIDS was going to be difficult for her. She was plainly embarrassed when she said, "We have no facilities here for caring for someone with AIDS."

Benita and Celeste both jumped in, Benita winning the right to speak, "Well, then, doctor, why not release him into our care. We'll take responsibility for him!"

"Yes, please!" Celeste interrupted, her voice eager as she appealed to the young doctor not much older than herself. "He's no worse than he's been for weeks. We can handle him."

The psychiatrist shook her head, "I'm sorry, I can't. Damon has been scheduled; he has to be thoroughly examined by two psychiatrists who will make their recommendation. Until then he has to remain here."

"Doctor!" I said, suddenly angry, "Not only does he have AIDS, he is also a haemophiliac. You are not equipped to look after either condition, just precisely how do you propose to take care of him?"

She bent down and picked up her clipboard and turned to the back of her notes; then she looked up at me confused, "It's not stated here he is a haemophiliac?"

"The bloody doctor who saw him last night didn't even know what a haemophiliac was!" I exploded.

The young woman pursed her lips, "I'm sure that's not true," she said quickly.

"Perhaps you can ask her?" Benita snapped, "My husband doesn't lie!"

The situation was getting out of hand and it was Celeste who came to the rescue. "Didn't Prince Henry send over his report?"

"No, it hasn't arrived yet," the young woman answered.

"Dr Springsteen?" I added.

She ruffled through her papers, "There's a note of a telephone conversation at seven o'clock last night," she studied the writing on the page, "It could be Springsteen."

"Well, Damon can do his own transfusions here, or we can come and do them for him. How long does he have to stay here, doctor?" Celeste asked, proving to be the most sensible and even-tempered of the three of us.

She looked gratefully at Celeste and shrugged, "I don't

know. But I have no authority to release him and there is no one here who can. There won't be any possibility of his being examined until the new year, when the review board and the senior psychiatrist return from holidays."

"Christ, that's a week away, at least!" I admit, I was annoyed at Celeste for calming things down just when I had the young psychiatrist on the run. It was my turn to nail somebody for a change, even if it was a psychiatric *ingenue.*

"Possibly two weeks, if he's well enough. Damon won't be the only case for review, we have several before him to process for release."

We were all dumbstruck. I'd been pretty sure that I could get him out in a couple of days at the most, that is, once we'd cleared up all the mistakes and misunderstandings of the previous day at Prince Henry.

"Two weeks!" I protested, "He's got AIDS! You said yourself you have no way of caring for someone with AIDS."

"We're preparing a cottage in the grounds for him so that he'll be completely away from the other patients," she said.

"Oh I see! You mean the nursing staff have complained?" I was getting very tetchy.

The young doctor looked as though she was about to burst into tears and I realised that what I'd said was bitchy. It wasn't her fault that the staff had objected to having Damon; after all, this was no different from the psychiatric ward at Prince Henry.

"Mr Courtenay, Ward 4 is not a nice place. Your son will be much better off in a cottage on his own. There will be someone with him constantly, someone to look after him."

"Does he have to be isolated? Perhaps there is a private room?" Benita suggested.

"Mrs Courtenay, Damon's record shows he resisted arrest and threatened two police officers with a dangerous weapon. Under normal circumstances he would remain in a high security ward, in fact in Ward 4." She turned and looked at me, "This way we can report him as having been placed in isolation, while at the same time he has the run of the grounds. The cottages are really quite nice."

"It was a spear gun, unloaded!" The moment I said this I realised how dangerous this must sound to the young doctor, "It was harmless. Damon's harmless," I added, my voice trailing.

She looked at me steadily, "I have no choice, Mr Courtenay."

I confess I was inclined to agree, Damon would be safer and better off on his own and I don't know why I was carrying on like this. Benita and Celeste turned and looked at me and I could see they felt the same way, the idea of Damon spending two weeks with the people we'd met earlier was disheartening to say the least.

"I have two friends who have AIDS," the young doctor said quietly, her eyes downcast, "I don't agree at all with the attitude of the nurses and orderlies, but isolating Damon is the only way of avoiding industrial trouble. I'm sure he'll be much better off in a cottage on his own." She looked up and smiled for the first time, it was a nice smile with the good, even white teeth of her fluoridated generation. I wondered why she didn't smile more often, perhaps working in a place like this made it difficult?

Damon's cottage was well away from the wards, set in the grounds among tall, old gum trees, though directly outside his cottage grew a magnificent English oak that must have been at least a hundred years old. It threw a patch of useful, dark shade over the front of the cottage. On one side, the sunny side of the cottage, an overgrown, pale blue plumbago bush sprawled under the kitchen window, giving the small dwelling an old-fashioned country town look.

Inside, the cottage was rather rustic, with the permanent dry smell of dust which comes from premises that have been left unlived in for a long time. The pipes growled and chortled before eventually delivering water to the bathroom basin tap and the basin surface directly under the tap showed a deep brown, sediment stain which stretched to the plug hole. The floor boards creaked, the mosquito wire on the front veranda needed mending and most of the windows jammed in their frames and wouldn't open properly, making it difficult to create a cross breeze indoors. On the second day in his official residence, I brought Damon a fan from home which helped him to sleep through the hot nights. Though it wasn't exactly the Ritz it wasn't too bad either, the sheets were changed every second day and the shower ran hottish and skittish, juddering and snorting along the pipes and doing a fair bit of sudden squirting and stopping and squirting again through the rosette, until finally it got going properly.

In recognition that his residence was situated some distance from the hospital kitchens, his dinner, the main meal of the day, always arrived completely cold. This wasn't a major concern, Damon ate like a bird and had lost his sense of taste and smell, as one of the many side effects of his time on AZT, and it was slow in coming back. Food, due to the severe thrush in his mouth, became a question of rough or smooth. In fact, there was very little they cooked at Rozelle he could eat, except for the odd, ubiquitous, white bread sandwich, so Celeste brought in his meals each day from home.

His minder was a man in his mid forties named Phil, ex-permanent army, a Vietnam veteran and wedding photographer, who'd only recently taken up a vocation as a medical orderly. He was a pretty basic sort of guy with a manner which suggested that, after leaving the army, he probably hadn't been a hugely successful photographer.

Still, Phil was nice to Damon, whom he soon decided was pretty harmless, and so he would happily leave Damon and Celeste alone for hours, while he snoozed on a camp bed on the veranda, with Damon's fan going full blast, or studied the form for the dogs at Harold Park, seated in an old wicker chair under the English oak. "Horses? Shit no! Too bloody corrupt. Dogs? A punter's got some sorta chance with them. Forget the bloody ponies. No way, mate!"

After the second day, Phil allowed "the love birds", which is what he called Damon and Celeste ("Like a pair of bloody budgies, them two!") to walk about the grounds whenever and wherever they pleased, providing they stayed clear of the administration block, where they might be spotted unescorted by him. "Stay clear of the admin, this place is full of gooks!" He meant, of course, the administrative staff and not the inmates.

I think Damon rather liked Rozelle, certainly he looked back on the week he spent there without the least resentment. What had been one of the most difficult weeks of my life, our lives, he'd coped with nonchalantly, secure with Celeste at his side and high as a kite, lost within his mania, which made him feel more powerful than God. We'd walk together through the unkempt, but still magnificent grounds, of the huge mental institution and he'd point out the beautiful Georgian and Victorian buildings, most rather badly in need of repair, and he'd talk about their restoration by Celeste who, of course, was to be the architect. He'd discuss with me his grand plans to rid the world of AIDS.

His was a magnificent obsession and, after a while, we all got so used to it we'd simply let the rhetoric flow. If Damon was going to be temporarily crazy, the illusion that he was doing something significant for the world wasn't the worst thing that could happen.

Some months later, when he'd finally recovered from his manic condition, he would confide in Celeste that he missed the certainty, the sense of invincibility, of his own strength in mind and body which the mania had given him.

As Damon grew increasingly frail and incapable in the final year of his life, he would sometimes say wistfully to Celeste, "It was so great, babe! It was the first time in my life I felt completely whole! I *was* the Mighty Damon. If only I could be well and have that same feeling again!"

With the help of Dr Roger Cole, his palliative specialist, and Dr Phil Jones, his doctor at Marks Pavilion, and by using a few old political contacts I'd made as a copywriter over some twenty years of doing election advertising, Damon was released on New Year's Eve, 1989. I must add that his AIDS condition would have played a large part in his early release, the staff at Rozelle were far from happy to have Damon in their midst; handling loonies was one thing, but being in contact with someone with AIDS, who was a bleeder as well, was quite another. The mind boggles at what they must have thought could happen. Anyway, they wanted him out of their care as quickly as possible and would have worked hard to untangle the bureaucratic knots involved in getting him an early release.

Damon was home again, just in time to see 1990 arrive. Steve, their old landlord, invited him to a party at the lighthouse flats to see the new year in and view the traditional midnight fireworks over the Harbour. The always generous Steve, aware of Damon's condition, offered to look after him for the evening and Celeste was delighted that Damon was home. But perhaps even more exhausted from a week of all-day visits to Rozelle, she took the opportunity to go straight to bed.

I have absolutely no doubt that as Damon watched the blaze and heard the crackle in the midnight sky above the Sydney Opera House he assumed the fireworks were intended as a rather nice "Welcome Home" from his loyal and adoring followers. Damon was home though, of course, he wasn't cured, he was as mad as ever. But we didn't care, we knew that time was running out and that we, and more importantly Celeste, didn't want him away ever again.

Benita contacted a private nursing organisation and arranged for a male nurse to be at Bondi with Damon twenty-four hours a day. For the next four weeks, three well-trained psychiatric nurses each worked eight-hour shifts to look after Damon. It was horrendously expensive, but I've never been more grateful for having a little money. The mighty Damon was safely home. Poor Celeste!

Professor Brent Waters returned from Canada in the third week of January and was able to persuade Damon, though not without difficulty, to go on to Lithium. It would be some four months, well into May, before he was well again, although we were able to dispense with the three psychiatric nurses after the first week of Lithium treatment.

As I near the end of Damon's story, I sense that so much has remained unsaid. The year of 1990 was filled with one disaster after another. AIDS is such a horrible disease, it never lets up for a moment, there is no intermission in a human tragedy which grinds remorselessly on, each day bringing with it a new horror and more suffering.

I'm not sure I want to go through the medical drama, the horrendous litany of opportunistic diseases that struck him down and which are an inescapable part of the last few months of the AIDS condition: perhaps I'll deal with it briefly a little further on. This book is Damon's book, the one he wanted me to write. It isn't intended to be a journal on AIDS, a handbook on a disease which threatens to kill millions of people; rather I'd like to think it is a love story, the story of two young people who loved to the very end and who continue to love, long after the mortal terms of their relationship have been completed. AIDS has been called the disease that brings love back to people, and love is what this story is all about.

If this book has any other purpose, it is an appeal for compassion and understanding and, most importantly of all, an appeal for love for those who have AIDS, however they might have contracted the disease.

AIDS is not a condition of which to be ashamed, it is caused by a deadly virus that has come, mostly, among our sons; an appalling virus we must be rid of, one which we must defeat by using all our genius for solving such problems. That we will eventually conquer AIDS, just as we have conquered all those other diseases, I am certain. But we will do so *only* when we begin to treat those who are brought down by it with love and compassion.

AIDS has not received the attention and the money and the fierce determination needed to wipe it out, because it is a disease which conjures up prejudice and bigotry and therefore is of low priority among hetero-sexuals of the human family.

The human male has always shown that, while he *mostly* seems to prefer sex with the female, in situations where it is not available to him for long periods, such as prison, a great many undeniably heterosexual males have been happy enough to take what they can get in the way of sex. In our own early history, sodomy has it's expected place. Colonial Secretary Goulburn, wishing to reduce the incidence of sodomy among the convicts on government farms, sent women convicts to the Emu Plains establishment and even drew up a timetable pre-scribing the maximum number of men they could take in an hour.

Unless we recognise its physicality as a communicable disease, and remove the social stigma, AIDS not only threatens to spread disastrously, but also to remain locked away from the human capacity to show compassion and love. AIDS creates, for the first time, a universal victim. This time the victim isn't a Jew or a black or a yellow person, this time the universal victim is our own son and daughter.

When we withdraw love and compassion and understanding from people with AIDS, we declare war against our humaneness. To attempt to censure what seems, and may well be, instinctive in humankind is an arrogant presumption which is destined always to fail. Gay people are not sinners condemned to burn in hell. We are entirely mistaken if we think God's stance in this issue is one of condemnation. Love, compassion and infinite understanding is the central credo of the God we profess to worship. God is on the side of the person with AIDS, and of thinking and feeling. I suspect God is actually on the side of commonsense.

AIDS is one of the great pandemics of the twentieth century, yet it has a characteristic inherent in it which could prove healing for our society. It has the capacity to unite families, who have been torn apart, by what we, in middle- and working-class society, have been taught so cruelly to regard as a sexually aberrant son or daughter, a sinner at the dining-room table.

In the final sense, we all belong to the same human family and so we must begin to see the AIDS virus for what it is, an opportunistic virus which travels through the blood of those it infects. It is no more and no less than this. It is simply a virus more deadly and more tricky than the flu virus or many another viruses, but still only a bloody virus!

Damon became infected because of contaminated blood

he received in a particular way, others become similarly infected in yet another way — blood was the only common factor — the virus didn't choose its host, it merely took the opportunity afforded it. AIDS leads to a lengthy, horrible death, because there is no hope, no real expectation of recovery. Perhaps more than most other diseases, it breaks the hearts of those who watch and wait for the death of someone they love. Waiting over a long period for the death of someone whom you love and who is suffering terribly, is a kind of psychological death in itself. Until AIDS is finally conquered we are *all* its victims.

If I have seemed angry at times in this book, it is not over the fact that Damon died of AIDS, but that his death was due to callousness and complacency, which didn't simply come from the ignorance of the medical bureaucracy. They, I feel sure, mirrored the ambivalent attitude society immediately adopted towards this disease when it was stereotyped as a homosexual affliction.

A recent survey shows that the average suburban GP, with few exceptions, is dismally misinformed about AIDS and holds attitudes about it which are not significantly different from those of the bulk of the population. However, I should also say that, today, there are people in the health-care professions, doctors, nurses, counsellors, priests, helpers, a legion of unsung heroes, who have shown they care deeply. But they are still too few.

Damon also asked me to write this book in an attempt to dispel the inclination he found in so many straight people to classify and vilify people with AIDS. The snigger behind the hand. The dismissive grunt. He wanted me to warn against the brutally thoughtless assumptions which are destroying the credibility of AIDS as a tragic disease for all humankind.

I recall words he used at a talk he was asked to give to a medical conference as a haemophiliac with AIDS. I thought at the time they were pretty sophisticated words for such a young man, I now realise how elegantly simple they in fact were. Damon said: "If we don't change our thinking about AIDS it will almost certainly spread rapidly among the heterosexual society. If we don't start to love the people with AIDS, it will eventually destroy our ability to love each other. If we don't love each other, we will not heal our differences or ever cure AIDS."

I have tried to do as he asked, but mostly I have tried to capture Damon's young life and the miracle of the love between Celeste and himself. There simply isn't enough love in the world that can survive in the climate of the last six years of the mighty Damon's life and the even mightier life of Celeste, who cared for him. Theirs was a love which was selfless and wonderful and clean. The kind of love Celeste showed for Damon makes possible a loving and generous God.

In the end, love is more important than everything and it will conquer and overcome anything. AIDS cannot withstand love, which will eventually demolish it with one hand behind its back, just as Mr Schmoo disposed of Steve's puny cat for the right to be the cat who wore the top hat and spats around the lighthouse flats.

Or that's how Damon saw it, anyway. Damon wanted a book that talked a lot about love.

30

Damon

Diary of My Mind.

At first I thought that I would write a conventional sort of a book. A book that started at the beginning, had a middle and an end. But that is not how it is going to be.

What you are going to get are my thoughts as they emerge from my mind. I don't know if anyone will ever read this. I'd like to think they might but in the end it doesn't really matter. Because this is for me.

I'm sitting here in bed in Prince Henry Hospital in Sydney. I have AIDS and things are beginning to go downhill. What approach do you take? Do you tell yourself that things will get better and that soon you will be well again? Or do you tell yourself that you are soon going to die? Well, the strange thing is, you do both.

I think that the human spirit finds it impossible to

contemplate the idea of not having a future.

This illness has changed the person I am. I used to be so in control, so able to handle any situation, so dynamic and strong. I was born with haemophilia and so I learnt to live with pain and limitations. But I was always able to compensate by sheer strength of will and an optimism that affected those around me. Now I feel helpless and vulnerable.

I picked up the AIDS virus from the blood product that I use regularly for control of haemophilia. It seems such a bitter irony that the medicine that has saved my life became the poison that may soon end it.

How do you come to terms with the fact that just when things should be beginning, they look like they might be ending? Why do I feel guilty and responsible? It may be because I seem to have no control over what is going on. Drugs are pumped into me, pills are popped down me and I'm just lying here letting it all happen.

I came into hospital because I had contracted pneumonia. Since I have been here I have begun to have severe pains in my abdomen. There seem to be two possibilities. One is a major infection of the bowel known as CMV. The other is a benign condition that simply may go away. That doesn't tell you much does it. That is because nobody really seems to know what the fuck is going on.

I am finding it very difficult to motivate myself. This is hardly turning into a fascinating story, but it is a start. Let me tell you a little bit about myself.

Damon is someone who always thought big. There was a slight problem and that was that he was never too concerned about details. I thought it would just happen, it would all come to me effortlessly. What has come is illness and unhappiness. Perhaps even death.

I have been thinking about dying. I don't want to suddenly reach out for a faith because I am scared. But something within me is saying that perhaps there is something more. Is it a fear-based concept or is it an inspiration?

There are thoughts that are going through my head right now. This is of no value other than to me. That doesn't matter. Can a life be saved? Can a life be completely turned around from a low, when everything is an effort and all that you do is an onerous task rather than a simple matter of getting on with the realities of life?

Is there a real concept of right or wrong? Is it a weakness in me to be jealous of those around me who I see are well, are happy and have normality? Or should I be grateful to be alive at all? Are there such things as miracles? Is it a positive thing for me to believe that I could simply get well?

The real question in my mind is this. Have I let myself get sick? Or is the sickness stronger than I am? Can I tap into a force within my mind to beat the odds, to survive?

Love is the most powerful force of all. It is an energy, it is a power. I must use it constructively. I must *stop* listening to the negative forces in my head that tell me that it is beginning to end. I want to give so much to this world to the people that I love. I mean Celeste.

I must rebuild slowly. I must establish a routine in my life. It must have some structure. If things are an effort, if they hurt, then I must do them anyway. There is strength in me yet. It must be slowly increased, it must be cherished and it must be used. I *still* believe that I can live.

They say that we only use a small percentage of our minds. I am going to explore the other side. The body is merely a vessel for the consciousness. If that consciousness can be tapped I firmly believe that the body can be controlled.

How to start? The first thing to do is to have faith in myself again. To take control. To get my brain working again. To live my life around a structured existence. I have been letting time slip away from me. Now I must read, I must write, I must contribute to the person that is me. I must walk my dog. I must help to run the house. I must support Celeste in even the smallest ways. I must learn to cook. I must do the washing. I must take her out to see movies, I must make an effort with my friends. I must learn to live again.

We *fall* into the dying mode. We wait for what we have decided is inevitable. It is going to require a true test of what the human being is capable of to beat this one. But anything can be done if the will is strong enough.

It is truly time to explore the spiritual nature of the person that is me. I use that word to describe that which is more than the heart, the bowel, the knee joint. That which makes us more than merely flesh and blood. For that is where the answer to healing and to thriving and to existence and to life is to be found.

31

Dihydroxypropoxymethylguanine means
You're in the Poo. Arrivederci Roma.

The last of Damon's mania was not over until late June though he gradually improved with a combination of Stelazine and Lithium carbonate. The Stelazine, which he hated, was discontinued around April though he continued Lithium until July.

These medical facts may appear unnecessary detail in a book like this but they may just help someone travelling the same sad way. Ignorance of the effects of medication is one of the many uncertainties of AIDS. So many drugs were used that we sometimes felt that the cocktail of pills, potions and liquids Damon was forced to take each day might have made him feel as sick as the infections it was meant to be fighting.

Stelazine, known in medical circles as a "chemical straitjacket", when taken in combination with Lithium is a real bitch; it flattened Damon out so completely that he seemed for a while to be a walking zombie. Damon crazy was difficult to handle and, while his cocked-up enthusiasm and desire to live sometimes took the most bizarre turns and his paranoia was extremely hard to cope with, he was still very much alive, an extreme form of the Damon we loved. Now he seemed dead. The effect of the Stelazine and Lithium combination was as bad as his earlier depression. Finally, with the Lithium treatment having some effect, Brent Waters took him off the dreaded "Stella the queller", as we'd dubbed it.

All this was happening while his AIDS condition continued to exacerbate, the invasive *Candida* in his mouth and throat had spread into the stomach lining making swallowing and even eating painful. Celeste supplemented his diet with high-energy milkshakes and yoghurt to help him swallow, while keeping his calorie intake up. Damon's bad bleeds returned and, with the approach of the cold weather, the pain from the arthritis, always present in his joints, now became unbearable.

We tend to think of arthritis as something of which old people complain, a stiffness and discomfort which is the price we pay for living past the age of sixty. In fact it is one of the most painful of all afflictions, so much so that Damon was taken off Endone and put on morphine. Later, the morphine would help to mask some of the pain from the multiple complications AIDS brings, all of which grew steadily worse, though its initial use was for the pain in his joints. Towards the end of his life the daily morphine intake was increased to 125 mg administered six-hourly. Though it was liquid morphine, taken orally, and so not as toxic as if it were injected directly into the blood stream, that dosage would be sufficient to support the daily habit of six or seven drug addicts.

In March, Damon started to get a recurrence of his old night sweats and, shortly afterwards, he went into hospital with severe diarrhoea which was diagnosed as *cryptosporidiosis*, a common enough stage in advanced AIDS but in many ways one of its most awful aspects. This particular infection meant that he had as many as twenty bowel movements a day, which consisted of a watery stool, and it became extremely stressful for Celeste to handle him. It seemed impossible that he could lose more weight, but he did, until he seemed no more than a skin and bone approximation of his old skin and bone self.

Of all the awful things that had happened this diarrhoea seemed, in many ways, the worst yet, for it meant that Damon was often suddenly and without warning incontinent and this was to continue with brief respites until the very end.

In May, Damon developed a dry and persistent cough and after a couple of days complained of difficulty breathing. When the cough started he'd immediately turned down the suggestion that he return to hospital, but when his breathing became laboured he reluctantly agreed. Damon hated hospital, he'd spent too much of his life in one or another and he would do almost anything to delay going.

Alas, it was a second bout of *Pneumocystis carinii* pneumonia (PCP), the respiratory infection which had taken him to Prince Henry's Marks Pavilion and the AIDS section for the first time. It is also the infection, you will recall, which had killed big John Baker.

PCP, while very common, is both dangerous and frightening and the patient is made to sit in an upright position with an oxygen mask attached, feeding him almost pure, humidified oxygen. The persistent cough which warns of the approach of the condition invariably makes it almost impossible to sleep and the oxygen dries out the mucosa of the nose and the mouth, which is very uncomfortable. Added to all this, the treatment was high-dose *cotrimoxazole* which can cause acute nausea and vomiting.

Almost the only thing we could do to comfort poor, miserable, old Damon was to pop little round marbles of ice into his mouth for him to suck, these helped a little to alleviate the discomfort caused by the oxygen.

We were extremely lucky that Prince Henry was prepared to take Damon through the worst of his infection, this is a dirty job which carries with it a great deal of despair, yet Rick Osborne and the other nurses at Marks Pavilion did their best to see that Damon was always comfortable and when things went suddenly and disastrously wrong from him, never left him stranded for more than a few moments.

What I am going to say next has no medical foundation whatsoever and certainly has no endorsement from the medical profession. When Damon returned to Bondi from hospital, though his bowel movements were still unpredictable, they occurred less often and it was thought they could be reasonably managed with home care. The idea that he would never be able to move more than a few metres from a toilet, bedpan or commode was almost impossible to grasp and Damon was devastated by this. It meant, in effect, that he was more or less condemned to remain at home, never able to set foot in public without wearing incontinence pads which can be worn, though somewhat conspicuously, under clothing. Knowing that at any moment and without warning you could shit your pants in public is a kind of emotional death sentence.

I called Ross Penman, a friend who is a well-known acupunc-turist, and explained to him what was wrong and asked him if he thought there would be any point in treating Damon? Quite why I did this I can't say; it must have just seemed like a good idea at the time or, perhaps, because Ross's services had been volunteered to me by the always caring and over-generous Ann Cameron, a top Sydney model and Ross's beautiful partner. I made contact with Ross in the hope that he might be able to help. With AIDS so many things happen so often and so fast that, after a while, you find yourself clutching at straws.

Ross Penman is a responsible and careful man and admitted he didn't know if he could help, but added that acupuncture was traditionally effective with some bowel conditions. He agreed to attempt to treat Damon and did so for two weeks, making daily visits from across the Bridge. In this period, the diarrhoea cleared up and it was never to return in the form of *cryptosporidiosis* again.

Damon seemed to be recovering slowly from this latest bout of PCP, though he was never far from the oxygen mask, when he was struck by a condition called *cyclomegalovirus gastritis* (CMV). Whilst it is entirely unimportant to know, the drug used to treat it is called by the unspellable name of *dihydroxypropoxymethylguanine* which is the only amusing part of this infection. CMV is an acute and very painful gastric condition and the diarrhoea was back with a vengeance.

Damon was very sick and we were all beginning to wonder whether he could take much more, whether this attack or the next would be the last. Only Celeste was convinced that Damon wouldn't die. It wasn't simply hopeful thinking on her part, she genuinely believed that the mighty Damon could pull through anything and that one day, despite all the evidence to the contrary, Damon would beat AIDS and get better.

An incident occurred while Damon was recovering which showed that, underneath all his misery and pain, Damon was still being himself. A young street prostitute was admitted to Marks Pavilion for a rest and a series of tests. Damon immediately befriended her and realised that she needed to be taken in hand. He was not yet over his mania and decided, with some considerable encouragement from the young lady, that she had all the makings of a model and an actress.

Rick Osborne, who has great experience as a psychiatric nurse and who, despite objections from other staff members, had personally fought to keep Damon at Marks Pavilion when he came out of Rozelle Psychiatric Hospital, was concerned for Damon's welfare. The staff at Marks Pavilion were all aware that the young lady was a notorious and practised liar and a troublemaker and Rick knew that Damon, in his present state, was no match for her guile. She was in the early stages of AIDS and used the hospital whenever she felt she wanted a rest from prostitution (who would blame her), a profession which, despite the warnings and pleas of Dr Phil Jones, the medical director of the AIDS unit, she continued to practise.

She was a pretty young creature who claimed to be seventeen, a street kid who'd run away from home at the age of eleven and who'd done it tough all her life; she was also a heroin addict who most probably contracted HIV through sharing a needle or, perhaps, from her pimp who had advanced AIDS. She was now on a program of methadone.

Rick, who'd been off duty for the couple of days during which the young lady had been admitted to Marks Pavilion, was waiting for me when I arrived after work to see Damon. He immediately asked me if I knew about Damon's interest in the young prostitute? I admitted that Damon had talked about her the previous evening.

"Please, Bryce, don't have anything to do with her. She's bad news!" Rick, a gentle and kind person, looked slightly embarrassed, "It's not because of what she is, God knows I don't care about things like that, it's just that she can do some real damage to Damon's fragile state of mind. Celeste is terribly upset and, of course, Damon won't listen to her; he thinks her anger and frustration is a woman to woman thing!" He looked at me directly, "Bryce, I'm a qualified psychiatric nurse, Damon's family and Celeste, in particular, are his only real link to reality, this person must not come between you."

I was immediately worried, Damon having already spoken to me about the young woman, asking me to help her to obtain a model test, and I'd agreed that I'd see her that very evening. I told Rick about this and asked his advice.

"Tell her you can't help her. Don't worry about her ego, she's got a hide like a rhino. I've already told her about Damon's mania." He looked suddenly apologetic, "I hope you don't mind?"

"No, no," I said, frowning.

"She thinks it's funny, a great joke," Rick added.

"I'll tell her there's nothing I can do," I promised.

But it wasn't quite as easy as this, when I got into Damon's room the young woman was seated beside his bed holding his hand. "Dad this is Tracey," he said excitedly, "Tracey, say hello to my dad."

Tracey, still holding Damon's hand, extended her free hand and smiled, she had a nice open smile and except for perhaps a bit too much make-up, she looked like any pretty seventeen-year-old.

"Pleased ter meetcha," she said in a cheeky and friendly voice; it was hard not to like her immediately. I took her hand, not looking at her directly, and noticed that her nail varnish needed attention.

"Dad, Tracey's had a bit of a hard time, but she's okay now. She wants to be a model and an actress." Damon appealed to me with his soft eyes, "You can help her can't you, Dad?"

"Well, er . . ."

Tracey released Damon's hand and jumped from her chair and took a couple of steps back from the bed so that I could see her figure. She had a nicely proportioned body and she stood with her hands on her hips, one leg forward, her toe pointed and just touching the ground, her left shoulder thrust towards me in what she took for a model pose. "What d'ya reckon, Mr Courtenay?" Her voice was filled with infectious laughter and she dropped her eyes, giving me an imperious and haughty look through her dark eyelashes. In a less shitty world she might have made it, in this one, Tracey's life was all but over, bar the pain and the awful despair to come. I wanted to weep, but instead I smiled (What a weak shit I am!), "We'll talk about it later, I'll see you on my way out," I said.

Tracey smiled and did a little curtsy, blew a kiss at Damon and left the room.

I don't recall exactly what I said to her, I tried to be kind except, of course, that what I meant was that I couldn't or more specifically, *wouldn't* help her. I remember her reply, which I had coming to me I guess and which showed she hadn't entirely lost her self-esteem.

She looked up at me and said in an angry voice, "Why don't you just do me a favour and fuck off!" Tracey checked herself out the following day. She'd gone in to say goodbye to Damon and found him asleep with the oxygen mask over his face. I guess she reckoned we owed her something anyway, so she took his Ray-Bans and his Walkman.

Damon came off Lithium in July and his disposition improved markedly. Though still very sick and frequently in hospital, his determination to get better again returned. He even seemed to put on a little weight. But AIDS is remorseless and in mid August he developed *Herpes zoster*.

Herpes zoster is better known to most people as shingles. If you've ever had the misfortune to have just one bad cold sore, you'll know how very painful it is, it attacks the nerve ends closest to the skin and the pain is unrelenting. Damon developed one hundred and eighty shingles below his knees on the inside of both legs, on the soft parts of his insteps, on the edges of the pads of his feet and between his toes. Without morphine, the pain may well have killed him; even with it, it remained severe, the pain slicing through the six-hourly morphine mask.

When the afflictions which continued to beset Damon didn't fill me with despair, I marvelled at the capacity of the human body to take the kind of punishment, the remorseless onslaught, AIDS delivers to it. How Damon was able to survive was a mystery, why he continued to want life to continue was even more bewildering. I am aware that the need to live in all of us is a tenacious instinct, I know this, yet how could this horror be seen to be living? There seemed to be no quality of life left for my son, who trudged though one severe affliction into another, his pain never ending. Surely, in the same situation, I would quietly take a handful of pills and end it all? Where did his strength come from? Was it love? Was he simply going along with Celeste who still believed, believed with all her soul, that Damon was going to make it? Was love this purposeful?

I hated myself for thinking like this, but I loved him so terribly and he *wasn't* going to get better and I couldn't bear to see him suffering the way he was. Later, I would have to face the actual prospect of putting him permanently to sleep and I was to find an ambivalence in me which made a mockery of these earlier emotions. I had requested that, if Damon had a heart attack, a common enough way for people with AIDS to die, the resuscitation unit not be used. But as Damon grew closer to the end I wanted to hang on to him, we all did, we wanted to postpone the moment and have him with us a little longer. If this seems unnatural, for we loved him so terribly we didn't want him to suffer, I can't explain.

The *Herpes zoster* was only to leave him shortly before he died. Treated with high-dose acyclovir, called Zovirax, and a locally applied anaesthetic, named Xylocaine, and bathed daily by Celeste in a saline solution in an attempt to dry out the blisters, his pain was somewhat reduced. Given the state of Damon's health, it came as an enormous surprise when Benita told me Damon wanted to go to Europe.

"That's bloody ridiculous, he's dying!" Taken by surprise, it was the first time I'd said it out aloud and Benita immediately burst into tears.

"He's missing Adam terribly. Adam wrote to him and suggested he and Celeste take him around Europe. Adam's got holidays coming up," she sobbed.

"Adam had no right suggesting such a trip! And you're telling me Damon *believes* he can make this trip? What does Celeste think?"

Benita teary-eyed but in control replied, "She says whatever Damon wants. If Damon says he can do it then he probably can."

"Christ! That's helpful. What if he dies while he's away?"

Benita burst into a fresh bout of tears, "Well, at least he'll have seen all those places! If it gets really bad, you and Brett can come over or we'll come back."

"I'll have to talk to Damon, make certain he knows what the bloody hell he's doing," I said, exasperated. "And to Phil Jones at the hospital and to Brent Waters."

I felt under a great deal of pressure. There was nothing

I would deny Damon, but he was so recently out of his mania that I still didn't fully trust his mind. He'd had one illness after another, how would he be treated in a foreign land, in a place where we knew no one and struggled to speak the language? Admittedly they would only go to the UK, France and Italy. Adam spoke fluent French and Benita a little Italian, but Damon spoke neither of these languages. It was taking a huge chance, tempting fate, and I wasn't at all certain that we should be doing so.

Dr Phil Jones of the AIDS unit appeared initially astonished at the suggestion but, after thinking about it, agreed that it might be possible. Phil Jones is a generous and open-hearted man who genuinely liked Damon. He thought for a while and then said, "Sometimes these things hold them together, give them a reason for continuing. It could be a good thing for Damon." Then he added, almost as though it was an unnecessary afterthought, "Of course, you *do* understand what could happen, don't you?" Brent Waters, as always, kept it simple, "If it doesn't concern him, where Damon dies is unimportant as long as you're all there with him. It's a helluva stupid idea, but it's worth it."

It was decided that Adam and Celeste would take him through France and most of Italy. Benita would meet them in Rome for the final part of the Italian leg and then return with them to London, where she would show Damon London and its wonderful feast of intellectual and visual treasures, a task few people in the world are better equipped to do than my wife.

I was working and, at the same time, trying to complete *Tandia*, my second novel, which was several months overdue and my London publisher and editor were growing anxious. It would have been impossible for me to accompany them and, with some private trepidation, I called Qantas and told them that I might need to fly out at very short notice, explaining the reasons to them. Then I did the same for Malaysian Airlines so that Brett and his wife, Ann, could fly out of Kuala Lumpur if a crisis should occur with Damon in Europe. Brett had gone into advertising after leaving university and was working as an account director in the BSB agency, Malaysia. Adam, upon leaving university, had trained as a journalist and was now working in London on a magazine in the *Financial Times* Group. Both airlines promised they would have us on board on the first flight to London after notifying them.

But before Benita, Celeste and Damon could leave, Damon was to face another huge crisis when, overnight, he was rushed into hospital with severe cramping in his bowel. At first the hospital wasn't even terribly sure what had happened. It seemed that an organism living in the wall of his bowel went out of control and caused a gas exchange which blew up the bowel walls. The gaseous mixture was unable to escape which meant simply that, if it were allowed to continue, the bowel would burst and Damon would almost certainly die. The problem was finally diagnosed as *Pneumatosis coli*, which I think simply means gas in the walls of the bowel.

Phil Jones, his doctor, was faced with an enormous dilemma. If he left the rapidly expanding bowel Damon would die; if he removed it, as a haemophiliac, Damon might bleed to death in the operation or, in his present state of health, the trauma might kill him. Even if Damon lived he would wear a colostomy bag for the remainder of his life.

It was certain death versus probable death and Phil Jones had no more than a few hours to act. He ordered nil-by-mouth and alerted the Blood Bank that he would need all the blood they could possibly scrounge overnight in New South Wales. The operation could wait no more than a few hours. In fact they would need to operate by mid morning the following day.

During the night Damon suffered terrible pain and we knew he was in great danger. Just before dawn he opened his eyes and declared the bowel pain was largely gone. Phil Jones and the specialist with him arrived early and examined Damon. His bowel condition was back to normal, the gas had subsided and all was well again. Well, in a manner of speaking, anyway. It seemed the mighty Damon was going on the Grand Tour after all.

The latest problem, even though it had been over so fast, seemed to affect Damon's confidence and he became worried about going away. Twice he went to see Brent Waters who noted his anxiety. In a call to me he said, "If he doesn't want to go, even at the last moment, don't try to persuade him, he's coming to terms with the the the possible consequences and he's not sure he wants to take the chance."

I thought I knew what Brent meant, Damon didn't want to die away from home. But, in this, we were both wrong. Quite recently I came across two paragraphs on his computer which somehow I'd missed and where he talks about going on the trip.

"At the moment, touch wood, I am comparatively well and am taking the opportunity to go overseas, to France, Italy and England. It is a daunting prospect and I am quite frightened, but in actual fact I see it as a great turning point in my life. For so long now I have been dependent on other people, and although I will be travelling with Celeste and my brother and my mother, there are still going to be times when I have to take things into my own hands. I have not had to do that for a long time and it is a daunting and frightening prospect. In fact, I have developed quite a negative attitude to the whole trip, because the prospect of having to take control actually scares me. On top of this I am of course worried that I may get ill over there, and although I know the medical facilities in those countries are of the highest quality, to leave my medical 'safety net' is in itself a great worry.

"The problem, however, compounds itself, the more negative feelings I develop, the more likely I am to get ill and so I must try to stop. I am a great believer that the mind and the body are in fact not separate identities at all and that one's psychological feelings have a great effect on one's physical health."

Damon wasn't afraid of dying, but only of not being able to cope. Finally, in the last week in September, his anxiety seemed to lift, no new catastrophe had occurred for over a month and I think he felt a little more secure. He told me that he definitely wanted to go on the trip.

"Damon, you can come back at any time. If you don't like it you can catch the plane home from the city that's the nearest."

"Thanks, Dad, but you don't have to worry, I'm going to like it. I'm going to like it a *lot*. I'll stay well, too, you'll see."

On 8 October 1990, they left by British Airways for London. On board with them went a large bag of the drugs Damon would need on the trip, enough morphine to last him three months and a chemist-shop-full of other stuff. In addition, he carried a fairly large Esky containing dry ice and dozens of bottles of AHF, the *Factor VIII* compound needed for his bleeds. In a small separate briefcase, Benita carried documents and letters from Phil Jones and Brent Waters, calculated to get them through customs at any of the borders they would be crossing and spelling out Damon's medical history and drug regime, plus letters of referral to doctors in London, Paris and the several places they would be visiting in Italy.

You will have read Benita's description of the part of the trip she shared with Damon. Adam now takes up the story as he meets their plane at Heathrow on a cool, London, October morning:

"I was pretty excited and had caught the tube to London Airport before dawn. I think it must have been the first tube out that day from Bayswater where I lived at the time. Damon's plane came in at six o'clock in the morning and, though I knew they wouldn't be through customs before at least six-thirty, I couldn't take a chance. I remember arriving at Heathrow just after five.

"About ten past six, I saw Damon walking through customs, he was the first person out and, although he was wearing a bulky sweater, he looked very thin in the face and I was shocked, but not as shocked as I expected to be. You know, the media shows you all these pictures and I didn't know quite what to expect. He'd lost probably two stone since I'd seen him almost a year ago, which is a lot on a person like Damon. But, I don't know, he was *still* Damon.

" 'Hi, Adam, I've missed you a lot, I hope you're ready to show me everything.' He grinned, his arms spread wide to accept me.

"I hugged him and, under his heavy sweater, I realised there was nothing much left of him; as I brought my hand down his side it was like feeling a skeleton through a woollen jumper. I could feel all his ribs and his pelvic bone. Later, I learned that he'd been in a wheelchair coming off the plane, but that he'd insisted on walking out to meet me. That was typical of Damon, he always tried to spare my feelings, even when we were kids.

"I remember when I was in my mid to late teens I suffered from an inane depression which forced me indoors to contemplate my navel for hours on end. The depression, which began over an unfulfilled love affair, overtook my entire consciousness and forced me inwards. Damon never contemplated the meaning of depression as a child. Pain ruled his life but not his thoughts. I know for sure now that he badly coveted the things I took for granted. Did I ever think of him when I was surfing? We'd talk a lot about my surfing, but did I ever wonder if somehow or another I should try to teach him how to surf, so he could feel the freedom of the waves which I accepted so casually? He gave me hints without saying anything. He played cricket with a soft ball. He played table tennis with his stiff arm and often he beat me. He made up for his body's disability with immaculate timing and a good eye. His timing was second to none, even when his body was slow to react. Put simply, Damon was a natural sportsplayer trapped inside an inadequate body.

"If it is at all possible to compare like to unlike then picture two brothers, each the benign inversion of the other. The one with moderately good physical ability, often crippled by self-doubt, and the other, unable to move dextrously, who never thought about anything except the next opportunity to compete or get on to the field. I'm sure he felt the irony, but his natural goodness knew that, if he were to point it out, I would have another navel-gazing attack and feel guilty, probably forever; he was far too sensitive and intelligent.

"Now, as I look back, the irony seems so clear but, of course, a kid in my self-preoccupied condition was incapable of perceiving it. So he let me know how he felt without getting too personal. Damon had an uncanny sense of another person's space and he never invaded it. But I know he loved me a lot and, I now realise, worried about me.

"Now, after a long and uncomfortable plane journey from Australia when all his joints would have been stiff and very painful from arthritis, he insisted on walking through the customs area to meet me. Damon, still on his feet, still basically in charge, still the younger, wiser brother.

"We all returned to Draycott House, the serviced apartments where my parents always stay when in London and where my mum had arranged a ground-floor flat. I remember that soon after we arrived Damon announced that he was hungry. Celeste seemed delighted, he'd eaten almost nothing on the trip coming over.

'I'd like three slices of Coon cheese, please,' Damon announced.

"He could have asked for a couple of ounces of fresh truffles and they'd have been easier to find. Coon cheese is almost as Australian as Vegemite and not to be found in London. It's a pliable cheese that comes in thin, tasteless slices, the exact size of a slice of bread, no doubt designed for school lunches. The unavailability of Coon cheese seemed to me, a born worrier, a not very propitious start to our Grand Tour. We expected him to be exhausted, to sleep the day through and perhaps even the night, but he seemed very excited, though in an understated kind of a way I was not familiar with. Damon's excitement was always contagious, it made you enjoy things more. After a short rest, he wanted to be up and about.

"London was all a bit weird to him but it was obvious he was trying very hard; occasionally I'd catch him gritting his teeth from some sudden pain, but mostly he showed nothing outwardly, his self-discipline quite remarkable. The first thing that really hit me, I suppose, was the slowness with which he walked. We walked through Hyde Park, it was so slow, but he just kept on going and going. That first day we must have covered two or three kilometres. I was quite amazed, knowing that he spent a lot of time in a wheelchair and that his legs and the soles of his feet were covered in painful herpes blisters. It was obvious he was making a big effort because his face was expressionless, not pained, rather his eyes were fixed — though he asked questions all the time. Damon always asked questions all the time, he was the most naturally curious person I've ever known.

"He was pretty good in London that first week, we went to the War Museum and to the Victoria and Albert and to the British Museum. Each day, we managed to do something nice and he was able to keep up, though of course at snail's pace, and when we got to the galleries and museums we always hired a wheelchair for him. Being me, I'd been enormously worried that I wouldn't be able to cope when we were together in Europe. Now, I felt pretty confident Celeste and I would manage when we left the following Monday for France.

"Damon decided to keep a journal of his trip, a task, as it turned out, which was well beyond his physical energy, but he managed to write a few pages. It begins in London."

11th October 1990

We arrived in London three days ago. It has for me at least, been simply time to get over jet lag and all that nonsense. We are staying in a rather lovely apartment in Chelsea. Tomorrow we leave for Paris and that is going to be exciting, frightening but above all, completely different to anything I have experienced before.

London was a gentle landing — the language is the same, the traffic works in much the same way and the people seem friendly and helpful. Of course, when I visited the V&A and the Tate it helps a lot to be in a wheelchair! But my real experience begins tomorrow, when we arrive in Paris. I wish myself luck, and am extremely grateful that I will be with Adam, who speaks fluent French. I'll speak to you from Paris tomorrow!

"But when we got to Paris Damon seemed to lose a lot of energy, it was as though the week in London had used up all his reserves. We seldom got going before eleven a.m. and, by three o'clock, he was exhausted and we'd return to the hotel, where he'd sleep until about eight o'clock, when we'd go out for dinner somewhere. By eleven he was ready for bed again.

"I remember one evening, it was a typical early autumn evening, a balmy night with no hint of the chill to come. Paris was at its most benign and we went out with friends of mine, Sylvie and Patrice Dana, to a restaurant named *Roulette de Mere*, near where I used to live in 1985 in St Germaine. Damon ate quite well of the typical French fare, a splendid *boeuf Bourguignon*. Sylvie and Patrice seemed to like him and he was amusing and asked the usual heap of Damon-type questions, wanting to know all about Paris in two and a half seconds. Towards the end of the meal he excused himself to go to the toilet, which was upstairs. I wanted to help him but Celeste cut in. 'It's not the going up,' Celeste said, 'it's coming down, he'll have trouble coming down.'

"I waited a few moments and went upstairs and waited outside the toilet door. I could hear Damon retching and then suddenly vomiting up his dinner. 'You okay, Damon?' I said in alarm and knocked frantically on the door of the toilet.

" 'Yeah, Adam, I'm okay,' I could hear him spitting and then the toilet flushing.

" 'What's wrong, can I help?'

" 'No, it's all right, I'll be out in a sec.'

"When he came out I handed him a paper towel, which I'd wet at the basin, and held a dry one for him, 'Thanks, Adam.' He grinned, wiping his mouth, 'I'm not used to the rich food.' Then taking the dry towel from my hands, he added, 'But it was really delicious.'

"I didn't know what to say, 'I'm sorry, I should have thought of that, they use a lot of red wine and garlic and I think they cook in pig fat here.'

"He immediately dismissed the subject, 'I like your friends Sylvie and Patrice, I like them a lot.'

"I helped him down the stairs and we left soon afterwards and, when we got to our hotel, Damon, who shared a room with Celeste, went straight to bed. Later downstairs, over a coffee with Celeste, I apologised for taking him to the restaurant with such rich food. She looked surprised, 'But why? He loved it! He really liked your friends.'

"I explained to her about Damon throwing up in the toilet. Celeste laughed and stretched over and put a hand on my shoulder, 'Adam, Damon throws up, not after every meal, but quite a lot. That's why I get so excited when he eats something, anything, and it stays down.' She grinned, 'Coon cheese stays down, I don't know why, it probably sticks to something down there, but it stays down.'

"But there is no doubt, Damon enjoyed Paris. His eyes were popping out of his head and he wanted to walk wherever he could. I'd now seen the shingles on his feet and I didn't know how he could possibly do so, I mean, walk. We'd stop for coffee at sidewalk cafes, which he especially liked. I think Damon really liked the idea of Paris, it was his sort of place — Paris, a red Ferrari, Celeste and a beautiful apartment in the 11th Arrondissement.

"We stayed four nights and on the fifth day we drove south to the chateau country. Our car, a little Ford Capri was loaded to the max and we were armed to the teeth with forms, letters in French and Italian and enough drugs, liquid morphine in particular, to land us in jail for a lifetime. The curious thing was that we were never stopped, not once; we sailed through every customs on the entire journey without a question being asked. Funny how that is? When you've got all the answers, nobody asks you the questions.

"We had just on a month to get from Paris to Rome before I had to be back at work at the *Financial Times*. We continued south and stayed in the Loire valley for a few nights and went on to several of the chateaux.

"Despite the fact that we'd taken it easy coming down south, Damon seemed tired and we stopped at Giens where I had two dear friends Laurence and Stephan, who'd booked us into a marvellous hotel situated on a point looking over the Mediterranean, where Damon rested for four days. Damon simply loved it, every morning began with coffee and fresh croissants on the balcony overlooking the sparkling sea.

"Damon's health was only just bearing up and he would have been better, had we allowed him to recover a little longer. We left Giens and travelled along the French Riviera all that afternoon and crossed the border into Italy in the early evening, stopping at a small, seaside resort hotel for the night. We were suddenly in Italy, where everything changed, and Damon went all funny again at being in Italy at last, after all the stories Benita had filled his head with since he'd been a child. But basically, I think he hoped to see a lot of Ferraris.

"The next day we drove to Florence and we arrived at sunset just after a rainstorm and, as we drove into

Florence, Celeste started to weep and be hysterical pointing to the clouds. 'Look Damon, the fingers of God!' she wept, and Damon grew the most excited he'd been for ages. They were looking at the sun stabbing its rays through the clouds and right on to the city and, I must say, it was pretty beautiful. It's a nice name for it, too, 'the fingers of God'.

"We stayed in Florence for a couple of days and went to the Pitti Palace and the Ufizzi and saw everything Mum had told us we must see on pain of death, though I think we were all a bit glazed-eyed after a couple of days. If you're not Benita, you can take only so much of that stuff.

"Instead, we watched the lunchtime oarsmen in their single sculls on the river Arno as we looked down from the Ponte Vecchio and ate heaps of the world's best ice cream, which was something Damon could eat heaps of without throwing up.

"Florence is a beautiful city but, except for 'the fingers of God' on our arrival, it was rainy and a bit cold and Damon wasn't well, so we did a lot of the actual indoor sightseeing in a wheelchair. Damon didn't enjoy it as much as Benita might have hoped. It is also one of Celeste's favourite places in the world and I think she wanted it to be perfect for Damon. *C'est la vie*. We were learning to take things as they came, it was the only way.

"We left the car in Florence and took the train to Venice. There really isn't any point in having a car in Venice. We decided to come back to Florence to collect it and then drive to Siena and thereafter to Rome. Damon went ape over Venice. I always knew, and Celeste has since reminded me, that for many, many years Damon had wanted to go to Venice. It had a remarkable effect on him, his energy seemed to return.

"I shall always remember Venice as the place Damon adored, the place he saw and fell in love with through the early morning mist.

"We took the train back to Florence and spent a couple more days there. Damon hardly left our hotel and was really quite sick. I was getting to know his dreadful illness, which makes you repay in suffering every ounce of energy it allows you on a tolerably well day. Venice had been two well days and so the return to Florence for two days and then the two days in Siena were the repayment sick days. Four very sick days for two when he could more or less get about. It didn't seem fair.

"We arrived in Rome and I think Damon had had about enough and wanted to go back to London. But, we were meeting Benita in Rome and I know he didn't want to spoil things for her."

* * *

Benita tells of Damon in Rome alone with her one quiet afternoon. Their hotel was in the Piazza della Rotunda which is the square containing the Pantheon, perhaps the most beautiful and exquisite building in Rome.

"Damon and I walked the few metres from our hotel and entered the awesome place. We found a quiet seat and I held his hand, while we looked above us at the great circle that slices off the very top of the dome and is open to the sky. It was that perfect time of day and, as Agrippa had intended, the sun shining directly down formed a great golden circle of molten light on the marble floor below. Together, we sat there drinking in the golden light, our feelings totally bonded by our love for each other."

Adam concludes, in his gentle way, "We saw the major sights of Rome and threw pennies into the various fountains and visited the Tivoli Gardens in the hills outside Rome. I remember when we got to the Trevi Fountain — it was one of our last stops — it was dry and under restoration. The Trevi is the famous fountain where, if you throw a coin into it, you will return to Rome. Being dry was symbol enough for me. I knew my darling brother would never return to Rome."

32

Eight Kilos of Pretend Coon Cheese.
Sometimes We find out Things about Ourselves.
Irwin the Good Needle Man.
Good night, sweet prince, may flights of angels see you to
your rest.

The completion of my novel, *Tandia*, was going badly. I kept thinking I had reached the final chapter, but the end never seemed to come. Big novels with a great many characters are like that though, at the time, I lacked the experience to know this. Characters, some of whom have been sustained for several hundred pages, cannot simply be dismissed, brought to an abrupt end; they are, after all, friends and enemies formed a long way back by the reader and, like real people, their lives must be brought to a logical conclusion. Besides all this, there are seemingly a thousand loose ends which have to be neatly tied together, before one can finally put a book to bed.

In the meantime, my London publisher was getting understandably concerned. The book was required for a March release and here it was, early December, and all they could get from me was a weekly fax stating that I was *definitely* on the last chapter, cross my heart. Finally, they suggested that I come to London and take an apartment where they could keep an eye on me and where I would do nothing else but write until the book was completed.

I liked the idea, it meant I could be back with Damon for the last part of his Grand Tour and, although I wouldn't be able to go out much with him, just knowing he was near me would be very comforting. I arrived in London on a Qantas flight on 27 November, determined to knock over the last chapter of my book and have time with Damon and Adam and to enjoy Christmas shopping at Simpsons and Harrods. But it wasn't to be quite so easy. In London I wrote another six chapters, five weeks' writing, before the book finally came to an end. My writing day began just before four a.m. and concluded at midnight, with half an hour's break for breakfast, the same for lunch and two hours for dinner and time to be with Damon.

The family touring party had arrived back from Rome in November, three weeks before I arrived, with Celeste leaving to visit Portugal and Spain two days before I got to London. This time she was on her own, though she had planned to meet up with Christopher, who'd arranged in Australia to meet her for part of the time. It was a much needed holiday which we were glad she could take. As Adam put it, "She can go as crazy as she likes and *ooh* and *aah* to her heart's content, she'll like that!"

The year was closing down as it does so neatly in the Northern Hemisphere, the weather was turning very cold and, with it, Damon seemed to be fading. It had taken him a week to recover from the trip to France and Italy, after which he'd had several "good days", when Benita would show him London. But it was becoming increasingly evident that he was very tired and weak and only just holding together. Most days he spent in an exhausted, troubled sleep, rising only in the late afternoon without the strength or will to go out. By mid evening he was ready to go to bed again.

The two-hour break I had for dinner was designed so that I could be with him, though this was getting more and more difficult, as his pain increased and he was increasingly dependent on morphine to contain it. Morphine is not a good companion and some evenings Damon would sit, glazed-eyed and uncommunicative, content to stare at the television, a prop which allowed him to avoid the effort of having to share in the conversation.

Some evenings he'd be a little better and we'd talk, mostly about his childhood, though sometimes he'd talk about getting better. On these occasions, I'd return to my study confused and saddened with the knowledge that Damon was dying, but that he still believed he would live.

Were the young simply convinced of their indestructibility? Was this why young blood so willingly shouldered a rifle and went to war, quite sure that the bullets the other side fired were not real or not intended for them? Did this sense of invincibility remain even when circumstances clearly showed otherwise? Was mortality something that entered the psyche at an older age but was no part of the fluid in the pituitary gland?

It was clear to me that Damon thought he could live, not by some miracle or act of faith, but simply by gradually allowing his mind to get the better of his illness.

But life wasn't all morphine and despair. Sometimes, in the late afternoon, he'd waken and put his head into the room which I'd converted into a study and suggest a walk to the shops in Kings Road. We'd rug him up until he resembled the Michelin man, then we'd venture out into the cold December evening. Damon walked so slowly that we'd practically risk frostbite covering the couple of blocks to the Kings Road.

I'd generally combine these walks with a bit of shopping, popping into the Safeway supermarket, leaving Damon in the warmth of the shop while I searched the aisles for what we needed. On one of these occasions, having completed my shopping, I found him at the cheese counter with a young female shop assistant who was happily wrapping up half an enormous round of cheese. "Dad, I've found it!" Damon cried excitedly, pointing to the huge half-round of cheese. "It tastes just like Coon!" He turned to the young lady behind the counter, "Will you cut off a piece for my dad, please?"

The shop assistant complied and placed a sliver of cheese on a strip of greaseproof paper, handing it across the counter to me. It tasted vaguely of soap, though it lacked that much true character.

"Dead cert, just like Coon, isn't it?" He turned to the assistant, "Coon's a cheese we get at home, in Australia."

The shop assistant arched one eyebrow, "It's not a very nice name for a cheese then, is it? Dead racist, if you ask me!"

I noticed for the first time that she was black. Damon,

who probably had never heard the derogatory name "coon" for a black person, just looked blank.

"In Australia, that word doesn't mean anything," I said hurriedly, trying to conceal my embarrassment. Then added, pointing to the cheese, "Don't you think that's rather a lot of cheese, Damon?"

"Yes, but it's on special and they're not getting any more in. We can't take a chance, can we?"

I lugged the eight-kilo (20 lbs) half-round of cheese home. It was pretty yucky stuff, but Damon seemed pleased with it. Later, when I made his usual cheese and tomato toast before he went to bed, I noticed that he didn't eat it. The following day he told me that Coon wasn't much good as toasted cheese, just as ordinary cheese. But the enormous cheese soon failed in this department as well. Our room maid was astonished when, a month later, as we were about to depart, Benita handed her the better part of eight kilos of cheese among other grocery items we'd accumulated.

Damon seemed to become increasingly ill as the weather grew colder and, soon, it was difficult to get him up on some days. He would often sleep for twenty hours, then rise; Benita or myself would help him to bathe and dress and place him in a chair when I'd make him toasted cheese (proper cheese) and tomato with the crusts cut off the bread. Sometimes all he wanted was baked beans on toast, which he could easily throw up before going to bed. Trying to feed him with stuff to keep him going was a nightmare for Benita and, more and more, his intake of food consisted of high-energy, protein-enriched milkshakes, high carbohydrate foods and drinks.

My memory of this time is warped. I would rise in the

morning at four a.m. and begin work and, sometimes, I'd hear him getting up. At first I went to him offering to help, but he'd simply want to go to the bathroom and he didn't want to be helped to do so. This was one of the few independent routines he could still manage and perhaps his self-respect needed it, though it would often take him half an hour to complete and return to bed. My daily vision of Damon became one of his frail little body in oversized pyjamas making his lopsided way every grey London dawn to the bathroom. His bedroom was next to my study and the bathroom was a little further down the hall, so he was obliged to pass my door on his way. I continued writing so as not to show him that I was aware of his presence. But it hurt like hell and the urge to rush to him was very difficult to resist. I could never quite bring myself to close the door, which I'm sure he would have preferred, just in case something went wrong and he needed help.

Damon, my beautiful little boy, had become a ghost who passed through my life at dawn and again just before midnight. I wrote and Damon died slowly in the room next door. It became a routine, the writing and the dying, each day a little bit more went out of Damon and each day my book moved closer to its inevitable end.

Two days before Christmas, Celeste returned. She'd had a lovely holiday but had cut it short a day because she was worried about Damon getting too tired. Mindful that Christmas was coming on, she feared that he might try to make too great an effort to co-operate and exhaust himself needlessly. Though she said nothing to us, Celeste came out of Damon's room after a couple of hours and it was clear from her eyes that she'd been weeping; it was also obvious that she was distressed at the way he had regressed in the time she'd been away.

Benita and I had never tried to compete for Damon's love with Celeste, but her return once again made it apparent to us just how much she meant to him. While he'd never once complained when she was away and he'd been adamant that she must not phone him, so that she could forget everything and have a proper holiday without worrying, her return gave him a joy we'd despaired of ever witnessing in him again.

It was the first time I had seen love as a healing process. Actual physical healing took place with Damon, which allowed him to make his last Christmas with us a happy, laughing, joyous day I shall remember as long as I have a mind and breath in my body. It was Celeste's real Christmas present to us all and we loved her very much for the gift of that one precious day.

Benita has spoken of that last Christmas with Damon. Soon after Christmas, Damon declared that he wanted to go home. He was very sick and he craved the sunlight and, besides, it was time to return. The mighty Damon had made it, he'd completed his Grand Tour of Europe! Now the sunlight and the hibiscus and bougainvillea and his favourite, battered old bush of yellow roses beckoned him from a small, antipodean garden. The little Bondi semi, with the shock of pale blue plumbago that grew beyond the front fence, was waiting to welcome him home.

I chose to stay in London and complete my book, another two weeks' writing and working with my editor. Almost without thinking, I allowed Celeste to travel home to Australia alone with a very, very sick Damon. She took the full responsibility of getting him safely home and looking after him in Australia without our help, until we returned in mid January. I can't explain why. I have often been accused of having tunnel vision, an ability to see only the project in hand until it is completed and, for a moment, I could not *see* Damon. Nothing I could possibly have done could have been more important than taking my son home. But I let a lousy, stupid book come first! I am bitterly ashamed of my actions and don't expect ever to be forgiven.

I have tried to tell Damon's story as honestly as I am able without offending people who are still alive or the families of those who are dead. I have changed names when it seemed considerate to do so. There are times in this book when I do unapologetically indict a person, persons or a system. There may also have been times when my emotion has over-ridden my detachment. If this is so, then this was not done deliberately, I have simply failed to see the other point of view. But the excuses I may have allowed others, because to do otherwise would have been hurtful, do not apply to myself.

Celeste, I am truly sorry, I beg your forgiveness.

The next part of Damon's story belongs to Celeste.

"It was such a lovely Christmas, I'd bought Damon a wonderful and most weirdly beautiful, nineteenth-century, brass writer's lamp which I'd found in an antique market in northern Portugal. I was sure I'd found something truly unique. Let me describe it to you. First of all it was meant to come apart, so I guess it was a traveller's lamp. It stands about twelve inches high on brass tripod legs, nicely curved, and from which a central pillar, a brass rod, rises to the full height and then a cross rod runs over the top about eight inches long. In the centre of this rod is this beautiful flying fish, which is the oil container, and on the tip of each wing are the wicks. Slotted into the upright rod at the top and directly behind the little fish is a cupped reflector, like the collar of a frill necked lizard, so that the light from the lamp reflects downwards, presumably on to the writer's or reader's page. At each end of the cross rod hang two chains, one carries a wick holder for dead wicks and the other a little container of fresh wicks. On the other side, the two chains carry a lamp-snuffer and a tiny pair of tweezers for removing a dead wick or inserting a new one.

"The whole contraption was just delicious and Damon said he liked it a lot, in between my jumping around and giggling, as I assembled it in front of him on a Christmas table groaning with food and this great turkey Bryce had cooked.

"It really is a very beautiful thing and I keep it in the living room and people go right up to it and exclaim *ooh* and *aah* and say, 'What is it?'

"'It's Damon's lamp, he's writing his book in heaven and he uses one just like that.' Sometimes they look at me weirdly, but mostly they seem to like my reply.

"We left London on 29 December, Adam took us to the airport. Damon wasn't well and was glad to be going home but it was one of his really bad days. I was enormously upset that Bryce and Benita weren't coming home with us because I knew that Damon was really sick and I felt really scared that I was by myself. I cried a lot on the flight and was angry, too. I felt that Bryce and Benita didn't have the guts to come home! When Damon said he wanted to come home I'd just naturally assumed they'd come back with us. Benita came over with us and now it was just me, there were no other people around. There was Brett, that was my whole family. My family had deserted me just when Damon was *really* sick and I knew it was going to be very hard.

"We were fortunate as we were travelling first class which was almost empty, and so I could make sort of a bed for Damon to sleep and I then found a corner seat in the cabin, where I could have a good cry. I remember I cried an awful lot on the trip home. Once you start it's hard to stop and I felt really alone. We came home via Singapore and flew over the major part of Australia during the day. We looked down at Australia's vastness for several hours and Damon, who'd just awakened, couldn't believe the size of our country, the sheer vastness of travelling for three or four hours while the scenery looks much the same; the great, brown desert underneath us seemed to stretch forever. I remember him saying, 'It's true, it *is* a sunburnt country,' referring to Dorothea Mackellar's famous poem. He used to recite it, I guess he learned it in school, then he'd say, 'I've only seen the green bits. One day we'll see it all, babe.' Now he was seeing it all in a rush from the air. It seemed almost as though life was tidying things up for him, giving him a sort of condensed, cinemascope, brown-bits view so he could say he'd seen them. Anyway we came down and suddenly got hit by the heat and, because I saw one in the airport, the cockroaches. We were back in the cockroach capital of the world.

"Bryce had arranged for Owen Denmeade to meet us at the airport and he was waiting with Amy and they took us straight home to Bondi, Owen chatting all the way nonstop. This probably sounds irrelevant but it was a strange time, almost surreal for me. The last few days in London Damon started having delusions. Not like his mania, you know — he'd think something had happened when it hadn't. Well, as we passed Bondi beach, you know the huge chimney that stands on the headland for the underground sewerage works, the Stinkpot? Well, for Christmas they'd fitted it out with thousands of fairy lights. I laughed for the first time on the trip home, it seemed to me, after the Christmas lights in Regent Street and Madrid, such a wonderful, funny, funny, Australian thing to do — fairy lights on the Stinkpot! It was the Australian sense of humour and it was good to be home. Lucy was overjoyed to see us, she was no longer a puppy but still very gangly-legs-going-everywhere-at-once. At first she didn't quite know who we were but was still overjoyed to see us. I suppose three months in a puppy's life is a lot of time.

"I phoned into the hospital to say we were back and that Damon was sick and I got him into hospital the next day. They didn't seem to know what was wrong and he wasn't admitted to hospital for a few days.

"It was a really sad New Year, there was a feeling of something happening, although I was still not prepared to admit that Damon was coming to the end, even though he was really bad. I remember, Damon was asleep and I was sitting in the kitchen alone and I heard the fireworks going off and the car horns at midnight and not knowing what that year was going to bring. I was feeling really low inside, I think the lowest I'd been except for perhaps when we'd left London, because as I said there was a feeling of something happening which I didn't understand.

"Five days later Damon went into hospital and was diagnosed with cardiomyopathy, that means a heart muscle disease. In Damon's case, the heart had been growing bigger and was pumping more slowly and this was why he'd gone downhill so fast and had so little energy. When they told me at the hospital I really felt totally abandoned by Bryce and Benita. I was quite desperate, I didn't know what to do. You hear about hearts and you think of them suddenly failing. The day he was diagnosed with the enlarged heart they let him come home, this wasn't anything they could treat. I remember Paula, the head district nurse, was there and Lindsay, who'd come in every morning to help after we returned. Paula is a no-nonsense type of person, very kind, but straight. She told me very definitely that Damon was going to die. That he didn't have very long to go and I had to watch out for the signs. I forget now what she told me to look for, I think I've erased it from my memory because I just couldn't, wouldn't, I refused to believe her. She asked me if there was anyone I had to call on? Who was keeping me together? And, of course, Bryce and Benita were still away, so I said, 'Lucy!'

" 'Lucy?' She looked at me for further explanation.

" 'Our dog.' At the time it didn't seem like a strange answer, though Paula looked shocked. But Lindsay jumped in and said she had a dog and she understood completely. Lindsay was wonderful and we became friends and she invited us to her wedding. Damon said it was definitely a wedding he'd go to. 'Of course I'll go to the wedding, I'd never miss *that* wedding!' He wasn't going to miss it no matter what. He said always to keep in touch with Lindsay because she was a very special person. But he did miss it, Lindsay was married two weeks after Damon died.

"Lindsay was fantastic, absolutely fantastic. For the remaining two and a half months of Damon's life she'd come in each morning and bathe Damon while I changed the sheets which needed to be washed every day.

"I'd fluff up the pillows and we'd treat his bed sores and powder him and change his pyjamas and I'd comb his hair. It was a concentrated time, we'd bathe his eyes and clean as much of the thrush as I could detach from the inside of his mouth and we'd treat his shingles. Working hard between us it all took about an hour.

"I remember, things started coming into the house. We had a large cylinder of oxygen for Damon's breathing. We had special attachments put into the shower and a special shower chair he could sit on. All the things for a complete invalid suddenly appeared that reminded me of when Daddy, my grandfather, was dying. All the paraphernalia, the wee bottles and wheelchair and the commode chair and the zillions of drugs; there were always lots of drugs in the house but now they seemed to multiply. They all looked like things for a dying person, things you'd have if that was going to happen to you.

"But still I didn't believe. I'd been told, but it still seemed impossible that Damon would die."

* * *

Celeste had phoned us in London when they'd diagnosed Damon's heart condition and we booked immediately to return to Australia. I remember working all day and all night with only two hours' sleep to get the final chapter of *Tandia* completed. We were on the first flight out in the morning, my publisher kindly sent a car to take us to London Airport. I handed the driver the manila envelope with the last of the pages of the book and asked him to deliver it to my editor on his return to the city.

Damon was in even worse shape when we returned and I began to perceive that we were beginning to live on borrowed time. I talked to Phil Jones at Prince Henry and he explained that there was no turning back, his heart condition was irreversible and that his heart would continue to enlarge until it became too slow and sluggish to pump, when the end would come.

Damon still had CMV in his bowel which caused him terrible pain and discomfort. He had infections in both eyes and he made a feeble joke about being able to wear his precious Ray-Bans legitimately in bed. The thrush was much, much worse than it had ever been and he started to develop several small bedsores and the huge bedsore which was to become an open wound, the size of a large man's fist. The *Herpes zoster* hadn't cleared up and now he could barely take even a few steps.

But he was still required to attend the AIDS Clinic at the Prince of Wales Hospital every fortnight. This was the second last such occasion we attended, just prior to the AIDS Clinic being shifted to Albion Street where it is now. Damon was finally ushered into the doctor's room. It was a stinking hot, summer day and he was exhausted from the business of getting to the clinic and the long walk in the sun from the parking lot behind the hospital. The long wait tired him even further. To add to all this, there was a new doctor examining him, someone he didn't know and who was unfamiliar with his case.

At first the medico seemed pleasant enough. That was until he saw Damon's shingles. He brought his hands up to his chest and smiled broadly, unable to contain his delight. "God! I've never seen anything as good as this! There must be two hundred blisters!" He rose quickly and crossed to a desk and searched through a drawer for a magnifying glass, returning to the examination couch with it. "On the legs and feet, under the sole, that's *very* unusual." He looked up and placed the glass down on the couch and clapped his hands in delight, thrilled at what he had seen.

"It's the best case of *Herpes zoster* I've ever seen. We must have a picture at once! I'll phone the photography department, you must go downstairs . . ."

He must have sensed something was wrong behind him for he turned to to see Celeste fighting back her tears and her anger. "He's exhausted. Can't you see he's exhausted, he can't take any more today, doctor!" Celeste was having trouble getting the words out, but now her anger grew greater than her distress for Damon. "He's not a case of herpes, he's Damon!" she shouted and then looked fiercely up at the doctor. "No! No you can't! You *can't* take a bloody photograph!"

Damon's tired voice cut in. "Let him, babe. What's the difference?"

The doctor, surprised at Celeste's outburst looked at Damon as though he was seeing him for the first time. He seemed about to apologise, but what came out was, "Are you sure, Damon?" Then he added, as though to explain himself, "These things are very useful for students."

Damon lifted his hand weakly, denoting his agreement and the doctor picked up the phone and made the arrangements. As he was about to terminate the call he added suddenly, "Oh, and take a few shots of the *Candida* around the inside of the mouth and the lining at the top of his throat, thank you." He put the phone down and looked up a little sheepishly. "Your oral thrush is pretty spectacular, might as well kill two birds with one stone, eh?"

The fortnightly clinics were awful, especially after the move from the hospital to Albion Street, though Damon only attended the Albion Street clinic on one disastrous occasion. It was the fortnight following the photography episode, he'd been in hospital the previous week and he was pretty sick but I think Damon felt that if he didn't attend the clinic it was a sign that he'd given up, that it was all over. The Albion Street clinic was really depressing, it was filled with people who had AIDS and Damon saw himself reflected in the faces of others. There was a strong sense of being in a space where a lot of people were dying. In Celeste's words: "It was really yucky! It was really yucky to see Damon in there with them."

She tells of the last clinic which was also their first visit to Albion Street.

"We arrived at Albion Street and Damon had a lot of trouble getting there. It's a hard place to get to and we couldn't find parking and it was another hot day and it was agony for him walking. The whole thing was just hard. It was really hard.

"Once there we waited for an hour and Damon was

feeling very sick and there wasn't a seat for him for part of the time and he was leaning against me and I could hear his heart beating against my breast. Damon's beautiful heart, that was always pretty big anyway, was getting larger and larger and one day it was going to burst. After another hour we were shown in to the doctor. The doctor clasped his hands together, the forefinger of each hand extended upwards, his elbows resting on the desk, then tapping the tips of the forefingers together he smiled benignly and announced, 'I'm sorry, Damon, I can't see you, they haven't sent your records over from the Prince of Wales.'

"The effort just to get there had been so enormous, it had taken — from the time I'd gotten him up and showered to the moment when the doctor said he couldn't see Damon — nearly six hours of unbelievable effort. Damon simply didn't have that kind of strength. On the pavement outside, holding his arm as we moved slowly, so terribly slowly, back to the car, I could feel the hot tears running down my cheeks. It was so unfair. Everything was so unfair! The system fucked up and nobody cared. Damon was just a thing you checked up because the system said you must. When the system went wrong, the thing with interesting blisters and spectacular fungus in the mouth and infected eyes with no eyelashes, the thing that shit itself because its bowels were being eaten up and which had a heart that was growing larger and larger and larger, when the system fucked up, that particular thing just wasn't attended to, in that particular fortnight.

"'We're not going back, babe,' Damon said quietly and then I knew he'd given up; the mighty Damon had spent all his courage, there was no more left."

* * *

But it wasn't all like this, the last two months brought Lindsay, who not only came every day but often came after work as well to help Celeste and just to be her friend. It also produced Dr Irwin Light.

Irwin Light is a GP with a mid city practice. He is also a friend with whom I quite often ran, a man of truly gentle nature given to putting on weight, which came from a love of good food and wine and a great weakness of character concerning both. Irwin is crazy about Bob Dylan, of whom he will tolerate no criticism whatsoever, and about most sport, though in particular cricket and rugby, both codes. It is said that on a miserable day at the Sydney Cricket Ground when nobody would dream of turning up to watch a Sheffield Shield game, the lone person you always see on TV sitting in the Members' is Irwin Light.

He is also one of the most knowledgeable of the "running" doctors, his advice is to be treasured, for he knows more about feet and knees and running injuries than anyone I've met in sports medicine. This is probably because he is a runner himself and, unlike most doctors who treat sport injuries, his advice isn't predictable. (Rest the injury for at least a month and then come back to running slowly.) Irwin understands that runners are meant to run and that his primary job is to keep them on their feet and on the road.

Though it should be added that, in the feet department, he sets the *worst* possible example. He has never been known to wear a pair of matching socks and, with his grey, three-piece suit, he wears running shoes to work, which, though well worn, are not the ones he runs in.

The shoes he runs in must be at least fifteen years old with a world record mileage under their canvas tops. They are soiled and broken on the uppers and his big toes stick out through them. The soles are worn so thin, it isn't absolutely certain they're there at all. Irwin's running shoes are *disgusting* and have been banned from entering the locker room; they must be left whimpering at the door when he arrives to run with us. One day someone will take a stick to them and put them out of their misery.

The paradox is that if he were to observe any of his runner patients wearing shoes half as badly in need of replacement, he would deliver a profound lecture on the twenty-seven fragile bones which make up the structure of the human foot and the consequence of pounding them incessantly on a hard city pavement. He would immediately forbid the miscreant to run again until the purchase of the latest pair of high-tech running footwear had been made.

Perhaps most annoying of all is that, in the ten years I have known him, Irwin Light has never been known to sustain a running injury.

Damon was now going into hospital for a few days at a time, more as a rest for Celeste than because they could do anything for him. Celeste would always want him back almost immediately he'd gone and we would have to persuade her that, in any sudden crisis, he would come home immediately.

After the conversation we'd had in hospital when Damon asked me whether he was going to die, he made me promise that, if it should happen, he would do so at home, in his own bed. The hospital had agreed that we keep him at home as much as possible but requested that a doctor be available to monitor his progress at least twice a week. In addition to this, Damon was still having regular bleeds, though now his hands were too unsteady and the veins in his arms and the top of his hands too restricted for him to treat himself. The job was also beyond Celeste or myself and we needed to have someone more skilled who could insert a needle in places unfamiliar to us.

I asked Irwin if he would be Damon's doctor, pointing out the inconvenience of him having to make a house call twice-weekly or being called to give Damon a transfusion at almost any time of the day or night. Irwin didn't hesitate for a moment and told me that he'd consider it an honour to be Damon's physician. He gave Celeste his personal beeper number which allowed her to reach him at any time wherever he happened to be.

Irwin knew Damon, though only as his foot doctor, in which capacity Damon had been his patient on and off for several years. Their relationship had started when Damon was a teenager and I'd asked Irwin if he'd examine his feet which had become somewhat malformed from the constant bleeding and the calliper he had been required to wear. Irwin had fitted him with orthotics which had made a tremendous difference and, every few years, Damon would return for a new pair. He knew Damon, perhaps not well, but sufficiently well to like him.

What I hadn't realised at the time was that Irwin was working at two jobs. He'd bought an additional practice which specialised in inoculations and business from shipping lines, seamen being sent by their companies when they needed medicals or attention. The downturn in the economy and the concurrent reduction in imports hit soon afterwards and the usual volume of ocean-going cargo ships calling on Australia diminished greatly, leaving Irwin to support the salary of a contracted doctor in his shipping practice who, as a consequence of the shipping downturn, was earning barely sufficient to cover her salary. This meant that Irwin needed to work weekends and two week-nights in an all-night practice at Kings Cross to earn sufficient income to meet his repayments at the bank. All this I heard only recently from another source.

Irwin made almost daily calls to Damon, both scheduled and unscheduled, even arriving on a Saturday morning after picking up his kids from sport and before, as it turned out, going to his second job. He also came late at night when Damon had a bleed and he proved to be an absolute wizard with a needle. Damon enjoyed and trusted him enormously and would brighten up when he arrived. Irwin was more than a doctor, he became a friend, confidant and counsellor and he did a great deal to add a little comfort to the last two months of Damon's life. Of all the doctors who featured in Damon's spectacular medical history, the last one to come into it, Dr Irwin Light, fanatical Bob Dylan fan, sports freak and physician, was to be the one he'd been looking for all his life. Damon loved Irwin most.

On a run along the coastline from Bronte to Bondi, months after it was all over, Irwin turned to me and out of the blue said, "You know, Bryce, Damon wasn't just an ordinary young man, he had more heart, more guts, more character and more courage than any patient I've ever treated. He never complained, he always had great dignity and he taught me a great deal. As far as I am concerned, he died absolutely covered in glory."

Two weeks before Damon died, on the Ides of March, unexpectedly, he suffered a massive fit and was rushed by ambulance to the Prince of Wales hospital in Randwick, the nearest Emergency to the cottage in Bondi. Celeste was with Lindsay when it happened and she remembers, as one so often does, a small detail in a large and traumatic event. It was awkward trying to get the stretcher carrying the unconscious Damon out of the side door of the cottage and along the narrow passage; Damon's elbow was scraped, not badly, a small flesh wound, though it left a streak of blood on the rough white wall which wasn't noticed at the time. The elbow was never to heal, his white blood cells were virtually nonexistent and there were no platelets left to bind over the torn flesh.

Sitting with Damon in the back of the ambulance Celeste, for the first time, began to embrace the possibility of Damon's death. It wasn't the fit, he'd fitted before. It was the fact that Damon became conscious while they were on their way to the hospital. He stared at her and Celeste took his hand and, fighting back her tears, said, "Hello, Damon, we're taking you to the hospital. You're going to be all right, darling." Damon continued to stare blankly at her, there was no corresponding squeeze of her hand, no sign of comprehension or recognition. Celeste was filled with a sudden horror. Damon was gone, the person she loved the most in the world didn't know who she was. That had never happened before, whatever had taken place it had always been the two of them clinging to each other, being there for each other no matter what.

The next hour in this long day into night is the subject of the opening chapter of this book and the beginning of Damon's story. We've come almost full circle in the life and times of the mighty Damon. Now all that remain are the last of the saffron days.

The day following Damon's fit, he was transferred from the Prince of Wales to the Marks Pavilion at Prince Henry to recover and there he spent several days which extended over the weekend into the following week.

On the Monday evening I was on my way to visit him when I met Rick Osborne in the passageway of Marks Pavilion and he greeted me with the good news that they thought Damon could go home on the Wednesday or Thursday. Then he looked directly at me and took a short breath as though making up his mind. "Got a moment?" He ushered me into one of the visitors rooms, but we didn't sit down. "Bryce, do you know what to do?" he began. I must have looked confused, getting Damon home was no real problem. Rick saw my confusion. "I mean, would it help if I came over to your place and talked to you and Benita some time during the week? There are things you are going to have to know."

My mind went numb and it must have been a few moments before I collected my thoughts, because he put his arm around my shoulders. "He won't be back here? This is it?" I asked foolishly, my heart starting to pound.

"You've already agreed that no attempt should be made to bring him back when his heart goes next time.

Bryce, Damon is going home for the last time." He spoke as gently as he could and I sensed that he wanted to be the one to tell me. That it was important that it come from a friend.

Later I was sitting with Damon, quietly holding his hand, knowing that it was soon time for me to go home, not knowing what to do, unable to face him, to tell him, when in a quiet voice Damon said, "Dad, it's time to bring Adam home."

There was nothing to say, I could feel the silent tears running down my cheeks and all I could do was squeeze his hand to tell him I understood. "It's okay, Dad," Damon said. We sat there for a long time and said nothing. There was nothing more to say, the mighty Damon had come to terms with his sweet, sad life.

Adam arrived on the Wednesday and Celeste went to the airport to pick him up, whereupon they went directly to see Damon. Both brothers cried a bit, Adam holding the tiny Damon in his arms like a child; they were overjoyed to see each other. Damon was to come home to Bondi the following day and Adam and Celeste made arrangements to arrive early and to get him home before breakfast.

There was one last incident which occurred on the same day and which I ought to preface by saying how it was atypical of Marks Pavilion. It also emphasised the kind way Rick Osborne had approached me three days earlier.

As Adam and Celeste sat with Damon, the palliative specialist entered the room. He was a new doctor, the much-loved Roger Cole having accepted an appointment to a South Coast Hospital. The new doctor seemed in a bit of a hurry and Celeste knew him only by sight. She introduced Adam as Damon's brother and the doctor gave him a perfunctory nod then, largely ignoring Damon and Adam, he spoke directly to Celeste. He asked her at length what drugs Damon was on and how he had reacted to them. Celeste, expert by now, gave him the answers. Then he started to describe the death process to her.

"This is what is going to happen, the patient is going to go through an increasing amount of very bad pain," he began.

He went on to talk about cardiomyopathy, explaining that the muscle of the heart enlarges until it is incapable of pushing blood around the body, so that the muscles become slack and cause a great deal of pain. He continued in great detail in front of Damon and Adam, who sat holding his brother's hand, too shocked and jet-lagged to react. The doctor was so removed from what was happening to the three young people in the room, on an emotional level, that he might as well have been addressing a class of first-year medical students.

However he must have finally sensed that something was wrong because he stopped in mid sentence. "You are a nurse, aren't you?" he asked Celeste.

Celeste explained that she was Damon's girlfriend and he seemed somewhat taken aback, but made no attempt to apologise, adding instead, "Well, I suppose it's just as well you all know."

We'd travelled the full twenty-four-year circle beginning with Sir Splutter Grunt; it seemed as though nothing had really changed for Damon — he was still a thing, a curiosity.

Adam and Celeste arrived very early the next day to bring Damon home on the Thursday, two days before the Easter weekend.

On Friday, Irwin Light arrived. He explained that he was taking his family down to Forster, a drive of some two hundred and fifty miles, where they had a weekender; he would be away for the day but would return the following morning to make sure Damon was all right over the weekend or in case he had a bleed and needed a transfusion.

Damon became very distressed and insisted that Irwin not come back. Irwin grew alarmed that Damon might die, but Damon persisted, until Irwin promised solemnly to spend the weekend with his family. "I'll look in on you first thing Tuesday, Damon. Try not to have a bleed, will you?"

Damon, for the first time ever shook Irwin's hand, he was exhausted from talking and his voice could barely be heard. "Irwin, thank you, thank you for everything." He paused and smiled weakly. "You're the best needle man ever, the best. Goodbye, mate."

Damon, as you may have noticed, has an unfortunate knack of getting ill on holidays and on the Saturday he was in such pain the liquid morphine was not sufficient to mask it. His palliative carer, the doctor with the death sentence, was away and so we couldn't get the hospital to authorise sub-cutaneous morphine. That is morphine delivered directly into his veins.

Lindsay, who'd spent most of the weekend helping Celeste, called Mark her fiance who was a doctor and Mark obtained the morphine and put a permanent butterfly needle into Damon's chest which allowed Celeste to administer morphine whenever he needed it.

We then got on the phone and started to call his friends. Those people who had been close to Damon all his life. They came each on his own. Bardy came up from Orange, a country town about 180 kilometres away where he taught music at a college. Paul came, big, lovely always laughing Paul Green. Andrew followed and then Sam, dear, sweet Samantha who'd finally triumphed against Damon at chess. On Sunday Christopher Molnar came, beautiful quiet Christopher who cared so much for Damon and finally on Sunday afternoon, Toby. Toby who had first found Celeste, Toby of the Ray-Ban Club, Toby who had been such a part of Damon's young life, Toby whom Damon loved so very much. Toby came to say goodbye. Damon always had such good taste in friends. All had been through school with him and now each said his own quiet goodbye.

On Easter Monday I woke very early and went for a run along the coastline. I stood on the rocks above Bondi and watched the false sunrise, the saffron dawn created by the reflection of the sun setting on the light side of the world from the clouds of volcanic dust the great Philippines volcano had spread across the stratosphere.

"On his last day Damon will have two sunrises and no sunset," I thought, trying to grin through my tears. "That's just like him, all start and no finish!" I tried to knuckle back my tears but I could barely see the narrow path along the cliff face as I started to run towards Tamarama Beach. I ran hard, until I felt my lungs would burst, and then I turned and came back to Bondi in the smooth, cold dawn. If I could run hard enough, maybe the dead feeling in my chest would go.

I got home just before sunrise and sat on the terrace and wept and wept as a beautiful Sydney autumn day arrived blazing over the Harbour. Then I put on the coffee and phoned Brett and woke Benita with the words, "We must go down to Damon."

We all had time to say goodbye, Brett and Adam and Ann and his mother, whom he loved so very much. I leaned close to him and kissed him and he stretched out and took my hand, "Thanks, Dad, thanks for everything." Then in a voice hardly above a whisper, he added, "Please write my book."

Damon was with Celeste when he died half an hour later of a massive and sudden heart attack. The mighty Damon in Celeste's arms. This time she had to let him go.

Trust Damon to die on April Fools' Day. It was so typical of him, trying to tell us he wasn't really dead, that he'd just gone away for a while, that it was all an elaborate April Fools' Day joke.

"Look, babe, I'm cured. It's all a matter of training the mind. I told you I could do it!"

Postscript

Life after Damon.

It is November 4th, 1993. Today, Damon would have turned 27. I call days like today "remembering days", days when it is impossible not to be washed over with vivid recollection, provoking laughter that comes out of the blue, or grief which grips my heart and my belly and pushes me into deep, dark holes which are sometimes difficult to climb out of. Of course, Damon touches me every day, it's just that remembering days sometimes beat me around a bit.

Damon's birthday is the right sort of day to remember what has happened in my life since he died. So I'm trying to put words to events past and emotions present. I call myself an artist, so usually I draw or I paint the images in my head, despatching my grief with wild brushstrokes or stabbing, scratching pencil lines. I cry a lot and get angry but I feel a whole lot better — lighter and clearer — when it's out there scrawled on a piece of paper in front of me. Mostly I burn these drawings, symbolically torching my sadness to let the goodness and love in my heart have a little more room to wiggle its toes.

It took me a while to start truly feeling the loss when Damon died. When Lindsay and I washed his body, the final loving we could provide, I didn't feel like I was quite there. It was dreamlike and unreal, as if I was looking at everything from a great distance and I couldn't really be sure that what I was seeing had actually happened. The man I held, lifeless and limp, couldn't really be Damon. It was like Damon had just got up and left the house, gone on a jaunt of his own or maybe a little holiday. He'll come through the front door soon, smiling and healthy again, with his eyes brimming with love and his head full of schemes.

Through the grief, shock and disbelief, the truth suddenly kicked me in the stomach. And with it, a lucid sense of relief and release. Damon's suffering was over. I know we all had that feeling, however hard it was to let him go. We coped together like a family, in a private sort of way.

The Courtenay's always will be part of my family, for we share experiences that have become stronger than blood ties. Bryce buried himself in *April Fool's Day*, an outpouring of words as much as it embodied an unburdening of soul. Benita and I spent time together, talking, crying and getting angry, and crying some more. We each held close our own personal, beloved Damon.

Despite the weight of all evidence, AIDS was never

going to kill Damon. That's what I always thought, even to the minute he breathed his last. It was that conviction, along with massive amounts of love, pure and simple, which kept me going. Now I see that I may have been described by those in the know as being "in denial". Being in denial means lying to onself — denying what is happening because it is too painful, or too inconceivable to deal with. Thinking that I may have been in denial about Damon's illness makes me angry — as though living with hope is somehow not natural. Without my hope and my dreams of a continuing happy life with Damon, I could never have had the strength to keep going.

Sometimes I feel really, really angry at Damon. Why the hell did he have to go and die? After all the time and the energy we spent battling AIDS, he goes and quits life. So we lose and the walls come tumbling down and now I'm all alone and sad and I'M PISSED OFF. How could you give up? I didn't give up on you so how could you give up on us. Where are you when I really need you, eh? You can't just go and shoot through when the going gets a bit hot. I'm still here, you know, and just to show you how tough I was I never gave up. And I never will give up, either.

I know that sort of thought process sounds irrational, considering the love we had. But maybe the anger is just a way to come to terms with my grief.

The death of my beloved Muzzy about four weeks after Damon's struck further pain into my heart. Damon had been the most important person in my adult life, but my grandmother had been the role-model of my child-hood, the story-teller and the great matriarch. She had been sick for some time and, while I loved her dearly, I had trouble finding the energy to help care for her as well as Damon, something I felt quite guilty about. Yet I am sure she would have understood. Her final gift to me was the money to pay my half of the little cottage in Bondi that Bryce and Benita had bought for Damon and me. That inheritance came also through my mother's generosity, and was in part offered in reparation for the misunderstanding and anger between us. I hope that one day all the little hurts between me and my mother will be finally resolved. Quoting a favourite saying of Muzzy, I guess that "time is the greatest healer".

After Damon died I didn't know what to do with myself. Suddenly my life had become totally and utterly different — unbearably empty. I had been dedicated to one person for a long time and I knew that I now needed to spend time dedicated to me and my life. I had to evaluate who exactly Celeste minus Damon was. Conversely, I needed to fill up my life with meaningful activity so that all the navel-gazing didn't get me too depressed. While Bryce and Benita were always there if I needed them, I knew it was time to be independent. I felt too fragile to go and get a job in a conventional way. Yet I was filled with the desire to work hard and to start afresh. What I wanted to do was to work with something I loved, and that was ceramics.

Celestial Ceramics had its humble beginnings at the Balmain markets, where I shared a stall with my friend Yvonne. I mainly work with handpainted tiles — they are the "bread and butter" of my cottage industry. When I'm not decorating and designing tiles I concentrate on my own artwork, although these days we are so busy with tiles it has become difficult to do anything else. The little studio in the back room of the house is busy with activity from early in the morning till late at night. Celestial Ceramics is a small creation with which I am justifiably pleased. I'm only sad that Damon hasn't shared it with me, for I would like him to be proud of me, too.

However, I do have someone else who I love and who loves me, and who I know is proud of me. Soon after I made the ridiculous decision not to share my life with another man for a very long time, Stephen and I met and we fell in love. There followed a slow, scary sort of courtship. We took our time, cautiously getting to know each other. Stephen began to get to know who Damon was, and I am sure they would have been great friends.

Stephen has been my greatest support through the grief of losing Damon, something I know must be hard for him sometimes. We live together now, sharing the same house Damon and I shared, filling the rooms where there was once sickness, pain and death with a new love and happiness. Stephen is also an artist and a film-maker, and between film projects he works with me on tiles — a perfect partnership.

Most of the time, I am extremely happy. I feel as though I have received a beautiful blessing, something that will last all my life. Sometimes, however, I still deeply long for the physical Damon, even though I feel him close to me all the time. He and I engage in a constant silent dialogue, a dialogue of thoughts and feelings rather than of words and touches. Some days I feel hopelessly old and a bit too wise for my years. I feel marked by the weight of my experience, rather than uplifted by my learning and love. And then Damon will rush into my thoughts and I will smile and lose my seriousness and be just like anybody else again. The lovely smiling image I have of Damon will remind me that love is an energy — it can neither be created nor destroyed. It just *is* and always will be, giving meaning to life and direction to goodness. Our love will never die.

Celeste

Bryce Courtenay

READS

April Fool's Day

This inspirational book is also available on tape and coming to a store near you soon.

Bryce Courtenay reads from his own powerful and passionate story. And it's all true.

Mandarin rrp $19.95
ISBN 1 86330 349 9

Bryce Courtenay

The Power of One

The book that inspired over 1,000,000 readers
world-wide.

In South Africa in the 1940s a young boy struggles to
realise his individuality in a society divided by hatred
and conflict.

A spellbinding story of cruelty, sadness, love and faith,
filled with unforgettable characters, and told with great
compassion and humour by phenomenally popular
author Bryce Courtenay.

'Quite simply it's pure magic'

Barbara Taylor Bradford

'A profoundly moving book, it'll have you breathlessly
burning the midnight oil!'

Cleo

'Bryce Courtenay's first novel is a triumph.'

The Sunday Times, London

'The ultimate international bestseller!'

The New York Times

Mandarin rrp $13.95 pb
ISBN 1 86330 297 2

Also available on tape read by Bryce Courtenay
Mandarin rrp $19.95 tape
ISBN 1 86330 273 5

The Power of One and *Tandia* are also available in a
handsome omnibus bound edition.
William Heinemann Australia $29.95 hb
ISBN 0 85561 504 4

Bryce Courtenay

Tandia

The Sequel to *The Power of One*

Half Indian, half African and beautiful, Tandia is just a
teenager when she is brutally attacked and violated by
the South African police.

Desperately afraid, consumed by hatred for the white
man, Tandia at last finds refuge in a brothel deep in the
veldt. There she learns to use her brilliant mind and
extraordinary looks as a weapon for the battles that lie
ahead: she trains as a terrorist.

Then Tandia meets a man with a past as strange as her
own. An Oxford graduate, Peekay is also the challenger
for the world welterweight boxing championship — and
a white man. And in a land where mixed relationships
are outlawed, their growing love can only have the most
explosive consequences . . .

'Courtenay proved in *The Power of One* that he is a
writer of considerable energy and ambition. Tandia is
more of the same, only more so.'

Weekend Australian

'A brilliant raconteur who piles up set piece after set
piece.'

Sydney Morning Herald

Mandarin rrp $13.95 pb
ISBN 1 86330 115 1

Bryce Courtenay

The Potato Factory

The Potato Factory is the story of Ikey Solomon, the true
character on whom Charles Dickens patterned his
notorious villain Fagin. Though Fagin, it transpires, is
in fiction a pale imitation of the Ikey Solomon of fact.

Ikey, 'The Prince of Fences', is a nocturnal creature,
brilliant, ruthless, unctuous and quick-witted. Hannah,
his brothel mistress wife, is rapacious, sharp-tongued,
amoral and filled with a burning hate for her husband
and a fierce love for her children. Mary Abacus, Ikey's
sometime mistress, born in St Giles, London's vilest
rookery, survives a young life of distress and misadven-
ture but is gifted with a knowledge of numbers and
possessed of a spirit that somehow never loses the
power to love and the determination that she will some
day succeed.

All three are transported as criminals to Van
Diemen's Land where the two strong and determined
women raise separate families, each with the surname
Solomon, the one legitimate, the other not. The destinies
of both family groups are irrevocably locked into Ikey's
greed, Hannah's hate and Mary's soaring ambition — a
potent combination that, when love is added, becomes a
vengeful and explosive mixture as each woman sets out
to destroy the other.

The Potato Factory is the first book in a trilogy that
spans the short and brilliant history of Australia and
tells of our painful journey into freedom. No nation ever

made a less propitious beginning, nor chose more alien
landscape on which to start its human journey. Yet few
peoples have stumbled to nationhood as free, nor welcomed through it gates a greater mix of colour, creed
and race.

Bryce Courtenay digs beneath the myths in a cutting
and powerful narrative that gets closer to the bone and
sinew of truth than perhaps any other fictional account
of our history. He tells us who we are and where we
came from in a richly peopled and compelling story that
touches the heart.

William Heinemann Australia rrp $35 hb
ISBN 0 85561 653 9